KIPLINGER'S
LOOKING AHEAD

KIPLINGER'S
LOOKING AHEAD

70 YEARS OF FORECASTS FROM
THE KIPLINGER WASHINGTON LETTER

Kiplinger Books, Washington, D.C.

**KIPLINGER
BOOKS**

Published by
The Kiplinger Washington Editors, Inc.
1729 H Street, N.W.
Washington, D.C. 20006

Library of Congress Cataloging-in Publication Data

Kiplinger's looking ahead : 70 years of forecasts from the Kiplinger Washington letter. — 1st ed.
  p. cm.
  Includes index.
 ISBN 0-938721-31-3 : $29.95
   1. Economic forecasting—United States—History—Sources. 2. United States—Economic conditions—Sources. 3. United States-Economic policy—Sources. 4. Kiplinger Washington letter.
HC103.K48 1993
330.973'001'12—dc20   93-30250
                                                CIP

Printed in the United States of America.

First edition. First Printing.

Book and dust jacket design by S. Laird Jenkins Corp.

Acknowledgments

This book is, fundamentally, the creation of dozens of people: all the reporters, editors and researchers who have contributed to The Kiplinger Washington Letter since its founding in 1923. Their forecasts of economic, political and demographic trends are the centerpiece of this book.

Because *Looking Ahead* is just a small sample of that work, the task of deciding which items to include was difficult. It required a detailed knowledge of history, because to recognize an interesting prediction, whether accurate or faulty, one has to know both what was happening at the time of the prediction and how the situation eventually played out. The task also required the judgment to distinguish the truly important trends of an era from the noisy sideshows that often dominated the daily headlines. In this daunting job we received invaluable assistance from our longtime colleague Sid Levy, a savvy Washington journalist who worked on the Washington Letter from 1961 through 1985, covering beats ranging from the White House to organized labor.

While the Kiplinger Letters are famous for their conciseness—just four pages of copy per week, about 2,000 words—70 years of publishing still adds up to more than 14,000 pages. Sid pored over every page of 70 volumes, scanning them for nuggets of noteworthy forecasting and making the first cut for inclusion in the book. In addition, Sid did extensive historical research and writing that served as the basis for chapter introductions, photo captions and timelines for each decade.

The idea for this book came from David Harrison, who heads the Kiplinger Books division of our company, and every aspect of the finished book bears his mark of good sense. Designer Susan Laird Jenkins created a format that nicely integrates the diverse editorial and graphic elements. Carol Mickey did the photo search, finding wonderful pictures and political cartoons to complement the text and provide a visual mood. Amy Arnold, Michael Faber, Joan McGee, Karmela Lejarde, Emily Melton and Dianne Olsufka organized, keyboarded and proofed the hundreds of Letter excerpts. Annemarie Albaugh, Rex Bell and Rosemary Neff ably checked and copy edited the introductions. Production was handled by our production director, Don Fragale, and the book was printed by Editors Press, Inc.

Our deepest appreciation to all these colleagues for their help on *Looking Ahead*, and a special salute to the current staff of The Kiplinger Washington Letter for carrying on the tradition so capably.

A. H. K.
K. A. K.

Contents

70 Years of Looking Ahead

In the fall of 1923, Washington journalist W. M. Kiplinger began serving his readers with a new kind of publication—a single page of forecasts of government policies affecting business. There were items on 15 different issues, each one written in a terse, breezy style that got right to the point, saving the reader's valuable time. "Fuller reports on any of these subjects will be furnished on request," said a message at the bottom of the page.

Thus was born *The Kiplinger Washington Letter*, the precursor of a new form of journalism, the modern newsletter. Today, 70 years later, Washington and the world economy are vastly more complex, and the volume of information pouring out of the nation's capital has increased enormously. In spite of this—no, *because* of this—the mission of the Kiplinger Letter is unchanged: to give busy decision makers informed judgments they can act upon, and to do it with simple, economical writing. "All readers are overburdened; they can't read all they should," W. M. Kiplinger wrote in 1935. (Imagine what he would think about the electronic information explosion of the '90s.)

Today hundreds of thousands of "overburdened" men and women in management rely on the forecasts in *The Kiplinger Washington Letter*. In their information diet it is not a substitute for a daily newspaper, business magazines or favorite radio or TV news program. The Letter is a companion to the news, helping subscribers make sense of it, figure out where events are leading and take steps to adapt to changing circumstances.

To commemorate the 70th anniversary of *The Kiplinger Washington Letter*, we've published this collection of forecasts from its pages. In many ways, it provides a unique look at the past seven decades of American history. While most histories, with the benefit of hindsight, attempt to explain what happened and why, this book simply shows what one publication was contemporaneously telling its readers was *likely* to happen.

That's why we thought of titling this book *Tomorrow's History*, or perhaps *Looking Back at the Future*. But we chose *Looking Ahead*, because that is what the Letter does every week. Here, scattered across the decades, are forecasts of soaring productivity and rising trade competition; the outcome of elections; the effect of the postwar baby boom on consumer spending and growth; the direction of the stock market; rising and falling interest rates and inflation; the impact of the interstate highway system on where and how people would live; the shift of population to the Sun Belt; new technologies ranging from computers to biotech; the economic rise of Japan before and after World War II; the inevitability of deficit spending and inflation in democracies; the steady march of government regulation in our lives; the resurgence of American manufacturing in the '80s; the worsening economic crisis in the Soviet empire.

You'll find that many of the crises and policy debates of the past have parallels to issues today, and seeing how judgments about them were formed in their day, both correctly and incorrectly, can help all of us better understand and deal with today's challenges.

Sound forecasting does not require clairvoyance or even intellectual brilliance. Any group of sensible people can assess the outcome of a situation remarkably well—IF they study it carefully, have access to reliable information, weigh conflicting evidence and, most of all, put aside their personal biases and wishful thinking.

We try to help our readers do their *own* forecasting. Looking ahead is something all of us have to do, in our personal lives and work. Most of our subscribers are managers of some kind of organization—business, civic, government, farm, law, accounting, educational, union, and many others. Managers must take calculated risks every day, in deciding whether to hire, invest, change direction, retrench or expand. They take these risks based on judgments about their markets, government regulation, demographic trends, technology, consumer tastes, political attitudes and much more, so these subjects are grist for our weekly Letters.

An air of inevitability

In selecting forecasts to include in this collection, we focused on predictions of events and trends that actually came to pass, becoming history. We also looked for some notable predictions that didn't pan out, because they are useful footnotes to history, revealing the sentiment of the times—and the iffiness of the forecasting process. (The memory of our errors keeps us humble, too.)

Many of the accurate predictions may seem obvious, because you know what finally happened. What you may have missed, however, is the enormous turmoil and uncertainty that surrounded many of the events. You may have also forgotten, or never have known, that the conventional wisdom expected a very different outcome.

Students of 20th-century history will recall, for example, that some economists predicted a return to deep depression at the end of World War II, while others—believed by Kiplinger to be smarter—foresaw a brief dip followed by a long, strong boom.

Similarly, during the recession and sluggishness of the late '50s, the Letter forecast a robust decade to come, which we dubbed "The Soaring Sixties."

Our forecasts are not necessarily the first to appear in print. Some actually are way ahead of the pack, but claims of uniqueness or firstness are hard to verify. And it is not our aim to be unique or first. We simply want to be right—not for our own sake, but as a service to our subscribers.

Just as we are very aware of our own fallibility, we are equally aware of the good forecasting being done by others. We are not economists, engineers, inventors, entrepreneurs or diplomats. But as reporters, we absorb the wisdom of many others, assimilate it into our own judgments and share it with our subscribers.

Keep this notion in mind as you read this book. If our staff and their predecessors made good forecasts of the coming U.S. involvement in World War II, the Marshall Plan, the deepening morass of Vietnam, the decay of Soviet communism, overvaluation of the stock market in '29 or '87, or the expulsion of Iraq from Kuwait, we were probably not alone in our judgments. If our accurate forecasts stand out in the memories of our readers, it may be because we state our predictions with firmness and clarity in a world rife with equivocation and obfuscation.

Our readers forgive our occasional mistakes, but having grown accustomed to forceful judgments from us, and needing to make decisions based on the best advice they can find, they don't tolerate wishy-washiness. The poet Carl Sandburg once noted, in an admiring review of W. M. Kiplinger's 1942 best-seller, *Washington Is Like That*, that Kiplinger made "a few mistakes here and there. Not in fact, but mainly in positive, sharpshooting judgments. Says something for sure when he could better say maybe." W. M. Kiplinger would gladly plead guilty to the charge, and we do, too.

Beginnings

W. M. Kiplinger, a wire-service reporter in Ohio, came to Washington in 1916 and was hired by the Associated Press bureau to cover economic issues. After a few years he became frustrated with the journalistic conventions of that era, which largely restricted the reporting of anything except the official acts and pronouncements of public officials. Reporters were not allowed to put forecasts and interpretive judgments into their stories, as is common today. If the secretary of the Treasury said he was going to take a certain action, that was the story. But if a well-connected reporter believed the secretary's statement to be a smoke screen, because the Treasury staff was secretly working on a completely different plan, the reporter had difficulty getting that contradictory information past his editor and into the reader's hands.

W. M. Kiplinger quit the AP in 1920 to become the Washington eyes-and-ears for a New York bank, giving it practical intelligence on the direction of economic policy, whether it was in the news or not. "They didn't want the outward signs of what was going on in the Treasury and the Federal Reserve Board," Kiplinger recalled in later years. "They wanted the inner workings. They already knew what *was* happening. They wanted to know what was *going* to happen. And if I replied that I didn't know, their answer was, 'Give us your best judgment, advise us, guide us.'" Kiplinger began sending his forecasts to his client in letter form—brief, blunt, conversational in tone, addressing the reader in the second person.

Over the next couple of years, Kiplinger and his small staff took on additional business clients. Their specialty was preparing, for separate fees, customized reports on particular subjects of interest to each client. But many of their clients were interested in the same general Washington issues—taxes, trade, regulation, monetary policy, government subsidies—so the agency decided to send them all a regular weekly report hitting key points. When the clients saw the usefulness of the report and asked that additional copies be sent to their friends and business associates, the weekly *Kiplinger Washington Letter* was born. That first, one-page issue was mailed to some 500 current and prospective clients on September 29, 1923.

A forecast from that first Kiplinger Letter was the subject of a front-page story in *The New York Times*, under the headline "New Washington News Agency Brands Rumors of Loan to Revive German Mark as 'Foolish.'" (That judgment, by the way, was sound at the moment, but within a year, the Dawes Plan began to encourage American banks to make massive loans to Germany and other weak governments around the world.) The *Times* article, which read more like a publicity release than a news story, was the work of Kiplinger's friends at the paper, for whose Sunday magazine he frequently free-lanced stories.

In the *Times* story, Kiplinger described his new publication like this: "I believe in plain, simple language, without a lot of useless verbiage. Our attitude will be completely non-partisan. We know how to separate hot air from sincerity, fiction from fact. We will not hesitate to deflate and debunk pure political hokum, regardless of party lines. That way, our clients will be able to assess realistically the intent and probable end-result of Washington activity. We will report what businessmen need to know to look ahead, plan ahead and make the decisions that help them stay ahead."

The early '20s were a time of exciting ferment in American society—in social mores, the arts, technology and virtually every other area. This spirit of experimentation was

---

THE KIPLINGER WASHINGTON AGENCY

ALBEE BUILDING

WILLARD M. KIPLINGER
MELVIN RYDER
C. B. HURREY
HENRY UTLEY MILNE

WASHINGTON, D.C.

NEW YORK OFFICE 15 PARK ROW

BUSINESS REPRESENTATION
GOVERNMENT PRACTICE
SALES INVESTIGATION
UNPUBLISHED INFORMATION
LEGISLATION REPORTS
FOREIGN BUSINESS
TRADE PRESS CLIPPINGS

THE KIPLINGER WASHINGTON LETTER   Sept. 29, 1923   ISSUED WEEKLY TO CLIENTS

Rumors of an international German loan are renewed - a loan to revive the mark. Bankers take them seriously in a few cases, but they are foolish. No German loan will come without plenty of advance notice and the paper mark will not come back. Begin to watch for the decline of the franc, too. Expiring Coal Commission recommends government regulation of the coal industry by the Interstate Commerce Commission. It will take legislation, and that probably won't come at the next session, opening in December. It will take a longer period of talk. An important case before the Supreme Court, which opens its fall session Oct. 1 is that of the First National Bank of St.Louis, involving the question of whether national banks may legally establish offices, or branches, within the same city; re-argument scheduled for Nov. 12. Muscle Shoals is still an issue, though the Gorgas steam plant was sold to the Alabama Power Co. Henry Ford's offer will remain to be fought over. The revenue act will be revised at the coming session of Congress, but mainly on technical phases. Washington will not give the farmers much relief; it can't. The proposal for a government-financed wheat exporting corporation probably means subsidy is an emergency shot-in-the-arm constitutionally good, or isn't it? Country bankers plan a suit to test the par collection rules of the Federal Reserve Board. In the end, they won't get anywhere. A report on the history of electric light is published by the Smithsonian Institution. It is significant of what museums can do for business, if "business" only knew what to ask for. Radio, what a lot of valuable research by government departments is available on this popular subject! But government documents suffer under their age-old reputation for mustiness.

The Japanese disaster means more business for American interests. It also means better relations between the two nations. Those are the two high points in the situation, so far as Washington is concerned, sentimentality barred.

Every banker who looks ahead should read the story of what labor banks are doing, embodied in the book, "Labor's Money", by Richard Boeckel, Harcourt, Brace & Co., $1.50. Read it whether you believe in the labor banks or not.

Another good book for banks, or foreign traders to have, is "WHO'S WHO IN WORLD TRADE", a directory and hand book of foreign agents, forwarders, attorneys, etc.,published by the International Bureau of Trade Extension, Washington.

Mexican claims: Nothing much can be done about them for six months or more, but every effort should be made now to get them in good shape for pressing.

Bankers meeting in Atlantic City at the convention of the American Bankers Association recommend amendment of the federal reserve act to eliminate politics from administration of the system. The recommendations are interesting and meritorious, but they will not be embodied in legislation very soon. Banks are getting ready to ask Congress for legislation to remove the tax exemption privileges from building and loan associations. They probably won't succeed.

FULLER REPORTS ON ANY OF THESE SUBJECTS WILL BE FURNISHED ON REQUEST.

alive in American journalism and publishing, giving rise to a surprising number of new publications that would survive, prosper and spawn many imitators. Founded within a year or two of each other were *Time* magazine, the first newsweekly; *The New Yorker,* an unusual compendium of stylish writing on everything from politics to the arts; *Reader's Digest,* the first successful magazine of articles condensed from other sources; and *The Kiplinger Washington Letter,* which would become the most widely read business letter in the world. As different as these publications were from each other, they shared a common trait: All were unique journalistic innovations with a strong commitment to their readers.

Through the 1920s *The Kiplinger Washington Letter* grew slowly in circulation, and the agency was supported mostly by special information services for clients and by W. M. Kiplinger's free-lance writing for a variety of national publications. From the first one-page edition, the Letter was expanded to two pages and later to four pages, which is still its length today. Circulation growth accelerated during the '30s, when the New Deal reinvented American government and business regulation, and the eyes of business were firmly fixed on Washington.

Kiplinger's weekly letter, the oldest continously published letter today, was not the first successful "newsletter" of modern times, as is often stated by others. When W. M. Kiplinger started his weekly service in 1923, *The Whaley-Eaton American Letter* was already five years old and thriving as an influential Washington publication. But Kiplinger's publication was quite different from *Whaley-Eaton.* For one thing, Kiplinger's mission was forecasting, while the *Whaley-Eaton* letter often prescribed and criticized public policy, in the manner of columnists and editorial writers. And *Whaley-Eaton* was written in conventional journalistic prose, while Kiplinger was experimenting with a new way of conveying a lot of information in a tight space.

The Kiplinger style

It was Kiplinger's stylistic innovations, widely emulated in other publications today, that eventually led to his being regarded as the creator of modern newsletter journalism. He recognized early on that a letter doesn't compete with publications such as newspapers and magazines. Readers have many sources for long, detailed accounts of subjects that interest them. What they wanted from his letter were brief, clear judgments on many topics.

His clients were busy; they expected him to sort through all the information, examine all the angles, and then give them his conclusion. If they wanted more information, they were free to call or write him and his staff.

To save the reader's time, and to cover more subjects in each week's issue, W. M. Kiplinger wrote in a highly condensed, almost telegraphic style. He used incomplete sentences, with phrases joined by dashes or three dots. He underscored the key points as a guide for the eye, and for emphasis, he would capitalize a whole word or phrase. Unlike most journalists of the day, Kiplinger wrote in the simple language of everyday conversation, often using slang. He avoided jargon, whether the jargon of government, business or economics. If regular folks commonly referred to third-class direct-mail solicitations as "junk mail," then the Kiplinger Letter would, too—even though direct marketers (including Kiplinger's own circulation department) considered the term to be pejorative.

The result of all this was a writing style that was very direct, emphatic and clear, getting right to the point simply and quickly. If the final product looked effortless, it wasn't. Kiplinger and his staff would write, rewrite and rewrite again until their ideas were stated as succinctly and clearly as possible. Carl Sandburg, himself a champion of simple American language, once wrote about W. M. Kiplinger: "Writes crisp. Smooth. But crisp. Imagine he's a good talker."

In the first decade of publication, Kiplinger's style evolved rather haphazardly, and the early letters are a stylistic jumble. By the mid '30s, however, the style had crystallized into a formal format he called "sweep-line," which we still use in the Kiplinger Letters today. In its purest form, a page of sweep-line writing consists entirely of one-line sentences or groups of phrases, each expressing a unified thought, starting on the left margin and ending on the right in punctuation (period, comma, three dots). No line ends in a hyphenated word or awkward phrase break. This enables the reader's eye to sweep across the line and take in the idea quickly. The main idea is always at the beginning of the line, with key words underscored. If it's done right, the reader can scan the page, reading only the underlined words on the left side, and get all the main points. As you browse in this anthology of items from the Kiplinger Letters, note the evolution of the style, and also note how rigorously the sweep-line style is still practiced by the Kiplinger staff today.

In purpose, format, writing style and general categories

of coverage, today's *Kiplinger Washington Letter* is virtually identical to its editions of 50 or 60 years ago. No other major publication of its age is as little changed. (Even *The Wall Street Journal*, which also sticks close to its roots, introduced photos and extra sections in recent years.) It's not that we lack imagination or don't occasionally consider whether some format change would improve the product. But we don't believe in change for the sake of novelty, and we can't picture a different format that would serve our subscribers as well as the original one does.

Besides, our Letter has a strong renewal rate, which is a rolling referendum on its usefulness to our clients. They're telling us, in the clearest way they can, that they like what they're getting. Although the world is a wider and more complex community today, the Letter is still just four pages each week. Our clients don't want *more* reading material; they want more *relevant* information, and they trust us to focus on what's important and skip the rest. As longtime champions of brevity in journalism, we're heartened by the new trend towards tighter, better-edited writing in newspapers and magazines. Long, rambling stories are often a self-indulgence on the part of the writer, showing little respect for the reader's valuable time.

How we work

More than any other publication we know, *The Kiplinger Washington Letter* is truly staff-written and collegially edited, and we believe this is a big factor in its reliability. Each of its 2,000 words per week is closely considered by an editorial staff of nearly 20 reporter/editors and researchers. The Letter undoubtedly has the highest ratio of editorial staff to finished product in all of publishing. The collective knowledge and experience of our colleagues, all of them seasoned journalists and knowledgeable in their fields, go into every issue.

Remarks of W.M. Kiplinger to the American Association of Teachers of Journalism, December 28, 1935, explaining his distinctive "sweep-line" style of newsletter writing.

```
This is shop-talk to teachers, to teachers of journalism.
The talk is by a writer of utilitarian matter.

Purpose is to urge a new style for the writing craft:
Sweep-line style, one full line to a statement or a thought.
Brevity, brevity. Essence. Main point. Scant detail. Speed.

The sweep-line style: A sweep of thought in a single line.
Your eye moves left to right, to the end, and THERE'S the whole thought.
The mind is relieved of the burden of carrying over to the next line.
The mind CAN carry over. The mind CAN do anything you require of it.
But relieve the mind, and ease the eye. It's a different writing style.

Other points of the style, beyond single-thought-single-line:
Key word or key phrase first in sentence or paragraph. Guide.
Impression is enough: No need to fill in tedious detail.
Reader does this for himself. Not exact? No. Often no need to be exact.
Don't insist on full sentence, nicely rounded, grammar rules.
Omit subject, object, verb, predicate, if suits you, if sense is clear.
(Is sense of THAT line clear? It's faulty grammar, but is it CLEAR?)
Emphasize with TYPE: Conversation is LIVE, print is dull.
In your talking you UP some words, down some words, and trail off...
You can simulate live conversation in type. Well, DO IT, then.
Meter, if you can, within your work time limit.
Try to avoid breaking words or thoughts at line-end. It's dis-
concerting to eye and mind.

In reader's interest, be brief: Say it in few words.
All readers are overburdened. They CAN'T read what they SHOULD.
You writers: You write twice as much as your readers need.
Sometimes you try to show how much you know, forgetting readers' time.
You publishers: You find it CHEAPER to fill your columns
with expanded writings. Brevity takes more money, more manpower.
But brevity, at higher cost of production, can be made to PAY. I KNOW.
(I have a staff of 8 men to turn out 1800 words per week. But it pays.)

You teachers of journalism: Is this cryptic style good?
No, not for straight news writing, not for bulk of reporting,
because of the urgencies of speed and mechanical make-up.
But for editorial writing, for policy writing? Yes, perhaps.
In these there's need of EMPHASIS, of gripping the reader's mind.
And column width can be adapted to fit the chosen style.
How far can you go in using this style? I don't quite know.
It's not a substitute for straight smooth writing of conventional type.
But it has its uses, mainly as a stimulant, antidote for stodgy style.

Urge it onto editors? No. Old dogs learn no new tricks.
Urge it onto editors-in-the-making? Yes. They will adapt it.
Your young men will grab the style when they feel the need of VIGOR.
Readers don't analyze or understand style, but they APPRECIATE.
They vibrate, they feel. This makes them receptive, and they THINK.
There's plenty of compensation for discarding formal writing.

          (This sample is an EXTREME illustration of the style)
```

In addition to contributing to the weekly Letter, our editorial staff has a duty to answer the information requests of our subscribers. Consistent with our founding as a Washington information service, we help our readers with any question they might have, whether it relates to something we've written or not. By phone call or personal letter, we give judgments on the status of pending legislation and regulations, the outlook for an industry or region, where to find an obscure piece of information, or anything else. Not only does this service reinforce our relationship with subscribers, it gives us a valuable sense of what our readers care about and need to know. We get a lot of good story ideas from our readers.

The process of creating a weekly edition of the Letter starts when we meet with our staff on Monday morning and discuss what they're working on and what would be a good lead story (page one) in that week's Letter. Everyone suggests story ideas, whether on their beat or someone else's. Over the next three days, the editors complete their reporting and submit their "items"—tightly written Kiplinger-style stories—to the editing desk, usually manned by executive editor Jack Kiesner. The person on the desk is in charge of selecting, rewriting and laying out the items into four pages of copy. Every item must meet what we call the "So what?" standard. It must have relevance to the business planning needs of our readers, and it should be something that the reader can *do* something about—by changing a plan, seizing an opportunity or taking other action.

On Wednesday the four draft pages, written on a word processor and laser-printed on white paper, are circulated to the whole staff to be critiqued. Everyone marks up the "whites" with challenges to facts or judgments, plus suggested changes of wording, style, punctuation or anything else. The best of the suggested changes are incorporated into a second round of draft pages, printed on green paper and circulated again to the whole staff on Thursday. By noon Friday, the marked-up "greens" have evolved into a finished Kiplinger Letter.

The signature on the bottom of page four—either Austin Kiplinger's or Knight Kiplinger's—indicates which of us oversaw the editorial operation that week. (If the Letter is signed "The Kiplinger Washington Editors" some week, it means that neither of us was available to oversee the Letter, but this is a rare occurrence in the era of fax machines.) The Letter is sent to the printer on Friday afternoon, printed and inserted into envelopes that night, and shipped by Express Mail early Saturday morning to regional postal centers around the country, for delivery Monday or Tuesday to several hundred thousand subscribers.

Keeping it timely

Throughout the week, we're watching to see whether any breaking news events might overtake our forecasts or change our judgment on something we're writing. Even though our Letters are trying to write next month's news—or next year's—there are times when something happens late in the week that is so momentous that it requires a scrapping or major rewrite of significant portions of the Letter in progress. The most dramatic of these events was the assassination of President John F. Kennedy.

As usual, the Washington Letter was just about finished on Friday morning, November 22, 1963. The lead page of the Letter that week happened to feature a candid appraisal of how Kennedy was doing after nearly three years as President. The Letter noted that his legislative program was going nowhere in Congress, his own Democratic colleagues were terribly disappointed in his leadership, and speculation was rampant in Washington that he might not be renominated, let alone reelected in '64. The Letter concluded, however, that the odds were still good that Kennedy would be both renominated and reelected, given the natural advantages of incumbency.

Austin Kiplinger was having lunch at our printing company, Editors Press Inc., in suburban Maryland, when he got a call from a colleague at the editorial office downtown, telling him that Kennedy had been shot. Austin rushed back to the office, gathered the staff and got started on a total rewrite of the Letter. Postponing the print run as long as possible without jeopardizing Monday mail delivery, they hurried to report, analyze and write their judgments about the changes that would be wrought by Kennedy's death. They finished by 3 a.m. Saturday and sent the Letter to press. It reached virtually every reader on schedule.

If any one Letter symbolizes our insistent focus on the future, it is that Letter, written on a day of tragedy and mourning. The Letter eulogized the slain president in the first three lines. The fourth line read: "But the government must...and does...go on. The U.S. must move ahead, and the world is watching." The rest of the letter was about the new President, Lyndon Baines Johnson—his style, his philosophy, and likely changes he would make in the Kennedy program.

Sources of wisdom

The Washington sources of the Kiplinger Letters are knowledgeable people in many kinds of work—civil servants, members of Congress, lobbyists, trade association executives, congressional staffers, think-tank analysts and others. Some of our sources are high-ranking, well-known people, but many more are middle-level aides. We're less interested in their rank than in their knowledge and record of reliability. We never quote a source or attribute an idea or judgment to anyone by name. If a Washington figure is interested only in seeing his name in print, then he won't give our staff the time of day.

Fortunately, we have many contacts around Washington who like the freedom to share their thoughts with us without risk of embarrassment from quotation. They give us their candid assessments of issues they're involved with, and sometimes this candor runs counter to their own public statements on the same issue. Publicly, the congressman or trade association executive expresses confidence that his pet bill will pass, but privately he tells us it hasn't the chance of a snowball in hell.

For our forecasting of business and economic trends, we rely on sources from many regions and lines of business. Our best information comes from owners and managers in business—men and women who are making daily decisions on hiring, borrowing, spending and managing. Many of them are subscribers we have talked with in the past and whom we have found to be astute analysts of their industry and their region. When we call them on the phone, we don't ask much about how business was last month, or even how sales are going right now, because that's history. We ask them what kind of *future* conditions they're planning for and what steps they intend to take next month.

We also talk with savvy economists who are making their own surveys and studying the leading indicators. We run all this information through the mill of our staff's collective judgment and institutional memory. Our staffers are expected to reach their own conclusion on what the outcome will be, and that conclusion won't necessarily be a consensus of the sources' opinions. Our colleagues are free to side with a minority opinion if they think it makes more sense, especially if the minority opinion has been right in the past.

A calm detachment

If there is something distinctive and consistent about the tone or "voice" of *The Kiplinger Washington Letter* over the years, it is the cool, dispassionate calmness of the analyses and forecasts. We try not to get caught up in the passions and anxieties of the moment, which would cloud our judgment on the outcome. Because of this matter-of-fact tone, when back issues of the Letters are read as history (or history waiting to happen), they often don't convey the heat and hostility of the raging public debate over, say, the New Deal, Joseph McCarthy, the civil rights movement, the war in Vietnam, Watergate or countless other tumultuous episodes in recent history. Our readers expect us to step back a little and give them a more-balanced assessment than they might get from the daily headlines.

We try to filter out of our forecasts the taint of personal preferences and wishes. Like all journalists, we do have preferences on policies, political candidates and issues, and there is usually a wide range of opinions among our colleagues here. But we don't practice advocacy journalism. We may predict the passage of legislation that many of us believe to be ill-advised, and we may predict the defeat of something that we believe would be beneficial. We don't endorse anything or anyone, and we try to prevent political or commercial interests from quoting our forecasts in support of their positions.

Sometimes our readers, especially new subscribers, mistake a forecast for an endorsement. They read their own wishes and biases into a forecast which, on careful reading, is simply that—a prediction that something is going to happen, whether we like it or not. They can't understand why we don't sound the alarm or join them on the ramparts. We explain that it is not our mission to espouse, praise or condemn. We do not deprecate the role of the impassioned advocate. It is simply not our role. We do not seek to be influential, like the syndicated columnist who hopes to affect the outcome by what he or she writes. We want only to be useful to our readers.

Our best check on whether we are maintaining our objectivity is the heavy mail we receive during a presidential campaign. We're not surprised to receive complaints from partisans on *all* sides that we are underestimating the electoral strength of their candidates or overestimating the opposition. On any given day we'll get letters from some subscribers complaining that we are part of the "liberal press"—and from other readers castigating us for allegedly promoting a "conservative" agenda.

Independent thinking

Since we're a forecasting service that tries to be ahead of the news, there is little overlap between what we're writing about in a given week and what is filling the daily newspapers and airwaves. After we make a forecast, we don't revisit the same subject for quite a while, until changing circumstances may cause us to rethink our earlier judgment. We often underplay stories that dominate the evening television news and the front pages of newspapers—for example, the Iran-Contra affair in the '80s. This intentional neglect could stem from any of several reasons. We might think the story doesn't have a signficant impact on American business and the economy, which is our readers' core interest. We might not have a relevant forecast to make. We might decide to focus instead on a little-noticed trend in demography, technology or regulation that we believe is much more important, in the long run, than the hot news story of the moment.

This approach to story selection and emphasis sets us apart from many of our colleagues in the Washington press corps. Because we're not reporting news, we usually don't attend press conferences on Capitol Hill or at the White House. We don't pay much attention to the intricate legislative maneuvering on complex pieces of legislation as they wend their way across the Hill, as long as the maneuvering doesn't change our judgment on the likely outcome.

Often our forecasts are not in line with the conventional wisdom. We don't automatically reject the majority view, but we subject it to the rigorous examination of skeptical reporters. We part company with the prevailing sentiment when it looks like a knee-jerk reaction.

This independence of thought helps us avoid the pitfalls of straight-line forecasting—predicting a continuation of present conditions without good reason. It helps us avoid excessive optimism when things are going well and despair when times are tough.

If our study of business cycles has taught us anything, it is that every excess is self-correcting. In the late '60s, when America was enjoying the longest economic expansion in history, the Kiplinger Letter warned that President Johnson's guns-and-butter fiscal policies were planting seeds of high inflation and recession in the next decade. Conversely, at the darkest hour of the severe recession of '81-82, when many pundits speculated on a coming depression, the Kiplinger Letter was urging its readers to be ready for a long, strong

expansion with declining inflation and lower interest rates. Later in the '80s, after five years of strong growth, some economists were proclaiming the repeal of the business cycle and forecasting endless national growth with only mild regional or sector recessions. We didn't believe that, and at the end of '87 we predicted five years of slower growth, punctuated by one national recession before '93.

Vagaries of politics

This independence extends to political reporting, too. We've learned from the mistakes of every reporter who ever covered a campaign—including our own miscues—not to assume anything.

We are acutely aware of the fickleness of public opinion and try to factor it into our forecasts. For example, in the afterglow of the '91 Gulf War, when George Bush's approval was running nearly 90% and most observers assumed his reelection in '92, we sounded a note of caution: The next election would be determined by the public's perception of the economy in mid '92, not its memory of Desert Storm. Similarly, many pundits wrote off a stumbling Bill Clinton in the spring of '92, doubting he would be nominated, let alone elected president. Independent Ross Perot was the choice of more than 40% of prospective voters at the time. But the Kiplinger Letter predicted that Perot would rapidly lose ground and Clinton would steadily rise from his third position in the polls to be a formidable candidate.

Our judgments were offered without regard for our own presidential preferences or those of our staff. This kind of analysis has enabled the Kiplinger Letter to make accurate calls, with just one exception, in every presidential election since 1924, including the very narrow victories of Kennedy over Nixon in 1960 and Carter over Ford in 1976. The one exception was the Letter's infamous miscall of the 1948 election.

W. M. Kiplinger was so certain of President Truman's eventual defeat that he made the call in mid '48, even before the Republican convention picked Thomas Dewey as its candidate. He reiterated that judgment through the fall, even as he noted that Dewey wasn't exciting the electorate and Truman was beginning to gain a little ground. On election night he hosted a dinner party at his home in Bethesda, Md., and he didn't even have his radio tuned in to the election results. He learned the shocking news of Truman's growing lead from a colleague who telephoned during the dinner party. Kiplinger returned to his guests with an ashen face, knowing that he had made the worst forecasting blunder in his 25 years of publishing. Compounding the error was a single-topic issue of the *Kiplinger Magazine* entitled "What Dewey Will Do," mailed *before* the election to impress its subscribers. In a special "shop talk" letter to subscribers a week later, Kiplinger ate crow and said the error resulted from the cardinal sin of forecasting—failure to continue reporting and analyzing right down to the wire. He took no solace in the fact that he had plenty of company in underestimating Truman, and he promptly refunded the subscription fees of many irate subscribers.

Looking ahead

While the Letter's editorial approach has remained constant since its founding, the tempo of change in Washington and the nation has accelerated over the years. Take, for example, the speed of turnover in the White House. In its first 38 years of publication, with W. M. Kiplinger as editor, the Letter covered the administrations of just five presidents. In the next 32 years, under the editorship of Austin Kiplinger, the Letter dealt with eight presidents, and only one of them (Ronald Reagan) served two full terms.

The last three decades have been marked by amazing turmoil: Assassination of a President. Resignation of a President. Vietnam. Student unrest and urban riots. Space exploration. Expansion of rights and economic power for racial minorities and women. Oil embargoes. Soaring inflation. Environmentalism. Millions of immigrants. The computer revolution. Restructuring of world business. Sweeping tax cuts—and hikes. European integration. War in the Middle East and the Balkans. The rise of Asian industry. The collapse of Soviet communism. Instant global communication. Surging foreign trade and global investment.

In our lifetimes we have witnessed a broad improvement in the human condition. It has come in fits and starts, never at the same pace or in the same way. Some critics today believe the improvement has stopped, but we disagree. We believe America is still making strides to better the rights, opportunities and material comforts of its citizens.

As we travel around the nation—reporting, listening and talking with people—we see firsthand the adaptability, resilience and imagination of the American people. It gives us confidence that America is still setting the pace as the most powerful cultural and economic force in the world.

This book concludes with our freshest judgments on where America is headed in the '90s. As with the forecasts from earlier times, their soundness won't be evident for a while, perhaps for years. We hope that, after you've read *Looking Ahead* and put it on the shelf, you'll take it down from time to time for a check on how things came out. At the very least, it will evoke memories of these times, and perhaps it will give you some perspective on the new challenges America will be facing at that moment.

Our best wishes to you in all your endeavors.

Austin Kiplinger

Austin H. Kiplinger

Knight Kiplinger

Knight A. Kiplinger

Washington, D.C.
September 1993

The Boston Daily Globe

MARGIN ACCOUNT DUMPING BRINGS STOCK CRASH
ANY FURTHER DIVES BANKERS PREPARE TO CHECK

BINGHAM FACES CENSURE THREAT

Second Slump More Drastic Than Thursday's But Volume of Trading Is Cut to 9,212,800— Curb Securities Hit Hardest in History

1920s

The Twenties was a time of amazing ferment in America: strong economic growth, unevenly shared; political and social emancipation of women; a flood of new labor-saving consumer goods, purchasable on credit; jazz music; spectacular motion pictures; a mania for pro sports; intellectual flirtation with left-wing ideologies; racial strife and mainstream support for the Ku Klux Klan; a penchant for private entrepreneurship with little interference from government.

The decade opened with two bold social experiments: a national vote for women and a ban on the sale of alcoholic beverages. The first endured. The second was a social disaster that would lead to the creation of organized crime to fill an undiminished consumer demand for booze.

World War I had imposed on the U.S. economy the first broad regimentation of private business in the nation's history—price and production controls, nationalization of railroads, farm subsidies, a corporate income tax, war-profits taxes, federal excise taxes and more. Personal tax rates soared. From a 1913 minimum rate of 1%, which covered relatively few prosperous Americans, the bottom rate jumped during World War I to 4%, coverage was vastly broadened, and the top rate—only 6% at the inception of income taxes—soared to 67%.

Postwar adjustment

After the Great War, Americans were eager to return to "normalcy," as President Warren Harding called it. The wartime economic controls were discarded quickly, and most income-tax rates were lowered later in the '20s. But normalcy was hard to achieve at first. The end of the wartime production boom brought a recession that lasted through mid 1921. Faced with declining sales, businesses reduced production, slashed wages and laid off workers.

This led to labor unrest and strikes across the nation. Poor blacks from the rural South flooded into border cities looking for work, and resentful whites attacked them in bloody race riots in East St. Louis, Ill., Washington, D.C., and other cities.

Many American workers believed their pay would be

1920			1921		1922	1923
SENATE REJECTS LEAGUE OF NATIONS.	LICENSED RADIO BROADCASTING BEGINS.	WOMEN GET THE VOTE.	CONGRESS CURBS IMMIGRATION.	MAJOR POWERS AGREE TO ARMS LIMITATIONS.	MUSSOLINI BECOMES ITALIAN DICTATOR.	36 KILLED IN U.S. COAL STRIKES. FIRST SOUND MOVIE SHOWN.

higher if there were fewer immigrants competing for the same jobs, and employers suspected immigrants of being partial to labor unions and other left-leaning causes. Nativist sentiment was fanned by the ascendance of Bolsheviks in Russia and a wave of anarchist bombings in the U.S. In 1921 Congress voted the first broad restriction on immigration in our nation's history, and over the decade the foreign-born percentage of the U.S. population, which had been rising for years, declined from 7% to 6%.

By 1922 American business had begun to expand, pushed by new technologies that would revolutionize life in America and eventually the whole world. The spread of electric power throughout urban and small-town America stimulated the invention of new electrical devices to make daily life more convenient and entertaining—washing machines, vacuum cleaners, refrigerators, toasters, radios, phonographs and more. Motion pictures, even without the voices of the new movie stars, became a national passion. A dazzling new invention that could transmit moving pictures and voices through the air was demonstrated in 1927, but another two decades would pass before commercial television emerged.

America on the move

More than any other technology, the automobile remade American life in the '20s. Mass production and falling prices brought cars within the reach of average Americans and in the process created entire new industries in petroleum refining, rubber, trucking, tourism, and construction of highways, filling stations, and roadside restaurants and tourist cabins. The spread of automobiles made possible the development of outlying neighborhoods called suburbs. In 1920 there were some eight million cars in America. By the end of the decade, the number had nearly tripled, to more than 23 million.

The '20s saw the birth of an aviation industry, too. World War I had romanticized the ace pilot in his biplane, but an outspoken Army officer named Col. Billy Mitchell was court-martialed in 1925 after he urged creation of a U.S. air force and criticized his superiors for going too slowly on developing military aircraft. The commercial implications of aviation, for the movement of mail, cargo and finally passengers, began to dawn on foresighted investors and communities. Aviation got an enormous lift—and the world a soft-spoken new hero—when Charles Lindbergh made a solo nonstop flight across the Atlantic in 1927. When the decade opened, there was no such thing as a commercial airline. By 1929 there were more than 40.

The consumer economy

The explosive growth of new technologies in the '20s—cars, consumer appliances, radio networks, filmmaking, aviation and more—fueled similar growth in advertising, retailing and publishing. Making and marketing the new goods of a new era created vast amounts of income, not just for the owners of the businesses but for employees, too. From 1922 through 1929, the U.S. economy expanded at an average annual rate of 5%, and it was a boom without inflation. Consumer prices actually declined slightly during the decade, due to international competition, stable food prices and surging productivity from automation. To stimulate even stronger retail sales, stores began offering their customers credit that could be repaid in installments. And the Ford Motor Company shocked the automotive business with a revolutionary new plan to lend its money directly to buyers of their new cars.

Middle-class American consumers sought to participate in the growing economy not just as customers but as owners, by investing in the hot stocks of the new technologies—automotive, radio, chemicals, steel, electric utilities, and so on. Share prices rose strongly on genuinely stronger earnings, and stockbrokers flourished. Small investors pooled their money to buy shares in multistock portfolios called investment trusts, the first mutual funds. Aided by cash in their pockets and new concrete roads leading south, thousands of Americans flocked to Florida in the early to mid '20s to buy houses or lots in new subdivisions, for vacations, retirement homes, permanent residences—or resale later at a higher price.

The boom of the '20s was not universally shared, either

CONGRESS GIVES AMERICAN INDIANS CITIZENSHIP.	LENIN DIES, STALIN TAKES OVER USSR.	ENGLAND ELECTS FIRST LABOUR GOVERNMENT.	CONGRESS EXPOSES TEAPOT DOME SCANDAL.	TENNESSEE CONVICTS TEACHER FOR TEACHING EVOLUTION.	FUNDAMENTALISTS TAKE OVER IN ARABIA.	FITZGERALD'S "THE GREAT GATSBY" PUBLISHED.

1924   **1925**

within America or around the world. In many factory sectors there was little growth in real wages over the decade. Inside the U.S., most Negro Americans lived in poverty on farms in the southern states, excluded by law, custom and limited education from participation in the growing economy. A large segment of the general population—the one-third of the labor force in the agricultural sector—never recovered from the economic slump at the end of the World War.

American farming had flourished during World War I. European production was decimated by war, and world grain prices exploded. The U.S. government stimulated farm production with subsidies, and farmers expanded their planting to meet the demand, borrowing heavily to buy more land and machinery. The whole process went into reverse when the war ended and production returned to normal in Europe. Prices fell, subsidies ended, U.S. farmers struggled under the burden of debt, and many tried to maintain their income by boosting production, which only accelerated the price collapse. Farmers pressured the White House and Congress for a variety of aid programs, ranging from easing of farm credit and higher tariffs on foreign farm goods to government purchases of farm surpluses. In 1921 Congress raised tariffs on agricultural products, the first of numerous protectionist measures in the '20s to restrict the import of a wide variety of raw materials and manufactured goods. After ten years of pushing for government purchases of surpluses, the farm lobby finally achieved this in 1929 with the creation of the Federal Farm Board.

Troubles abroad

If middle-class prosperity was not broadly shared within the U.S., it was even less common elsewhere, even in industrialized Europe. After involvement in Europe's war, most Americans were uninterested in foreign affairs, whether the rise of communism in Russia and China, the first tremors of fascism in Germany and Italy, or frequent U.S. interventions in Nicaragua. America emerged from World War I a true superpower, the strongest economy on earth. But it didn't use its economic might to help rebuild either its allies or its former foes.

Since its founding, the United States had been a debtor to the rest of the world, but in World War I it became the world's chief creditor. It was owed $10 billion by its allies (England, France and Italy), and the allies in turn demanded enormous reparations from the defeated Germany. To repay loans and reparations to America, the nations of Europe needed access to the booming U.S. market to sell their manufactured and farm goods. But U.S. farmers and manufacturers didn't welcome the competition, even though they were selling their goods strongly in overseas markets. As European manufacturing got back on its feet and began sending more goods to America, U.S. firms successfully petitioned Congress to put ever-higher tariffs on imported goods, stunting growth in Europe. Great Britain sold off large amounts of gold to repay American war loans. Wall Street financiers lent their capital to European nations to help them repay the U.S. government. (Many of the loans would go into default in the worldwide depression of the next decade.) The Weimar Republic of Germany was battered by high inflation, and it secured from the U.S., in the Dawes Plan, a modest easing of reparations and enormous private American loans to keep repayments on schedule. Meanwhile, strident nationalist voices in Germany, among them those of rising politician Adolf Hitler, urged repudiation of the reparations.

Laizzez-faire

After the tight economic regulation of World War I, most Americans wanted political leadership that would let them go about their business without hindrance. Help from Washington, however, was always welcome, and it was avidly sought by industry and agriculture. Republican Warren Harding died in 1923, leaving only a legacy of political corruption, notably the Teapot Dome scandal, which involved oil leases on federal lands in Wyoming and California. Things quieted down under the stewardship of Calvin Coolidge, who decreed that "the business of America is business." Most Americans agreed.

Laissez-faire was the rule. The principal government assistance to business was tax reduction and protection from

ARMY AIR CORPS CREATED.	RAILWAY LABOR ACT ESTABLISHES MEDIATION SYSTEM.	IN U.S., FIRST LIQUID-FUEL ROCKET.	FLORIDA LAND BOOM COLLAPSES.	U.S. MARINES LAND IN CHINA TO PROTECT AMERICAN PROPERTY.	LINDBERGH FLIES SOLO, NEW YORK-PARIS.
1926				**1927**	

foreign competition. From 1926 through 1928, there were major cuts in income and inheritance taxes. Many business owners decried overcapacity and low prices in their fields, and they longed for relief from antitrust laws that barred them from combining and colluding with competitors to firm up prices. World War I veterans demanded a special bonus for their service, and in 1924 Congress voted one and made it stick over Coolidge's veto.

Employers were free to deal with their workers as they wished, without laws stating minimum wages, maximum hours or working conditions. Private pensions were rare, and there were no public retirement benefits either. Most unions were weak, led by men nearly as conservative as management. The "open shop," meaning nonunion, was the norm, and organizing workers was difficult.

Governmental regulation of the economy, such as it was, centered on tariffs and farm policy. The fairly new Federal Reserve Board watched over banks and credit. The Federal Trade Commission concerned itself with antitrust laws. There was considerable business-promotion vitality in the Commerce Department, headed by the highly respected Herbert Hoover, an engineer and businessman who had impressed the world with his management of postwar European relief. When Coolidge decided not to run for reelection in 1928, the Republicans turned to Hoover.

A faltering boom

Cracks began to appear in the U.S. economy by mid decade. Residential construction peaked in '25 and then declined, and commercial and industrial construction fell off in '29. The Florida land boom started to cool in '26, and two devastating hurricanes that year led to a collapse in prices. Lenders concerned about rising debt, especially to foreign nations, began to demand higher interest rates. By 1928 unemployment was rising in manufacturing, profits were being squeezed, and real wage growth had flattened.

In a decade dominated by newly rich industrialists and New York financiers, Washington was an observer of the passing parade. Federal officials were usually reduced to fretting over unstable situations they couldn't or didn't want to control, like the spread of consumer installment buying, the plight of the farmer, the Florida land boom, or—most of all—the sharply rising stock market.

The speculative fever didn't really take hold, especially with small investors, until 1928, late in the economy's long growth cycle. In 1926 average share prices were about 62% above 1920's—solid but not spectacular appreciation. But those prices more than doubled over the next three years. The volume of shares traded on Wall Street doubled between 1927 and 1929. There were no limits on what portion of a stock purchase could be financed with margin loans, and investors borrowed freely to chase hot stocks, such as RCA, which shot from $85 to $420 during 1928. Most of the margin loans came from banks, which were free to invest in stocks and give loans to brokers.

Free-falling stocks

A few alarmed experts, notably banker Paul Warburg and financial analyst Roger Babson, issued warnings. Federal Reserve officials in Washington privately hoped for a therapeutic "correction" to cool the fever. Savvy investors began selling in early October 1929, and demands for more collateral went out to overleveraged speculators. After a particularly steep drop, the captains of Wall Street tried to stem the sell-off with well-publicized purchases, but to no avail. A few days later—on Tuesday, October 29, 1929—the market collapsed. Investors collectively lost some $8 billion in one day and a cumulative $30 billion over the following few weeks.

In late November President Hoover convened a Washington conference of business leaders to try to convince them to maintain current production and employment as long as possible, and the conference adjourned in agreement. While he sounded confident and optimistic in his public statements, Hoover privately told the conferees he was gravely concerned that the Wall Street crisis would spread into a broad business slump of indeterminate length and depth.

1928				1929		
HOOVER ELECTED PRESIDENT.		STALIN LAUNCHES FIRST FIVE-YEAR PLAN.		CONGRESS PASSES AGRICULTURAL MARKETING ACT.	STOCK MARKET CRASHES.	
	EARHART BECOMES FIRST WOMAN TO FLY THE ATLANTIC.		CHIANG KAI-SHEK CRACKS DOWN ON CHINESE COMMUNISTS.			STALIN COLLECTIVIZES FARMS IN USSR.

September 29, 1923

      Rumors of an international <u>German loan</u> are renewed — a loan to revive the mark. No German loan will come without plenty of advance notice, and the mark will not come back. Begin to watch for the <u>decline of the franc</u>, too.

      <u>Washington will not give the farmers much relief</u>; it can't. The proposal for a government-financed wheat exporting corporation probably means subsidy, is an emergency shot-in-the-arm.

      Banks are getting ready to ask Congress for legislation to remove the <u>tax exemption privileges from building and loan associations</u>. They probably won't succeed.

October 6, 1923

      Treasury is working on recommendations for <u>legislation to simplify income tax procedure</u>.

      <u>Prohibition is not a closed issue</u>: drys do not measure accurately the organized propaganda and unorganized sentiment against it; wets underestimate the non-vocal strength for it. Big anti-prohibition collections are being taken.

October 13, 1923

      Look out for <u>raising of foreign tariff walls against American exports</u>; we have information that this may happen.

October 20, 1923

A great wind of <u>tax revision talk</u> blows up, preceding the coming Congressional storm; Treasury wants many amendments in procedure and maybe reductions; Smoot stands pat against much revision, fearing Pandora's box; Borah says reduce; western radicals say lift the burden on poor men; Democrats say nothing but plan something embarrassing to administration; dozen other groups come forth with special programs; <u>soldiers' bonus</u> and its tax question brother stand in the offing.

<u>Soviet government downfall</u> — perhaps eventually, but not now, our reports indicate; American government has ample information on Russia to answer all specific trade inquiries; no need for accepting vague rumors or propaganda.

December 15, 1923

Look for legislation regulating <u>commercial aviation and radio</u>.

A new campaign to <u>raise tariff duties</u> on many articles now imported from Europe is being organized secretly by group of American manufacturers. We think there is no chance of adoption. One feature of campaign is to charge <u>retailers</u> with high profits on cheap imported articles.

<u>Agriculture</u>. Fight now brewing between Secretary Wallace's plan for <u>government corporation to finance exports</u> of grain, pork and other agricultural products and Eugene Meyer's plan to have War Finance Corporation do it. Just now we think Wallace plan has more chance. Secretary Hoover says on <u>wheat</u>: "It seems necessary gradually to reduce acreage."

December 20, 1923

<u>Russia</u>. Many able Russians now visiting England, whose views can be trusted, say that state capitalism in Russia (the new economic policy, or "N.E.P.") is failing; prices remain oppressively high. Nevertheless, <u>soviet government has come to stay</u>, with certain modifications. Another important development: <u>New generation of Russians are different</u>; they are keen, active, and out for money-making; not like the old Slavic dreamers. Bolsheviks are going strongly after government recognition and foreign credits.

V.I. Lenin led the Bolsheviks
to power in Russia.

1924

"Silent Cal" Coolidge opens the baseball season.

March 1, 1924

<u>Scandal</u>. Preponderating opinion in Washington is that oil investigation will be dominant issue in political campaign. We don't quite agree; think rather that business prosperity, expressed in variety of ways, including insistence on clean government, will be the stuff of issues; clean government alone is too unanimous an issue. Coolidge will clean house, but deliberately, in his way. Daugherty will resign.

March 22, 1924

<u>More investigations are planned</u>. Teapot Dome so far has shown only nasty loans to a cabinet officer, but will pass into <u>new stage of showing party campaign contributions</u> for purposes of influence; this is the most fruitful field of any or all investigations, but both parties are afraid to go deep, for they will soon be looking for contributions.

April 26, 1924

More tourists in town this week than any time in Washington history; they file through the President's office silently, watching him work. <u>How would you like to be President</u>?

May 3, 1924

Certainly a beneficent government activity: Secretary Hoover's department will investigate reasons for <u>shrinkage of underwear</u>.

June 13, 1924

<u>BRIEF SUMMARY OF DAWES PLAN, to refresh your recollection</u>: Germany pays reparations by annual <u>installments next ten years</u>, total well above twenty billion gold marks.
<u>Reparation payments are to be from these sources</u>: (1) General budget; (2) interest from railroad bonds, railroads to be mortgaged for eleven billions; (3) transportation taxes; (4) interest from industrial debenture bonds, German industries to be mortgaged for the purpose, like railroad; (5) a loan of 800,000,000 gold marks, this year only.

August 22, 1924

<u>Immediate benefits from Dawes plan? No. Long time benefits? Yes</u>. There's feeling here that business interests are overestimating revival of business attributable to early operation of Dawes plan and consequent stabilization of Germany and Europe. Results will be very gradual, stimulate export of raw materials from U.S. only as industrial structure of Europe is built up.
<u>Now for nip-and-tuck international industrial competition</u>. American government will begin this fall in various ways to warn American industry that it must gird its loans for more active competition than at any time since pre-war. Stabilized industry in Central Europe will push industry in France and England, and all together will go after markets in which American interests now have their own way. There is much talk in Washington these days of "super-competition" in world trade.
<u>As a consequence, big tariff agitation is coming at next session</u>. Various business interests have been in informal consultation with government agencies in recent weeks, disclosing plans for campaigns to get tariff rates boosted on certain manufactured products next winter. Don't get over-optimistic about success of these efforts.

October 3, 1924

> More airplanes, for war, and commercial flying—you will see this become one of the big national issues during the next eighteen months. Some officials want to put commercial flying first, have government subsidize or otherwise help it, and trail fighting flying behind; think it will go better with this country. Fairly certain that there will be more aerial mail routes; get one for your city.

November 22, 1924

> Stock market boom worries officials here, but they can't do much about it. General conclusion reached was that funds from interior are largely supporting the spectacular market, that commercial credit is not being affected seriously, that funds of reserve banks are not being drawn upon heavily, that sudden move to raise rediscount rates might shock the country, bringing effect psychologically rather than by direct financial mechanics.
>
> You ask what Washington thinks of the stock market. Well, this is a situation in which Washington opinion is not worth much; Washington did not think the market would go as long and as high as it has; now thinks surely the break is near.

February 20, 1925

> Aviation. General feeling in Washington is that General Mitchell went too far in criticizing army and navy, but that agitation will be beneficial for future of aviation; important developments are expected in commercial aviation within the year. New things expected in dirigibles.

March 13, 1925

> Private manufacture of aircraft will be stimulated by new decision of government to stay out of manufacture and repair field.

March 20, 1925

> More on amending anti-trust laws: A series of more-or-less confidential discussions is now going on in Washington looking at industrial combinations under certain emergency conditions. Principal argument for this plan is that many industries are now working on an uneconomic basis, wasting resources, duplicating effort, engaging in cut-throat competition which temporarily brings price reductions but which in long run is not in public interest. Men engaged in these discussions have not yet worked out satisfactory plan for protecting public interest against artificial price fixing; working on this now.

1925

General Billy Mitchell's outspoken views about military air power led to his court-martial.

FLORIDA REAL ESTATE AGENT—Can't ye just see it? The sunken garden here, the garage there, and the kiddies playing around the house!

August 28, 1925

Real estate booms in Florida and in many localities throughout the United States are beginning to attract attention of government policy-makers, who fear over-expansion, and subsequent set-back which might affect more lines of business than real estate. Reports now coming in that some established business enterprises have difficulty getting capital because it is being used in Florida. Will Federal Reserve System do anything to check? Well, there are no signs of it. Some government offices are being depopulated by emigration to Florida; nothing like it here since the war.

1926

January 4, 1926

Political situation on agriculture is really quite serious, according to all the quiet talk here. Fears disturbing to business interests arise less out of issue of disposing of exportable agricultural surpluses, than out of threat of agricultural bloc in Congress, led by Senator Capper, Republican, to demand downward revision of tariff. Truth is, in our opinion, that this will not happen at present session, but the growing threat of combination of Democrats and Western Republicans on tariff revision, is going to cause real uneasiness in next three months.

March 15, 1926

St. Lawrence outlet from Great Lakes, rather than development of New York Barge Canal route, is favored in private conversations by most officials here. They are disappointed at sudden precipitation of "all-American issue" in the dispute over routes, feeling this is set-back to effort to develop relations of cooperation between U.S. and Canada.

September 13, 1926

Too many bothersome reports required of corporations by government agencies, federal and state, outside realm of taxes. One corporation has had to file between 350 and 400 reports already this year, mainly with state governments. Some are proper, some are of doubtful use, many are comparable but requiring different arrangement of figures.

September 20, 1926

Politics. The President's return to Washington is stimulating political speculation: (1) Will Coolidge be a "third term" candidate? Impression is growing that he will be. Our own inclination is to think developments will be such that he will voluntarily withdraw, but this is only a guess. (2) Is Hoover a candidate? Not actively. An influential junta of business men want him, but the politicians are not taking him up, and he is not courting the politicians. Anything like a "Hoover boom" would embarrass him in his work, and would start political attacks on him.

September 27, 1926

Some means of unifying the various banking systems of the country, national and 48 states, is under the very closest study in high quarters here. Discussion is revolving around a plan of having Congress legalize as "secondary currency" checks drawn on member banks of the Federal Reserve System, and penalize by a tax (mentioned as 10%) all checks drawn on non-member banks.

November 22, 1926

Installment selling. A year ago Washington economic opinion was noticeably fearful of installment selling, and several high officials were considering issuance of statements discouraging its further growth. Some of these same men now tell us they have reached the conclusion that installment selling is economically sound and permanent.

They note various exceptions, most mentioning clothing as an undesirable object for installment selling. They have ceased trying to distinguish between "luxuries" and "necessities."

Chiang Kai-shek headed the Chinese government.

January 17, 1927

   Systematic campaign for corporate income tax reduction to 12-1/2% is now on. Business leaders are seeing members of Congress and administration officials. Word from inner circle is that it will not be done, but pressure may change this.

April 4, 1927

   China. In spite of official denials, it is known here that plans are being made to send large detachments of the army to reinforce the marines in the event of a further outbreak. The split in the nationalist faction into communist and anti-communist groups is looked upon as a most serious development with grave dangers to American interests.

May 16, 1927

   The statement from the White House, to the effect that the methods employed in the pacification of Nicaragua are not important if the desired result is obtained, is further ammunition for the anti-administration Republicans and Democrats who are planning a violent attack on the administration's Latin American policy in December. Certain large industrial corporations interested in South American trade are planning protests to the State Department to secure a less high-handed policy, which is resulting in increase of anti-American sentiment south of the Rio Grande with corresponding damage to American trade.

May 31, 1927

   Securities market. We note an undercurrent of feeling here that securities markets generally are too high, but nobody in authoritative position seems to have any definite idea as to when they may break. The talk outside Washington is that the administration will not allow a break. This is freely characterized here as too bullish. The truth seems to be that the administration would not be averse to a quieting down of the market, so that it would feel free to reduce rediscount rates. Furthermore, a decline is preferred in the next few months, rather than next year, for political reasons.

June 20, 1927

   As a result of the Lindbergh flight, inquiries to the Department of Commerce for information on how to establish airports have tripled. Cities are now scrambling for the first time to be designated as stations on the regular air routes as now laid out or projected.

August 22, 1927

   Will American loans abroad stimulate foreign industrial competition with our own industries, making us eventually an "importing nation" with an unfavorable trade balance? The Department of Commerce thinks "it is impossible to predict with assurance that the United States will ever have an unfavorable balance of trade." The Department of Labor gives currency to the view that American capital is likely to turn to foreign production, on account of lower labor costs, and thereby undercut social standards in this country.

August 22, 1927

Investment trusts. The mushroom development of hundreds of small investment trusts in the last few months has been called to the attention of a number of officials. The official comment is that "the federal government has no concern with investment trusts." The unofficial and personal comment is to the effect that too many investment trusts are being organized hastily, with inadequate personnel and experience, and that only the fittest will survive. One man remarks, "The movement has some points of resemblance to the Florida boom."

October 10, 1927

Business. During the past week we have noted in the private conversations of government officials and economists and of business men visiting here, a distinctly increased fear that the securities markets will slide off from their present high levels. The majority think any decline would not be precipitate, but a thoughtful minority are fearful of a bad slump, frightening out the numerous small investors and speculators who are supposed to be maintaining the present market.

Farm lands. We hear the opinion in unofficial but authoritative quarters that farm land prices generally have not reached bottom, and will have no great upward movement for some years. Comment comes in connection with the big corporations, one formed, others forming, to buy up foreclosed farm lands from banks, insurance companies and mortgage houses, operate the farms or sell on easy terms to individuals who have good records as tenants. Plans of these corporations are receiving commendation in agricultural quarters here.

October 31, 1927

Selling the fear of bolshevism, collecting funds from prominent business men to fight red activities, has become such a business that officials are called upon frequently to give advice. They say bolshevism is over-rated; that many anti-red propagandists are merely making a living at it.

November 7, 1927

    <u>The new Ford financing scheme</u>: Surplus of Ford capital will be employed in the partial ownership of hundreds of thousands of cars, the drivers being co-owners. The instalment basis will be widened tremendously, with all its stabilizing influences and its dangers. (Washington opinion of gradually growing away from the former fear of instalment buying.) The feeling here is that <u>the plan represents a stimulant to general business conditions for the future</u>.

1928

April 9, 1928

    <u>The big economic issues of the next five years</u>, with its accompanying political aspects, will revolve around the <u>status of city workers</u> — such things as steady employment, stabilization of industry to provide this, better city housing, cheaper distribution as a step toward lower prices, maintenance of the tariff (though perhaps at a lower level for the sake of promoting export trade), and the "full gasoline tank," which is the modern counterpart of the full dinner pail of the early 1900's.

    Political and economic issues move in cycles: Free silver for the west was followed by the full dinner pail for the east. Equality for agriculture, now nearly attained, will be followed by a wave of attention to industrial workers, and the current unemployment is one of the first symptoms of the new set of issues.

    <u>The present unemployment is not temporary</u>. The things which have caused it will continue to cause more of it — mainly readjustment of industry, machine methods, shifting of plants from one line to another.

Early assembly line in a tire factory.

April 30, 1928

<u>Difficult business ahead, next five years</u>?
The United States will be faced by increasingly stiff competition from the reviving industries of Europe within the next few years, and the evidence of this will be quite apparent in 1929. Now it is regarded as abnormal and temporary, and the belief is that surely improvement is just around the corner. This view is false and misleading, and will slowly be abandoned.

The more optimistic feel that American mass production methods will adequately counter-balance the effects of European competition. But even the men with this view look for many forced combinations and consolidations of American firms in the process.

The thought also takes the form of a prediction that the United States will remodel its anti-trust laws, to permit more latitude in combinations and cooperation through trade associations or institutes. This development will come after the fact, not before. (Remedial legislation never is seriously considered until the situation requiring remedy is well upon us.)

From a political angle, it is frequently said that the party which is in power between 1929 and 1933, will have more than its share of troubles, and will have difficulty maintaining itself in the presidential elections of 1932. There are those who say Mr. Coolidge recognizes this, and therefore will not consent to serve another term.

August 6, 1928

There is frank disappointment here over the failure of Federal Reserve influences to keep the stock market down during the past month. <u>The market is called "dangerously high"</u>. There is division of opinion as to the reaction on basic business of a drastic decline; the weight of opinion seems to be that business expansion in the fall will feel the effects of the digression of funds to an inflated stock market, and of the postponement of capital projects due to high money rates.

September 10, 1928

<u>Stock market is still regarded as precarious</u>. Decline has been expected weekly, and the lack of this development does not seem to kill the Washington expectation that it will come. Begin to hear much talk to effect that stocks as a whole have not been spectacular like the leaders.

November 12, 1928

<u>Stock market</u>. Private views of Washington authorities are pretty well represented by one comment. "The public is buying activity rather than values." All official and unofficial comment out of Washington touching upon the stock market is "warning." We would give you bullish reports if we could find any. Can't.

1929

President Coolidge, Treasury Secretary Andrew Mellon, and incoming President Herbert Hoover.

January 14, 1929

Authorities who give direct consideration to the condition of credit and who keep an indirect eye on the stock market continue to speak freely in private conversations of the "<u>dangerously high position of the stock market</u>."

July 29, 1929

If brokers' loans continue to rise, then Board will "consider new steps", with rediscount rate increase as the first of several alternatives. The feeling here seems to be, however, that this will not be necessary. In quite a few conversations the remark is made that "<u>stock market will correct itself shortly</u>." The inference is that present price levels are too high.

October 7, 1929

<u>Stock market</u>. The Washington attitude is that the drastic decline in securities prices is a most beneficial development. Veiled warnings of it have emanated from authoritative quarters here for some time and have been reflected in our recent letters.

Now the feeling seems to be that the <u>market will be irregular for a while, the average going even lower</u> some time within the next 30 days, then starting a "slow but sane climb."

<u>Business conditions</u> are considered generally satisfactory.

October 28, 1929

<u>Washington policies had nothing directly to do with stock market break</u>. There was no tightness of credit for securities, no shortage of money for business (excepting for building, mortgage money, which Washington can't control directly), and no startling government development. "It was New York's show, not Washington's." Private opinion of high Washington authorities who cannot be quoted but whose views have been reflected in previous letters, turns out to be justified. Seven weeks ago they agreed with the tone of Roger Babson's warning, as we reported, but thought he had gone too far, and it turns out that he was right.

The Boston Daily Globe

BOSTON, TUESDAY MORNING, OCTOBER 29, 1929—THIRTY-SIX PAGES — TWO CENTS

MARGIN ACCOUNT DUMPING BRINGS STOCK CRASH ANY FURTHER DIVES BANKERS PREPARE TO CHECK

BINGHAM FACES CENSURE THREAT

Norris Gives Notice of Motion Today on Lobby Charges

Connecticut Senator Hotly Answers Critics, Biting Reply by Caraway

WARDEN FOILS PRISON BREAK AT THOMASTON

MRS CURLEY STORY DENIED BY COAKLEY

BANKERS CONFER ON STOCK CRASH

Second Slump More Drastic Than Thursday's But Volume of Trading Is Cut to 9,212,800— Curb Securities Hit Hardest in History

ATTENDED BANKERS' CONFERENCE

Investment Group Ready to Enter Market Today With Buying Orders to Support Prices

Banking Officials Optimistic Over Future For Business and Not Alarmed by Break

SENATOR BURTON DIES AT 77 IN CAPITAL

November 18, 1929

   Summary of the 600 letters: Business is "fundamentally sound," which is the expression used by many. Cancellations of orders are not numerous at the present time, but there are enough to cause much scattered concern about the immediate future, and it is the prospect for new orders one, two and three months hence that is worrying manufacturers.
   A spirit of caution on future commitments is displayed in scores of letters from all kinds of manufacturers, jobbers and retailers. They may not be trimming expenses now, but they are prepared to do so after the turn of the year "if circumstances warrant." This is akin to the "psychology of pessimism" which many say is not warranted, but which they fear may get started anyway and do some unnecessary harm.

December 9, 1929

   Incoming correspondence shows this question in everyone's mind: Did the business conference here last week really accomplish much practical good, or was it merely the finale of a series of conferences designed to whip up enthusiasm artificially and temporarily?

   The conference results will NOT be to prevent a business recession of some undetermined proportions during first half of 1930. The decline will be materially less, however, than if this conference had not been held. Recovery will be quicker. Many competent observers believe only two or three months will be required for "adjustment," but our impression is that it will take longer.
   A serious depression is not on the business horizon. Indeed, there were plenty of hard-headed unsentimental men at this conference who sincerely believe that 1930 will be what they call a "good year."

1930s

TWO TIMES IS ENOUGH FOR ANY MAN

The decade of the Thirties dawned just two months after the worst stock market crash in history, and it came to a close as Germany's military juggernaut rolled across Europe in the autumn of 1939. In the ten years between, America and the world struggled unsuccessfully to restore living standards to pre-Depression levels, failing to achieve this even with massive government relief and employment.

Not surprisingly, the Crash of '29, with its damage to purchasing power and consumer confidence, led to a contraction of business activity. But there wasn't a widespread feeling that the contraction would be long and severe. There was little historical precedent for major government efforts to end a slump because recession was considered a normal, if painful, phase of the business cycle that had to run its course. The Hoover administration acted accordingly.

But as the recession deepened into depression in the three years after the crash, Hoover, prodded by Congress, tried more economic remedies than Washington had ever before undertaken. Work advanced on new hydroelectric projects in the West, the Boulder and Grand Coulee dams. The new Farm Board bought up agricultural surpluses to support prices. Hoover declared a one-year moratorium on European war debts to the U.S. Urging consumers and businesses to go out and spend, Hoover set an example by accelerating federal spending on roads and government office buildings. A new federal bank was created to forestall home-mortgage foreclosures. The boldest initiative of all was the Reconstruction Finance Corporation, which gave emergency federal loans to banks, corporations and railroads.

Deepening depression

But while these depression-fighting programs were being put in place, severe and largely unnoticed damage was being done to the U.S. and world economy by more-powerful U.S. policies on world trade and monetary regulation. Although many in Congress believed that tariff reductions would help the world economy, they

1930	1931	1932
SMOOT-HAWLEY TARIFF ACT PASSED.	EMPIRE STATE BUILDING OPENS.	HOOVER SETS UP RECONSTRUCTION FINANCE CORP.
DEMOCRATS WIN CONTROL OF HOUSE.	EUROPE ABANDONS GOLD STANDARD.	ROOSEVELT WINS IN LANDSLIDE.
	JAPAN INVADES MANCHURIA.	UNEMPLOYMENT REACHES 25% OF LABOR FORCE.
	SPAIN ESTABLISHES REPUBLICAN GOVERNMENT.	

were not able to withstand manufacturers' pressures for higher barriers to imports. In 1930 Congress passed, and Hoover signed, the high Smoot-Hawley Tariff, which deepened the depression in Europe and stifled foreign markets for U.S. goods. In monetary policy, the Federal Reserve Board sharply contracted the U.S. money supply for three years after the crash, rather than expanding credit to stimulate a recovery.

The economic decline wasn't steep at first, raising false hopes that the economy would bottom out and begin growing again in a year or so. The gross national product fell about 10% in 1930, and most employers just trimmed hours rather than laying off workers and cutting wages. But the spreading despair cut deeper into business and consumer spending, and soon widespread layoffs and wage cuts were rippling through the economy. By the end of 1932, GNP and industrial production had fallen 46% from the 1929 level, and joblessness had skyrocketed from 1.5 million in '29 to an estimated 12 to 16 million in '32—nearly a quarter of the labor force. With no unemployment benefits, many families fell into abject destitution. Many depositors, seeing their neighbors lose everything they had in bank failures, withdrew deposits in bank runs, compounding bank failures. More than 2,298 banks collapsed in '32, triple the '29 number.

Hoover and Roosevelt

For all his efforts to buck up confidence and stimulate the economy, Hoover came across to the average American as aloof and unconcerned. He confidently insisted that recovery would begin soon and estimates of unemployment were exaggerated. He urged better-off consumers and businesses to boost their spending as an act of confidence and benevolence. He opposed direct government relief, in goods and cash, because he feared it would dry up private giving to charities and, by creating dependency on a dole, impede the normal business recovery. When World War I veterans marched on Washington, demanding early payment of a bonus not due until 1945, Hoover allowed Army troops to rout them and destroy their

shantytowns. Meanwhile, states across the nation were experimenting with social programs far bolder than Washington's, such as unemployment insurance in Wisconsin and New York's program to create public-works jobs for the unemployed.

In the presidential race of '32, Democratic candidate Franklin D. Roosevelt spoke of a "new deal for the American people," but he never spelled out what it might consist of. The federal budget deficit had soared during the three-year plunge in GNP and tax receipts. Roosevelt ridiculed Hoover for excessive government spending and promised to balance the budget. While his record as governor of New York suggested an activist streak—supporting public old-age pensions, labor legislation, public utilities and unemployment insurance—candidate Roosevelt campaigned like a fiscal conservative. He won in a landslide, with the voters choosing not a coherent program but a personality that projected courage, hope and unspecified change.

Tumultuous change

In the four-month interregnum from election in November to inauguration in March, FDR's "brain trust" of professors and young liberal activists drafted a blueprint for a new American society, which would be directed by a federal government with powers unprecedented in peacetime America. They worked in secret, with hints of new intiatives leaking to the press in fragmentary trial balloons. Presenting their programs with confidence to a desperate Congress and American people, the New Dealers won passage of bold and untested programs within three months of taking office.

In his first term, FDR secured passage of laws that shored up banks, created social security, made direct cash payments to the poor, hiked income and inheritance taxes, insured bank deposits, regulated stock speculation, set production limits on agriculture to boost prices, enhanced the organizing and strike power of unions, subsidized housing, spread electric power through rural America, and put millions of youths and adults on the public payroll. The first New Deal also repealed

			U.S. AND RUSSIA			
	CONGRESS		RESUME			
FIRST WOMAN	APPROVES NEW		DIPLOMATIC	ITALY SIGNS		SECURITIES
NAMED TO CABINET,	DEAL PROGRAMS,		RELATIONS.	PACT WITH		AND
FRANCES PERKINS,	INCLUDING NRA.			GERMANY	DUST	EXCHANGE
LABOR.				AND JAPAN.	STORMS	COMMISSION
		HITLER	PROHIBITION		DEVASTATE	CREATED.
1933		BECOMES	REPEALED.	**1934**	MIDWEST	
	FDR CLOSES	GERMAN			FARMS.	
	BANKS, TAKES	DICTATOR				
	U.S. OFF GOLD					
	STANDARD.					

Prohibition, authorized 50% tariff cuts if other nations reciprocated (which few did), and took the U.S. off the gold standard to stimulate price inflation.

The centerpiece of the New Deal was the National Recovery Act, which allowed—indeed, pressured—firms in major business sectors to reach industrywide agreements limiting production, setting prices and combining resources, with exemption from antitrust laws. Big business had lobbied GOP administrations for similar authority in the fierce competition of the '20s but had always been rejected. Now, in exchange for government-sanctioned collusion, businesses agreed to unprecedented gains for labor, including collective bargaining rights, a minimum wage and a shorter workweek. There was widespread business support for the NRA, especially at the U.S. Chamber of Commerce, but most members of the National Association of Manufacturers opposed it.

Economic activity bottomed in 1933 and began a long, slow climb. The causes were many—the natural rhythm of business cycles, the first flows of federal money from Washington, a new confidence that it was safe to spend and invest again. It is not clear that the New Deal's economic restructuring, especially the NRA and production limits in agriculture, actually aided the recovery, and at the time even some liberal economists (at the Brookings Institution, for example) argued that they hurt. The strongest period of growth in the 1930s occurred between '35 and '37, after the Supreme Court struck down as unconstitutional a major section of the NRA and later the farm program. Unemployment remained high throughout the decade, and private job creation was weak.

Trouble for FDR

While FDR battled conservative opponents of the New Deal, he also had to watch his left flank. His programs were attacked as inadequate and halfhearted by unionists, pro-communist intellectuals, and share-the-wealth populists ranging from Louisiana Governor Huey Long and Dr. Francis Townsend

to the anti-semitic "radio priest" Father Coughlin. But FDR's landslide reelection in '36 emboldened him to accelerate his overhaul of American government, and more social legislation was enacted. FDR and his confidants began to discuss privately an unprecedented third presidential term.

His consensus was already coming unraveled, however. Business owners and conservative Democratic politicians were tiring of the new regimentation and the cost of the welfare state. Middle-class Americans were frightened by the new aggressiveness of labor unions, which used sit-down strikes to take over factories and force the organizing of the steel, rubber and auto industries. Angered at the interference of an old and conservative Supreme Court with his New Deal programs, FDR proposed in '37 a plan to enlarge the court with liberal appointees, but he was rebuffed by Congress. (Within the next three years, FDR got to appoint five pro-New Deal justices through normal attrition.)

By 1937, GNP had almost climbed back to the level of 1929, but it was a recovery precariously dependent on massive federal outlays. FDR decided to slash federal relief and public-jobs spending to balance the budget. At the same time, the Federal Reserve tightened credit to cool off the recovery, and the new social security program took $2 billion of payroll taxes out of the economy but hadn't yet begun paying benefits. The federal budget did balance in '37, but the economy went into a tailspin. Private payrolls dropped 35%, industrial production 33%, and GNP 13%. The "Roosevelt recession" was halted in '38, ended only by a resumption of enormous federal welfare spending. After five years of remaking the U.S. economic system and reducing human suffering, the New Deal had still not found a way to sustain private-sector growth.

With waning public enthusiasm for new social legislation, the New Deal laid blame for the continuing depression on excesses of free-market capitalism, including industrial monopolies, concentrated personal wealth and high executive salaries. Embittered by rising opposition

1935	1936	1937
SOCIAL SECURITY ACT VOTED.	"GONE WITH THE WIND" PUBLISHED.	FDR SPRINGS "COURT PACKING" PLAN.
"PORGY AND BESS" OPENS IN NEW YORK.	SPANISH ARMY REBELS.	
NAZI GERMANY OCCUPIES THE SAARLAND.	STALIN LAUNCHES GREAT PURGE.	
NEUTRALITY ACT PASSES.	MAYNARD KEYNES' "GENERAL THEORY" IS PUBLISHED.	
AFL UNIONISTS SET UP COMMITTEE FOR INDUSTRIAL ORGANIZATION.		
ITALY INVADES ETHIOPIA.		
CONGRESS APPROVES NATIONAL LABOR RELATIONS ACT.		

from moderate and conservative Democrats in Congress, FDR tried to purge several of them in the congressional elections of '38. He was rebuffed by the voters, who elected not only most of his Democratic foes but also scores of new GOP members. Increasingly, he turned his attention to worsening military crises in Europe and Asia.

The rise of fascism

The Great Depression of the 1930s was truly worldwide. The United States and Great Britain tried to bolster capitalism by creating mixed economies with elements of the welfare states, and democracy was maintained throughout the social experimentation. But many other distressed nations, industrial and less developed, succumbed to dictatorships of the left and right during the '30s. The tentative capitalist initiatives of Bolshevik Russia in the mid '20s gave way to brutal collectivization under Joseph Stalin in the '30s. Japan, a small island nation whose economic growth required secure overseas markets for its manufactured goods, yielded to rule by generals, who began their conquest of Asia with the invasion of Manchuria in 1931. By '37 Japan would be in full but undeclared war with China, where Mao Tse-tung was waging a communist peasant revolt against both Chinese warlords and the Japanese invaders.

Mussolini consolidated his rule in Italy, then attacked Ethiopia in '35 and Albania in '39. The most ruthless fascist of all, Adolf Hitler, came to power in '33 and soon began expanding German domination into neighboring lands, always threatening military force but rarely having to use it openly. Germany took over the Saar in '35, the Rhineland in '36, the Sudetenland and Austria in '38, and Czechoslovakia in '38-39. England and France watched in dismay, but to avoid war, they acquiesced to Hitler's aggression at the Munich conference in September of '38. The Spanish Civil War of '36-39 became a virtual rehearsal for the coming world war, with German and Soviet troops fighting each other and American volunteers lending a hand against fascism, too.

American isolationism

The American people observed the proceedings in Europe with concerned detachment. With the horrors of the Great World War fresh in the memory, they were averse to getting embroiled in new crises in Europe or Asia. The American isolationist mood strengthened throughout the '30s as world affairs grew more tense. From '35 through '37 Congress passed a variety of neutrality acts to bar U.S. arms sales and even loans to belligerents.

FDR and his Secretary of State, Cordell Hull, officially supported American neutrality, but they came to believe confidentially that all of Europe, including Britain, would fall to the fascists if U.S. financial aid and armaments were not offered. They also knew that the U.S., whose military forces were small and weak, was prepared neither to offer modern armaments to the allies nor to fight a war itself—even if American opinion supported involvement, which it didn't.

Tensions with Japan accelerated in '37 after Japanese planes sank a U.S. gunboat in Chinese waters, for which Japan apologized and paid $2.2 million in damages. Washington debated trade sanctions and other measures to slow Japanese expansion but did little.

In August 1939, Hitler took the final necessary step toward domination of Europe. Shocking communist sympathizers in the U.S., who had believed that Soviet Russia was a determined foe of German aggression, Stalin and Hitler signed a nonaggression pact. In September, Hitler stunned the world with a blitzkrieg conquest of Poland, and in November, Stalin invaded Finland. Great Britain declared war on Germany three days after the invasion of Poland, and soon FDR asked Congress to repeal the American neutrality act. Congress reluctantly agreed but insisted that U.S. merchant ships be banned from belligerent ports and combat zones, which included the entire North Atlantic.

The '30s came to a close with most of the industrial nations—except the United States—engaged in, or preparing for, the widest and most devastating war in world history.

CIO WINS AUTO AND STEEL CONTRACTS.

ECONOMY SLUMPS AFTER RECOVERING 1929 LEVELS.

JAPAN LAUNCHES FULL-SCALE WAR AGAINST CHINA.

U.S. NAVAL EXPANSION ACT PASSED.

1938

CONGRESS VOTES MINIMUM WAGE LAW.

BRITAIN SEEKS "APPEASEMENT" OF HITLER AT MUNICH.

FDR DECLARES NATIONAL EMERGENCY.

1939

EINSTEIN INFORMS FDR OF A-BOMB POSSIBILITY.

GERMANY AND RUSSIA SIGN NON-AGGRESSION PACT.

HITLER INVADES POLAND.

U.S. DECLARES NEUTRALITY.

June 21, 1930

Nothing is being said about flexible tariff INCREASES. This is the first time in many years that the whole tone of Washington agitation was for rate reductions. Even among members of Congress you hear the same thing: "I hope they reduce some of the rates we voted."

June 28, 1930

There is a sort of tacit agreement around Washington that business must now 'take its medicine' and work out of the doldrums slowly and gradually, without any new artificial stimulation.

So far as we can ascertain in various quarters here, there are no Washington plans for doing anything new to boost business.

November 15, 1930

Washington is besieged these days, by applications for government cooperation, through commission or other means, to solve over-production problems of this-or-that industry. Administration is very conservative, reminding industries that they must not lean on government, and that business sentiment at large is supposed to be quite hostile to government in business.

December 6, 1930

For several weeks we have been consulting privately with official and unofficial authorities on international affairs and have found, somewhat to our surprise, that the possibility of European war within three to five years, involving U.S. either directly or indirectly, is playing a big part in administration policies. This is not jingo talk, and all conversations are conservative, guarded and hedged. Obviously public discussions are not possible, but it is well for you to know that moderate anxiety exists here.

Germany is the critical big power. Germany has all the troubles of other countries, including growing unemployment, plus the war guilt reparations loan. Germany's internal politics are unstable, may result next March or April in overthrow of present conservative government, due to internal economic desperation, of which the German people make the most.

Field Marshal Paul von Hindenburg, president of Germany, accepting the salute of Nazi brown shirts, with Adolf Hitler and his principal aides in the background.

December 13, 1930

Government will wiggle through its first deficit year by additional temporary borrowings. Probably this is a good thing, for it will (a) draw on the excess lending capacities of the country, (b) spread the tax load to more favorable future years, (c) teach us that the federal Treasury has no resources which we as taxpayers do not supply, and (d) put the new phase of agitation for European war debt reduction in close proximity to our individual pocket-book nerves.

December 27, 1930

The current battle is not between the Republican and Democratic parties, but between the conservative and so-called liberal or so-called radical influences in both parties. To define "liberal" or "radical" would take a book instead of a letter. We use terms in their economic sense rather than their personal conduct sense: "Conservative" means property rights, materialism, belief that satisfactory materialism is the rich soil out of which grows the spiritual qualities of a race or nation, belief in slow evolution rather than revolution. "Liberal" or "radical" implies a distinction between so-called "property rights" and so-called "human rights." There isn't any clear difference but many people think there is. A thousand dollars of capital normally represents a thousand hours of hard work and abnegation, but this isn't understood, and all conservatives make the mistake of forgetting that it isn't understood. Two out of three voters are conservative; three out of four party political leaders are conservative.

February 7, 1931

Business-at-large does not seem to be as much disturbed as Mr. Hoover over the "bad principle" of using government funds for human food and other relief; there has been quite a growth of sentiment throughout the country that "the emergency is greater than the principle."

1931

April 25, 1931

There's a strong feeling throughout the country that Washington officialdom is asleep at the switch. A good many conservatives want the President to call a "conference." Liberals want a special session of Congress, and are starting a new campaign for it, though there will be none, of course.

May 23, 1931

<u>Whispers of approaching crisis in business</u> are common throughout the country. We get them from incoming confidential correspondence, from unofficial reports to government officials, and from our periodic trips to other localities. Much business thought is that we are in the lull before the storm. The storm clouds seem to consist of fears of a collapse of the wage scale before autumn, fears of a further cut-throat dog fight on prices, fears of labor strikes, fears of an increase in unemployment, fears of a collapse of public morale.

Meanwhile the standard of living in this country will not fall materially. On the 5-to-10 year pull, it will resume its rise.

August 8, 1931

<u>Direct government appropriations for the unemployed</u> are definitely planned by progressive elements in Congress, and are greatly feared by the conservatives, (a) because the "dole" system will lead to increased taxation directed as a social instrument against wealth, and (b) because the threat or promise of government appropriations will cause the withholding of private contributions to charity fund campaigns in the fall.

Most radicals and liberals want to draw on public funds, raised by taxation or by public borrowing, the borrowing to be covered by taxations in subsequent years. Despite all the public statements against relief appropriations, we believe it may prove very difficult to avoid them next winter.

August 22, 1931

<u>Bills for guarantee of bank deposits</u> will be put forward in the next session of Congress.

We note among members of Congress a note of frank recognition that <u>drastic remedies of a socialistic nature</u> will be demanded next winter. The diversity of demands and the lack of cohesiveness among the various groups are the greatest deterrents.

<u>The fundamental character of the changes</u> through which we are now passing is probably just beginning to be recognized. There will be expressions in political terms during the next year, not by demand for different form of government but by demand for gradual reorganization of the social order - unemployment funds, shorter work periods, more government undertakings rather than fewer, more government regulation rather than less, more government spending and higher taxes. (We are discussing PROSPECTS, not merits.)

Politics. The prospects are 3-to-1 that Republicans will renominate Hoover, and 2-to-1 that Democrats will nominate Roosevelt. Administration scouts after touring the country bring word that Hoover could not be re-elected today, but they count on better business and better sentiment to improve his chances a year hence.

September 26, 1931

The dollar has a good chance of becoming the world exchange unit. Washington authorities are restrained in their private opinion on this point, however.

October 3, 1931

"Panic." The business community of the country as a whole seems to be on the verge of a panic. Yes, the President and his Cabinet and all his other advisors are fully aware of the situation. They are not uninformed as to either the discouraging facts or the depressed sentiment. They are in direct touch with the prevalent "all-gone feeling."

Do they share the all-gone feeling? YES and NO. Some of the President's direct advisors consulted informally during the past week indicate that they are at their wit's ends. They are fatalistic. They are working day and night on suggested "remedies." They are conscientious. Nothing is ignored and nothing is overlooked.

Do they think "things will be worse before they are better?" Generally speaking, Yes. They think that public confidence is sliding to such an extent that some further slide cannot be stopped by any artificial or sentimental dam.

October 31, 1931

"Inflation" is a loose word entering into all conversations. The thing desired is strengthening of prices. Expansion of bank credit is conceived to be the means of accomplishing this, thereby cheapening money and credit, thereby raising prices.

Foreign situation continues full of uncertainties despite British national government victory. Some kind of a British protective tariff will be adopted, full of compromises, including probably preference for British empire, mildly disturbing for U.S. trade, but not necessarily serious. German political and economic conditions are very precarious. French are feeling the strain.

December 19, 1931

 <u>Political nervousness next summer and fall</u> should be minimized by the fact that both parties will be essentially conservative. Hoover will head the Republican ticket, notwithstanding current gossip to the contrary. Either Roosevelt or Baker will head the Democratic ticket.

1932

January 16, 1932

 <u>Inside gossip among Democratic politicians</u> shows no impressive harmony. Roosevelt is being damned with faint praise — "an amiable fellow, but wobbly, without convictions."

February 13, 1932

 <u>Governmental tendencies</u>: More and more a swing to state socialism in banking and credit. Swing toward relaxation of anti-trust laws, accompanied by a higher degree of government regulation of industry. Swing toward regulation of railroads under I. C. C. discretion rather than under statutory formulae which have proved unworkable. Stricter regulation of banking. More government regulation all along the line.

July 30, 1932

 <u>Roosevelt is now less "feared" by business interests</u>. He is regarded as reasonably safe, though somewhat "experimental."

August 6, 1932

 <u>Elections</u>. Advices reaching us from a multitude of quarters show a preponderance of expressions that <u>Roosevelt has the edge</u> over Hoover, on basis of CURRENT sentiment. An anti-Hoover counter influence which we shall try to appraise systematically lies in the possibility that the business upswing and inflation may get so far by October as to support a charge that <u>Hoover policies are wild</u> and unsound, leading to post-election grief.

August 20, 1932

    <u>Government is putting money, credit, effort, organization,</u>
all its resources back of a concerted effort to mobilize all national
economic forces. It is a bold experiment in use of government credit.
Callers at the White House are touched by the <u>President's grim</u>
<u>determination that the experiment shall succeed</u>.

September 24, 1932

    British, French and German bankers and politicians, to whom
we talked on a recent trip to Europe, reflected a rather surprisingly
strong <u>confidence in America's economic recovery ahead of Europe's</u>.
    We felt shocked at the <u>frank war talk</u>. Well-informed men spoke
of war as "almost inevitable within 5 years."

November 26, 1932

    <u>Mr. Roosevelt</u> did much talking "off the record" here this week.
<u>Impressions of him</u>: <u>He is a likeable person, a good fellow</u>. He has a
minimum of dangerous ego. He talks freely, and in a manner which
suggests that he agrees with you.
    <u>He is not well-informed about details of many current issues</u>
with which a President must deal. You can not quite decide whether his
lack of information on things which you thought everyone knew will prove
a strength or a weakness. Comparing him with Mr. Hoover on another
facet: Mr. Hoover thinks more in cold terms of what OUGHT to be done.
Mr. Roosevelt thinks a good deal in terms of how the thing will look to
Congress, or to the public, how much is politically feasible, what he
can "get away with." <u>You think of Mr. Hoover as a technician-statesman,</u>
<u>and of Mr. Roosevelt as a politician-statesman</u>.

CHRISTMAS EVE PREPARATION.

December 24, 1932

    <u>Drift toward government control</u> over private business operations will proceed more rapidly.

    <u>Experimental economic legislation</u> will be forced by bloc and sectional interests, modifying Roosevelt's party program in many ways.

    <u>Prohibition</u> will be amended.

    <u>New farm relief experiments</u>, approaching nearer to fundamentals, will be launched.

    <u>New bank legislation will be passed</u>, extending branch banking, and imposing stricter government control. Many more weak banks will be eliminated.

    <u>Federal budget</u> will approach (but not reach) balanced status through new tax laws and economies.

    <u>Government expenditures</u>, national, state and local, will be reduced.

    <u>Wages</u> will decline further; also the cost of living.

    <u>Employment</u> gains will be small, and these mainly through spreading available work.

    <u>Crisis phase</u> of depression will recede but the after-effects will be prolonged throughout 1933.

    <u>There will NOT be</u>: (a) Revolution. (b) General dole system. (c) Serious breakdown of government credit. (d) General moratoriums. (e) Technological eradication of present price system.

    <u>Economic laws will not be permitted to operate normally</u>. New political experiments will be adopted to modify normal economic operations. There will be MORE rather than less government control over and interference with private business. This will be due not so much to growth of radical sentiment as to the demands of various conservative business groups themselves. This trend toward politico-economic experimentation is the most significant thing on the 1933 landscape.

    <u>1933 probably will mark the turning point of national policy</u>, the cross roads on numerous political issues. It will be the most important year of either the past decade or the next decade. But 1933 will only fix the trends and will NOT bring permanent settlement of many major issues.

January 14, 1933

"Buy American" is an emotional and sentimental phenomenon. It will have small practical result. Don't we want to SELL abroad? If we want to sell, we must also buy. We can't do just one.

January 28, 1933

CREDIT inflation by large new government loans is PROBABLE. It is now reasonably certain that the substitute for wholesale currency inflation will be the further extension of government loans through R.F.C. and other agencies to a wide variety of situations, - farmers to refinance mortgages, mortgage lenders to let them refinance mortgages, banks, insurance companies, railroads, public works, relief, many others. Various different kinds of plans will head up in this general policy.

Budget will be off balance, therefore, by 2 billions or more. Investment market must count on trying to absorb something like this. Whether government bond market can stand the strain is a subject of dispute among technicians. Some say yes, some say no; we don't know. Tremendous growth of state capitalism is implied, of course.

February 25, 1933

A bit of encouragement also may be gained from the fact that this banking crisis is setting into motion the forces of reform and true reconstruction of the banking machinery which everyone knew MUST be done, but which heretofore has been delayed by natural inertia, by false hope that the final crash could be avoided.

March 4, 1933

Next week will show whether Roosevelt hopes are sustained. If so, well and good. If not (and our feeling is in this direction), then there must be a general banking holiday for at least a week.
Purpose of general bank holiday: To freeze the situation for a while, to chloroform the panic, to allow time to plan remedies.
Unification of banks into a single national system, the Federal Reserve System, also has been advanced YEARS by new developments. Deposit guarantee is the bait and the lash which will bring them in.

March 10, 1933

<u>Mr. Roosevelt has met and won the Press</u>. He wooed the press
men, using simple human candor, enlisting them as aides, explaining
everything in "strict confidence," electrifying them with the
entrustment of moral responsibilities, making them feel they were
co-partners in the responsibilities of government. Hard-boiled old
Washington correspondents are all-stirred-up over this new President.

March 25, 1933

<u>Along with credit expansion will come "budgetary inflation."</u>
We aren't going to balance the whole governmental budget, and we might
as well get this into our heads. We are entering a new era of
government capitalism, truly revolutionary. Government capital will be
used to do those things formerly done through channels of private
capital.

April 1, 1933

<u>Big program of public works now seems assured</u>, as one means of
getting "direct action," of making sure of activity. Emphasis will be
not on federal works, public buildings, etc., but on LOCAL UNDERTAKINGS.

<u>Here is the point of view of the President and his cabinet</u>,
stated somewhat roughly and imperfectly, but essential to your
understanding of what is going on in Washington:
<u>The old order of laissez faire has broken down</u>. Business, if
let alone, would not bring itself out of depression for 5 or 10 years.
Federal government now stands out as the strongest element in picture.
Federal government, therefore, must and will dictate to business, and
business will follow political leadership of the Executive branch.

Going beyond credit, the plan is to "regiment" industries.
This is to be done piece-meal, step by step, as necessities develop.
First came banking, and it is in process of being regimented.
Meanwhile sale of securities is being put under government regulation.
Agriculture is regimented by the pending farm bill. The big significance
of this is not merely that it provides for leasing of fallow lands, and
for tax on processors to pay the leasing bill. The big significance
is that it makes the government, the Secretary of Agriculture, a
dictator to engineer or rationalize the whole agricultural industry.

The most latitudinous regimentation of all, applicable to all industry,
will come through a new program for trade practice conferences, by which
ANY trade or industry can come before Federal Trade Commission and agree
on standard rules, practices, even standard wages, working conditions.

From preceding you can see what Roosevelt is trying to do.
First, now, he is trying to make hasty reforms in MECHANISM of business.
This involves political dictation, or suggestion, to integrated groups.
Political force has definitely taken lead from private business force.
Second, later, he and his government will apply budgetary inflation.
By budgetary inflation is meant expansion of government credit into
realms ordinarily occupied by private credit. Government, of course,
has no credit and no capital, except that supplied by private citizens.
But the relatively few owners of big gobs of capital will trust
government with it more than they will trust anything else.

It is obvious that business men must shift their thinking
into a new pattern. The old order will not come back. It is difficult
to say precisely what the picture will be a year or two hence. Private
business will continue, but the rules will be different. We are moving
toward socialism, not by predetermined plan, but by necessity. No one
can see the details clearly.

Out of his own hatchery!

April 29, 1933

Can inflation be controlled? We all hope it can, and, therefore, we think it can, but frankly none of us here KNOW. During past week we have gone to a dozen big-bugs and asked HOW. They give vague answers. They recognize that public pressure during any inflation movement is always for more-and-more inflation, as a drinking man always wants just one more drink. They believe the pressure can be resisted.

Our own opinion? We are on the fence. We haven't lived long enough to KNOW. We believe inflation to be full of later dangers. Remember, inflation will be harder to stop than to start.

Labor. Organized labor now has the chance of a generation to fix wages into the general scheme of production costs, and to promote collective bargaining. Labor leaders do not seem to see it, however. You, as employer, seem safe in assuming continuing stupidity of Labor.

October 21, 1933

High corporation salaries. Yes, they are to be cut down, not so much by specific government action as by publicity and public sentiment. It is one of the current steps toward "levelling of wealth."

War in Europe within next year or two seems to be taken for granted by the more sophisticated international observers. Don't ask us WHEN or WHERE, for we don't know. Washington doesn't know.

Administration thinks in terms of major economic reforms, recasting of the system, not merely of speedy recovery, or even of recovery by the slow operation of natural economic forces.

December 30, 1933

Is the Roosevelt program socialistic? Certainly YES, the trend is more and more in this direction. But the ultimate aim is not thorough-going socialism. It's merely a step-by-step procedure, each step being taken for some immediate practical reason. It isn't doctrinaire. Carl Marx isn't in the mind. The purpose behind new socialistic policies is not to embrace socialism, but rather to save capitalism.

Ratification of the 21st Amendment in December 1933 ended prohibition and brought happy scenes like this all over the country.

A new party is being born out of the Great Experiment. It keeps the Democratic name, but it has slight resemblance to the traditional Democratic party on almost any issue you want to select — tariff, taxation, state rights, for example. If it creates prosperity in the next three years, as it probably will, it will be invincible in 1936. It will draw to itself the more liberal elements of the Republican party, and it will alienate its more conservative elements, who will go into the Republican camp. Meanwhile the Republican party will develop a real code of principles, which at present it hasn't. Both parties, using the same old names, will become essentially new parties.

January 27, 1934

Industry unions, as distinguished from the old craft unions: There was much talk about the desirability of new forms of labor organizations, including ALL workers within a plant or an industry, rather than only unions formed along craft or functional lines.

1934

February 3, 1934

War with Japan is a vague fear, a whisper-topic at tea time, hardly a real fear in broad daylight. Within next year or two, it's possible, but not probable. Bigger navy is aimed mainly at Japan, of course. But hope of officials is to appeal directly to peoples, and to override the jingo press of both countries.

March 17, 1934

Washington influence sooner or later will be on the side of independent organization of your employes, without any interference with them on your part.

June 2, 1934

Drought: Its continuance through this week made it nationally serious. Two weeks more will make it a major national disaster. Even with moderate rains soon, it will cut buying power tremendously in dry areas, increase the cost of federal relief, put new drag on recovery.

The fledgling auto workers' union electrified the country with a sit-down strike.

July 14, 1934

    Keep this in mind: Our traditional tariff policy is changing. The high tide of protection of domestic industries is now at hand. The future tendency will be in general direction of LESS protection. This new tendency will affect adversely many American industries which are technically less efficient (or high-cost) in production than the competitive industries in other countries. New emphasis is on importing more, buying more, thus giving foreign countries more power to buy from us. Thus some domestic industries will gain exports, while other industries will suffer from competition of imports.

    Imports from Japan, manufactured goods, are causing much apprehension among manufacturers. Yet the government's idea is to admit moderate amounts of Japanese goods, on the theory that these will result in increased world purchases from us.

July 28, 1934

    Ultimate war: If official opinions could be reduced to betting odds, they would be 2-to-1 against war within next year, but 3-to-1 for war within next 5 years. No one tries to say where, when or why.

August 25, 1934

    Unionization of virtually ALL industries seems pretty clearly indicated. Will unions use their power wisely? Tendency is for labor leaders to abuse power (as employers are apt to do). Special labor tribunals with power to enforce decrees would be authorized to supervise both unions and employers. (This is looking ahead 5 years or more.)

November 24, 1934

    Private capital and credit is plentiful, but government is frightening it with one hand while soothing it with the other. Fright psychology continues to be dominant. Hence few new jobs. Hence new government efforts to prime the pump.

    Government is desperately anxious to reduce public relief rolls, knows relief work is wormy with local waste, graft and character deterioration. Public works seems the only way of getting quick relief from relief.

January 5, 1935

New banking legislation is being formulated. More direct control by Reserve Board over Reserve Bank governors, open market and rediscount policies. Insurance of deposits up to $5000, with limitation of assessments on banks. FDIC to have power to expel an insured bank from deposit insurance fund, or to refuse admission to an "unnecessary newly formed bank."

January 19, 1935

Social insurance, Wagner-Lewis bill, prospects, perspective: Unemployment insurance: Payroll tax in 1936 will be 1%, not 3%. Old age pensions: 1% in 1937, graduating up to 5% after 20 yrs. Half of this by employer, half by employe, deducted from wages. Retirement benefits don't start till 1942, for those aged 65 then, limited to $30 a month, but this is likely to be raised to at least $40 by later amendments. Townsend plan for $200 a month has startling amount of support in House, might even pass House if it came to a vote, but will NOT pass Senate.

March 23, 1935

War in Europe: Our government does not expect it this year, hopes it will not come next year. The unofficial private cautious talk is to the effect that European war is inevitable within four years. The surface talk is that U.S. will stay out, be neutral, but the more thoughtful comment is that neutrality and avoidance are very difficult.

March 30, 1935

Civilian Conservation Corps. Allowance for this has been doubled. It is a "work army of young men." It has relieved unemployment, done it in a constructive manner, built character, created the materials of a future army if and when we need it. It has done a good job. There's rather universal approval.

June 1, 1935

How to get around Supreme Court? There are several ways. By packing it, but there's no thought of this at present. But legislating against its power to declare congressional acts unconstitutional, but this isn't being taken seriously. By much more extensive use of the federal taxing power — this will be considered seriously.

July 20, 1935

Court decisions have been preponderantly against New Deal. More-and-more covert criticism of courts is heard within New Deal. Things seem headed toward some sort of executive attack on the judiciary.

To many, New Deal programs smacked of dictatorship, to others, reborn hope. Then the Blue Eagle was shot down.

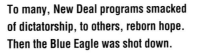

August 3, 1935

Meanwhile manufacturers are putting in labor saving machinery.
The advance in technological processes has been rapid during depression.
More machines to do men's work — fewer jobs. But there's compensation
in new jobs in the production of machines. Furthermore, note that in
mass production industries, where machines play the biggest part,
the unemployment has been least. Eventually, shorter work periods.

New industries to take up slack in employment, or new phases
of established industries: Plenty of them ahead. Perhaps cheap safe
airplanes. Certainly home equipment lines will expand. Standard houses
by mass production methods will go big within 5 years.

August 10, 1935

Germany. Bitterness against Nazi regime has become noticeable
among ALL classes of population, but early breakdown is NOT indicated.
The Army remains dominating factor, and Army is interested only in more
time to complete the rearmament program, which will make Germany the
controlling force on the continent. Nazi chieftains will fight
ruthlessly, will risk war rather than give up on domestic issues.
But — internal economic situation is bad. Debt is mounting, public
works are hampered, only armament industries are going full blast.

War. Basically the forces making for war are still dominant.
Italy will not be influenced much by diplomats and the League of Nations.
Apprehension is still felt in Geneva that Italy may quit League in fall.
Undoubtedly the majority of the Italian people are opposed to the war.
Russia is potentially in danger from Germany on west, Japan on east.

September 7, 1935

Social security legislation: Remember that this is long range
relief substitute. Ultimate employer-employe payroll tax of 9% is device
for socializing the cost of unemployment and old-age relief — cost now
covered largely by borrowed money. This will seem much more important to
you in 1937 than now. It is PERMANENT, despite possible Supreme Court
reversal, since both political parties will support it and will find way
to put it into effect.

September 14, 1935

Huey Long's death, considered impersonally and politically, is of great importance in modifying trends.

It means setback to American fascist movement, which, although not bearing fascist label, has been growing in many states.

It means the weakening of third party for share-the-wealth.

Roosevelt can now woo and win big part of the wealth-sharers. But he can do it more adroitly, less precipitately, without Huey Long.

October 19, 1935

Basically there's more dynamite in the situation than in 1914 — danger of general European war, and world war. This is a flat statement of the private views, cautiously expressed, among authorities. Britain, France, Russia (and U.S.) are trying to hold what they have, in way of territories or economic advantages. Others are trying to win back what they lost. Haven't been able to do it by economic means, because of growing world tendency toward nationalism and trade barriers. So they are being FORCED to resort to war — Japan, Italy, Germany.

November 9, 1935

Germany plans to drive against Russia, wants slice of Ukraine for colonization. Simultaneously, Japan will go after slice of Siberia, and Soviet gov't probably will have to concede it.

November 30, 1935

German army and arms will not be ready to fight until 1937. That's why well-informed persons think in terms of European war, 1937. Discussion is in this vein: Europe is headed directly toward war. It CAN be avoided, but PROBABLY WILL NOT be avoided.

Japan: There's rather general belief that Japan will grab more of China and some of Siberia. Russia can't defend. Japan's newest move into China is considered unwise and premature.

Whether U.S. can stay out of European war or world war is open question. Many sophisticated observers doubt it. That's why the biggest single issue in next session of Congress will be NEUTRALITY. Current neutrality measures are described by officials as "just practice."

The sleeping giant begins to feel it

1936

Always the Last One Up

January 18, 1936

What does all this mean? — beyond just fiscal arithmetic.
It means that our government has a 7-year unbroken record
of living beyond its means. Every OTHER government in OTHER times
which went approximately this long with perennially unbalanced budgets
eventually went further, - into some serious financial grief.
U.S. may be an exception; officials say it is; but exceptions are rare.

March 21, 1936

Recession when spendings stop: Business analysts point out that
recession usually results when a gov't shifts from spending to economy.
Thus there are forecasts of temporary slump beginning sometime in 1937.
This is something to think about, but it is too early to plan for it.

May 23, 1936

Change the complexion of the Supreme Court by appointment
of "liberal" justices to fill the vacancies that will be coming along.
Roosevelt WILL change the Court's complexion if he makes appointments.

June 20, 1936

Thus endeth four years of the most remarkable Congress in modern
times. Remarkable for the number of big pieces of legislation enacted.
Remarkable for the quantity of legislation nullified by Supreme Court.
Remarkable for laws tending to exalt government over private business.
Remarkable for subservience of the Legislative branch to the Executive.

September 19, 1936

It seems pretty clear that Germany plans to strike eastward
through Czechoslovakia and South Poland as soon as her armies are ready,
and justifications are manufactured.

October 31, 1936

> Our best final judgment is that Roosevelt will be reelected.
> Long-range contemplation of tremendous political problems ahead
in next 4 years, not settled by the election, suggests that the lucky man
is the presidential candidate who loses next Tuesday.

December 5, 1936

> General observations on Roosevelt, which seem timely now,
and which are based on conversations with men to whom the President
has talked intimately: He is ambitious to be The Great President Who
- Conserved the capitalistic system. - Made it work better for the
masses. - Staved off communism and fascism by LIMITED dosage of
"semi-socialism."

January 9, 1937

> Central bargaining vs. plant-by-plant bargaining: Unions are
likely to succeed in their insistence on central bargaining.

1937

January 23, 1937

> Wage-&-hour legislation on which many elements are now focusing
is along these lines: Let Congress specify that some government agency
determine what constitutes sub-standard wages ("sweatshop wages") for
each business line, by localities or regions. Also determine what hours
of work are excessive. Specify by law that longer hours or lower wages
than these standards shall constitute unfair methods of competition.
> Is this constitutional? Some lawyers say YES, some say NO.
Congress is of a mind to pass such a law and "see what happens."
> We believe wage-&-hour legislation will take this general
direction, and that you should begin now to plan on it.

February 13, 1937

> There's no chance that 6 extra judges will be authorized.
The Supreme Court membership will not be raised to 15.
> Balance of power in the Court will shift to the liberals.
This conclusion leaps over the complex tangle of questions of HOW.
> This means that you should prepare your mind and your plans
for a Supreme Court which will approve SOME but not necessarily ALL
of the Roosevelt ideas on legislation. Not just a rubber stamp Court.

"To Furnish The Supreme
Court Practical Assistance"

March 6, 1937

> <u>Third term</u>: The President now says publicly that his ambition
> is to retire at the end of this term, but there are implied IFS....
> IF he can complete his program of rebuilding, and IF the Supreme Court
> will let him do this. Otherwise....

March 20, 1937

> <u>Figure on further concentration of power in federal government</u>.
> This tendency in the past will be continued steadily in the future.
> <u>Figure on MORE federal government regulation of business</u>.
> Not merely in wages-&-hours; these are only preliminaries. But also
> in the broad policies of business, - production, prices, profits, rates.
> <u>This will amount to government participation in business</u>. The
> President's term in "partnership."
> <u>How</u>? By wage-&-hour laws. By other laws regulating employment.
> By some new NRA, integrating and regulating whole-industry policies.
> By some stiffened AAA, controlling agricultural production, distribution.
> By government financing of business, coincidental with next depression.
> BIG industries will come first in this development of gov't regulation.
> <u>Figure on regulation of labor unions as a PART of industry</u>.
> This is absolutely certain. When? Don't quite know. The beginnings
> in year or two, the full development several years off.
> <u>Taxation will increasingly become an INSTRUMENT of regulation</u>.
> Force business to do certain things. Force earnings distribution, etc.
> Tax not merely for revenues; tax also for general business regulation.
>
> <u>Dictatorship</u>? That is possible, but it seems to be improbable.
> Still, we ARE headed toward something resembling "authoritarian state."
> <u>Communism</u>? No, but in its stead, rather steady approach toward
> social controls which some people call "socialism" — probably gradual.

April 10, 1937

> <u>Third term for Roosevelt</u>: It is noteworthy that third-term talk
> has now come out in the open, and is discussed frankly by commentators.
> The opinion of most is that it is possible and politically feasible.
> Many who think this are opposed to it, but they recognize the realities.

April 24, 1937

> <u>Anti-lynching bill</u> is salt in wounds of southerners — painful.
> It dramatizes Farley-Roosevelt transformation of the Democratic party —
> advertises the power of negro voters which the Democrats will
> cultivate hereafter just as the Republicans did in the past.

May 1, 1937

> <u>The neutrality act is a hodgepodge</u>, not insuring neutrality.
> When the next war comes, public sentiment will determine whether or not
> this country shall be truly neutral. The law itself is futile.

May 8, 1937

> <u>Washington boom-curbing gestures</u> will be less in next few weeks.
> Some advisers think they have been overdone, think the public will blame
> administration for the <u>moderate business recession now being forecast</u>
> by most economists and statisticians here.

July 10, 1937

<u>The Court a year hence</u>: Sound-&-fury over Court bill
should not blind your eyes to the probability that additional vacancies
will develop, and that, therefore, <u>Roosevelt WILL have "liberal" Court</u>.

September 4, 1937

<u>Inventions which may make deep changes in things in the future</u>:

Mechanical cotton picker	Synthetic rubber	Plastics
Air conditioning equipment	Prefabricated houses	Television
Artificial cotton - cellulose	Facsimile transmission	Auto trailer
Artificial wool - cellulose	Gasoline from coal	Photo electric cell
Steep-flight airplanes	Tray agriculture	

<u>Inventions</u>: Trend is toward further increase - no diminution.
<u>Jobs</u>: New processes abolish old jobs, but also make new jobs.
<u>Technological unemployment</u>: There's no way to measure it as yet.
There's no way to determine the NET job effect of new processes.
<u>Volume of production</u> should be increased 20% above 1929 level —
IF unemployment is to be cut to 1929 level. (Some dispute about this.)
<u>Industrial research is needed</u> to keep industries from freezing
into particular patterns. Many industries do good work in research.
<u>Social changes from new inventions</u> never come without warning.
There's always a period of advance notice. Thus planning is needed.
<u>New equipment for old</u> is economically and socially desirable,
but there's always inertia, great resistance to change.

September 11, 1937

<u>China-Japan war will be long</u>, intense, highly disastrous affair
in Orient, according to those studying the situation. Aggressive war
may run a year or two, with many years of sporadic fighting thereafter.
<u>Washington is surprised at power of resistance shown by China</u>.
Odds seem to favor Japan to win, technically and in military sense.
"But price will be high. Japan may be overstrained economically."
<u>Tight blockade of China coast</u> by Japan now is fully expected.
This raises official fears that blockade will lead to provoking
incidents.
<u>Washington sympathies</u> are clearly pro-China. But actual policy
is so strongly pro-peace that the chance of direct U.S. involvement
in China-Japan war seems small.

September 25, 1937

<u>Business volume</u> is roughly in midst of long sideways movement.
The movement started last spring, will continue perhaps 9 months longer.
Within this sideways movement are minor ups-&-downs. Each little up
suggests a boom, but isn't. Each down suggests a depression, but isn't.

October 9, 1937

<u>Prepare for war</u>? NO, this isn't in the minds of officials.
That is, war involving the U.S. forms no part of their calculations
for the present, or for the visible future.
<u>Take the world lead against aggressors</u>? Quite definitely, NO.
This is the one thing which Roosevelt-&-Hull are determined to dodge.
They are leery lest European diplomacy leave the U.S. holding the bag.
Yet, as for dealings with Japan, it is hard to see how U.S. can avoid
being jockeyed into position of taking more responsibility than others.

October 23, 1937

New Deal now faces its greatest test, for it must "manage"
the first real business recession since New Deal reached adulthood.
All sales talk in the past has been of motives, intentions, reforms,
planning from above, and schemes to protect against fluctuations.
Will they now WORK to maintain stability claimed for them in the ads?
Is there enough wisdom and ability in government to apply them?

October 30, 1937

It is branded, of course, as the "first Roosevelt recession."
It arises from forces created within the time of the Roosevelt regime,
which has led the public to believe that it would prevent fluctuations.

Growing unemployment is a specter. Congressmen appeal to WPA
to send more help to home districts. At the same time they talk of need
for budget balancing. Of the two pulls, relief will be stronger.

November 6, 1937

Recession is a pause in the long-range upswing, not the end,
say the technicians. Main reasons are given as these:
The conditions which usually accompany the end of an upswing
are not with us now. Business debts are low. Credit is cheap, plentiful.
Banking resources are not strained. There has been no building boom.
There has been no violent speculation in securities or other spheres.
Implication is that upswing will be resumed by the end of 1938.

November 20, 1937

For next few months new New Deal "reforms" are out the window,
insofar as Congress is concerned.
The thing which counts most in Congress now is business aid.
There's genuine alarm over the visible bad business factors back home,
the reductions in operations, the recent sudden rise in unemployment.
This, in minds of congressmen, is "bad for politics." To help politics
they must help business. That's the way they think.

December 11, 1937

The 1940 elections depend largely on the degree of prosperity prevailing in 1939-40. If it is high, the New Deal will succeed itself. If it is low, a more conservative regime is likely to come into power. This assumption is held by most political-minded men within the New Deal. Consequently there is a conscious and deliberate effort to work toward rising business in 1939-40.

Keeping it out of balance

December 31, 1937

Unemployment census will show shock total, rumored to be above 12 millions. "Five years of reforms haven't cured unemployment."

Big salaries of corporation officials are about to be attacked by New Deal publicity, accompanied by the suggestion that they be reduced voluntarily, especially by corporations firing workers, cutting dividends.

"Concentrated wealth:" A good deal will be heard on this from government quarters in next few months. Expect tax attack on it.

January 8, 1938

War: Hull off-the-record is talking discreetly to gov't men and other insiders, implying without specifically saying so that the U.S. must prepare to come to grips with Japan and other aggressor nations. He feels strongly, using terms not used in church, that time is close, probably within this year, when U.S. must lay down a stiffer challenge.

1938

January 29, 1938

Internal political effects of a war are quietly discussed here: Pull New Deal out of a hole? Make Roosevelt President again in 1940? Make Hull President? Promote inflation? Advance socialism?

February 12, 1938

War profits legislation: Likely to be entangled, postponed. But, anyway, if there's a war, a drastic law will be cracked through in a hurry, taxing war profits close to the point of confiscation, and giving the President something resembling dictatorial powers. Thus the fate of this bill at this session is not so important.

War: U.S. and British navies know each other's plans, and agree. They swap "shop talk." That's probably the basis for "understanding," which is informal, and "diplomatically deniable." Congress will vote the bigger navy, after sharp challengings by aggressive pacifist forces. War talk is working up.

FDR and Secretary of State Cordell Hull sought ways to help victims of Germany and Japan without provoking a domestic war-powers crisis.

March 12, 1938

Depression is rapidly undercutting the Roosevelt prestige. The technique of economic planning, now put to test, isn't effective.

"Hoover depression" kicked out Hoover. "Roosevelt depression" may do the same for Roosevelt. That's the Republican basis of hope.

March 26, 1938

Government is scared, alarmed, more conscious of possibility of a continuing depression than it has been at any time previously. This applies to Congress, to executive officials, even to the President. Swing of sentiment within gov't is definitely TOWARD the dolorous views which have prevailed in business and financial quarters for some time.

Old Reliable!

April 2, 1938

The all-gone feeling, like 1932, is with us again. The fact is
that business sentiment, confidence, psychology, is at a new 6-year low.
Causes are mixed: Some are economic, some are purely political.
Distrust of Washington, particularly of the President, plays a big part.
Rightly or wrongly, this is a concrete influence for depression.
Antidote for hysteria is unemotional examination of the FACTS.

May 28, 1938

The money power: When any men, in either business or gov't,
acquire great money power, they are apt to use it to force THEIR ideas
on those who receive the money. They act with fair degree of sincerity,
for they think that their ends are just, and that ends justify means.
Farmers are in the grip of the money power. They are subsidized
by gov't to do certain things, some of which are good, some questionable.
To keep the money coming, many farmers vote for those who pay the money.
Business itself gets much of the money. Many cash outpourings
find their way back through business tills, especially of merchants.
Politics is a business to the politicians. Just as business men
do whatever is necessary to make a profit, so politicians do whatever
they must to be reelected. Most follow the course of greatest pressure.
Pressure FOR spending is heavy from those who receive the money.
Pressure AGAINST spending is less effective. It is unorganized.

June 18, 1938

To have gov't buy up surpluses, food-&-clothing, work them off
on the poor...not only farm products but also consumer goods: This idea
is growing. Officials would like to hit on some big dramatic plan,
but several agencies will work out little plans, big in aggregate.
Surplus Commodities Corp. already is stepping up its buying —
flour, dry milk, canned fruit juice, prunes, etc. Others coming.
Commodity Credit Corp. may get into the picture in a big way,
already is financing purchase of 50,000,000 lbs. of butter from co-ops.
Exports of wheat, cotton, possibly other crops: Some new scheme
for increasing exports, even by subsidy (possible under the AAA law),
is under study by Wallace and Hull.
Manufactured articles, too: WPA is rushing studies of both needs
and production possibilities...cotton mattresses, overcoats, overalls,
mackinaws, work shirts, gloves, mittens, other clothing.
The idea: Use gov't money to put men to work in private plants,
thus a substitute for WPA. Give the goods to the needy, direct relief,
thus increase consumption. More production, consumption, employment.
How to do this without upsetting private trade: There's the rub,
the unsolved problem. Trades should watch developments closely.

Mule-drawn wagons were still commonly used to transport goods in the South, as at this cotton gin.

July 23, 1938

    <u>Doctors and the New Deal</u>: The President's health conference here this week fanned into flame the issue of socialized medical care which has been smouldering for several years. The outlook is that gov't will work steadily toward more socialized health services for masses. One reason is the need for useful jobs which the reliefers can perform. It is assumed that large WPA corps will be permanent, and aim will be to develop new public services (such as health) as means of employing the unemployed in ways to give taxpayers "something for their money." Program is BIG - Billions. Plan is to start at 850 millions a year. Most doctors will fight it, and may take their turn as "whipping boys."
    <u>But socialized medical care IS on the way</u>.

July 30, 1938

    <u>Government-owned broadcasting station</u> is planned for the future. Present purpose is to spread "good neighbor" propaganda to South America.

August 13, 1938

    <u>Rehabilitation of the "backward South" with federal aid money</u> will become one of the New Deal's major objectives in the next 2 years. Motives are social, economic, AND POLITICAL.
    <u>Politically it's part of plan to undercut conservative leaders</u> in the South, to wean the masses away from such leadership of the past. New Deal will appeal directly to the millions of poor people in South — tenant farmers, share croppers, mill hands, lumber workers, roustabouts. The New Deal implication will be that these classes are being hoodwinked by their present conservative representatives in Congress.

September 3, 1938

    <u>War issues</u> in various forms will get into our internal politics during next session of Congress. Some of our left liberals think of war as a means to the end of promoting gov't control of all private industry. There's no doubt gov't would GET control, and KEEP much of it after war.

September 17, 1938

    <u>IF war were to come, what would happen here</u>? There's much talk of all angles and phases. Plans are tentative, contingent, far from sure. But we report the responsible talk...which contains a bit of guidance.
    <u>U.S. would keep out of war</u>, directly, for a considerable time. Seems probable that it would take <u>nearly 2 years</u> to create circumstances which MIGHT draw us into war as a belligerent.

"Shhhh! He'll be quiet now—maybe!"

October 1, 1938

There's relief but no great joy here over European settlement.
Relief comes from avoidance of immediate war, with U.S. repercussions.
But the reasons for no great joy are these:
The aggressor nations won. Their prestige is now increased.
This may be temporary, but it's a fact which cannot be easily blinked.
Additional crises will come...from Germany, Italy, Japan.
The year 1939 is sure to bring one or more of them.
"We don't want war." That's clear in all official discussions.
There's no tongue-in-cheek about the attitude. Every official knows
that American public sentiment demands that we keep out...if possible.
Keep out HOW? On this point a great change is occurring,
probably throughout the country, and certainly within officialdom.
Preparedness for war as a means of enforcing peace: This idea
has had a sudden great growth...main U.S. result of German-Czech crisis.
As a direct consequence of events in Europe in past few weeks,
industrial preparation for any emergency is taking on new life in U.S.

October 22, 1938

Many national banks must tighten up their practices from now on.
Bad or questionable practices prevailing or tolerated in past
will be criticized more vigorously by bank examiners...pressures applied.
These practices relate to paying dividends which otherwise go to surplus;
sliding along with too small capitalization; failing to get new capital
from RFC by preferred stock sales - procedure to be forced on some banks;
making unsound loans to insiders; fixing bad assets to seem good assets
by accounting devices, these applying particularly to real estate loans;
covering up the true inside situation from bank directors themselves.

October 29, 1938

Government spending is popular with many of the new Republicans
to be elected to Congress. On this, there's less fundamental difference
between the two parties than appears on the surface, in campaign talk.

November 19, 1938

Industry mobilization speed-up will be main 1939 business phase.
Educational orders for industry, to train factories to turn out
equipment on big scale after M-Day (Mobilization Day), will be expanded.
Many companies will be told explicitly during next year or so
just what will be expected of them, how they must change production,
by order of War or Navy Dept. at some undetermined future time.
Airplanes are to be multiplied spectacularly. But the boost
to general business will come from making of 55 other "critical items."

November 26, 1938

To put it bluntly, we are entering a preparation-for-war era.
That's not news. You know it already. But point in saying it
is to emphasize in advance that many Washington policies in next 2 years
are going to be presented in the wrappings of national defense (or war).
To business it means this: Reforms which the New Deal wants
will be pressed as corollaries of the unity program for defense (or war).
Whether they are "good" or otherwise depends on individual perspective.
But point is that administration will claim they are needed for defense.
Perhaps they are, perhaps they are NOT, and that's the thing to watch.
More control of business by gov't will be aim in many plans.
Not labeled "economic planning" as in past. But now for "defense."
The President has new base of operations for business reforms.

On the other side, remember the taxes. Recent gov't publicity
has been designed to create impression that taxes would not be raised.
It has been said that present rates applied to expanding business base
would yield "enough" revenue.
We are inclined to think this is a wrong steer.
Think it more likely that taxes WILL be raised.
Special "defense tax" is being considered within the Treasury,
to be superimposed upon, or added to, the income tax. "Percent plusage."
Only "temporary," of course. But note that most temporary taxes
in the past have soon become permanent...like the excise taxes.

Third term for Roosevelt: Both Garner and Farley are opposed,
although for purposes of publication Farley would certainly deny it.
Roosevelt, therefore, will not be a third term nominee.
This seems to us to be the probability...barring unforeseeable war.

January 21, 1939

Repeal of New Deal laws: In Mid-West, which Republicans swept,
there's widespread impression among business men that repeal is imminent
for many New Deal laws, particularly labor laws. This is erroneous.
We do not foresee repeal of ANY major New Deal law within next 2 years.

January 28, 1939

Influence of Europe on politics here: There's no great dispute
over defense measures here, no big questioning of increase of armament.
The issue, now rapidly taking shape, in many different ways,
is over whether we shall give active economic support to the democracies
in advance of any overt and demonstrable threat to U.S.
The President is definitely steering toward such a policy.

VOTE
STRAIGHT
REPUBLICAN
TUESDAY, NOV. 8, 1938

1939

February 4, 1939

War jitters: From Washington squabbles over our foreign policy
some people are getting the impression that European war is imminent.
Isolation idealists protest against ANY foreign entanglements.
They say the way to avoid war is to avoid going toward the war zone.
They say the President's policy is to steer toward this danger zone.
Retort is, of course, that the safest course is the bold course,
and that the President's course is bold, designed to keep us out of war
by throwing our influence on the "right side"...IN ADVANCE of war.

Now a new element appears — suspicion of President's motives.
The plain fact is that many members of Congress, in BOTH of the parties,
suspect the President of welcoming a war crisis for third-term reasons.
It is disputable whether the suspicion is right or wrong.
It is NOT disputable that the suspicion will figure prominently
in many important decisions to be made by Congress in next few months.
The suspicion will determine the course of much legislation.

March 18, 1939

1940 elections: Anti-Roosevelt Democrats are doing much talking
about the lack of any contender against Roosevelt for the nomination.
They fear a movement to "draft Roosevelt."
Most politicians think Roosevelt IS a candidate.
Most think he will not be renominated..."unless there's a war
crisis." That's why they harp on limiting his power to make a crisis.

April 15, 1939

The President's position is clear. He wants to go just as far
as he can to support Britain-France-&-allies against Germany-Italy-Japan.
His implements are utterances, political alignments, AND NEEDED GOODS.
Ostensibly these steps are intended in ADVANCE of war, in LIEU of war,
in the hope of PREVENTING a war, but taking a chance that they WON'T.
Also taking a chance of U.S. involvement...earlier rather than later.

IF war comes, WHAT effects here? Humanitarian considerations come ahead of business phases, but we are reporting only on the latter.

Business stimulation: Most analysts think this would result from war in Europe, assuming that U.S. were not an active belligerent. At least for first year. In the end, of course, net loss to all.

April 22, 1939

President's policy makes U.S. an antagonist of the aggressors. U.S. is no longer "neutral." In Washington these are considered FACTS, although out around the country they don't seem to be fully recognized.

If there's a war, will the U.S. get into it? A ticklish question. Most persons here, after explaining they deeply hope it will NOT, conclude by admitting reluctantly they fear it WILL.

Public opinion controls, but it can be manipulated..up..or down.

May 13, 1939

The "draft Roosevelt" movement is about to start...next 30 days. It will pop up in various parts of country, and seem to be spontaneous. Actually it is directed from Washington, by attaches of the White House, without explicit approval of the President, but without his displeasure. Politicians who know how to interpret the intentions behind actions have no doubt that Roosevelt is a definite behind-scenes candidate.

September 2, 1939

Third term for Roosevelt is more of a possibility than it was. There's much political capital to be made for him out of the position of facing the world, with the U.S. behind him. People are reluctant to strike down statesmen when they are facing outward.

September 9, 1939

The long war theory:
Reasoning: Britain & France are not fighting merely for Poland, but are fighting against Hitlerism, are determined to make an end of it. Thus only the passing out of Hitler himself could terminate the war.

This is generally what most Washington authorities now think.
Gov't plans are being based on the assumption of a long war.
"Long war" means a year or more, with the end not predictable.

Soviet Foreign Minister Molotov signs the nonaggression pact with Germany as his German counterpart, von Ribbentrop (center), and Stalin (second from right) look on.

September 16, 1939

It is our opinion that the Executive branch of our government is putting up a front of intention-talk about staying out of the war, but is actually preparing to go into it.

Sorry if this shocks you, but it seems to us to be the fact. There's no use in being timid about stating it. Implication is subject to pro forma denial, but it will become apparent in the next few weeks.

As for the longer-range price trend, most gov't analysts agree that world-wide and domestic pressures will be on side of higher prices, until the war and the war-born inflation have run their course.

There's a new fundamental factor...war-inflation psychology. This is replacing the depression psychology. Turning point is past. For years the prudent have clung to cash and "safe" investments...scared. Shift from this to equities, tangibles, would change the whole picture.

So concepts about "normal" inventories must be revised UPWARD. "Normal" inventories will be larger in the future than in the past.

Rush of war orders from Britain & France is expected shortly.

Draft plans are nearing completion. Important feature of them is that care will be taken NOT to draft essential workers in industry.

September 23, 1939

The arms embargo will be replaced by some form of cash-&-carry.

If war goes on, as is expected, most estimates are that U.S. production for 1940 will be the highest of any year since 1929...might even exceed...in volume, not in profits.

September 30, 1939

Business is spurting upward even faster than had been expected. It's a real boom psychology.

And yet it's based on HOPES more than actual consumption. Domestic orders are for stocking up, getting ready for new business which is expected to flow from war orders.

November 18, 1939

Supreme Court will be dominated for many years in the future
by Roosevelt New Deal men, leaning to idea of a flexible Constitution
and to idea that new laws of Congress should have the benefit of doubts.
Thus Roosevelt wins his fight against the Court..."by natural means."

November 25, 1939

Wendell Willkie is not taken seriously; it's compliment-talk.
Of course, under a conservative administration, he might be in the
cabinet.

December 23, 1939

What's ahead in 1940? Can't foresee all, but can foresee some,
or at least can make the EFFORT to assemble a pattern of expectations...
the trends of 1940, extending perhaps beyond the calendar year itself.

United States in 1940 will not get into the shooting war,
but WILL become more firmly committed to the side of Britain-&-France.
U.S. will become more involved MORALLY. If war continues into 1941,
the chances that the U.S. will stay out will be considerably diminished.

Gasoline will be more powerful, will have higher octane rating,
due to new processes, and competition among rival brands.

Aircraft industry will reach a new high phase of maturity.
Technical improvements and mass production, stimulated by war orders,
will lead to great expansion of commercial aviation in the next decade.

Television will make some little gains, but no big splash.

Silk stocking industry will begin to decline, due partly to
trouble with Japan, partly to synthetic chemical substitutes for silk.

Superhighways, great trunks, city-to-city, and around cities,
crossing over other highways, will get a lot of talk, and some progress,
but the era of superhighway construction is still some years off.

Inflation will be in the air, in the trend, creeping along,
due to gov't deficits, war wastes, cheap credit and lots of it.

But wild inflation is probably not due within the next year.
It's a possibility of next 5 years...to watch...but not a certainty.

1940s

The first half of the Forties was given over to fighting a world war, the second half to recovering from it—and gearing up for a new military threat, communist aggression in Europe and Asia.

Hitler set Europe ablaze in '39 and '40, attacking Denmark, Norway and the Netherlands, then overrunning Belgium and France. German bombers pounded Britain to weaken it for an invasion by sea, but the British air force showed Hitler that England would not be defeated easily. Meanwhile, the Soviet Union forcibly annexed the Baltic nations. In 1941 Nazi forces overwhelmed Yugoslavia and Greece and established dominance over most of Eastern Europe. Then, disdaining the nonaggression pact with Stalin, Hitler attacked the Soviet Union.

The U.S. rushed to Britain as much aid—old destroyers, airplanes and cash—as the Roosevelt administration could manueveur past Congress's neutrality laws. In 1940 Congress passed a military draft, the Navy began patrols in the north Atlantic, and the U.S. imposed a limited trade embargo on Japan, which was continuing to press for domination of Asia. In 1941 the U.S. increased its aid to Britain and began providing naval escorts for allied convoys, and that fall Germany attacked a U.S. destroyer in the Atlantic.

Slowly the U.S. was being drawn into the world conflict, despite the resolute isolationism of most Americans. "America First" was both the slogan and the name of the growing antiwar movement, and "Keep America Out of War" its battle cry. Broadly supported by the American people, it carried great weight with Congress. American aviation hero Charles Lindbergh, convinced that the U.S. was no match for German air power, gave respectability to the isolationist stance.

Relations with Japan deteriorated to the point that, in July 1941, the U.S. demanded Japanese withdrawal from China and Indochina, froze Japanese assets in the U.S., and cut off all U.S. trade with Japan, depriving it of a large share of its oil supply. Speculation on impending war with Japan buzzed around Washington throughout the fall and winter of '41. But nothing could prepare America for the shock of the Japanese attack on Pearl Harbor, Hawaii, on the morning of December 7, 1941. The antiwar movement evaporated overnight, and

1940	1941	1942
FIRST PEACETIME DRAFT.	U.S., BRITAIN SIGN ATLANTIC CHARTER.	U.S. WINS BATTLE OF MIDWAY.
FDR WINS THIRD TERM.	LEND-LEASE FOR BRITAIN AND U.S.S.R.	JAPANESE-AMERICANS SENT TO DETENTION CAMPS.
GERMAN BLITZKRIEG: FRANCE SURRENDERS.	JAPAN STRIKES PEARL HARBOR, U.S. DECLARES WAR.	U.S. ACHIEVES FIRST NUCLEAR CHAIN REACTION.

the American people rallied behind FDR, who had defeated Wendell Willkie for a third term in 1940. The war became a two-continent effort for America when Hitler foolishly declared war on the U.S. soon after Pearl Harbor.

Wartime controls

American business had grown accustomed to, if not comfortable with, the routine of New Deal government regulation, but that was nothing compared with the tight control of the civilian economy that spread in 1942 and '43. The first wave of wartime production for allied aid in 1940 had given the economy an inflationary kick, and rising commodity and consumer prices led to a halfhearted price-control program in '41. After Pearl Harbor the controls were given real teeth. Steel, aluminum, copper and other war materials were allocated by Washington. Price controls went on industrial and civilian goods and rents, and soon there was rationing of tires, gasoline and meat—and black markets in all of them. Silk and nylon stockings disappeared in favor of parachute production.

The economic controls were controversial and unpopular at first, in part because the war was going badly for America. Dissent translated into sizable gains for the Republicans in the congressional elections of '42. Unions were demanding higher wages to offset rising prices, but FDR resisted. When John L. Lewis and his mine workers defied the president and went on strike in '43, FDR seized the mines and ordered the men back to work. Anger over the growing power of unions led to the first legislation in many years that restricted, rather than broadened, organized-labor rights. Meanwhile, black Americans were migrating north to fill factory jobs in defense work, and there was widespread white resentment of the hiring and advancement of Negroes. There were 34 deaths resulting from the Detroit race riot in the summer of '43.

Economic boom

For seven years FDR and his New Deal colleagues had tried to stimulate private-sector jobs and raise real wages. What the New Deal couldn't accomplish, the war effort did. Unemployment vanished, and millions of women went to work as replacements for men in the service. Over the course of the war, industrial output nearly doubled, and the Pacific Coast of the U.S. became an industrial powerhouse from Washington State to southern California. Real wages in manufacturing rose 70%, and people paid down debts and bought war bonds with their savings. With the world starved for America's food, the net cash income of U.S. farmers quadrupled, and government programs tilted from forced scarcity to incentives for production.

The government, of course, was the ultimate buyer of much of this output. Federal spending exploded from $9 billion in 1940 to $93 billion in '45. Taxes skyrocketed, too, on personal and corporate income, estates, and gifts. At the start of the war, only eight million Americans paid any income tax at all; by the end there were 50 million on the taxpayer rolls. War bonds became an anti-inflationary device for soaking up the savings of workers who had few consumer goods to buy, and the American people lent $100 billion to their government. But the surge in federal spending on the war so swamped the rise in tax revenues and bond proceeds that the national debt hit $258 billion by the end of the war, nearly 125% of annual GNP.

The war was going well for the allies in '44, with the Normandy invasion in June followed by the liberation of Paris in August. This took the wind out of the Republicans' sails, and FDR was reelected to a fourth term in November. For his vice-president he replaced the out-of-favor Henry Wallace with Harry S. Truman, a U.S. senator respected for his honesty.

A new world order

As the war effort continued, the allies met frequently to discuss what kind of political and economic framework for aid, to both allies and defeated foes, would ensure future world peace. They set the requirement of unconditional surrender by Germany and Japan. In the summer of '44 the allies met at Dumbarton Oaks in Washington, D.C., to sketch the outlines of a new international organization that would be called the United Nations. Ideas for economic stabilization, including the International Monetary Fund and the World

						FDR DIES, TRUMAN BECOMES PRESIDENT.
	INCOME-TAX WITHHOLDING BEGINS.	D-DAY INVASION OF NORMANDY.	GI BILL OF RIGHTS ENACTED.	BRETTON WOODS CONFERENCE ON POSTWAR FINANCIAL COOPERATION.	YALTA CONFERENCE: RUSSIA JOINS WAR AGAINST JAPAN.	
GOVERNMENT BANS RACE BIAS IN DEFENSE PLANTS.						
1943		**1944**			**1945**	

Bank, emerged from a conference at Bretton Woods, N.H., that same summer.

As an ally, Russia was a party to negotiations over the future of Europe. Roosevelt and British Prime Minister Winston Churchill mistrusted Stalin's intentions toward Eastern Europe, but they believed they needed his help in defeating Japan. At the Yalta conference in February of '45, Stalin promised that new governments in partitioned postwar Germany, Poland and other liberated Eastern European nations would include non-communist elements, and that there would later be free elections. In April 1945, a frail FDR died, and Truman continued the allied discussions at Potsdam, in Germany. He agreed to a major postwar role for Russia in Germany and Eastern Europe, in exchange for the secret pledge of Soviet help in defeating Japan.

The war in Europe would soon be over, and allied troops jockeyed for position in Germany and Eastern Europe. U.S. troops probably could have seized Berlin and Prague, but Soviet troops got there first. It soon became clear that Stalin had no intention of honoring commitments he had made to self-determination in the liberated nations, and as things turned out, the U.S. didn't need Russia's help in defeating Japan.

On July 16, 1945, U.S. scientists secretly detonated the first atomic bomb. Shortly afterward, the allies, meeting in Potsdam, called on Japan to surrender or "face the prompt and utter destruction" of its homeland. Japan did not respond. To avoid an invasion that probably would have cost many thousands of lives, Truman authorized the use of the terrifying new weapon. A single atomic bomb was dropped on one Japanese city, Hiroshima, on August 6. Japan did not surrender at once. Three days later, a second bomb was dropped on another city, Nagasaki. It was not until five days later that Japan capitulated. The age of atomic energy, a force for destructive and peaceful uses, had arrived.

Boom and inflation

At home in the U.S., attention was focused on the staggering task of converting the nation from a seminationalized, tightly controlled wartime economy to something like a free-market economy once again. During the war, there was hot debate among economists over what the postwar U.S. economy would look like. The most common view held that the sudden cessation of military production and return of now-jobless GIs would thrust the U.S. back into depression. A minority argued that, after a brief recession for civilian conversion, there would emerge a strong boom with plenty of inflation, driven by the long-deferred public demand for housing, cars and consumer goods.

And that's what happened. Postponed marriage and childbearing surged, beginning a spike in births that would earn the term baby boom. Suburban housing boomed, and former GIs hit the books in college. Wartime advances in electronics, aviation, plastics and synthetic fibers fed the consumer boom with new products and services. More than two decades after its invention, television emerged as a popular technology that would spark profound changes in American thought, mores and political behavior.

At the end of the war, the government sold off to private firms, at attractively low prices, enormous industrial capacity in machine tools, aluminum, synthetic rubber and other businesses. The pent-up savings of wartime deprivation flooded into consumer markets, driving up prices. Truman convinced Congress to remove wage and price controls, which would stimulate production and eventually bring price stability. But in the short run, wages and prices exploded.

Unions struck the coal mines and railroads (with an irate Truman seizing control and threatening to draft the strikers into the army), and some wage settlements ran as high as 19%. Truman and Congress flip-flopped on price controls, angering farmers, consumers, unions and almost everyone else in succession. A disillusioned public gave the Republicans big gains in Congress in '46, and in '47 an increasingly conservative Congress passed the Taft-Hartley bill over Truman's veto, sharply curtailing the power of unions.

A man of firmly held convictions, Truman battled with Congress over all his liberal legislation, including civil rights for Negroes, freer immigration and support for public housing. By '48 he was so broadly unpopular that it was widely assumed he would lose the election to Thomas Dewey, and this outcome was forecast by the Gallup and

	U.N. CHARTER SIGNED BY 50 NATIONS.	JAPAN SURRENDERS.	STRIKES IN STEEL, AUTOS, COAL MINING.	COMMUNISTS RISE AGAINST FRENCH IN VIETNAM.	TRUMAN LIFTS WARTIME CONTROLS.
GERMANY SURRENDERS.	U.S. DROPS A-BOMBS ON TWO JAPANESE CITIES.			ENIAC, FIRST PRACTICAL DIGITAL COMPUTER.	REPUBLICANS WIN MAJORITIES IN CONGRESS.
1945			**1946**		

Roper polls. On election day, Truman failed to get a majority of the votes, but he won a plurality over a fragmented field of four candidates. Over the next four years he would continue to press Congress, largely unsuccessfully, for "Fair Deal" reforms for national health insurance, federal aid to local schools and slum clearance.

Soviet aggression

Americans dreamed the defeat of fascism would bring years of world peace, but that was not to be. While the U.S. tackled the tough domestic problems of postwar conversion, Stalin went on the offensive in Europe, and Communist insurgents gained strength in China and Southeast Asia. Great Britain and France were flat on their backs economically and unable to block Stalin, who had turned East Germany and other Eastern Europe nations into dictatorships and was putting pressure on Greece, Turkey and Iran. In '46 Churchill warned that an "iron curtain has descended across the Continent," and in early '47 Truman asked Congress for massive economic and military aid to Greece and Turkey. In '47 State Department staff under George Kennan urged the "containment" of Soviet aggression, and that spring they secretly recommended a program of massive European assistance that Secretary of State George Marshall unveiled in a speech in June.

Stalin turned up the heat with the seizure of Czechoslovakia in '48, followed by a total rail and highway blockade of Berlin, a city deep within Soviet East Germany that was divided between allied and Russian authority after the war. U.S. statesman Bernard Baruch had warned in '47 that a "cold war" was at hand, and now, with a crisis over Berlin, there were fears of another hot war against a new enemy. The U.S. responded to the blockading of Berlin with resolve but not military force. Every day, close to 1,000 cargo planes flew across East Germany and dropped all the goods Berlin needed to survive—coal, food, medicine, clothing. After nearly a year of the airlift, the Soviets lifted the blockade.

Meanwhile, the Marshall Plan stabilized governments throughout Europe. But in Asia, deemed a less vital interest of the U.S., the communist Chinese under Mao succeeded in pushing Chiang Kai-shek's troops off the mainland in 1949.

Communist ideology had long been anathema to most Americans, but during the Great Depression and the rise of fascism in Europe, communism held a certain appeal in American colleges, government agencies, labor unions and artistic circles. But when the Soviet Union emerged as an expansive threat after World War II, America's tolerance for communist sympathies evaporated. It was discovered that pro-communist Americans held sensitive positions in the U.S. government, and there was substantial evidence that some of them had spied for the Soviets. The Truman administration, encouraged by Republicans in Congress, began a purge of communists in government in '46.

In 1948 Alger Hiss, who had been a mid-level State Department official in the '30s, was accused by a repentant American communist of passing secret documents to the Russians, and Hiss was convicted of perjury on strong evidence. In September 1949, the world was shocked to find that the Soviets had developed an atomic bomb. The following year, Klaus Fuchs, a scientist who had worked in the top-secret American atomic program at Los Alamos, N.M., confessed to passing important scientific information to the Russians from '42 through '49. His confession led to the conviction and execution for treason of American accomplices Julius and Ethel Rosenberg. By 1951 more than 200 government employees had been fired by the Truman administration for alleged communist ties, and another 2,000 resigned.

As the tumultuous decade of the Forties came to a close, trouble was brewing in Korea. After the defeat of the occupying Japanese, control over Korea was divided between the U.S. (in the south) and the Soviets (in the north). In 1948 Washington proposed to Moscow a mutual pullout, and a year later both complied. But the Soviets left the communist regime in North Korea heavily armed. There were suspicions that the North Koreans had thoughts of unifying the whole country under their rule.

	1947	1948	1949
TAFT-HARTLEY LABOR ACT PASSES OVER VETO.	MARSHALL PLAN LAUNCHED.	SOVIETS BLOCKADE BERLIN, U.S. AIRLIFT COMMENCES.	
		ISRAEL PROCLAIMS INDEPENDENCE, REPELS ARAB ATTACK.	NATO ESTABLISHED.
		TRUMAN DEFEATS DEWEY.	PEOPLE'S REPUBLIC PROCLAIMED IN CHINA.
			U.S. COMMUNIST LEADERS CONVICTED IN N.Y. COURT.
			COMMUNISTS COMPLETE TAKEOVER IN EASTERN EUROPE.
			"DEATH OF A SALESMAN" OPENS ON BROADWAY.

Innocence abroad

January 6, 1940

      <u>Big war in spring</u> is now the expectation of military experts.
      Our gov't believes this, and is making domestic plans to fit.
Mainly air attack on ports & ships, not frontal attack on land.
      <u>Germany is likely to get the best of it</u>, in the early phases,
and the allies the worst of it, say the best-informed officials here,
and they say it with regret.
      <u>Some new gesture against Japan</u> is ahead. Perhaps naval display
in the Pacific. Time uncertain, possibly within next 2 or 3 months.
Purpose: To add jitters to the nerves of Japan already showing jitters.

January 13, 1940

      <u>At secret meeting</u> of dozen or so New Dealers last Monday night,
immediately after the Jackson Day dinner, at the Mayflower Hotel,
it was decided to organize actively, at once, a "spontaneous movement"
to burst upon the Democratic nominating convention...<u>to draft Roosevelt.</u>

February 24, 1940

      <u>Theory of planners is that end of war will bring depression</u>,
price collapse, liquidation of war industries, and huge unemployment.
The planners hope to minimize the shock, and possibly even avoid it.
There's no One Big Plan, but many partial plans, and most of these
point toward <u>creation of a great new international banking mechanism</u>.
      <u>Spread U.S. gold, credit & capital around the world</u>.
      <u>It is NOT premature</u> to get in mind these long-range plans now.

March 30, 1940

      <u>Television</u>: RCA's commercial permit probably will be reissued,
following clarification by Communications Commission of its position.
FCC wants it understood by public that television is still experimental.
Wants to head off big wave of set-buying and later consumer resistance
to inevitable improvements. Wants a little more time for experiments,
to discourage manufacturers from rushing into production prematurely.
      <u>Frequency modulation broadcasting</u>, a revolutionary practice,
may be given the go-sign by FCC within the next 30 days. Officials say
this system will not interfere with established broadcasting stations.

April 27, 1940

      <u>There's a close watch on public opinion</u> with respect to war.
Letters from ordinary citizens are read with great care at White House.
      <u>Public sentiment against U.S. in war is still overwhelming</u>,
according to these indicators. But there's also much evidence that...
      <u>More-&-more people are beginning to think we MAY get into it</u>,
despite the desire to stay out. It's a vague feeling, but it's growing.

May 4, 1940

      <u>Government policy between now and elections next November</u>
will be to continue to support the allies' cause in back-door ways...
financial and economic. This can be done by administrative policies
which are largely of technical nature, which will raise no hue & cry.

Third term: It is now accepted by all political observers
that Roosevelt will be nominated by the Democratic convention in July,
UNLESS he says NO at the 11th hour. He has it within his hands.

May 18, 1940

Willkie: Fact about him is that he has come up fast from zero,
and is now rated as a "possibility," though faint. Politicians remark
that times have changed, since radio can "make" a candidate so quickly.

June 8, 1940

Some sort of more highly integrated economy, national planning,
national control, regimentation under government, is probably expectable
for a period of years ahead, regardless of which way the war comes out,
regardless of whether U.S. gets into it, even regardless of elections.
(Under Republicans, the push toward integration would merely be slower.)

June 15, 1940

Various anti-war organizations..."respectable, not communazi"...
are now organizing a crusade, with the following claims and keynotes:
Aid to allies, such as we are now giving, can not be limited.
It is quite likely to lead, step by step, to the sending of MEN abroad.
Democracy in the U.S. will be threatened, perhaps permanently,
by putting the U.S. into foreign war. Authoritarian government at home
is the price to be paid. Internal weakness will hatch dictatorship.

August 17, 1940

<u>Conscription</u>: Expect the enactment of some sort of draft law, but with the provision that both registration and calling up of men be delayed until after the elections.

<u>Destroyers</u> to Britain. Chances are a way will be found.

<u>Battle of Britain</u>: Officials here think Britain MAY hold out, but wouldn't bet much on it. British claims are believed more accurate than German claims. But actual DEFEAT of Germany seems unattainable... UNLESS U.S. joins in war full-tilt, which seems unlikely before 1941.

September 7, 1940

<u>Will the U.S. get into the war?</u>...as an active belligerent? The answer is not surely YES, but no one can say that the answer is NO.

<u>Practically we are already a nonbelligerent ally</u> of Britain, as is shown by official acts and utterances. "Neutrality" is thin.

<u>Thus we are already in the war</u>, regardless of the nice points of international law which define when war becomes legal war.

<u>There isn't much doubt that we shall go FURTHER</u> into the war, aiding one side against the other...step by step. At each of these steps it will be argued in justification that this is not war, but defense.

<u>Roosevelt's election</u> undoubtedly would expedite the trend.

September 14, 1940

<u>Cost of national defense</u> will be met largely by gov't borrowing, despite the new higher taxes...and the still HIGHER taxes NEXT year.

<u>Public debt</u>, now 44 Billions, may grow to 60 Billions or more before the armament splurge is over. Then it probably will rise further as the result of spending project to prevent a post-armament crash.

<u>Pay the debt</u>? Fiscal officials don't seem much worried about it. Gradually there is developing the vague thought that at some future time devices will be found for "handling" the debt, or interest charges on it, perhaps through some new Federal Reserve credit manipulation.

A flood of new money made by such handling of the public debt could make wild price inflation, but experts would try to prevent this by imposing strict governmental price controls.

September 28, 1940

<u>Embargo on exports to Japan</u> will be extended to other items. The hope is that our series of economic squeezings will give her pause. Our government has no desire to START a war. Neither has Japan. But both nations have fists up, chips on shoulder. Some "incident" might set off war.

October 5, 1940

<u>War crises</u> play definitely into the hands of Roosevelt.

<u>"Don't change horses in midstream"</u>: Many voters are influenced by this plea, and it's an important factor for Roosevelt...net.

October 12, 1940

<u>War with Japan</u> is a serious possibility...not yet a probability.

<u>ECONOMIC war on Japan</u> is almost certain...embargoes, boycotts.

<u>Expanded help for Britain</u> is a fixed and definite policy.

<u>Main chance AGAINST the slide toward war lies in public opinion</u>. There's a possibility that people will be shocked by sudden spectacle of actual-war-soon, and see that it is not mere Washington gesturing.

Elections, of course, are retarding many formal steps toward war, and activity will be far greater after elections...if Roosevelt wins.

Wendell Willkie, FDR's Republican opponent in 1940.

Whether Willkie could or would stem the war tide is a question. He would have opportunity to pause, look around, take inventory.
In either event, the chances seem to be on the side of war.

Japan: Our gov't clearly does not WANT war with Japan. Japan does not WANT war with us. But circumstances are shaping for clash, and there WILL be war unless one or the other backs down.
Is U.S. bluffing? YES and NO. The answer is NO in the sense that our gov't is prepared to act if Japan forces the issue so clearly that failure to act would seem like ignominious crawfishing.
Answer is YES in the sense that our gov't thinks the chances are 2-to-1 that Japan WILL quiet down...and ease up on her aggressions.
Flaw in latter theory is that the Japanese militarists in power are touchy, stubborn, psychologically clumsy. They may risk a showdown.

December 7, 1940

Prevailing assumption is that America will inherit major job of providing money, materials, transportation, and much of the management for the world-wide post-war reconstruction. Assumption also is that...
Great world-wide activity will follow the end of the war, after the first shock, after temporary period of readjustment to peace. It is quite possible that national income will reach 100 Billions a year at some stage, as compared with current level of around 74 Billions.

Japanese Emperor Hirohito (left) receives his war minister, Admiral Hideki Tojo.

December 14, 1940

Outlook for years ahead is for deficits and mounting debt. No end is even faintly in sight. Even after the war (or the emergency), armament outpourings may be channeled into peace-time gov't projects to prevent a crash, to provide a bridge. And so...continuing deficits...

January 25, 1941

The old talk of "business as usual" is being abandoned.
The new talk is of "deprivations ahead." It's not a new tune but it's a new emphasis. Defense is going to change a lot of things.
Theoretically our economy can furnish BOTH guns AND butter, but practically there must be many compromises. Hence "deprivations." Shrinkages here, expansion there. Adjustments.
The WHOLE economy is to be geared to defense (or war) efforts.

1941

February 1, 1941

    <u>Censorship has started</u>, like war-time, on press, radio, movies.
It's voluntary, by request, not mandatory. <u>It covers certain Navy news</u>,
unless such news is announced or authorized by the government itself.
Editors are complying without much complaint, but it is recognized
that the "request rules" will be extended later to other kinds of news.

February 8, 1941

    <u>Total of NEW taxes</u> to be imposed will be one billion or MORE.
The Treasury will not set a figure, but implies a billion as minimum.
Thus federal taxes will rise above 10 billions from about 9 billions now.
    <u>All classes catch it</u> in higher taxes...both rich and poor.
But the upper-middle or the "well-to-do" will be the special targets.
    <u>It will be a further step in the redistribution of income</u>.

March 1, 1941

    <u>Price control plans</u>: There's new talk of need for legislation
to deal with individual situations where commodity prices get out of line
because of "unpatriotic practices by industry." (Precisely those words
are used more-&-more often by officials. They show the spirit here.)

May 3, 1941

    There's a great disparity between the public attitude
out around the country and the attitude of Washington officialdom.
Out around the country there's much talk that Washington is hysterical,
and our officials know they are so regarded, but they say they are NOT.
They retort hotly that the country is "asleep," and too much "unaware"
and consequently "unprepared" for the rigid government war controls
which must be imposed "soon." They say "business-as-usual is out,"
and they are amazed business men do not yet understand.

July 19, 1941

    <u>Automobiles</u> will be cut way down...not 20%, not 40%, but MORE...
perhaps 70%. New cars by this time next year will be really SCARCE.
    <u>Sharp civilian shortages</u> are just around the corner.

August 2, 1941

      <u>This is the month for curtailment of civilian goods production</u>
on a really big scale. Orders to cut will take effect in late August.
      <u>The program is really RATIONING</u>...a broadening of priorities.
      <u>The depth and extent of the cuts</u> have not been fully disclosed.
      <u>Reason for reticence by gov't</u> is fear of a buyers' stampede.
Hence the reluctance to tell the public the full truth at this time.

      <u>Japan</u> will push on, but just where is not known. Our State Dept.
is strong for view that economic measures will strangle Japan in 6 mos.
especially if Chinese go aggressive, as they probably will, because...
      <u>U.S. men in U.S. planes</u> may soon be bombing the Japanese...
flying under foreign colors...getting experience...in a common-law war.

August 30, 1941

      <u>American expeditionary forces</u> abroad are foreseen...eventually.
Our government is not being candid with its people.

September 13, 1941

      <u>War economy is upon you</u>. It is well beyond the twilight zone.
      <u>War economy means this</u>: Full absolute power by gov't to dictate
all transactions within the nation, and also all dealings abroad.
That covers a lot of territory, but it means exactly that.

October 18, 1941

      <u>Naval war with Japan</u> now threatens, but is merely the opener,
and the major objective is Hitler.

October 25, 1941

      <u>Japan is called an "incidental war</u>," or a "preliminary war."
      <u>Navy influence</u> is now pretty much FOR it, to get it over with,
to make the Pacific back door safe...and then face Hitler.
      <u>Most say it would take 6 months</u>, and a few say only 3 months.
This is the preponderant expert military opinion here. Officials say
Japan recognizes this, and so still welcome a chance to save face.

November 8, 1941

      <u>War with Japan</u>: Opinion here is SLIGHTLY that it will not be.
      <u>Reasons given</u>: Military and economic steps are being taken
which could strangle Japan and burn her cities, and Japanese know it.
Our measures are stiffening, not easing. Also there's a counter-plan
for U.S. economic aid to let Japan shift from her present war economy.

November 29, 1941

      <u>War with Japan</u>? Over this week end no one here really knows.
Our gov't is standing pat, not giving an inch, preparing for war.
It is assumed that if Japan does not fight within the next 30 days
she will not fight, for the A-B-C-D fighting power is mounting rapidly.
      Within Washington there is no attempt to conceal the tension...
a recognition that crisis has been reached in U.S.-Japanese relations.

Japanese special envoy Saburo Kurusu (left), with Ambassador Kichisaburo Nomuro, brought a conciliatory message to Washington 17 days before the attack on Pearl Harbor.

December 6, 1941

     <u>War with Japan</u>? Officials as late as this afternoon, Saturday, simply did not know, but their cautious private observations indicated that they are prepared for the worst. Much seems to hinge on Moscow. If it holds, maybe no war. If it falls, probably war.

December 13, 1941

     <u>What war will do to business</u>:
     <u>It will make gov't control of business COMPLETE</u>.
     More than 100 laws now, and more coming, make the President the commander in chief of business...powers that he can invoke at will. He can delegate authority to many gov't agencies to do almost anything.
     <u>Consumers must learn to do without a lot of things</u>.
     <u>Wages will rise gradually</u>, due to the dearth of skilled men, and also to <u>inflation</u>, which gov't can restrain but not stop.
     <u>Taxes will rise</u> next year, and in addition there will be some form of <u>forced savings</u>...forced investment in war bonds.
     <u>In all your plans, you must assume a war for several years</u>.

December 20, 1941

     <u>A temporary postwar depression probably can not be avoided</u>. This means for perhaps six months...or something like that.
     <u>Boom activity for years after war</u>, to make up for war losses, is the theoretical expectation. Especially a boom for those industries which are cut down during war...and notably the durable goods industries.

December 27, 1941

     <u>Revival of U.S. civilian industries</u>...push private spending for houses, automobiles, refrigerators, and other things now restricted.
     <u>World reconstruction</u>...much feeding of starved Europeans, and U.S. materials for the physical rebuilding of parts of Europe.
     <u>How pay for all this? How raise the billions</u>?

SAVE FREEDOM OF SPEECH

BUY WAR BONDS

Very high taxes, of course...permanently, for years and years.
Don't know how high, but certainly as high as now.
But not ALL of the cost by taxes. Cover some of it by borrowing.
Continue deficit financing, run gov't in the red, as in past 11 years.
Balance the budget? NO, not for years. No balance in sight.
Planners say debt doesn't hurt so long as we don't try to pay it off.
They say attempt to reduce debt sharply would bring on a depression.
Present price levels on the average will be nearly doubled
at some stage during the next few years...the war and postwar years.
So the outlook is for inflation during war, and more after war.

January 31, 1942

Women probably will be used for noncombatant military service,
as volunteers, uniformed, military pay, WITH the Army, not IN the Army,
to do types of work which they can do as well as or better than the men.

1942

February 7, 1942

Score for whole of 1942 is expected to be on the side of Japan.
Next year, 1943, is expected to be turning point the other way.
Some of the more optimistic appraisers think war will end late in 1943.
A majority doubt this, and think the war will still be active in 1944.

March 14, 1942

Shrinkage in standard of living: You should count on this
gradually over the next year. Officials say public should "wise up,"
that many things now thought to be essential will not be produced.
And in addition, taxes and bond-buying will take larger share of income,
so, many persons will be unable to buy things which will be available.

March 21, 1942

There will be some new restrictions and limitations on profits.
Judging by the private talk of many members of Congress, we are inclined
to think it will NOT be a flat percentage limit on war contract profits,
but instead a stiffening of ALL taxes, especially excess profits.

April 4, 1942

<u>Hiring of Negroes in southern shipyards</u>: Gov't will insist.

April 25, 1942

<u>Gasoline rationing is not a phony</u>.   Neither is rubber shortage.
<u>Gas rationing will extend to most of the rest of the country</u>,
beyond the Atlantic seaboard...sometime this summer or fall.
<u>Most civilians, which probably means you</u>, will be hit hard,
will have to restrict their driving to barest needs, or to emergencies.

July 11, 1942

<u>Reminder to take home to the wife</u>: Tell her there is evidence
that many <u>domestics will quit jobs in homes</u> and take higher-pay jobs.
This is already occurring in many communities, and is sure to extend.
It means that many an upper-income household will have to trim its sails,
the housewife doing more chores, and reducing the scale of operations.
And, of course, pressure of circumstances will force up domestics' pay.
This will come about especially in industrial cities and adjoining areas,
and within a radius of 50 to 100 miles.
<u>It's part of the deep change in personal living that lies ahead</u>.

September. 5, 1942

<u>There must and will be a lot of food rationing</u>...very complex.
Rationing will spread out the available supply so as to be fair to all,
without regard to people's buying power. It will restrain the "rich,"
but not the non-rich families who will be living better than in past.

November 7, 1942

The elections show the passing of the crest or the high tide
of the social and economic reforms commonly characterized as "New Deal."
Political style in the future will be for a slowing down.
But there will be no real swingback to old conservative ideas.
Instead, merely a pause for digestion.
Strong central gov't during war, of course.
And strong central gov't AFTER war, during years of rebuilding,
for the crises of postwar period will be as great as the crises of war.
Some higher degree of world cooperation will be found feasible.
Economic planning from the top will be kept in one way or other,
and the main basic industries will be "guided" by gov't policies.
Essentials of capitalism, private profit, private initiative
will be retained, but modified by the new push toward "planning."
"Social aims" will be uppermost under any party or regime.
These will limit but will not stop those private activities and functions
which have "moneymaking" as their motive. All the postwar planning now
includes much talk of profit incentive as a practical driving force.
It will be a perplexing world, and doubtless a better world,
but first we've got to win the war.

December 26, 1942

<u>That Axis will be defeated is no longer doubted by anyone here</u>.
(Few months ago there WAS some doubt it could be done under 5 years.)

Scrap-rubber drives gave civilians a chance to help the war effort.

    <u>Peacetime will bring several years of great business activity</u>, starting after the temporary letdown...don't know just how many years.
    <u>The industries now starved by war</u> will rush to catch up.
    <u>House building and home furnishings & equipment</u> will go strong to take care of deferred marriages and the un-doubling-up of families.
    <u>New products, new processes, new industries</u> will come out of war, or out of the stimulation which war has given to technology.
    <u>Synthetic rubber</u> is here to stay.
    <u>Synthetic "silk"</u> will replace most of the former natural silk.
    <u>Thousands of new things are coming</u>...not published during war.
    When you put all the facts together...these facts and others... you can see that this war is likely to lead to a better future world... IF we work and think and fight to make it so.

January 2, 1943

    <u>As for the postwar internal system, the internal economy</u>... we think certain general trends are foreseeable, and in our last Letter we reported some of them. One of the most interesting facts is that within gov't, even among so-called New Deal "liberals" and "reformers," there is a bit of a rise in the appreciation of private enterprise. There's even much more talk of the desirability of "private profit," not so much as an end but more as a lure, a bait, a motive power.

1943

January 16, 1943

    <u>Labor influence in Congress is still high</u>, but has leveled off, is not increasing, and for first time in 10 years <u>labor is on defensive</u>. The majority sentiment in Congress, both parties, is still pro-labor, pro-unionization, pro-Wagner act, pro-high wages, pro-labor rights.
    <u>But Congress is whetting its knives against union racketeering</u>, which covers such abuses as building big union fortunes from high dues, union secrecy, political contributions, jurisdictional fights & strikes, limitation of output, featherbedding, rules requiring extra useless men. These practices are regarded as comparable to the abuses in business which have been remedied in the past by New Deal reform legislation.
    <u>The trend is definitely toward compulsory reform of unions</u>, but the timing is uncertain. Reform movement will get going this year, may come to partial fruition next fall, but probably not until next year.

United Mine Workers President
John L. Lewis called coal strikes for
higher wages, drawing the wrath of
Congress and the public.

January 23, 1943

<u>Lewis will insist on even higher wages</u> for all coal miners
on grounds that living costs have outrun present rate of wage raises.
<u>Gov't will crack down, threaten gov't operation of coal</u>.
<u>The thing will spur Congress toward a law to forbid strikes</u>...
strikes during the war...and other labor issues will be dragged in.

February 27, 1943

<u>Congress is on warpath against New Deal home-front management</u>.
<u>Hidden factors, not mentioned in public debate</u>, play a big part:
<u>One is the fourth term</u>. It is on all minds. Some leaders say
that much opposition to the New Deal would end overnight if the President
were to declare himself unequivocally against a fourth term.
<u>One is Mrs. Roosevelt</u>. Her political activities are disliked
so much in Congress that any project she sponsors is sure to be fought,
not necessarily on merit, but just because she is for it.
<u>If the war is over before elections</u>, then chances are 4-to-1
that a Republican will be the next President.
<u>If the war is not over</u>, then Roosevelt probably will run again.
<u>If the war is not over, and if Roosevelt is 4th term candidate</u>:
There's close division of cold objective opinion about such an election,
but even many Republicans say it would be hard to beat the President
while the country is still at war.

First lady Eleanor Roosevelt.

April 10, 1943

<u>No one expects a swing back to "the old days</u>," back to the 20's.
Many of the basic reforms of the New Deal will stick and be permanent.
There will even be some advances in schemes which are called socialistic,
but the GENERAL veering is toward what might be called "orthodoxy."
<u>The gov't will be a partner, not the boss</u>...in the new economy.
The mainsprings will be private, not governmental. The gov't will be
more cooperative in spirit, less punitive...collaborator, not dictator.
<u>World organization</u> will trend toward international collaboration
of one sort or another, under either party within U.S. Precisely how,
and the form, and the degree and extent are not yet clearly discernible.
Global policies will be on practical rather than ideological grounds.
<u>Tariff barriers</u> will be moderated by new schemes, new formulas,
under either party in the U.S. Expect international barter and pooling.
<u>Some sort of international financial agency</u> (or "world bank")
will be agreed upon to stabilize currencies and influence flow of trade.
<u>World super investment company</u>, with gov't-AND-private capital,
is planned, may come, but probably not on the grandiose scale now talked.

At Cairo in November 1943, FDR promised China's Chiang Kai-shek (left) to continue the war against Japan. (At right, British Prime Minister Winston Churchill and Madam Chiang.)

August 21, 1943

<u>Postwar world politics will be run by the "Big Four" nations</u>: U.S., Britain, Russia, China.

<u>These will control a "Council of Nations</u>," which in due course will include all or most nations, with the Big Four pulling the wires. Not exactly a "League of Nations," but a looser, less formal setup, with the Big Four dominating.

<u>Carve Germany up into many small states</u>? No, it's not favored by any of the big conferees. And it seems to be accepted as inevitable that Russia, not Britain or U.S., will swing biggest stick over Germany.

<u>Is this the war to end all wars</u>? No one seems to think so, despite the hope so. "The world is still too laggard in its thinking."

August 28, 1943

<u>Russia is sore</u> about a lot of things, both past and present, but mainly over the thought that U.S.-&-Britain are high-hatting Russia by not giving proper place in counsels, underrating her postwar power. Russia's strong position in the war and our desire to keep her in it provide a big pile of chips which Stalin is now playing by acting mad, hoping to get us scared into coming his way...as he MAY.

And we, in turn, think Stalin is bad-mannered, inconsiderate, but we need him, and so will do something to meet his point of view, hoping to lure HIM into coming OUR way...as we MAY.

<u>Buffer states in East Europe</u>: Russia thinks U.S. and Britain want to set them up against communism, but Russia won't stand for it.

October 2, 1943

<u>U.S.-British invasion date will be moved up</u>, for two reasons:
(a) To discourage any possible Russian intention to stop at some line.
(b) To put us closer to Germany in case peace negotiations DO start.

January 1, 1944

<u>Invasion across the Channel</u>: Preparations are in final stage. Military men don't say when, of course. But it should NOT be assumed that it will necessarily be delayed until spring just because of weather. There is no perfect time for invasion of a heavily fortified area, and the weather could be considered good any time from February on.

February 12, 1944

Oil pipeline in Arabia will have no effect on current shortage, but will be peacetime "insurance" for U.S. users of petroleum products. It probably will be approved, but only after opposition by the British, and also some U.S. oil interests. It is a big postwar issue, because...

British don't like it, for it puts the U.S. into a trade area which heretofore has been dominated almost exclusively by the British. Truth is, British are afraid of becoming a second-rate world power. Russia, they think, will be stronger throughout Europe after the war, and the U.S., they think, will be dominant in the Western Hemisphere. So the British are scurrying around to find new ties, new TRADE ties, to team up closer with the Dominions, Western Europe, Norway, Sweden. And there's increasing talk of British preferential tariffs for them. This wouldn't suit the U.S., with its ideas of FREER world trade.

Length of war in Pacific: Most opinions range around two years, running into 1946. Military men think it MIGHT run only 1 1/2 years more, to late 1945, but this would be with ALL the breaks...too much to expect. The subject comes up now because a lot of people are over-optimistic, due to showing in Marshalls. But the Pacific job gets bigger and bigger as we advance and lengthen supply lines. It's hard, slow, costly.

February 19, 1944

Training for discharged servicemen-&-women will be authorized by Congress...some will return to school this year, more NEXT year.

March 4, 1944

Women, older men, Negroes: It is now mathematically certain that the supply of new workers must come more and more from these groups, quite regardless of employers' preferences.

Russia: Our national policy is to "get along with Russia"...
one way or another...even to stand for some things which we don't like.
This is a cornerstone of policy at present, and doubtless will continue
no matter who wins the elections next fall.

Expediency dictates that adequate recognition be given to Russia
as biggest country, second biggest industrially, raw material producer,
aiming at a living standard comparable to that of the U.S.

All policies are being shaped to fit into the general pattern
of good relations and big trade with Russia for many years after war.
Some people are looking askance, but anyway it is the fixed policy.

March 18, 1944

Russia is on the political offensive in Europe,
as on the military offensive.

Relations between U.S. and Russia are a bit difficult right now,
but are not "strained." We are trying to be "very nice to Russia."

March 25, 1944

The President is overworking himself. He is part-time director
of Manpower, Stabilization, War Mobilization, Food, Prices, Treasury,
Labor, War Production, and foreign policy.

It's more than any one man can do, and do well. Many high officials
are whispering about the situation...both sympathetically and critically.

April 29, 1944

The situation in China is very bad...dissension, war lords,
inflation, growing feeling that the Allies are laggard with their help.
Internal collapse is feared...seems on the verge...just hanging on.
It would drag out the Japanese war, and be serious.

So we are moving fast to help...big things are in the making...
toward Philippines, toward China Coast landings.

May 20, 1944

Television: Gov't will stick to its policy of going slow
on postwar development for a while. Near-miracles are possible now,
thanks to war developments (secrets), but gov't will continue to insist
that the industry take more time, give the public even more miracles.

May 27, 1944

CIO Political Action Committee (Hillman) must now be recognized
as a major force in elections. It makes the claim that it is bipartisan,
but actually it is pro-Roosevelt, pro his foreign policy, pro New Deal,
and in effect it is anti-Dewey, and anti-most-Republicans.

The CIO-PAC has $700,000 to work with, and can get plenty more,
from surpluses in union treasuries, and thus indirectly from union dues.
It is exempt from the $5000 legal limitation on campaign contributions,
for it makes no contributions to any party...merely uses its own money
in the interest of "free speech" and "education"...political education.

By long-range standards, years ahead, all this is significant.
Formerly union labor's power was in collective bargaining...ECONOMIC.
But now the CIO is demonstrating that the power can also be POLITICAL.
If it works well, then the union cause need not form a "labor party,"
but can make one of the regular parties into EQUIVALENT of a labor party,
without making labor carry the responsibilities of a regular party.
So this year's elections will set the pattern for many years to come.

Allied Commander Dwight Eisenhower confers with French leader Charles deGaulle. At top right, victorious Allied troops march into Paris August 25, 1944.

July 22, 1944

Truman is good medium-grade man, won't help ticket, won't hurt.
Brawl over Vice Presidency did the party no good and much harm.
Voters don't care a whole lot WHO runs for Vice President with Roosevelt,
but the politicians do, and they do the work of getting out the vote,
or they refrain and sulk on the job, and this brawl will make many sulk.

August 12, 1944

Allied conditions to be imposed upon Germany AFTER the surrender
have been agreed upon generally. We have talked with representatives
of a number of the governments involved, can report that in our opinion
the conditions, the high points without the details, will be as follows:
Complete military occupation of ALL Germany...Russians in east,
British in north, Americans in south...perhaps French in west, but minor.
How long has not been determined, for this must depend on developments.
Total disarmament of Germany. All military and naval equipment
to be given to bordering countries, so they can police from the outside.

August 26, 1944

Tremendous food problem is ahead...the problem of TOO MUCH food.
We can not eat it all, we can not sell it all...and looks as if
we may not be able to lend-lease it all, or give it all away for relief.
There's so much food in storage and in sight from future crops
that the officials just don't know what they will be able to do with it.

October 7, 1944

Big U.S. foreign loans to build postwar trade are sure to come.
Plans are in the works inside gov't right now for such loans...via gov't,
or the new world bank, or by extension of powers of Export-Import Bank.
It's in self-interest, to make work for our factories & workers
while the world, including U.S., is getting back on its business feet.
Idea is not to subsidize exports generally, or to give our stuff away.
Most of the world will be broke, unable to trade without credit.
Theory is that if we help finance peace, we can make it stick.

Nov. 4, 1944

Situation in China is critical. There are war lords and graft,
and bickering at the top. Chiang Kai-shek is not wholly blameless,
but he's the ONLY man with a fighting chance of holding China together.
If his regime falls, then China goes to pieces, and the war is prolonged.

February 10, 1945

Berlin is doomed to the Russians, and the time is now figured as "soon"...which might mean in "a week or two" or up to "several weeks." Russians are believed to have the force to smash through from the Oder.

The end of the full-scale fighting is expected "by this spring." This is necessarily vague...could mean March or April, could mean May.

February 17, 1945

Russia gets the most advantages of a tangible nature.

The U.S. winnings are largely of an idealistic character, such as free elections and an approach toward democratic processes in European countries. U.S. thinks this will help to curb war.

What Germany gets (without fully understanding this as yet) is assurance of postwar treatment that is less harsh and repressive than some of the extreme proposals, such as Vansittart's in Britain or Morgenthau's in the U.S. In due time Germany can be strong again, but not in arms, and not in Nazi-ism.

April 14, 1945

President Truman is not seasoned for his huge responsibilities, and he would admit it, for he is a modest and genuine man.

But Truman is no dummy...he has courage, can't be pushed around. Under him the country will not go to the dogs.

One fact about Truman is that he has a deep sense of DUTY. He doesn't talk about it much, but those who work with him always notice that when he makes up his mind as to what his duty is, he is bullheaded, and often he overrides considerations of temporary political expediency. It was so in his work on the Truman committee. He showed real courage. When praised for it he squirmed and said he gave no thought to courage.

May 19, 1945

Relations with Russia are strained, and the outlook is not good. Russia doesn't understand the West, the West doesn't understand Russia. Relies on her own force in neighboring countries, regardless of Allies. May want to control bulk of Europe...a suspicion, which may not be true.

Long-range, the situation is serious, must be ironed out by Big 3. Truman and Churchill will be firm and definite with Stalin, not soft. If they fail, the chances for a lasting world peace will be dimmed.

FDR's funeral cortege in Washington, April 1945.

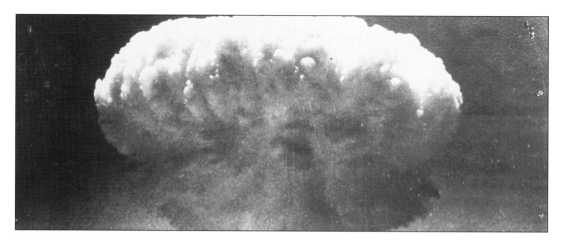

June 2, 1945

      <u>Cities of Japan</u> are going to be destroyed within a few months.
Our bomber force is sufficient to reduce them to rubble like Berlin,
but faster and worse, due to "technological improvements" in bombing.

July 7, 1945

      <u>Mass migration during war means great change in markets postwar</u>,
and businesses must resurvey their markets...national, regional, local.
      <u>Many families will stay</u> where they have moved during the war.
      <u>West Coast will gain most heavily</u>.
      <u>Farm population</u> has shrunk during war, and will stay shrunk.
      <u>Rims of cities</u> will expand fast...the suburban areas.
      <u>New families</u>, new homes, new households after the war.
      <u>About 2 million marriages</u> have already occurred during the war.
      <u>Probably 3-to-4 million more</u> will occur soon after men return.
      Most will want homes and all the things that go with them.
      <u>Despite war, births are highest in history</u>...3 million a year.
That many births in '43, about the same in '44 and probably in '45.
War has speeded some marriages, retarded others...net, raised the births.
      These basic facts are important any way you want to look at them.
People are producers and consumers and customers. A growing population
means more production, more consumption, more activity, and more jobs.
      The postwar economy, despite all difficulties, will be dynamic.

August 11, 1945

      <u>The telegrams cancelling war orders have already been typed</u>,
and they will be sent out by the thousands over the next few weeks.
Cut will be from rate of 48 billions a year to 20 billions...in 2 months.
Then further cuts will be to somewhere around 12 billions...in 6 months.
      <u>This means idle factories, idle workers</u>...a double dose.
      <u>And then a strong upsurge, almost a boom</u>, from mid-1946 on.
This will run for 4 or 5 years...to fill in the wants of wartime...
to rebuild what a vicious war has destroyed.

      <u>Practical application of atomic power in industry is not near</u>.
We have talked this week by long-distance phone with big-shot scientists
throughout the U.S. They are cautious, but this is what they think:
      <u>Coal, oil, electric power, water power</u> won't be revolutionized
within the next 20-30-40 years..."within our time."
      <u>Homes will still heat</u> with whatever they heat with...not atoms.
      <u>Autos will not run with "atom pills"</u>...at any foreseeable time.
      <u>True, incidental discoveries</u> WILL be applied in industry soon...
soon in the scientists' sense...which means in the next 10 to 15 years...
but the <u>industrial revolution from atoms</u> is for our great-grandchildren.

September 1, 1945

New industrial processes will mean gradually improved quality and lower prices...such things as better welding, centrifugal casting, powder casting, metal spinning, metal spraying, high-speed milling.
All these things came out of the war.
It's 50 years of progress in 5 years...development of know-how, the practical application of discoveries, technical ideas, techniques.

October 6, 1945

U.S. & Britain are likely to give in to stiff-necked Russians, and bow to the idea of Russian domination of the Balkans and Baltic, simply because Russia's stake in those parts is bigger, more tangible than that of either the U.S. or Britain. But the trouble is that...
The world will then have a new political balance of power...
Russia on one side, with her adherents...U.S. & Britain on the other side.

November 3, 1945

Problem of atom bomb & how to control it is making no progress.
Indications are that within a few years ALL big nations will have it.
This makes for a new armament race, and the U.S. is the leader in it.
Scientists see world control as the ONLY guard against world destruction.
Politicians are dawdling, haven't waked up. It's about time they did.

December 1, 1945

The politics in strikes: The unions have now become big dogs, but the law and government philosophy still treat them as under dogs.
In brawls among themselves and with management the victim is the public.
The public indignation is rising...it is not anti-labor but anti-strike.

February 16, 1946

There are now only two great world powers...the U.S. and Russia.
Britain is weak, and poor, and defensive...and so are her prewar allies.
The U.S. policy has been to appease Russia...to bow and knuckle.
Now boiling beneath the surface here is agitation for a changed policy.
Brynes is under new pressure to stop kowtowing whenever Stalin says boo.
He is now being told that "toughness now is better than trouble later."
Stiffer policy is imminent. Loan to Russia will be challenged.
Conditions will be imposed...to cut down Russia's military forces.
The challenge will be direct to Russia...not through United Nations.
Will this economic pressure work? Will Russia become less aggressive?
Must we keep up a military power to compete with Russia? Don't know.
Know only that this is a very solemn situation.

1946

February 23, 1946

      <u>Relations with Russia are bad</u>, will get worse in next few months. The strain is greater than our gov't expected, even a few weeks ago.

      <u>Russia's land-grabbing policy</u> is what's behind the tenseness. Both U.S. and British officials insist that Russia's program of expansion must be stopped "before it is too late."

      "<u>It's very much like Hitler's march into the Rhineland in 1936</u>. Hitler should have been stopped then. Stalin should be stopped now."

      <u>So...our gov't is preparing to get tough with Russia and say NO</u>. Our policy, now being formulated, with consultation with the British, will be to say that Russia may control the Baltic, and dominate Poland and the Balkans, and use Dardanelles, and have a corridor through Iran to a port on the Persian Gulf, and retain possession of the Kuriles.

      <u>But NO</u> on letting Russia take a part of Turkey.

      <u>And NO</u> on control of the Middle East.

      <u>And NO</u> on the East African bases which control the Suez route.

      <u>And NO</u> on Russian domination of Manchuria and Korea.

      <u>That is our position and it will suddenly be disclosed...soon</u>... which means within the next month or two...with preliminary signs sooner.

      <u>Will Russia fight</u>? No, she will back down...for the present.

March 2, 1946

      <u>Looks as if new jobs will open up fast throughout this year</u>, due to boom in production caused by the big demand for goods at home, plus the tremendous demand from abroad.

      <u>Here's the surprise: By year end there will be a labor shortage</u>, a shortage of workers QUALIFIED for the vacant jobs. (At the same time there may be persons unemployed, but not fitted for the job.)

      <u>That is called "over-employment"...and that is what's ahead</u>. <u>Result will be a mad scramble of industrial activity in the U.S</u>. Just now this is not evident to the short-sighted, harassed by strikes, harassed by the OPA, but it is plenty evident to the long-sighted men. The scramble will start as soon as the major strikes are settled.

      <u>Physical volume of production will break all peacetime records</u> during this year, 1946...despite the troubled and inauspicious start.

      <u>Nothing from now on is deflationary</u>...that danger is past.

      <u>Every influence from now on is inflationary</u>...both here at home and throughout the world...for about two years...until 1948.

June 29, 1946

<u>Current political talk</u> among men who make politics a business
is along these lines:

<u>Truman is sure to be renominated in '48</u>, for there's no one else
who might win. Stories that he might refuse are not taken seriously.

<u>Dewey must be counted in</u> for '48 presidential nomination,
even though a lot of his own party people feel no warmth toward him.
At least he will have big say-so in the picking of any other candidate.

<u>Generally the weather ahead looks like Republican weather</u>...
if they don't blunder in national strategy, as they've done for 15 years.

July 27, 1946

<u>China is headed for long civil war</u>, Russia backing communists,
U.S. reluctantly backing Chiang Kai-shek...could become "another Spain."

<u>Palestine</u> will not be composed by conference of Arabs and Jews.
The best to be expected is partition of Palestine, which means no peace.

August 24, 1946

<u>Families on the average have much more to spend than prewar</u>.
Income is TWICE as much as in 1939, TWICE as much money is available.
Of course prices are about a third higher, but even with this adjustment
the average consumers have the money to buy at least 50% more goods now.

<u>The rich have come down</u> since prewar. Still lots of big incomes,
but with the heavy taxes the rich are sliding in their spending power,
sliding down toward middle. Thus limited market for fancy luxury things.

<u>The poor have come up since prewar</u>. The low incomes are higher
all along the line, and many former lows have ascended to middle.

<u>The middle incomes have come up</u>...both in size and in numbers.
Even with allowance for inflation of incomes, the report leaves no doubt
that middle-income markets are about to show a very great expansion.

President Harry Truman campaigning in Washington.

October 12, 1946

<u>Drives against communists in U.S. will come from many quarters</u>
in next few months. Gov't officials expect to move against communists
in State Dep't especially, but they are waiting until after elections.
Most of the labor unions are preparing to challenge their own communists.

November 9, 1946

<u>The Republican sweep this week is having a sobering effect</u>
on Republican party leaders here. The rejoicing is quiet, restrained.
They expected to win the House...they only HOPED to win the Senate.
They just didn't count on gaining control of both.

The people voted in protest...against too much government...
too many controls...too much labor coddling...and too high prices.
It was really a delayed reaction from 1944 when the war and Roosevelt
put a dampener on the protest that was already widespread.

It was a vote AGAINST the Democrats, not FOR the Republicans.

November 23, 1946

<u>Eisenhower for President</u> has often been mentioned half-heartedly.
But from now on he is sure to be considered a good deal more seriously,
mainly because the CIO convention gave him such a rousing commendation.
His political ideas are not well known, but in due course they will be.
He doesn't carry a party label, but probably will emerge as a Republican.

1947

January 4, 1947

<u>Labor law is the hottest issue</u>. Time of enactment, about April.
What Congress will NOT do to labor, under spirit of restraint:
Will not vote any compulsory arbitration, or prohibit the closed shop,
or ban industry-wide contracts, or force labor unions to incorporate,
or provide any special antitrust law for labor.
What Congress probably WILL do: Establish "union responsibility,"
perhaps deny bargaining rights to unions which violate their contracts.
Permit injunctions by gov't where it's "in the public interest."
This is the "anti-John Lewis" provision...endorsement of Truman policy.
Give employers "free speech"...let them talk with the workers.
Forbid secondary boycotts...and probably sympathy strikes.

The man at the switch

February 1, 1947

<u>The next few months mark the end of an era in labor relations</u>.
<u>Heretofore</u> labor advanced by a coalition between unions and the gov't.
The gov't nurtured the whole labor movement, and especially the CIO.
<u>Hereafter</u> the unions must go it alone, really bargain, get what they can
without direct back of paternalistic bureaus as allies in a cause.
<u>This shift in policy</u> makes labor into an equal dog instead of a top dog.
It is a turn toward old-style labor unionism...but with stronger unions.

February 8, 1947

<u>The two-term limit for Presidents</u> will be voted by the Senate,
as amendment to the constitution, and will be ratified by the states.

February 22, 1947

<u>Communists within gov't</u>: A new list of 53 names is in possession
of two responsible committees of Congress...Senate Foreign Relations...
House Executive Expenditures. They are being guarded against publication
in order not to damage any persons UNTIL fuller proof is available.
<u>State Dep't names will get first attention</u>...second-string men,
not high up, but high enough to be able to influence foreign policy.
The State Dep't attitude heretofore has been that it should never fire
on mere suspicion...and there's seldom any PROOF of communist membership.
The new pressure will be, however, to fire on evidence that the person
changed his acts or attitudes in accordance with the party line shifts.
These party line shifts are always occurring...and are easy to detect.
<u>Witch hunt?</u> All these moves against communists COULD degenerate
into an unrestrained hysterical attack on any & all liberals or leftists.
So a cautionary note is being sounded among the investigating agencies...
to avoid smearing, to stick to communists and party-line followers.

March 8, 1947

<u>Our foreign relations right now are approaching a major crisis
and full truth is not being told by the State Dep't or by the President</u>.
Congress and the public are being spoon-fed with fragmentary information
in a sort of conspiracy to conceal the unpleasant facts and implications.
<u>It's about Greece, but Greece is only the starter</u>. We are about
to take the responsibility for Greece, because Britain cannot carry it.
<u>The object is to "contain Russia,"</u> to hold Russia where she is.
This is stated in precisely those words by responsible high officials.
<u>But we can not stop with Greece</u>. Soon we must also bolster Turkey.
Also Italy...in almost as precarious a position as Greece.
<u>British collapse is at bottom of all this</u>...Britain is busted.
<u>We are making tentative moves to take over British obligations</u>
in many parts of the world...Greece, Mediterranean...other areas later.

Londoners receiving American orange juice concentrate, courtesy of the Marshall Plan.

<u>All these things do NOT mean that war with Russia is IMMINENT</u>.
Neither nation wants it, neither can afford it, not even the rich U.S.
We can not have a major war across the oceans without some strong allies,
and there AREN'T any strong allies. War at this time could bust the U.S.
<u>Instead, our gov't policy is to challenge Russian expansion</u>...
hoping against war. Greece represents concrete challenge at this time.
<u>To hold Russia where she is</u>...this is likely to lead to war.
<u>To let Russia expand freely</u>...is almost sure to lead to war.
<u>Is there any third course?</u>...midway between Russian expansion
and Russian "containment"? Is agreement between the two powers possible?
Perhaps...there MAY be in the future...but at present it is not visible.

April 12, 1947

<u>Use of radio waves for heating & cooking</u> is a growing business,
but these waves interfere with others and even cause some radio static.
Gov't will limit wave lengths, unless industry lessens the interference.

May 3, 1947

<u>Our gov't is readying a 5-yr. program to help certain countries</u>.
And these countries will be cultivated as "allies"...in case of any war.
Not just relief, but rehabilitation, self-help. Greece is merely one.
Over the long-pull of the next 5 years it means 10, 15 or more billions.
This program exists...unannounced...will be made clear within the year.

An early microwave oven.

October 4, 1947

<u>The big crop of war babies is now jamming the elementary schools</u>
which haven't expanded to match the birth rate. Conditions will worsen
in the next 2 or 3 years, for the wave of 6-&-7-year-olds is rising fast,
and schools can't be built fast enough, and the teachers can't be found.

October 11, 1947

<u>Communist agitations</u> from now on will step up...throughout world
and also here in the U.S. There are many evidences of increased activity.
The reorganized Comintern. The new communist alliance formed at Belgrade.
<u>Strikes will increase in Europe</u>. They will hurt Marshall plan,
for it will be argued that we shouldn't help when workers go on strike.
This is what communists want...to kill off Marshall plan reconstruction.
<u>More talk of U.S. "imperialism" & "expansionism"</u> will be heard,
and the commies will accuse U.S. of "trying to export its depression."
<u>Forceful direct action tactics</u> will replace peaceful tactics.
More strikes, riots, sabotage, breakdowns...less resort to elections.
<u>Watch Italy & France especially</u>...they are main commie targets.

October 11, 1947

      <u>Communist tactics here in the U.S.</u> will be something like this:
      <u>Some big new "front" organization</u>, headed by respectable names,
will be created within a few months to agitate against the Marshall plan,
and will horn in on other movements which challenge the Marshall plan.
This will embarrass these other movements, for they are not Communist.
      <u>Communist-dominated unions in this country</u> will follow the line,
will whip up members to fight Marshall plan, and give funds to "fronts."
      <u>Leftish unions will get militant</u> when their contracts expire,
and part of the purpose will be to slow up the production for Europe.
Aim will be partly political...not just to gain more for the workers.

October 18, 1947

      <u>Movies on the pan next few weeks</u>...issue of communist influence.
Jack Warner will deplore hiring of reds. Louis Mayer will not go along,
saying you can't tell who's a red, or what the gov't policy is toward them.
Rightist screen writers will attack subtle communist propaganda in films.
Leftist writers will come later and call the rightist writers "fascist."
Pawed over will be "Mission to Moscow," "Song of Russia," and others.
Quite a brawl...going to extremes both ways...stirring up the public.

      <u>First imports from Japan are arriving</u>...Christmas tree stuff,
toys, binoculars, hat bodies, porcelain, china, aluminum & gold leaf.
It is U.S. policy to promote Japanese trade in these and other things,
in order to reduce costs on our taxpayers for relief and occupation.
This is just a small beginning, but Japan is on her way to recovery.

November 1, 1947

      <u>Civil rights report on racial, religious, color discrimination</u>
is bound to stir up big fights in Congress and in state legislatures.
But Congress will not vote the new FEPC, anti-lynching or poll tax laws,
for Southern Democrats can prevent. (Negro vote will trend Republican.)
      <u>Many congressional appropriations</u>...education, hospitals, etc...
will contain anti-discrimination provisions, touching local communities.
Some legislatures in northern & eastern states are expected to legislate.

December 6, 1947

      <u>In Palestine the British are counting on moving out next spring</u>.
      <u>There are bound to be greater disorders</u> in Palestine in future,
Arabs fighting Jews. The Jews are backed by the American charity money.
The Arabs are backed by American oil money. American money backing both.
      <u>Bloodshed is inevitable in Near East</u>...some of it American blood.

December 20, 1947

      <u>Now it's "two worlds"</u>...openly hostile...without even a pretense
of friendly collaboration. Every move everywhere is toward a showdown.
This means, within the coming year, an intensification of the "cold war."
At times, on the fringes, it will be "hot war"...in danger of spreading.
      <u>Both sides are inching toward crises...tests of the other side</u>.
Such crises, such tests of intent will come often within the next year.

1948

February 7, 1948

<u>This oil shortage is not temporary...will run next winter, too.</u>
<u>Production is up, but demand is up MORE</u>. Demand is skyrocketing.
We simply are not producing enough in this country, not importing enough
to take care of all the oil burners, the diesels, the buses and trucks,
the tractors, the heavy pleasure driving...all taking oil or gasoline.
<u>Imports are the only quick answer</u>...but even these take time.
The U.S. is now importing more oil than it exports...first time ever.
<u>Middle East is best possible source</u>...Saudi Arabia, Iraq, Iran.
These are in Russian danger zone. This nation is playing politics there
to protect oil supply.

February 28, 1948

<u>Some Democratic politicians are now talking of ditching Truman</u>,
substituting someone like Vinson. They may give up the idea, but anyway
it's going to be difficult to elect Truman...and that's understatement.

March 6, 1948

<u>Atom bomb</u>: Russia probably WILL get the bomb. The time when Russia
may acquire it was formerly estimated at 5 years. New calculations, not
published, have reduced the time to 3 or 4 years.

March 20, 1948

<u>There are those who think this nation should initiate a war</u>,
and do it soon, on the theory that Russia is less prepared than we are.
Such talk comes mainly from people who do not know the business of war.
It does NOT come from our military men. They think it's too dangerous.
<u>There's a fragment of hope</u> in the designs for an "armed truce."
The theory is that both sides get to be so strong they fear each other,
and neither makes war. This has often kept the peace for a few years.

April 17, 1948

<u>Tiny new Fords</u> will be imported to U.S. from the English factory,
3000 cars, 3000 trucks...and will test demand here for really SMALL cars.
Many manufacturers can shift to smalls or midgets...if people want them.

The new state of Israel was
proclaimed on May 14, 1948.
David Ben-Gurion (standing) was its
first prime minister.

May 22, 1948

The U.S. will proceed to arm Western Europe...some late in year, more next year...under Vandenberg resolution, which Congress will adopt. Policy is bipartisan, will not change...even if there's a new President. It is pretty close to a military alliance, something new in our history.

June 5, 1948

New crisis with Russia is imminent in Berlin. U.S. will proceed to organize a "strong Germany"...Western Germany, the industrial part... thus a divided Germany. Russia will scream that this violates Potsdam, and Russia will retaliate by organizing an Eastern Germany...communist.
Get out of Berlin...this will be the Russian drive from now on. We will refuse to withdraw under bullying, and this will make a crisis. There will be a rash of "incidents," pointing up the danger of staying.
Berlin is regarded as a test of American and Russian intentions. It is the showdown. If the Russians wish, they can force Americans out, and this would be a sign that Russia is willing to risk an early war. If the Russians show any sign of compromise, it means a postponement.

June 12, 1948

The Republicans will be in convention at Philadelphia in a week.
They WILL nominate either Dewey or Vandenberg...this seems sure. Dewey is the leading candidate at this stage, but hasn't enough votes to win without trading. Vandenberg is the leading compromise candidate.
A deadlock is possible but not probable. After a few ballots the bosses will trade among themselves, and will finally do the picking.
Next President of the United States will be known 2 weeks hence.

October 2, 1948

Month from the time you read this, Dewey will have been elected. All the reports and all the figures show overwhelmingly that he is in. Practically nothing can change the result within the remaining period.

October 23, 1948

The campaign is dull. On both sides, it simply reeks with apathy. Voters are yawning over Truman's invectives...and Dewey's platitudes.
Dewey was winning a majority of the voters, but not the enthusiasm that usually goes with the winner. People aren't whooping & hollering. Millions of independent voters, who are always THE determining factor, want to vote against Truman and his stale party, so they vote for Dewey, but somehow they are reserved...lukewarm...and they feel no inner heat.

When the Soviets blockaded Berlin in June 1948, the U.S. responded with the Berlin airlift, until Moscow relented nearly a year later.

November 10, 1948

<u>We said Dewey</u>. This was a tremendous blunder, and we are sorry, and especially sorry for your sake...that we gave you such a bad steer.

<u>Should good reporters have known all these things...in advance</u>? Yes, should have. Trouble with all reporters, including ourselves, was that they didn't get deep enough into the precincts in the last 10 days.

<u>It wasn't partisan bias</u>...reporters try first of all to be right. It wasn't lack of integrity. And it wasn't the polls, except secondarily. It was simply that an 11th-hour Truman swing, and a Republican apathy, down at the grass roots, locally, were not detected by the "experts."

<u>Future consequences</u>: Political observers have learned a lesson, the hard way, and will be extra-cautious next time. (Certainly WE shall.) People generally will be skeptical of all election forecasts for a while.

November 20, 1948

<u>Manchuria and most of North China are goners</u>, taken by commies. Thereby Russia will get access to enormous new sources of raw materials. It is a major victory for Russia, and a major defeat for Western Powers.

December 18, 1948

<u>Traitors were deep inside the gov't</u>...as shown by spy evidence. The executive branch of the gov't let them be, did NOT clean them out. The FBI either did not know, or else was not allowed to take any action. So there is distrust of the executive branch, and this is why Congress will continue the spy investigations, despite open opposition by Truman.

On "vacation"

December 24, 1948

<u>Future political trends</u>: For the long pull, the decades ahead, such a population of more city people will become less individualistic, more mass-minded, social-minded, political-minded. People are likely to turn gradually to more social & political control over the economy. Not state socialism or ownership, but gov't participation in controls.

January 22, 1949

Next, a world development program...economic...financed by U.S.
This is something POSITIVE against Russia...Truman Doctrine is NEGATIVE.
Time element: The program will run for decades, even generations.
Cost element: Not merely billions as now, but TENS of billions.
Gov't capital AND private capital...for world-wide development.
Machinery for this now is being worked on by State Dep't and the ECA.
Also know-how, technical aid...a big element, beyond mere money.
Eyes are on Africa...the biggest and richest undeveloped area.
Secondarily on Indonesia, S.W. Pacific. Also on Latin American countries.
But plenty of private profits are intended...even big profits.
These are the ways by which we can get back some of what we have spent.
Of course it will take decades or generations for the thing to work out.
Like Britain in the past century...when British money & brains
went into backward countries...to invest, build, develop, open things up.
The great idea now is that America will succeed to Britain's former role.
Thus, in 10-20-50 years, American companies, with men, brains, capital,
will be all over the world...developing, making money, raising standards.

February 19, 1949

Phonograph records: Retailers are dumping their present stocks,
waiting for manufacturers to get together on new long-playing records.
Television sales are going strong, but some dealers are saying
they can't get manufacturers to tell them about new channel prospects.
This makes confusion, tends to retard some sales.

April 23, 1949

All China is headed toward communist control. No stopping of it.
Our gov't might have prevented it a couple of years ago, but too late now.
Then Indo-China, Burma, Siam...communists will move into them.
British policy is to resist a bit. U.S. policy is to wring its hands.
Berlin blockade will be lifted...by early summer, maybe sooner.
And, of course, U.S. will also lift its blockade between E. & W. Germany.
Then 4-Power talks will be resumed on Germany...on the unification of it.
Russia will be for it...including the Ruhr. The U.S. will be against it.

Mao Tse-tung, soon-to-be China's ruler.

May 7, 1949

Television: Dollar volume of TV sales now exceeds radio sales.
Prices of television sets will come down faster over the next few months,
as savings in the cost of tubes and other parts are passed on to buyers.

September 3, 1949

Color television is not ready for public use, despite reports.
Lots of bugs yet. So color won't come for another year...at earliest.
Present sets will not be made obsolete by color...can convert.

September 24, 1949

Ford's willingness to grant pensions breaks the industry line...
and other big companies will now be pushed into setting up pension plans.
The government is behind all this. Truman is turning on the heat
in the steel industry, and will follow through with heat on many others.
Businessmen feel a gripe at being forced...but they ARE forced.

Oct. 1, 1949

While the shadow lengthens.

Any international control of atom bombs by UN is a long way off.
The U.S. has refused to destroy its stockpile, as the Russians proposed.
Russia has rejected international inspection, on which the U.S. insisted.
The bomb is not likely to be ruled out as a weapon of war anytime soon.
Whether both sides will refrain, as from poison gas...a hopeful theory.

How far ahead is the U.S. on atom bombs? Probably several years,
but no one actually knows. U.S. dope has been wrong, may be wrong again.
World balance of power is changing. Formerly we had a wide edge.
Now we still have an edge, but it isn't as wide. We are nearer the line
at which Russian power will approximately equal combined Western power.
That's dangerous...for history has proved that when an aggressor nation
finally acquires the advantage in the balance of power...it goes to war.
Our foreign policy is sure to shift. Bomb gave us an advantage
in persuading wobbling nations to our side. We could offer protection.
Now this advantage is lessened. We'll have to compensate in other ways,
and one of the ways is the continuance of a great deal of economic aid.

October 8, 1949

Saw TV colorvision the other day. Impressive, like home movies,
but it will be a year or two before many homes can have colorvision sets.
The FCC will decide next year which one of the color systems to approve,
but it will take time for set-makers to get bugs out, start mass output.

November 5, 1949

Take a look at future gov't expenses and what they do to taxes.
Start with foreign aid. Marshall plan is not working as intended.
We are doing our part, but Europe is not doing what we expected in return.
Here at home, the biggest expenditures are for our own military.
These COULD be trimmed, or shifted in part to building up Europe's arms,
but sentiment is still strong for building our own, relying on no others.
Add the trend toward more for internal purposes, social causes.
More for social security pensions, public housing, education, health,
gov't power, public works, etc., etc. Each is regarded as "desirable."
Each has powerful public support...focused on particular pet projects.
So the chances are on the side of expansion of these internal costs.
But all these expenses added together are bigger than the income
which comes from taxes. Gov't this year is running a 5 1/2 billion deficit.
Raise taxes next year? Truman will ask it but won't get it voted.
Then how about the subsequent year? Taxes WILL be raised then, we think.
But there's some practical limit beyond which taxes can not be raised.
This limit is probably lower than what's required to balance the budget.
Result, deficits for some years yet, unbalanced budgets on & on.
This may not be what people wish, but it's the course that's being taken.
Deficits make inflation, when continued over a number of years.
So more inflation is in prospect...the trend irregularly upward.
Right now little more deflation...then inflation...eventually the crisis.

December 3, 1949

Next 10 years, what's in store?
"If no war." This had to be the assumption...otherwise no basis.
Generally prosperous business for the decade, taken as a whole.
Stimulated by technological gains, population growth, and other forces.
Some sort of slump by the middle-1950s...but no deep depression
like the early 30's. Then a good recovery, running through late 50's.
Political trend, leftward. Left-swing has not yet run its course.
The trend will continue under either party...faster if under Democrats.
Taxes will stay high, spending will stay high...by either party.
Living standards, higher...net...despite a creeping inflation.

1950s

The Fifties opened with another deadly Asian war, just five years after the end of the Second World War. As the decade came to a close, America was struggling with a sluggish economy, pressure from Negroes for equal rights, and seesaw relations with its nuclear rival, Russia. And in the ten years between, the '50s were hardly placid.

The economy boomed and slumped, jet airliners shrank the nation's travel time, and suburbs and superhighways spread across the nation. White and black students began attending school together in the South, under court order. Television, transistor radios and rock 'n' roll changed the look and sound of America. The first inklings of a social revolution were seen in the growing sexual candor of movies, novels, TV and a new kind of mass-circulation magazine—*Playboy*—which featured a unique mix of nude pinups and serious articles. Many women, especially college-educated housewives, were beginning to feel unfulfilled in their homemaker roles. A demagogue named McCarthy tainted the nation's reputation for fair play and decency with indiscriminate attacks on the loyalty of government officials and private citizens.

The Cold War grew more and more chilly. The Soviet Union sought to extend its domination and influence throughout the world, from the Middle East and Europe to Asia and Central America, supporting leftist rebellions and stirring up anti-American sentiment. The U.S. military and Central Intelligence Agency tried to counter these activities with covert efforts of their own, such as helping overthrow a pro-communist regime in Guatemala in '54. The U.S.-Soviet rivalry of the '50s was the driving force behind mankind's first steps into outer space, with each nation seeking international prestige and military advantage from the launching of satellites atop ever-more-powerful guided missiles.

War in Korea

In January 1950, Secretary of State Dean Acheson indicated that Korea, divided into communist and non-communist sectors since '45, was not vital to the security interests of the U.S. Six months later, communist

			SENATOR		ROSENBERGS AND OTHERS	
			MCCARTHY	SENATE	CONVICTED AS	NATIONWIDE TV
NORTH KOREA	FIRST U.S.		LAUNCHES	COMMITTEE	SPIES FOR	INAUGURATED.
INVADES SOUTH,	MILITARY		RED-HUNT.	PROBES	RUSSIA.	
TRUMAN SENDS	ADVISERS TO			ORGANIZED		
TROOPS.	VIETNAM.			CRIME.		SALINGER'S
						"CATCHER IN THE
1950		UNIONS STRIKE		**1951**		RYE" PUBLISHED.
	WAGE-PRICE	RAILS, TRUMAN			TRUMAN FIRES	
	CONTROLS	ORDERS			MACARTHUR.	
	REIMPOSED.	SEIZURE.				

North Korean troops invaded South Korea, and a U.N. force dominated by Americans went to the aid of the South. By November, General Douglas MacArthur's offensive had taken control of all of Korea, north and south, but the cost was high—nearly 30,000 U.S. casualties.

Then communist Chinese troops poured into Korea and pushed the Americans back. When MacArthur sought authority to take the war into China and then criticized Truman's refusal, the President fired the popular general in April 1951, making MacArthur a martyred hero with a passionate public following. Deadly fighting and tedious negotiations dragged on for more than two years. In '53 the Korean War ended with the same north-south division intact, but communist expansion had been blocked.

America turns to Ike

With the Korean War came sharply higher U.S. defense spending, an accelerated economic boom and a return to consumer price controls. The Truman administration, saddled with an unpopular war, was hurt further by scandals involving bribery and influence peddling. The '52 election pitted Illinois Governor Adlai Stevenson against retired General Dwight D. Eisenhower, a World War II hero with no political experience. Many Americans were charmed by the wit and intellect of Stevenson, but more were weary of the turmoil of the Truman years, longing for national unity. The voters selected Eisenhower in the first presidential campaign and election to be widely covered by television, and he beat Stevenson again in a 1956 landslide.

Conservatives, reveling in the first GOP White House victory in 24 years, soon discovered that Ike wasn't always their kind of leader. He spoke like a conservative but acted like a liberal—at least a liberal Republican. Many of his legislative victories were provided by Democratic votes. Federal subsidies to farmers rose sixfold during his two administrations. In 1957 he signed the first national civil rights law in eight decades, and he threw the weight of federal law and troops behind school desegregation in Little Rock, Ark. He resorted to Keynesian deficit spending to stimulate a sluggish economy, running budget deficits in five of his eight years in office.

In foreign policy, Ike and his Secretary of State, John Foster Dulles, talked tough against communist aggression, with pledges of rolling back the iron curtain and "massive retaliation"—including the possible use of nuclear weapons as punishment for regional Soviet expansion. But time and again, accurately sensing the nonconfrontational mood of the American people, Eisenhower stuck more or less to the Democratic policy of containing the Soviet empire without major military offensives. He chose not to send U.S. troops to Indochina in '54, when communists took control of North Vietnam from French colonial rule. When Hungarian freedom-fighters led an uprising against Soviet rule in Hungary in '56, they expected American support. But none was forthcoming, and their revolt was crushed by Soviet tanks. When pro-Soviet Egyptian leader Gamal Abdel Nasser seized and closed the Suez Canal in '56, Israel, Britain and France sent troops to reopen it, but the U.S. joined Russia in criticizing the allied intervention and calling for a cease-fire.

Two years later, Eisenhower did send a small force of U.S. troops to Lebanon to bolster its government against pro-Soviet Arab rebels, easing the way for a neutralist successor regime. And when islands off the Chinese mainland were shelled by Mao's communist government, and Formosa seemed to be threatened by a communist invasion, Ike gave just enough support to Chiang Kai-shek's regime to quiet the crisis.

McCarthy madness

The early years of Eisenhower's administration were dominated by the wild accusations of communism in government and American life made by Senator Joseph McCarthy, a Republican from Wisconsin. Most of the genuine security risks in government, such as Alger Hiss, had been identified and expelled from government long before McCarthy made his first unsubstantiated charges in February 1950.

But over the following four years, McCarthy and like-minded demagogues tarred many loyal Americans in

1952	1953	1954
TRUMAN SEIZES STRUCK STEEL MILLS, SUPREME COURT OVERRULES.	STALIN DIES.	SENATE CONDEMNS McCARTHY.
NEW IMMIGRATION LAW REMOVES RACIAL AND ETHNIC BARRIERS.	SOVIETS EXPLODE THEIR FIRST H-BOMB.	SUPREME COURT RULES AGAINST SCHOOL SEGREGATION.
IKE BOOSTS AID TO FRANCE IN VIETNAM.	ARMISTICE IN KOREA.	FRENCH DEFEATED, VIETNAM DIVIDES NORTH-SOUTH.
EISENHOWER ELECTED PRESIDENT.		

government, academics, the arts and entertainment, and virtually every other field with accusations of communist sympathies—charges which were often either untrue or unimportant. People whose only involvement with communism may have been youthful ideological flirtations in the 1930s found themselves blacklisted and fired from jobs, their careers ruined. Civil libertarians in both parties objected to McCarthy's ruthless tactics, but his popularity mounted. When McCarthy began an assault on alleged disloyalty in the U.S. Army in 1954, he finally overreached. The tide turned against him, and by the end of the year his fellow senators had condemned him for misconduct.

Space and arms races

America's feelings of vulnerability to Soviet communism were heightened by a stunning shock in 1957—Russia's launch of the world's first earth-orbiting satellite, Sputnik. Two years later, a Russian satellite would be orbiting the moon. While the U.S. launched its own satellite in '58 and formed a new space agency, the Russian triumphs awakened the U.S. to the Soviets' technological prowess and stimulated a broad reappraisal of the American educational system.

The same kind of powerful missiles that could launch satellites were outfitted with nuclear warheads, giving both superpowers the ability to annihilate each other's major cities in long-range attacks. Most government leaders, in both America and Russia, apparently believed that the greatest security was offered by nuclear parity—that is, the deterrent value of likely mutual destruction—so each nation strived to match the other's nuclear buildup. The growth of nuclear arsenals was paralleled in the '50s by the rise of a nuclear disarmament movement supported mostly by the political left.

Economic growth

On the economic front at home, the war in Korea added a heavy dose of military spending to an already booming consumer economy, heating up inflation and leading to limited price controls. The economy continued to grow through 1957, driven by soaring factory productivity (known by the new buzzword "automation"), strong household formation and a high birth rate. The world's other industrial nations, in Europe and Asia, were still rebuilding, with American aid, from the devastation of World War II, and they weren't yet giving the U.S. much competition in world trade. Home entertainment was a boom industry, with television sets sprouting in every home, color television on the way, and long-playing records (soon to be in stereophonic sound) displacing the old 78s. A network of interstate divided highways, planned and funded largely by the federal government, would soon knit the nation together as never before—and stimulate an extraordinary real estate boom at every new interchange.

Meanwhile, urban planners and local officials launched the "urban renewal" movement. Rather than revitalize decaying neighborhoods with selective restoration of old buildings, they razed large sections of inner cities and downtown shopping districts. Many of the new buildings, especially the high-rise public housing projects, would be demolished as crime-ridden eyesores barely 20 years later.

New technological advances

Electronics were going miniature, with tiny transistors replacing vacuum tubes in radios and phonographs. Room-sized computers that read paper punch cards were beginning to replace the bulky file cabinets of American business. Peaceful uses for atomic power were beginning to appear, in medicine, transportation (nuclear-powered ships) and electrical generation. The first electric generating plant powered by atomic reaction began commercial service in 1955, raising hopes that nuclear power would eventually replace coal and oil as the major fuel source for making electricity.

The scourge of polio was finally conquered by vaccines, and antibiotics were controlling a wider range of infectious diseases. Retailing was going through a revolution of self-service supermarkets and drug stores. Detroit sold millions of ever-bigger, ever-more-powerful cars to an appreciative American public, but a few dissident buyers

1955	1956	1957
U.S. AGREES TO TRAIN SOUTH VIETNAM'S ARMY.	MINIMUM WAGE GOES TO $1 AN HOUR.	ANTI-SOVIET RIOTS IN POLAND, HUNGARY.
	WORK BEGUN ON INTERSTATE HIGHWAY SYSTEM.	BRITAIN, FRANCE SEIZE SUEZ CANAL.
	FIRST TRANS-ATLANTIC PHONE CABLE.	EUROPEAN ECONOMIC COMMUNITY FORMED.

were starting to eye the small, fuel-efficient cars imported from Europe.

The economy of the '50s expanded nicely, with only two recessions that lasted less than a year each, in '53-54 and '57-58. Productivity soared in manufacturing and agriculture, and the poverty rate plummeted for both white and black Americans. But the '57-58 recession was harsh, with unemployment climbing to 7.7%, the highest level since 1941. Declining steel and auto production was accompanied by distress in agriculture, where overproduction depressed prices throughout the Fifties. Some forecasters feared a return to '30s-style depression, or at least many years of anemic growth. Others foresaw the opposite—a major boom taking shape in the decade ahead, based on demographic and productivity trends already visible, especially the high birth rate that started after World War II and continued throughout the '50s. But in the gloom of the '58 congressional elections, liberal Democrats swept dozens of races, and the Democrats fattened slender majorities into commanding control of both houses. Despite a White House ethics scandal that forced the resignation of Eisenhower's powerful aide, Sherman Adams, and despite concerns about the President's health after two heart attacks, his personal popularity remained surprisingly strong.

Communists in Cuba

Meanwhile, a volatile situation was brewing in the Caribbean, just south of Florida. "Agrarian reformers" in Cuba, led by Fidel Castro, were battling the repressive Batista dictatorship, and in January 1959 they overthrew the regime. There had long been broad support for Castro in the U.S., with the wishful feeling that he would establish democracy in Cuba. Within a few months, however, Castro established instead a communist dictatorship, armed and funded by Moscow and poised to export leftist rebellion throughout Latin America.

The decade closed with the eyes of the world focused on tension between the two great nuclear powers. In '58 and '59, the Soviets once again threatened to push the western allies out of the divided city of Berlin, as they had failed to do a decade before. Public anxieties over the specter of nuclear war led to civil-defense drills in elementary-school classrooms, and some families had elaborate bomb shelters installed in their backyards and basements.

Peaceful coexistence

But the two superpowers also took the first steps toward a thaw in the Cold War. Cultural exchanges were begun, and high officials of each nation paid unprecedented visits on each other. In 1958 Vice President Richard Nixon toured the Soviet Union, and Soviet Premier Nikita Khrushchev toured the United States, visiting with Eisenhower at Camp David. From this attempt at peaceful coexistence came the first tentative steps toward slowing down the arms race. Russia unilaterally suspended tests of new nuclear weapons, and the U.S. followed suit.

The path to a less-dangerous world would not be straight or smooth. All over the world, from Southeast Asia and Africa to the Middle East and Latin America, onetime colonies were establishing fragile new states. Their peoples were often bitterly divided between allegiances to democracy and communism, and the two superpowers were very willing to arm opposing factions. The Cold War would soon breed many regional hot wars, fought by proxies in faraway lands.

SOVIETS LAUNCH SPUTNIK.

LITTLE ROCK SCHOOL-DESEGREGATION SHOWDOWN.

U.S. LAUNCHES ITS FIRST SATELLITE.

MAO ORDERS "GREAT LEAP FORWARD" IN CHINA.

NASA ESTABLISHED.

1958

CASTRO TAKES POWER IN CUBA.

ALASKA AND HAWAII BECOME STATES.

ST. LAWRENCE SEAWAY OPENS.

1959

1950

January 7, 1950

<u>Civil rights, no final action</u>, due to hypocrisy on both sides.
Democrats will push FEPC, but they KNOW it will be filibustered to death.
They could get anti-lynch and anti-poll tax, and Republicans would join
in voting for them. But Democrats don't want Republicans to get credit,
and Republicans prefer to be in position to charge Democratic failure.
So civil rights will get the run-around, and remain a talking issue.

January 14, 1950

<u>Unbalanced budget in times of good business was formerly a sin</u>.
<u>But now it's a virtue</u>...or is so regarded by the administration.
This is the new-style of gov't thinking...you'll soon hear more of it.
It will influence Congress...FOR spending...and AGAINST higher taxes.
<u>The red ink in gov't operations is here to stay</u>...
<u>New attitude is that it's ALL RIGHT for gov't to run a deficit</u>.
No need to worry about it. Even 5 billions a year for some years is OK.
Shouldn't cut expenses. As for social welfare, costs should be EXPANDED.
Spending by gov't stimulates business. Mustn't do anything to frighten.
Might make a recession. Can't afford that, especially in election year.
<u>Keep business steamed up</u>, expand the economy. The time will come
when this expansion will yield more total income and more taxes from it.
THEN the budget will balance itself. The time of this is not specified.
Not this year, not next year, hardly the year after...but just sometime.

January 21, 1950

<u>Hydrogen bomb</u>, many times better (or worse) than the atom bomb,
is stirring up a great moral controversy, because it would kill civilians
on a tremendous scale, and be far more inhuman than 'simple' atom bomb.
Nevertheless, the decision probably will be to go ahead with production
on the theory that Russia may develop it. The U.S. wants to keep abreast.

February 18, 1950

<u>The selling talk for it is this</u>: We all want peace with Russia.
Russia will talk peace ONLY IF we build up more strength and armed force.
Russia listened and backed off in the days when Byrnes was talking tough,
but then we had a big advantage with the A-bomb...now we have lost it.
So...we must get a move on, and go further and faster with our armament.
Thus the talk for bigger defense is wrapped in the mantle of peace.
<u>What it means internally</u>: More defense money will soon be asked.
<u>Higher taxes? Not necessarily</u>. <u>Higher deficits? Yes, probably</u>.
One more step in direction of inflation...long range...the years ahead.

March 18, 1950

<u>Reds in the State Dept</u>? Sen. McCarthy has stirred up suspicions
that were kicking around even before the Hiss trial. His methods to date
are shot-gun & meat-axe...his facts meager...proving nothing conclusive.
No help from gov't, only resistance. May find pay dirt later, hasn't yet.

July 8, 1950

<u>Korean war may last a long time</u>. Military is preparing for it.
According to present outlook, Korea will take a lot more men & materials.
<u>The draft is essential</u> to get the men...for Korea and elsewhere.
<u>National Guard</u> probably will be called up, too...time uncertain.

Yeah—so help me God!

LOYALTY OATH

An American Army convoy retreats across the border back into South Korea.

October 21, 1950

    <u>Eisenhower for President</u>? He CAN be Republican nominee in '52, but the politicians are warning that he had better announce himself. He can't win by being silent and expecting to be drafted at 11th hour. It takes year or more to round up delegates...for an AVOWED candidate.

December 2, 1950

    It now looks as if...
(1) War in Korea will not be won militarily by the U.S.-UN.
(2) Bombing of Manchuria will not be authorized by the UN.
(3) Settlement will be by diplomatic negotiation...compromise.
(4) Such a settlement will be delayed for weeks within the UN.
(5) Meanwhile our forces in Korea will be pushed farther back.
(6) War with China must still be rated as a strong possibility.
(7) Defense program on the home front will be stepped up fast.

    <u>Will MacArthur be replaced</u>? We do not know. But what we DO know is that he isn't liked by the White House, State Dep't or Gen. Marshall. They would be happy to replace him but are afraid of the public reaction.

April 21, 1951

    <u>Passions over MacArthur</u> are deeper & hotter than any we've seen in our whole reporting experience, which goes back to President Wilson. Even the brawl over the League of Nations was mild compared to this one. MacArthur has the man-on-the-street with him...not just some highbrows. The torrid talk is weighted overwhelmingly pro-MacArthur, anti-Truman. Seldom before has a President of the United States been so on defensive.

May 19, 1951

Eisenhower, '52: Rumors persist, especially among New Dealers, that he may be persuaded to run for President on the Democratic ticket. In our opinion he will NOT. Our information is that he is a REPUBLICAN.

June 30, 1951

West Germany is to be rearmed. French opposition is weakening, so the U.S. will go ahead when it can...and pour weapons into Germany.

July 14, 1951

The final terms of cease-fire will be galling to the U.S. side. We shall probably give up territory won by arms, and fall back southward to a zone related to the 38th parallel. It won't look like any victory.
What we've succeeded in doing is this: We stopped the aggressor. We slaughtered pretty heavily. We did it in the name of collective action with other UN nations. By compromise & consultation we held UN together. We gave Russia a lesson...that the U.S. is not as soft as Russia thought.

September 8, 1951

Money, machinery, materials will go to Japan for reconstruction, economic & military. In a few months Japan will have an arms industry. Then she will get substantial trade concessions...broad fishing rights in U.S. & Canadian waters, unlimited shipbuilding and textile output. This means competition with U.S. business...to keep Japan on our side.

1952

February 2, 1952

Stevenson, Gov. of Ill: Much talk of him among top Democrats. They stress his experience in foreign affairs, ability as a vote-getter. And what's more, he talks states' rights...big help to him in the South.

February 23, 1952

Amazing spectacle about this country is its productive capacity, which has gone up more than anyone foresaw, to give both guns and butter. For the present this is fine. But if & when defense ever comes to an end, it means that productive capacity will be out of kilter with consumption.
This has the makings of a crash...several years off...not now.

May 3, 1952

You'll see more Japanese goods in stores...all sorts of stuff. Textiles. Light bulbs. Novelties & gifts. Bicycles. Canned fish.
Means more competition for U.S. producers, by cheap Jap labor, and the Japanese are not averse to selling at a loss to grab a market. More & more industries will demand that gov't act...boost the tariff.

Crime & sex in comic magazines will be investigated by Congress, to see whether they go "too far," and whether they ought to be curbed.
"Offensive" programs on TV & radio will get careful going-over.

May 17, 1952

A sorry mental state in this country: No full war and no peace. Indifference, half-heartedness. Want defense, yet grumble about taxes. Leaders in Washington at sixes & sevens, so they provide no leadership, either moral, intellectual or spiritual. A vacuum. People are confused, with nothing to rally around, nothing to spend their zeal upon.
But all this is temporary. It will end when elections are over. Meanwhile go ahead and do your stuff in your own way. That's initiative.

May 24, 1952

Electronic brain: Gov't scientists now predict simplified models
for practical business uses...inventorying, accounting, mailing lists,
sales, market research, other records. But it's still a few years off.

June 7, 1952

Korea is a fringe war for us, and Indo-China may become another.
The French say they can't afford the money & men to fight in Indo-China,
and want to dump the whole mess in our laps...as Britain dumped Greece.
But any such shift now would be embarrassing to Truman administration,
so the French are willing to wait a bit, take only more military aid now.
After elections we're supposed to take over the WHOLE cost of Indo-China.
No U.S. troops to Indo-China, but much more air & naval help...
ships, airplanes, and maybe men to train pilots...for which U.S. pays.
Thus the U.S. will have to spread its strength out...further and thinner.

June 14, 1952

Television is proving to be a tremendous new political force.
Candidates win or lose votes on the basis of their looks on the screen.
And TV men are having to fight for their right, or the public's right,
to be in on everything, to see it at first hand, not just be told about it.

July 12, 1952

The woman vote: Signs point to more women voters this election.
The significance, electionwise, is open to question. Common theory is
that most husbands & wives vote the same, because under same influences.
Nevertheless Republicans are going to make special appeal to the women
on the issues of corruption, public morals, inflated prices, and Korea.

Newly nominated by the 1952 GOP
convention: Dwight "Ike" Eisenhower
and Richard Nixon with wives Mamie
and Pat.

August 23, 1952

Small cars, the near-midget varieties, are selling quite well.
Station wagon types of low-priced cars are becoming more popular.
Air conditioning for big expensive cars will be ready next year,
but the trade expects to sell very few of them...until they get cheaper.

Advertising on TV is zooming, and is hurting radio ads a little,
but is not yet affecting advertising in either newspapers or magazines.
Both of these are on the rise, and promising to go higher in coming year.
Eventually, however, TV threatens to be MORE of a challenge to ALL media.

October 18, 1952

To our readers abroad: You say you're puzzled by our elections?
Yes, puzzling, even here. National popular vote probably will be close,
but electoral vote not so close...because based on states, not nation.
Democratic party is preferred abroad, as a known factor, but...
Republican party is not "isolationist," as you have been told.
It would continue foreign aid, but would insist on more "self-help."
Our people are groaning under taxes, and our resources are not unlimited.
This country is not going to pieces because of the nasty oratory.
We fuss extravagantly every four years...and then resume a basic unity.

Note the private medical program, about ready for announcement.
It's supposed to block socialized medicine as proposed by gov't.
Embraces all medical & dental care, hospitalization, health insurance.
Individuals could subscribe for the service, pay share of pooled costs.
Or companies could subscribe for employes, and pay a part of the costs.
Who's behind it? Leading physicians, leading businessmen, others.
Organizing nationally, but also must organize locally to give the service.
It's a form of social medicine, but run privately, not by gov't.

November 15, 1952

    <u>There's confidence in Eisenhower</u>...intangible, hard to define.
People don't expect any miracles from him, but they do feel hopefulness,
which somehow they had lost under the governmental regimes of the past.
They are not explicit, they fumble at explanation, say it's a "feeling."
The feeling isn't just economic or political, certainly isn't partisan.
It's something deeper down in them, in the realm of the spirit, spiritual.
It COULD be the rebirth of confidence that people have been praying for.

November 22, 1952

    <u>Our alliances abroad are showing signs of rapid deterioration.</u>
    <u>NATO-West Europe</u>...lagging far behind the earlier defense goals.
U.S. is delivering much less than promised, and our allies are trimming,
cutting industrial expansion, length of conscription, and arms budgets.
So, U.S. must supply MORE...or else cut back on whole defense timetable.
    <u>Iran</u> is on the verge of anarchy, and needs more help from U.S.
    <u>Indo-China</u> is too heavy for the French. They want to pass it on.
Especially they want American officers to train their own native forces.
And they are crying for more arms aid from us...including more planes.
    <u>Italy</u> is threatening not to support NATO, if aid is continued
to Tito, Yugoslavia. The Italians are blunt about it...strong language.
    <u>Germany vs. France</u>...frictions worse than public has been told.
    <u>Japan</u> demands more trade outlets...if not to U.S., then to China.

**French troops interrogate a Vietcong
prisoner.**

November 29, 1952

    <u>Generally, this is a team of businessmen.</u> All of the top people
have actually run businesses of their own...know the practical problems.
They are trained doers, as distinguished from theoretical ideologists,
who were most conspicuous in the cabinets of both Roosevelt and Truman.
    <u>Businessmen for 20 years</u> have felt relegated to the sidelines.
Now they are in the game. Can they govern? Can they adjust to politics?
And look to the interest of ALL the people? Probably can...we shall see.

December 20, 1952

    <u>Expect still another year of world tension, but not a world war</u>.
Within the year we shall increase our strength...AND our moral position.
We've made mistakes, and we've been clumsy in our diplomatic dealings,
but, after all, this nation has demonstrated its willingness to give out,
to help others. And this is not just for safety & self-interest, either.
It stems from the internal spirit of humanitarianism, missionary style.
The motives are not advertised as religious, and yet at base they are.
This nation is aware of its faults, but it can also count up its virtues.
They are numerous, and they are rooted pretty deep down in the spirit.

January 3, 1953

    <u>Incentives to business</u> will be a major influence on tax policy.
New officials are convinced that the upper-bracket rates on individuals
and the excess profits tax tend to stifle the incentive to take any risk.
They will urge that tax relief be voted to encourage more risk-taking...
say that bigger volume of business might mean even MORE taxes for gov't.
Congress will be sympathetic, and will vote small tax cuts for this year.

Americans were urged to build back yard air raid shelters.

February 7, 1953

<u>We are taking the initiative in the cold war</u>, and hope to win it
as the best existing means of avoiding an all-out world-wide hot war.
Every move was weighed so as to fall short of exciting Russia. Negative.
<u>Now less timidity, less fearfulness...more boldness...positive</u>.
Now let Russia wonder what-next, and sit on an anxious seat of her own.
Anxious about the fronts, such as Formosa. Anxious about her satellites.
We shall deliberately cultivate trouble for Russia behind the Iron Curtain,
for trouble-internal can make the Moscow men reluctant to start any war.

March 7, 1953

<u>In China, Mao, red dictator</u>, regards himself as Marxist expert,
second only to Stalin, and has contempt for all the men around Stalin,
Can't be subservient to them...will pull away...but not in any big hurry.

March 21, 1953

<u>Electric power from atom heat</u> is probably 10 to 15 years off...
on economic scale that will let it compete with coal, oil, water power.
It probably will be applied in other countries before it is applied here,
because their fuels cost more than ours, so A-power could compete better.
England, for example. Or Argentina & other countries that now lack fuel.
In U.S., coal, oil and power dams won't be outmoded for many-many years.

July 25, 1953

<u>Gov't policy is to let the adjustment run</u> and rely upon business
to work out remedies...and not to rush in too soon with gov't measures.
The present Republican regime, unlike the preceding Democratic regimes,
believes in private initiative at maximum, and gov't efforts at minimum.
Let gov't keep hands off, long as possible. Let the super-boom slack off.
<u>That's what officials SAY they will do, BUT</u>...it is our opinion
that public pressures will force them to act...more than they now intend.

August 1, 1953

<u>Unification of Korea</u> will be given lip-service by our diplomats,
but no one expects it to occur in near future. The reds are too strong.
Early withdrawal of foreign troops from Korea can not be accepted by UN,
for Red Chinese insist that they are "volunteers," not "foreign troops."

August 15, 1953

U.S. troops to Indo-China? The official line is that we WON'T,
even if the Red Chinese invade. But there's new pressure from the French,
and new talk within our gov't as to WHETHER we can afford to keep out,
and WHETHER U.S. public would approve a going-in. We sense a wavering
in gov't attitude. This is not a forecast, but it IS a note of warning.

August 22, 1953

Russian H-bomb explosion was perfectly timed...for the commies.
France, Italy & Germany are shaking under internal commie influences...
and are weakening in their willingness to build up a West European army.
Threat of the H-bomb in Russian hands will make them even less willing.

Negro employes of firms having gov't contracts or subcontracts:
To protect them against discrimination is the aim of the new committee,
headed by VP Nixon. Forfeiture of contract will be the penalty imposed
in cases of proven discrimination. The same for other minority groups.
The theory is that if discrimination is abandoned by gov't contractors...
and there are thousands of such firms...many others will fall into line.

"Think maybe we'd better say
something about it?"

August 29, 1953

Here are some conclusions, realistic but distasteful:
Red China is going to be opened up to world trade, including U.S.
It's a big future market. Wants to industrialize. We'll have to go along
and in due course we'll also be scrambling for our share of the trade.
Probably, with time uncertain, Red China will be admitted to UN, too.
Japan will industrialize, and will go after the markets of China.
Just how, don't know, but inevitable...with or without approval of U.S.

So...true budget balance is not in sight for 2 years, maybe 3.
Treasury talks its "hopes"...doesn't figure on Congress...too many ifs.
The chances are that genuine budget balance will not come before '56.
Startling...to those who've thought the Republicans OF COURSE
would balance the budget promptly. They won't. It's still some time off.

Senator Joe McCarthy at a Senate hearing with aide Roy Cohn (second from left).

September 12, 1953

> <u>McCarthy</u> is too much a one-man show to suit officials.
> So senators of both parties have a plan to limit his funds next year.
> They hope thus to harness him. (They also call it "belling the cat.")

September 26, 1953

> <u>Baseball</u>: Soon after the World Series is over, the Supreme Court
> will hear arguments on whether baseball is a business or merely a sport.
> If it's a business, players' contracts probably violate antitrust laws,
> and this might leave players free to sell themselves to the rich teams.
> Would wreck the game, so Congress is ready to vote antitrust exemption.

October 24, 1953

> <u>Indo-China</u>: We are paying two-thirds of the expenses of the war,
> not far under a billion dollars this year, which is not generally known.
> Most of the troops are native, most of the officers in charge are French,
> but it has become "our war"...to keep communists from whole big areas.
> Shows how we adopt...gradually, step by step...distant wars as our own.

November 7, 1953

> <u>American exports of goods have been sitting pretty</u> since the war
> because they didn't have much competition. Other nations were bad off,
> didn't have industrial capacity to compete, or the money for financing.
> <u>Now things are changing</u>. There's a growing European competition.
> Some of our exporting industries are dozing...they MUST compete harder.
> As for our gov't, it is "studying" the trends...leisurely, late as usual.

November 14, 1953

> <u>Has the administration "gone McCarthy?"</u> And adopted his tactics?
> Eisenhower men say NO, say they will use rifle on reds, not blunderbuss.
> They profess to approve McCarthy's general aims, but not his methods.
> Despite the distinction, it seems that the Republicans have rediscovered
> that red hunting is good politics. Former reluctance is being abandoned.

November 28, 1953

Color TV: New system for whole industry will be OK'd by gov't within the next 2 or 3 weeks, replacing the CBS method approved earlier. First sets will show up about Feb-Mar., costing in range of $800-$1000.

Prices of black & white sets will drop sharply in months ahead. The bargains will persuade lots of families not to wait it out for color.

Movies, jolted by TV, now face another blow from tape recordings that carry both sound and color TV, and can be used over & over again. Means TV producers won't be buying as many movie films in a year or so.

New anti-polio vaccine will be given limited tryout next year. Expected to reduce severity of polio, maybe make some children immune.

Salt-free foods: Food & Drug will order accurate labeling so that people who are on diets can tell how much salt is in their food.

Artificial sweeteners: FDA also wants food makers to disclose to customers whether products contain sugar or a substitute sweetener. So in next few months it will write new rules tightening up on labels.

Bug poisons on crops: Gov't thinks public needs more protection from residue on fruits & vegetables, will write tighter rules in '54.

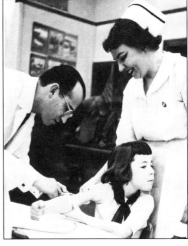

Dr. Jonas Salk administers his new polio vaccine.

December 19, 1953

Electronic office machines: They will be really practicable, even for small & medium businesses, within 5 years, or 10 at the most. Too costly for most businesses at present, but progress in past 2 years suggests very rapid development, resulting in substantially lower costs.

Insurance companies eventually will have elaborate machines to write out policies, send out bills, figure tables...all automatic.

Big stores will have them to keep all the records of customers, all the charge accounts, total up the monthly bills and send them out.

Newspapers & magazines will use them on subscription records, and for all the details of mailing lists, billings and solicitations.

Banks can be almost entirely mechanized as for record-keeping, with automatic figuring...deposits, withdrawals, interest, everything.

Inventory control machines, a running record of what's on hand, covering hundreds of plants and thousands of items, pieces and parts.

All these are definitely in the works. Need further refinement, but are past the mere-dream stage. Formerly it was generally thought they'd require 10 or 15 years. Now better figure on 5 or 10 years.

An early mainframe computer.

1954

January 23, 1954

    <u>U.S. is making progress against the red threat in Latin America</u>.
In Guatemala, commies ruled the roost, ran labor unions AND the gov't.
Now one of the biggest unions has tossed out its top communist leaders.
U.S. had a hand in it, but to avoid the charge of "Yankee imperialism,"
got other Latin American governments and labor unions to do the job.
Next steps: Kick reds out of more unions, then out of Guatemalan gov't.

February 13, 1954

    <u>In long years ahead we foresee wages up, then costs & prices up</u>.
Union leaders must always get MORE, will not be limited by productivity.
Thus a slow game of leapfrog, wages & prices...and a creeping inflation.
    <u>Add governmental or monetary inflation</u>, probable over long pull.
Gov't is certain to run more in the red in the times of economic downs
than it runs in the black in times of boom. Won't have the guts to tax.
    <u>So we expect further inflation</u>...over the next 10-20-30 years.

Civil rights attorney Thurgood Marshall mounts steps at Supreme Court, where he successfully argued for the end to legal school segregation. He later served as an associate justice.

March 13, 1954

    <u>More about McCarthy</u>...to answer questions that are being asked,
and to make light rather than heat, of which there's already a plenty:
    <u>First, will Eisenhower squelch him</u>? No, he won't, for he can't.
He can speak out against him, and is doing so with a rising emphasis,
but McCarthy is free to retort, and, being brassy, he's not squelchable.
Besides, Eisenhower can't afford to alienate a lot of loyal Republicans
who back McCarthy. He hopes to MEND the party split, but probably can't.

April 24, 1954

    <u>Congress isn't ready to take on the load of Indo-China now</u>.
The truce with Korea gave the members a chance to cut down gov't spending,
and to trim defense, because a lot of stuff isn't being shot up in a war.
Many members already say, firmly: "We MUST NOT get into another Korea."
Republicans remind that Eisenhower's promise to end Korea won many votes,
and warn that "it would be political suicide to go into Indo-China."

May 15, 1954

    <u>One question</u>: <u>Are we accepting fringe wars</u>, formerly shunned,
and shelving the policy of "massive retaliation," bombing of Russia?
The explanations are long and involved, but the simple answer is YES.

May 22, 1954

    <u>Negro and white children to be mingled in schools</u> under ruling
by the Supreme Court that segregation violates the federal Constitution.
In District of Columbia, which has about as many Negro children as white
within D.C. boundaries, the integration will be done this coming year.
Balking in the South and long delay...legal tangles must be unsnarled.
    <u>Biggest thing for the Negro race</u> since emancipation from slavery.
In a generation or two it will lift bulk of Negroes to better education,
better jobs, better pay...and make millions into better customers.

May 29, 1954

<u>Other new practical uses for atom</u>, recently disclosed:
<u>Better-keeping meat</u>: The scientists are now perfecting a process
to pasteurize or purify meat, so that it will stay fresh in stores...
for weeks instead of days...without discoloration...or change of flavor.
<u>Potatoes</u>: New radiation keeps them fresh for many months longer.
<u>Rust-free oats</u> are under experimentation...helpful to farmers.
All these are still in the experimental stage, but moving fast.

June 12, 1954

<u>As for Indo-China, things are going badly</u>.
<u>Will the U.S. go in anyway, without the others</u>? We will NOT.
We insist on fighting collectively and not alone. Hard to do it via UN,
partly because of Russian veto, partly because other UN methods are slow.

June 26, 1954

<u>Cigarets, cancer, heart trouble</u>: The Dept. of Agr. tobacco men
are now sure that the talk will cut tobacco smoking and tobacco growing.
The slide has already been under way, and they think it will continue.
<u>The adverse publicity also is resulting in fewer NEW smokers</u>,
thus depriving the industry of replacement customers, relied on in past.

July 24, 1954

<u>Negroes & public schools</u>: Negro organizations are getting set
to bring suits against many cities and states that don't end segregation
by this coming fall...say that's "plenty long enough to make the shift."
<u>Next, transportation, gov't-financed housing</u>. Negro groups say
the jim crow laws on buses, even local, must end. They are now planning
to try to get ICC help. They will also try to get federal & local gov'ts
to end segregation in gov't-financed housing, gov't-financed hospitals.
Many communities will have new problems beyond just school integration.

August 14, 1954

<u>McCarthy censure</u>: Senate committee members are sincere, genuine,
not limelight-lovers. Hearings will be sober & sedate...no TV or radio.
Question is whether McCarthy-the-Senator, rather than McCarthy-the-man,
cast reflections on the Senate...in the minds of the general public.
Our opinion is that if committee recommends censure, Senate will so vote.

September 25, 1954

 Automatic machinery is zooming...machines that run themselves... operated by a few engineers and mechanics...replacing a lot of workers. The trend is old, but the rapid growth is new...especially in past year. Progress in the future is assured...at the zooming rate of the present.
 There's a new word for it..."automation." It means automatics... automatic control of single machines or whole production lines of them.
 It's a new phase of the industrial revolution...a rushing phase. No telling now how far it will go. We shall be writing you more about it.

October 9, 1954

 Midget cars: No one in Detroit is interested in them, saying the American people won't buy enough midget cars to justify making them. Prefer bigger used cars. "If they want midgets, let them buy foreign cars."

October 30, 1954

 Now it's time to wake up on Europe. Postwar reconstruction there is just about finished. A boom is about to start...the same sort of boom we had here in U.S. after the war...resulting from the pent-up demands. European peoples now want all the things which we in U.S. wanted and got.

November 6, 1954

 Net, the Republican party moved a bit toward middle-of-the-road, toward acceptance and embracement of some of the New Deal philosophy.

November 13, 1954

 Note that extremists have lost ground in both political parties, both extreme Republican conservatives and extreme Democratic liberals.
 What we have are two strong parties, both hovering near center, the Republican with much wider scattering toward the ideological right, the Democrats with a broader extension toward the left. Less disparity in the strength and appeal of both than has prevailed for past 22 years. Like two good teams...No. 1 vs. No. 2...it promises a wholesome contest.

 Big new plan for roads & highways: Old plan for 50 billions is already out the window...too low and too slow. Now it's 100 billions, maybe 60% or 70% from federal gov't, the rest of it from state & local. Idea is to get started in '55, speed up in '56, spread it over 10 years. Raise the money by setting up a gov't corporation, letting it sell bonds. Thus finance it outside the gov't budget and avoid building up a deficit.

December 24, 1954

 Future demand for housing is shown by marriages, plus incomes, plus money costs and other economic factors. By all of these measures the outlook is favorable, except for a couple of short-range cautions.
 Another big boom, starting in early 60's, is almost sure. The wave of births in past 15 years will become a wave of marriages then, creating demand for millions of homes...a bigger boom than at present.

January 22, 1955

Fight against discount houses is being stepped up by merchants. More are now featuring their own private brands (made by regular mfrs.), even cutting prices on them (which is not permitted on regular brands).

Fair trade as a way to keep prices up is slowly disintegrating. Manufacturers are too slow or too reluctant to enforce the set prices on discount houses, and so regular merchants let their prices slip, too. This has been going on quietly for some time. Now it's out in the open.

As for fate of discount houses, some of the smalls are failing, but some of the bigs are prospering...with mass buying, mass selling.

Another wrinkle, more imported goods: Better profits on these offset some of the losses that merchants take on goods sold at discount. Merchants are finding that imported stuff is popular because different, and so there's quite a movement toward it. Most stores buy via agents, but more & more big stores are opening their own purchasing offices abroad. Expect to see an increase in foreign-made goods in the stores this year.

Influence of women: All builders everywhere say women now choose the house more often than a few years ago. Thus the catering is to women. Men are tending to become mere silent partners...limited to the paying.

February 12, 1955

Defense is going to stay at about present levels indefinitely. The level is now 34 billions a year. It will hover there for some time.
New kind of war must be prepared for, and it's mighty expensive. Nuclear weapons mean new strategy and new tactics. Bigger battle areas. Faster dispersal and regrouping. Trucks are too vulnerable for some uses, must be replaced by tank-like vehicles. Need new and better radio stuff. New diesel tanks. Bigger, faster guided missiles. Bigger, faster planes. Atomic plane carriers. More atomic subs. New war machinery, all around.

March 12, 1955

Russian farmers will be permitted to visit Iowa corn-hog farms. Delays in our gov't approval is due to red tape and legal technicalities. Also to some internal nervousness about public sentiment on the visit. Most people seem to think that it would be a good thing...for our side... to show the visiting Russian people how well we farm, how well we live, even under the "tyranny of capitalism, imperialism and Wall Street rulers."

Nautilus, America's first nuclear sub.

May 7, 1955

Automatic machines that "read" are about to be tested by gov't, and by banks, retail stores, publishers, insurance and oil companies. The machines "look" at a paper, and "read" typewritten words & numbers, then transfer information to punch cards, calculating or other machines. Could make big changes in office practices. More on this after testing.

Atomic radiation to preserve food is making very rapid headway, and threatens to start a revolution in food processing in a year or two. Housewives may be able to buy meats, vegetables, fruits, maybe even milk that will keep completely fresh on pantry shelf in airtight containers.

May 14, 1955

Expansion has gone pretty fast since the war ended 10 years ago. It will go as fast or faster in next 10 years...that is the probability. It will help to make solidity. Not everything will boom all of the time. There will be ups & downs, as usual...troubles and soft spots, as usual. But now it's fairly clear that we face a decade of "dynamic economy"... with business values and human values. It's not a dream, it's reality.

Germany is going to be a leading contender for trade with U.S., especially now that she's free. German engineers & technicians are good, as everyone knows, and they are working hard at developing new products, lots of less costly things to be thrown onto the world markets...soon.

May 21, 1955

On pensions, unions are demanding and getting more concessions:
(1) Complete separation of private pensions and gov't pensions, so that the private pensions won't go down as the gov't pensions go up.
(2) A switch from insurance to trust funds, to finance pensions.

A banner commemorating AFL-CIO merger.

June 4, 1955

Urban redevelopment, slum clearance: Congress will vote more, 500 millions more to dish out to cities to help buy up and clear slums. More cities are doing it...the motives being social, health, humane... plus higher values, higher tax yields, rejuvenation of the WHOLE city.

June 11, 1955

Farm land values have been sliding for several years.
Now reversal, farm lands starting upward...one big reason being non-farm use of land...suburban growth, spread of industry to farm areas, and growth of highways...these are making farm lands into "real estate." More & more farm land is getting to be in easy reach of growing cities. The line between suburban and rural is dimming, suburban zone extending. This nudges up farm land averages...now 2% higher than only one year ago.

July 16, 1955

Employe savings & stock purchase plans are offshoot of inflation and really spreading fast. Not truly new, tried in forms in the past, but now they are getting quite a nudge, and here are some of the reasons: As an inflation hedge for employes. To tie employes closer to company. To meet the growing desire to own stocks, equities. And, in some cases, to soften the growing demands for guaranteed wage programs.

The first U.S. nuclear power plant at Shippingport, Pa.

July 23, 1955

　　<u>Atomic power for commercial sale, actual use, arrived this week</u>.
It ranks with Edison's first incandescent lamp at Menlo Park in 1879...
or Bell's telephone, 1877...or Marconi's wireless, 1896...or the airplane
by the Wrights, 1903...or Morse's telegraph, 1844...or the steamboat
by Fulton, 1807...McCormick's reaper, 1834...Whitney's cotton gin, 1793.
　　<u>The event got buried in the news</u>. We thought it was so important
that we went to see it, can tell you about it, and thus in future years,
when atom power is common, you can recall the start of it...back in 1955.
　　<u>You will see such plants</u> outside many cities before very long.
Not a stunt or experiment, but the real thing.
　　<u>Competitive...in 5 to 10 years</u>...with coal, oil and gas.
Not everywhere at first, but in those areas that don't have cheap power.
Then gradually extending to areas where competition will be tougher.
Won't replace coal, oil or gas, but will serve to supplement them.
　　Regardless of details, it now appears that atomic electric power
is moving faster than was thought. The resulting revolution is nearer.

July 30, 1955

　　<u>The new peace spirit has a vagueness which worries some people</u>.
They'd like to believe it but can't quite do it, lest it be an illusion.
It seems too good to be true, and so they conclude that it ISN'T true.
　　<u>Our answer</u>: We are aware that this is not the arrival of peace,
that there is harmony only at the edges, that many problems are unsolved,
that the reds are wily and not to be fully trusted, that some fringe wars
are still not unlikely, that strong defense is still essential to safety.
We've made allowance for unknown factors and things that may go haywire,
and have tried to balance up both the good and the bad in the picture.
　　<u>With all that, we think the peace spirit has great genuineness</u>,
that it will grow and deepen, and that a new era is probably at hand.
　　<u>Think furthermore that it's the beginning of a world-wide boom</u>,
and that the boom in U.S. will be carried even higher in next few years.

　　<u>Reasons for thinking these things</u>: We in the U.S. don't want war,
and there is now much evidence that the Kremlin doesn't want it either.
　　Consider this naive if you wish, but we trust reports that we get
from behind the iron curtain: There's critical shortage of food in Russia
and of other civilian essentials. There's ferment within the satellites.
The new rulers have GOT to work at peace...for their own internal reasons.

October 29, 1955

<u>Jobs for Negroes</u>: Very little on the movement gets into the news but the fact is that there's an active and organized effort to push it, and that <u>it heads up in the White House itself</u>...in a gov't committee which is directed by Vice President Nixon. Whole thing is done quietly.

<u>Political implications in it</u>: Both parties vie for Negro votes, especially in cities of North & East. Democrats will resurrect FEPC talk. Republicans will claim that they are doing better with quiet persuasion.

Handle with care!

November 12, 1955

<u>We shall never use the H bombs</u>, for they are much too dangerous.
<u>Russia will never use the H bombs, either</u>, for the Russians know from their own experiments how after-effects can hurt their own people. The information on what the Russians think has come via secret channels which may not be discussed, but which we know to be reliable.

<u>As for A bombs, much the same</u>, but to a lesser extent or degree. Any massive use of A bombs by the thousands (and this is now possible) would result in damage to millions of people throughout the whole world.

November 19, 1955

<u>Biggest worry is Japan</u>. Imports are up sharply on many things... glassware, pottery, bicycles, textiles, tools, optical goods and others. And Japanese quality is improving...Japanese gov't is insisting on it.

1956

January 21, 1956

Eisenhower's budget record covering 4 years shows these things:
<u>Republicans are spenders</u>...almost as much as the Democrats were. Budgets have been trimmed a bit here & there, but not very significantly. This is due to politics...pressures on Congress and the gov't agencies for all sorts of outlays. To trim them makes enemies and loses votes. The line of least resistance is to let expenses run...and please people.

<u>But Republicans may have spent less</u> than Democrats WOULD have, if they had been in office. Democrats learned under the Roosevelt regime that spending is "popular," even at risk of budget unbalance & inflation.

February 4, 1956

<u>Shopping centers are going to get bigger...whoppers are coming</u>. Multimillion-dollar deals, with two or more department stores, and room for flocks of satellite stores, chains & independents, and supermarkets. Some will even have office buildings, medical centers, hotels & parks. Plus big amphitheater for fashion shows, concerts, etc. Acres of parking. And underground passages for truck deliveries. Even competitive stores.

March 10, 1956

<u>Integration of Negroes in schools</u>, like slavery a century ago, is a great emotional issue, but we'd like to report on it unemotionally
<u>We've rechecked with Negro leaders</u>, NAACP, Nat. Assn. for the Advancement of Colored People, to see whether they intend to be aggressive or whether they might relax and go slower, and thus avoid race frictions.
<u>We get this answer</u>: They fully intend to continue the pressures, and "not to let up for a minute." "Waiting might mean slipping backward."
<u>Passive resistance, no violence</u>: Negro leaders stress this method in all talks with all followers. They want no bloodshed on either side. At the same time, being educated and sophisticated, they do recognize the possibility of violence, and they are willing to run the risk of it.

Ike with civil rights leaders at the White House. He is flanked by Rev. Martin Luther King (left) and A. Philip Randolph (right). Attorney General William P. Rogers is second from right.

In Congress and in whole federal government, we think we foresee at least a decade, perhaps more, of political turmoil over Negro rights. Republicans will hang together, somewhat loosely, for Negro privileges. Democrats of North and South simply can not stick together on the issue. Emotions are sure to split off the South politically...somehow, sometime.

March 17, 1956

Israel-Arab situation is precarious...described as "touch & go." If war comes, it is likely to come this summer.
The trouble is all about the growth of Israel, past & future.
Russia is promoting the trouble, urging Arabs not to compromise with Israel or with the West, and to fight if necessary. Russian hope is to gain control of the Middle East...with its oil and warm water ports.

April 28, 1956

Instalment buying is spreading, reaching to more & more lines. People are buying not only big stuff on credit...autos, appliances, etc... but also more soft goods lines...clothing, rugs, carpets, draperies, etc.
Retail credit men are not afraid of the trend, as others are. They met here this week to swap views, and were emphatic in conclusions: Most people are good risks, pay bills promptly, with few delinquencies. Over 95% of people who buy on credit come along and pay bills on time.

May 5, 1956

New super-highways are booming land values. Reports to gov't say land has shot up tremendously along routes in some of the states. So if you plan to relocate your plant or business, don't delay too long.

August 4, 1956

Suez is dynamite, could blow up into a hot war at any moment.
Peace or war is up to Nasser. Issue is NOT nationalization... Britain, France and rest of the allies will accept that, if grudgingly. But the allies insist the Canal must be kept open, at reasonable rates.
Britain & France are ready to fight, if Nasser closes the Canal. U.S. doubtless would be drawn in...with ships & planes in Mediterranean.
Our opinion, based on some diplomatic maneuverings now going on, here and in other capitals, is that it won't come to outright fighting, that Nasser will keep the Canal open to everybody, and rates reasonable. But the issue fans old resentments...revives old cries of colonialism... domination by big powers. And it makes Mid-East problems more difficult.

Colonel Abdel Gamal Nasser, leader of Egypt.

The Battle of The Manhole Covers

October 27, 1956

    <u>Beginning of the end of Russian empire</u> is biggest event for West since the war, and starts a chain reaction. First Poland. Then Hungary. (Note that in Hungary there is stiff opposition even to nationalist reds.) Next <u>East Germany</u>. Then <u>Czechoslovakia</u>. Those will come within a year.

November 24, 1956

    <u>"Reopening" clauses on mortgage interest</u> are under discussion by a few lenders...clauses requiring a review of rates every 3 years, with the borrower to pay more if general trend of interest is upward. (But long-range, it might force rates lower...so, idea will be dropped.)

December 1, 1956

    <u>Now is a turning point in air warfare</u> most important in years. It means some changes in defense contract business...plants in your city.
    <u>Fewer fighting planes, more guided missiles</u>. Fewer air bases. More new metals, electronic processes. Less competition for engineers and scientists, less hoarding of technical brains by competing services. Still plenty of demand for them, but not quite as frantic rush to hire.
    <u>Army, short-range missiles</u>...<u>Air Force, long-range missiles</u>... this new alignment of functions after years of inter-service squabbling. Within gov't there's much relief...and many good words for Sec. Wilson.

December 8, 1956

    <u>There's great unrest within Russia</u>. We've heard so for some time and now we have information from reliable sources behind the Iron Curtain.
    <u>Trouble in Russia, not just in satellites</u>. Student rebellions. Factory slowdowns, and even strikes. Farmers holding back food supplies. Everybody everywhere showing a little less fear of the red secret police.
    <u>Even loyalty of the army is in doubt</u>...the army inside Russia.
    <u>All 5-year plans are behind schedule</u>...in satellites AND Russia.

    <u>Does all this foreshadow break-up & revolution in Russia itself</u>? As we see it, the answer is yes...but the time of it is not foreseeable. The Kremlin bosses have power to hang on, to make trouble where they can, partly to look stronger than they are, partly to hold an uneasy control. But the fever of freedom is spreading...within Russia...slowly & surely. May take years. Meanwhile a wobbly Kremlin won't dare start any big war.

1957

January 26, 1957

    <u>Middle East</u>: Why is the U.S. getting involved? Is war likely? Lots of people write to ask whether the real danger is being exaggerated. Is it merely political scaremongering? What happens if we stay out? What do we stand to lose? Is it oil? Or foreign trade? Or what?
    <u>First, the WHY</u>: Our gov't is convinced that communist control of Mid-East would knock the props out from under West Europe's economy, and over the long pull would seriously damage our own economy as well.
    <u>Oil & raw materials are at stake</u>...oil first, the rest later on. Middle East nations are weak economically, despite the rich oil supplies. Britain and France have subsidized them to maintain political stability. But now Britain and France are being pushed out by the new nationalism. There's a vacuum. Russia is ready to filter in, take control of the oil, put Europe at her mercy, and force the U.S. to make up the oil deficits.

<u>U.S. is counting on economic aid to prevent war</u>, or fighting.
Still, our armed forces will be kept in readiness...just in case.
<u>Will the plan work?</u> <u>We think it will</u>. It has done quite well
in a number of places...Iraq, Iran, Pakistan, India, Burma, S. America.
Living standards are better, people are less ripe for red infiltration.
<u>The cost</u>...<u>200 millions a year</u> at the start, still more later.
But that's a low price for waging peace...less costly than waging war.

February 2, 1957

<u>And now many industries are eyeing defense as a gravy train</u>...
big money in contracts...for big companies, with subcontracts to smalls.
Now there's high pressure by business, with entrenched vested interest,
to get more appropriated, more spent. This is natural and understandable,
and yet the over-all fact must be faced...that pressure is overwhelming,
that it's always in one direction, up, and that it means tremendous taxes
on all people...for things that are essentially non-productive.
<u>Defense is practically out of control</u>. Gov't is not its master.
It is the master of gov't...with powerful private interests back of it.
A very dangerous situation, and it's sneaking up on our gov't,
and our economy and our public thinking...almost unnoticed.

February 9, 1957

<u>Point is that ordinary gov't costs less than you might think</u>.
The big and growing realms are (1) defense and the cost of wars in past,
(2) federal funds for all sorts of social programs, aid, public works.
<u>Congress will surely expand welfare programs in the years ahead</u>.
This may call for more taxes, IF total economy doesn't keep expanding.
<u>Something somewhere has got to be shrunk, and it may be defense</u>.
No one dares advocate this at present, for defense is still sacred cow,
but as defense keeps on swelling and as no one seems able to check it,
defense is bound to be an issue...honestly, passionately controversial.

<u>Note how the Washington climate is shifting</u>...into old patterns,
that remind people of the New Deal. Concentration of power in Big Gov't.
Federal funds for state aid. Gov't responsibility for economic health.
Big spending. Wartime taxes still persisting. Talk of economic controls.
Talk of higher taxes...to supply public needs...via the federal gov't.

<u>All these trends are explained vaguely as "Modern Republicanism."</u>
This tag is meant to differentiate it from the Democratic New Dealism.
But...more & more there is getting to be basic and inherent similarity.
Note the little steps, the trends. Note them while they are evolving.
It's part of your long-range business steering job to watch the weather,
and the weather out of Washington is veering.

Downtown Washington, D.C. grows as
federal bureaucracy expands.

February 23, 1957

      People ask WHY gov't won't cut taxes & spending. OK, here's why:
The whole system is geared to spending MORE...on practically every front.
Every gov't administrator, big or little, wants more for HIS functions...
and is backed by like-minded lobbies in Washington, lobbying for more.
Every member of Congress tries to get more for his district, his voters.
Even the average citizen, perhaps even you, has some special interest,
and wants gov't to spend more for that, and economize on other things.
Almost no one dares stick his neck out for cuts...on any specified front.
The total forces for spending exceeds the total of forces for cutting.
And, mind you, this applies to the general public as well as to gov't.

March 2, 1957

      Football is under antitrust, baseball isn't, says Supreme Court.
This is a preposterous situation, and is already leading to speculation
that Congress will now put baseball under antitrust. But it WON'T.
      What will happen say lawyers who keep close tab on the courts:
Courts will put baseball under antitrust. But they also will approve
the "reserve clause," which lets the clubs sign up players for life.
This clause will be held legal...essential to protect "poor" teams.
      So both football & baseball will go along pretty much as-is.

      Small American cars are again under study by U.S. manufacturers.
They were planned in '46 & '47, but were shelved in favor of bigger cars.
Then imports doubled last year, so manufacturers are taking another look.
Still, imports are only 2% of U.S. output, and many private surveys show
that most Americans prefer the bigger domestic cars. So the chances are
that small U.S. cars will be shelved again for at least 2 or 3 years.

"Me and my shadow"

March 16, 1957

      Civil rights, Negro rights: Many congressmen think Ike's plan
is too vague...could be misused by overzealous officials in the gov't,
perhaps even turned against people because of religion or nationality.
If a majority of congressmen voted their convictions, bill would fail.
But the Democrats need to pass it to win back the Negro votes they lost,
and the Republicans need it to try to woo more Negro voters. In the end,
after bickering, fighting, backbiting, name-calling, it WILL be voted.

April 20, 1957

They are all baffled by Eisenhower, his liberal administration. They can't quite believe that a Republican could get himself involved with so many "left-wingers." (They all applaud Brother Edgar Eisenhower.)
For comfort, the conservatives look to Nixon and hope for 1960, when they think they can put Nixon over as nominee, a "real Republican." Our own opinion is that although Nixon will gladly accept their support, he can not be counted among the conservatives. He's now a "moderate," patterned after Eisenhower...who showed the Republicans how to win.

May 25, 1957

Here are generalizations for the future, the next few years:
Higher prices, meaning inflation, will creep upon us further.
The budget is pretty close to being out of control...of ANYONE.
Gov't spending will increase, about as shown at top of this page.
Federal taxes will be generally sustained...only slight cuts.
Local & state taxes are sure to increase from year to year.
Substantial tax relief is not in sight...for people or businesses.
One qualification: Unless there's a sharp limitation of arms.
This could come about...but not within 5 years...possibly in 10.

July 6, 1957

Brand-new products will come in a flood, and the main reason is that business is spending billions in research to develop new products. One big company, deep in such development, tells us 75% of its profits in the early '80s will come from things that are not even known of today. And, of course, a lot of products now standard will fall by the wayside.
Home gadgets, fabulous: Stoves that cook in a flash...no heat.
TV screens on the wall, picture-thin...color and 3 dimensions.
Private planes, helicopters...many more for long & short hauls.
Autos...twice as many in the '80s. Lower. Faster. Smaller.
Traffic jams? Yes, and they're sure to get worse for a few years.
Travel: N.Y. to Paris in 2 hours...N.Y. to Los Angeles, the same.
Weather, more controlled. Clothing, astounding new fabrics.
Houses, new materials & designs. Two-house families...city, and country.
Health, long strides. Cancer, licked. Heart disease, curbed.
Geriatrics, remarkable advances for oldsters. Mental illness, more help.
Life span, substantially longer. Many diseases licked...for young & old.
Plus thousands of things that nobody can even think of today.

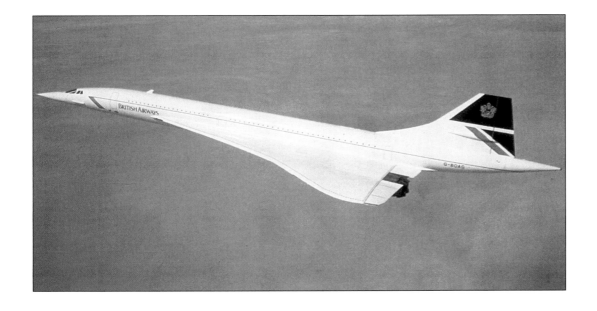

Self-service supermarkets were becoming the norm.

August 3, 1957

  <u>U.S. exports to Europe will be hurt</u> by coming new trade barriers being set up in France, Belgium, W. Germany, Italy, Holland & Luxembourg. Results from a "common market" policy being worked out by these nations, to free-up trade and reduce tariffs among themselves, and curb U.S. goods.
  <u>What can be done about it</u>? Some big firms are enlarging plants they have in Europe, so that when new restrictions are put into effect they'll be able to get around them...by simply boosting production abroad.

August 10, 1957

  <u>Self-service in retail stores</u>: We found many more merchants experimenting with the self-service idea, finding it generally good, planning to extend it. Examples: Men's shirts, hosiery, some appliances, stuff that's more or less standard and well advertised. Also, as usual, market-basket stuff such as groceries, drugs, cosmetics, magazines. Also the 5¢ & 10¢ goods. Everything must be well displayed & packaged. Anyway, self-service is a definite trend, and likely to develop faster.
  <u>Regular stores are beating discount houses</u> in many localities by doing their own discounting...not only in their own bargain basements but in separate warehouses...unattractive places without usual frills.

August 24, 1957

  <u>Who's the leading Republican candidate for 1960</u>? We'd say Nixon. He's running hard, doing everything to make himself suitable, cultivating the right people & causes. Eisenhower back him? Not sure, but probably.
  <u>And who's the leading Democrat</u>? At present we'd say John Kennedy, young senator from Mass...prominent in labor hearings, with his Bro. Bob. He's a middle-of-the-road Democrat...the New England brand of "liberal."

September 7, 1957

    <u>Next five years, for example</u>: They look like slow gradual growth,
not as fast as the growth of the past ten years which made a great boom.
There might come a period of letdown, but it would be only temporary...
a sort of pause, not really serious, not any deep slump or depression.
    <u>In five years, a great NEW boom</u>...starting around 1962 or 1963.
This is no crystal ball vision. It's factual, even the time is factual.
    <u>It will be a GREATER boom than that of the past decade, postwar</u>,
and the reasons for this are perfectly evident, too. There's no mystery.
    <u>Start with past births</u>. They make a firm fact, to be projected.
    <u>Extra-high births of the '40s & '50s</u> produce a population bulge
in the '60s & '70s...of young men & women, marrying or ready to marry.
It's as simple as that. Marriages make homes, and homes make business.
    <u>Then add another fact...the momentum of new products, new ideas</u>,
that flow from technical, scientific, mechanical development in the past.
    <u>The rise in total goods & services</u> is statistically measurable.
Through the '60s, about 4% a year, and through the '70s approaching 5%.
This refers to GNP, or gross national product. A great flood of stuff.
    <u>It means more things for more people</u>, rising standard of living.
This increase in living standards has been rapid in the past 10 years,
and it will be even more rapid in next 10 or 20 years...further & faster.
    <u>Then consider gov't policy ahead</u>, for it determines the climate,
and the climate is important, for it can either stimulate or retard.
    <u>The political climate is bullish</u>...both parties and all groups.
They are committed to a "full employment," an economy going at full speed,
with the gov't playing as a sort of partner...to make it go like that.

    <u>But there's bad news too, inflation</u>...higher prices all the way.
Prices are now high, and they will go higher. In 10 years, 15% higher.
In 20 years, 35% higher. In 25 years, 50% higher. <u>The dollar shrinking</u>.
    <u>The No. 1 cause: Wages being forced up faster than productivity</u>.
This is a sore point among the professional unioneers, and they deny it.
They put the blame on excessive profits. But profits stay about level,
or even shrink in relation to total volume, while wages keep on going up.
    <u>Furthermore, the whole world economy is headed toward inflation</u>.
People en masse, everywhere, want more goods than are being supplied.
In one way or another governments are inflating their supplies of money,
injecting varying degree of phoniness into the money. It loses value,
and so the prices of things go up. We buy a lot from other countries.
Their higher prices enter into our costs, and add to our own inflation.
    <u>It's a world-wide circle</u>...cause & effect...world-wide inflation.

    <u>As for the political forces here at home, they are inflationary</u>.
No matter what the men of any particular regime may say, they are pressed
to expand public spending on this & that cause...all causes being "good."
One or more of such regimes, regardless of party, is apt to run deficits.
In next 20 years our gov't is practically sure to live beyond its means,
and this will be inflationary...on top of the other causes.
    <u>Theoretically there's a way out</u>...to tax, to balance the budget.
But there always comes a time when people relax and enjoy extravagance.
They vote for a regime that gives them the big spending that they want,
not mindful of the deficits...or the inflation that comes in the wake.
    This is not cynical...it's realistic...it's the way things are.

    <u>OK then, if we are in for inflation, what's to be done about it</u>?
    <u>Buy & own THINGS, tangible things of permanent value</u>. Examples:
Your family home. Or land or other real estate...city, suburban, farm.
(And pay special attention to investments in resort or leisure locations.)
Prices of practically all things will rise. Even diamonds, rare jewels.
    <u>Buy & own stocks, equities</u>, for generally they will go higher.
Stable stocks if you want income, growth stocks if you want to hold them.

Russia's Sputnik satellite was a wake-up call for Uncle Sam.

Awake at last!

October 12, 1957

<u>Is world war imminent</u>? <u>No</u>.
Does it bring war any close? No.
<u>Did the Russians outsmart us</u>? <u>Yes</u>, of course they did.
Are their scientists good? Yes. Our own scientists have said so,
but our military men and our civilian officials have pooh-poohed them,
and it is by this level that our public has been misled.

<u>Do we have as good a satellite</u>, or better? <u>Frankly, don't know</u>,
and we do not quite trust what we are told by the head man about this.
<u>What about all this talk of going to the moon</u>, and first?
It sounds fantastic, but scientists who seem to have feet on the ground
tell us that it's the real thing, that it's possible, and can be done.
They differ as to time. One says in 12 months. Several say 2 or 3 years.
Most assent only to "years," and let it go at that.

November 30, 1957

<u>Small foreign cars are just a fad...the opinion in Detroit</u>.
Majority view is that the fad will fade, as it has done in the past.
(Our opinion is that the U.S. companies are being too complacent,
and that there will be a much bigger market for smaller second cars.)

1958

January 4, 1958

<u>And now look ahead, realistically</u>: Missiles solve no problems.
Even the best of them solve no problems...for both sides can have them.
Each side can devastate the other side, and simultaneously be devastated.
Each side knows that a missile war will bring no victory...just suicide.
<u>This is why the ONLY solution is disarmament in the years ahead</u>.

February 8, 1958

<u>Russian sputniks made us into a nation of neurotics on defense</u>.
Some of the anxiety was natural & proper, but most of it was whipped up
to make propaganda for extremes in defense. This undermined moderation.

<u>From that frenzy we are now delivered, thanks to our own shot</u>, with our own satellite. Now we are only semi-neurotic, which is better.

<u>What still makes jitters is the fear of sudden missile warfare</u>. <u>That's wholly unwarranted</u>. It's neither imminent nor probable. Russia just does not have the stuff to do it with...and neither do we.

Besides, we do have the power of retaliation, and all set to go, because of our bases, our man-driven bombers, and our plenty of bombs.

April 12, 1958

<u>Department stores, hiring of Negroes</u> as salespeople and clerks: A nationwide movement is on for "merit hiring." Some stores have done it on experimental scale. Results fair to good. Recently in Washington, D.C. the Negroes, prompted by their churches, boycotted a few selected stores for a single day...or, as they put it, "abstained" from buying for a day. There was no trouble, no violence, no "incident," but the stores felt it.

Now some stores in the upper echelon are "considering" hiring of Negro women behind the counter, not right now, but by next Christmas.

July 26, 1958

<u>As a nation, we'll have to get used to being "world policeman,"</u> a role we didn't choose and don't like. It's one of the responsibilities that goes with leadership...can't avoid it. It's a matter of survival.

<u>What we long for is peace, but what we will have is cold war</u> for a decade or more. Often it will approach hot war, as in Mid-East.

October 25, 1958

<u>Foreign auto makers are gleeful over the new U.S. models</u>... fatter, longer, costlier...leaving small imports a rich market here. Ads will play up the "economy" of their cars, against our "gas-eaters," and they'll push for upper-income trade that wants to be different.

<u>Exports of U.S. cars are falling off</u>. Our prices are too high, and foreign gas costs too much for most people abroad to run big cars.

A '59 Cadillac exemplified Detroit's continuing love affair with big cars.

December 20, 1958

<u>Next, take a look at potential costs of the new Space Agency</u>,
now a civilian scientific agency, separate from the military missiles.
It is in charge of moon shots, outer space platforms, and the like.
Now it has a "mere" 327 millions, but will soon be asking for billions.
Congress does not understand it, for laymen can't, but Congress jumps
whenever anyone says "Russia, boo," or otherwise pushes the panic button.
<u>This is why space "exploring" is headed toward the billions</u>,
the cries for pioneering science out-shouting any murmurs for economy.
The question, "Can we afford it?" The answer given, "We MUST afford it."
And now the moon is not enough. Early next year it will be Mars & Venus.

December 26, 1958

<u>The face of America is going to change rapidly & radically</u>.
<u>Cities spreading, fanning out</u>, to take on new enterprises.
<u>Highway networks are growing faster</u>...to relieve the congestion.
But the highways often make new congested areas not originally imagined.
Commuting distances longer, so more families with two cars, "of course."
<u>Further flight from the farm</u>...bigger farms, more machinery...
and wage lures from nearby plants...many of them in the farm areas.

<u>Local civic problems greater</u>, with expansion of the cities.
<u>Higher local taxes</u> to support all the special services demanded.
More police & fire services. Better water supply. Health, sanitation,
big expansion in those facilities. More electric power. More telephones.

<u>A further revolution in merchandising is coming in the 60's</u>.
More chains. Larger stores. Many stores taking additional lines.
<u>The food store more & more a "general store</u>," with other things
than groceries. Super-super-market...the end of this trend is not yet.

Farm mechanization fed the flight from countryside to city.

DR. FIDEL CASTRO

January 10, 1959

U.S. investments in Cuba seem safe, despite Castro upheaval. Castro did accept red help but now he's called back some solid citizens to staff gov't posts. Sugar crop is OK. The country will be solvent. Companies planning to do business in Cuba may still do so in safety.

1959

February 14, 1959

Then there are the credit cards, growing by leaps and bounds. Persons with cards charge on them...scope widening on what's chargeable. Businesses that are patronized pay a commission to credit card company. But some companies have their own credit cards and save the commissions. The cards do seem to spur sales & patronage...they have "snob appeal."

March 28, 1959

Kennedy has the lead, which is his weakness, for all the others are trying to knock him out without being caught at it in any open way. The professional politicians have their fingers crossed on Kennedy... "He looks too immature." Many of them think of him as winner of VP.

Religious issue (Kennedy) haunts Democrats. They say so frankly. They fear Catholic voters if he isn't named, and Protestants if he is.

The election itself: Democrats have edge...IF they don't split.

May 16, 1959

Note the imported stuff in the stores...more than ever before. Most of it is of good quality, not shoddy, not substandard as formerly.

They are made especially for U.S. consumers. Foreign producers are scientific about shipping goods here. They don't just ship anything, they size up the needs & wants of U.S. shoppers. They manufacture things that will SELL here...specially designed, packaged and priced to sell. They have Americans in their plants abroad to advise on the production, and they know how to advertise their things, using American agencies.

More countries are coming into our markets...with new products, or their version of products that other countries sell here successfully.

All this is good for our consumers, our stores, our merchants.

But it's hard on our manufacturers, producers and their workers. American companies are fighting imports by trying to shave their prices, sometimes possible, sometimes not. Also by having their own plants abroad and then "importing" their own goods. Also by buying the foreign goods, finished or unfinished, thus getting the advantage of the lower prices. A few examples: Steel wire & bars. Lumber. Plywood. Bearings. Motors. Building materials. Packaging machines. And lots of others.

An American compact—the 1960 Valiant.

May 30, 1959

> The 1960 model autos: New designs are all set, all decided on.
> New small U.S. cars: Each of Big 3 will have one...to compete
with Rambler and Studebaker Lark, and also with the popular imports.
> Names: General Motors, Corvair. Ford, Falcon. Chrysler, Valiant.
Corvair out early in Oct...Falcon later in Oct...Valiant not until Dec.
> These smalls won't be "sports cars"...as some of the imports are.
They will be pushed mostly as "family cars," but a new sales approach
will also feature a "second car" angle...one for the wife or teen-ager.

June 6, 1959

> We call the decade "The Soaring Sixties." Economic advancement
will be greater than at any time in our entire history, even greater
than the boom of the last decade, the boom that ran from '47 to '57.
> Great changes, shifts and dislocations...not universal gains.
Most lines up but some lines down...squeezed by the growing competition.
Good times for the majority but not for all. Many troubles, new problems.
> Next 3 or 4 years, normal growth, average growth, but not a boom.
Perhaps a pause, or even mild slide, in 1961-62...then healthy recovery.
> The boom should start in 1963-64, and run through the decade,
accelerating at a fast pace in the final half, the last five years.
Pauses in the progress, perhaps a pause in 1965-66, a mild recession.
But the period as a whole will be essentially boomy, the trend upward.
> Growth of total economy, 47%...REAL growth in physical volume.
In 10 years, GNP, Gross National Product, will be around 700 billions,
showing a startling rise from its present level of about 475 billions.

> A creeping inflation, prices rising throughout the whole decade.
The price level 10 years from now probably 15% or so higher than now.
This is not a horrendous inflation picture, but it must be reckoned with
in all business and personal plans...especially in investments.

> No big world war...for neither side will dare to start it.
Perhaps a couple of flare-ups in Mid-East or Asia, but not spreading,
and not big enough to upset our economy. Nothing as big as Korea was.

June 20, 1959

> Atomic fall-out from missiles: The imminent hearings in Congress
will not bring out the full truth about the discovered dangers to health.
> There are still "secrets" that prevent or restrict disclosures.
The secrets are subjects of whispers, but the military men suppress them,
or deny them, or call them "irresponsible." But they'll soon come out,
and they'll show that ANY nation will damage the health of its own people
if it uses A-or-H bombs against another. Both sides already KNOW this.
That's why it's reasonable to assume that neither side will ever use them.

July 4, 1959

> A fresh wave of Japanese imports will soon head toward the U.S.
Japanese are now making a dent in U.S. sales of cameras, optical goods,
radios, sewing machines, textiles, etc. They find selling here so good
that they are rushing more stuff designed especially for the U.S. market.
> Washing machines...first break into the big appliance field.
> Transistor TV sets...portable, small, prices way below domestic.
> Portable typewriters...plus adding machines and calculators.
> Small pleasure boats, plastic & plywood...and at lower prices.
> Autos...two more makers of small cars are eyeing U.S. market.
> Quality? Still some sleazy stuff. Be on the lookout for it.
But we've examined samples of many new lines and quality seems good.

July 18, 1959

It's basically a communist situation in Cuba, reds pulling wires that make Castro jump. They could take over, but prefer undercover role. Communists are also at work elsewhere in the Caribbean and Latin America, notably Central America, Venezuela, Ecuador...and our own Puerto Rico. All governments are worried, but our government avoids taking the lead because of extreme sensitiveness to the communist charge of imperialism.

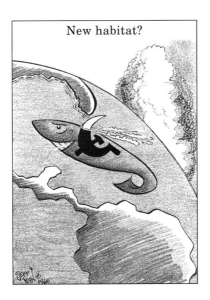
New habitat?

August 8, 1959

Just back from Russia with Nixon.

People were often skeptical about what we told them of U.S. Told them simple facts, but they couldn't understand...hard to believe.

They want peace, and they often asked why WE threatened THEM. Told them we too want peace...but their leaders tell them otherwise.

Will the Russians rise and rebel? No, not the slightest chance. They are SO much better off than they were. They accept it thankfully. They are apart from their rulers...they can't imagine a free democracy. As individuals they don't count for much...it's the state that counts... and the state is a sort of massive IT. (All incidents drive this home.)

Vice-President Nixon confronts Soviet Premier Nikita Khrushchev at a Moscow trade fair.

September 26, 1959

Revolutionary new office machines designed for SMALL businesses are coming on the market fast. Simple electronic devices. Bookkeepers. Cash registers that keep records and make change. Devices for copying, duplicating, sorting, checking, making up payrolls. New magnetic inks to simplify coding, account handling, inventory control, other records. Printers that will print letterheads and form letters in one operation. Equipment that photographs copy automatically, makes multilith plates for printing...in two minutes...at low cost. Telephone writing machine that transmits a note, even a scribbled note, if nobody answers phone. Scores of other machines that do paper work..."the curse of business."

October 31, 1959

Much more cargo will be shipped by air in another five years... even heavy things. Airlines are getting ready to buy new planes to do it, and rates will be adjusted so as to compete better with trucks & rails.

See some of the advantages to businesses: Smaller inventories, less need for huge warehouse space. Fresher stocks, less shelf-aging. And deliveries on most things will be speedier...fewer delays in transit.

It will be a major challenge to trucks & rails on freight hauls. Air freight is small now, a drop in the bucket, because of limitations on weight and high costs. But it's growing...and this will be cumulative.

November 7, 1959

Mail by wire, facsimile service, Western Union, after Dec. 1, between New York, Washington, Chicago, San Francisco and Los Angeles. It will transmit exact reproductions of letters, bills, graphs, charts, invoices, legal documents up to 7 x 9 inches. (But not photographs.) Central offices will handle at first...later direct to individual firms. Cost depends on length. One full page, from coast to coast, $7.90.

To test it we sent our last week's Letter of four full pages from Washington to New York. Time per page 17 min...cost per page $4.10.

It's going to be useful in business. Shall report further.

"Get lost"

THE DEMOCRATS LET CUBA BECOME A RUSSIAN SATELLITE

CASTRO CAME TO POWER UNDER A REPUBLICAN PRESIDENT

1960s

PITTSBURGH
student co-ordinating
committee

MARCH ON
WASHINGTON

The Sixties: a decade of rapid social change and violent domestic conflict—assassinations of revered leaders, cities in flames, college campuses under siege. Previously in American history, such turmoil had usually been rooted in economic distress, but the Sixties enjoyed the longest economic expansion ever—nine years of strong, uninterrupted growth, with big gains in productivity and personal income and declining rates of poverty. But the boom took place during, and was in part fueled by, the most unpopular war in American history, Vietnam. And the expansion of the '60s also took place during a period of mounting impatience with racial and economic inequality. Rather than buy domestic peace, the boom fueled an acceleration of expectations that couldn't be fulfilled, especially among poor urban blacks. And some white suburban youths, indulged materially and emotionally by parents compensating for the deprivation of their own Depression childhoods, rebelled against their own middle-class affluence and success to become passive "hippies" or left-wing radicals.

The Sixties was a decade of contrasts: humanitarian concerns and extreme self-indulgence; celebration of peace and love amid violent protest; broad, rapid gains in the rights and prosperity of black Americans, but devastating riots in urban ghettos; reckless experimentation with illegal, mind-altering drugs amid a growing passion for natural foods, consumer protection and auto safety. As in every era, media attention on rebellious behavior gave a mistaken impression that it was more widespread than it really was. Hippies, ghetto rioters, violent student protesters and free-love advocates were a small minority in the '60s, but depictions of their actions and ideas seemed to dominate the headlines and airwaves.

Over the course of the decade, the U.S. plunged into the first foreign war that it would eventually lose. Nearly a century after the Civil War, black Americans finally won the full rights and privileges of citizenship. And picking up the loose threads of feminism from earlier decades, American women began moving away from the home-and-family orientation of the '50s to press for equal status with men in

	SOVIETS SHOOT DOWN U-2, DISRUPTING SUMMIT.	CHINA-RUSSIA RELATIONS TURN SOUR.			PEACE CORPS ESTABLISHED.	
WAVE OF CIVIL RIGHTS SIT-INS HITS SOUTH.						
		CONGRESS PASSES VOTING-RIGHTS LAW.	KENNEDY ELECTED PRESIDENT.	BAY OF PIGS INVASION FAILS.		BERLIN WALL GOES UP.
1960				**1961**		

the workplace. A remarkable new pharmaceutical, the contraceptive pill, gave women unprecedented control over unwanted pregnancy. It also contributed, along with changing social mores, to a surge in premarital sexual relations.

Increasing federal control

During the first 60 years of the century, federal control over the American economy had ebbed and flowed through three wars and many phases of the business cycle, but the broad trend was always toward more control. In the '60s the trend accelerated faster than at any time since the New Deal.

Government regulation surged. Money poured out of Washington in countless new social programs, at the same time that defense spending on the war in Southeast Asia soared. A government dedicated to providing guns *and* butter sowed the seeds of inflation that would explode early in the '70s.

The first year of the new decade, 1960, was a time of humiliation for America. The U.S. admitted to aerial spying on Russia when the Soviets shot down one of our U-2 planes, and a scheduled summit between U.S. and Soviet leaders was canceled. Russia openly embraced its client state in Cuba. When anti-American rioting erupted in Japan, America's most cooperative friend since 1945, the Japanese government canceled an imminent visit from President Eisenhower. The economy, sluggish since the last recession in '57-58, began contracting again in the spring of '60.

JFK's New Frontier

John F. Kennedy, a charismatic young Democratic senator with modest prior accomplishments, sought the presidency with an unusual blend of conservative and liberal proposals. He attacked the Republicans for a weak economy, and he urged deep cuts in income-tax rates and protectionist tariffs. He accused the Republicans of softness toward the Russians and called for stepped-up defense spending to close an alleged "missile gap" of Soviet superiority. On the domestic front, he urged equal rights for

blacks, new initiatives against poverty, federal support of the arts, and a renewed individual commitment to public service.

Kennedy was elected by a razor-thin margin of electoral votes and popular support—just two-tenths of 1% of the votes cast. In his three years in office, Kennedy couldn't convince Congress to adopt much of his program. He did win approval for tariff cuts, and he pushed the U.S. into an ambitious program of space exploration.

The U.S. began closing in on Russia's space lead when Alan Shepard became the first American in space in 1961, and John Glenn became the first American to orbit the earth the following year. In the last year of the decade, the U.S. finally put men on the moon, astronauts Neil Armstrong and Buzz Aldrin.

Despite a dramatic desegregation campaign throughout the South in the first years of the '60s, Kennedy failed, as had Eisenhower, to win congressional enactment of an open-accommodations law giving blacks equal access to all public commercial facilities in America—including buses, restaurants, hotels and theaters.

In foreign policy, Kennedy took a generally tougher stance against communist expansion than Eisenhower had. With a dim prospect of success, Kennedy gave approval to a secret plan, conceived by his predecessor's Central Intelligence Agency, for an invasion of Cuba by anti-Castro Cuban expatriates. Undersupported by the U.S. military and expected by Castro's forces, the invasion ended in slaughter on the beach at the Bay of Pigs. Later in '61, the Soviets built a wall along the boundary between East and West Berlin, to stem the tide of East Germans trying to flee communism. Kennedy called up American reserve soldiers and sent battle-ready troops to West Berlin, and many Americans feared that war with Russia was at hand. The crisis subsided, but the Kennedy defense buildup continued.

Cuban missile crisis

When U.S. intelligence detected the recent installation of Soviet missiles in Cuba in the fall of '62, Kennedy ordered a quarantine of Cuban waters and moved to intercept a Soviet ship. The world held

ONE-MAN, ONE-VOTE APPORTIONMENT UPHELD.	CUBAN MISSILE CRISIS: SOVIETS BACK DOWN.	NUCLEAR TEST BAN AGREED TO BY U.S., U.K., U.S.S.R.		KENNEDY ASSASSINATED. JOHNSON SWORN IN.
FIRST U.S. MANNED ORBITAL FLIGHT.			KING LEADS CIVIL RIGHTS RALLY IN WASHINGTON.	
1962	FIRST U.S. COMMUNICATIONS SATELLITE.	CARSON'S "SILENT SPRING" PUBLISHED.	**1963**	

its breath, fearing it was on the brink of nuclear war. But in the face of Kennedy's resolve, the Soviets agreed to remove all offensive missiles from Cuba. Meanwhile, across the Pacific in Indochina, Kennedy sought to bolster pro-American regimes in South Vietnam and Laos against communist insurgencies from North Vietnam and within their own societies. He first sent military advisers and later small forces of troops trained in guerrilla warfare.

Kennedy's administration was tragically cut short by an assassin's bullet on November 22, 1963. The task of completing much unfinished business fell to his vice-president, longtime Senate leader Lyndon B. Johnson. Under Johnson's prodding, and in part as a memorial to the slain President, Congress enacted Kennedy's proposed deep cuts in tax rates and passed an open-accommodations civil rights law.

In 1964, the Republicans nominated a pure conservative, Senator Barry Goldwater of Arizona, who called for balanced federal budgets, a slowdown in welfare spending, and a tough line against communism. The Democrats appealed to public concerns that Goldwater would immerse the nation in a major war in Southeast Asia. Candidate Johnson, while secretly planning a broad expansion of the war in Vietnam, talked like a man of peace and won in a landslide.

Escalation in Vietnam

Over the following two years, with broad support in Congress and from the American people, Johnson matched the communist escalation in Vietnam by pouring U.S. aid and soldiers into Southeast Asia. Spurred by civil rights protests and later rioting in the black ghettos of Los Angeles, Newark, Detroit and other cities, Johnson convinced Congress to fund the "Great Society," an enormous expansion of federal aid for urban development, education, transportation, nutrition and medical care. Stringent new clean-water rules were enacted, and for the first time ever, the government guaranteed medical care for the elderly and the poor through new programs called Medicare and Medicaid.

LBJ's "Great Society" was popular with the voters, but the war in Vietnam fell out of favor. The U.S. death toll mounted—some 500 deaths a week in early '68—and a guerrilla war in the jungle looked less and less winnable. Opposition rose in every segment of U.S. society, but especially among affluent youths and intellectuals on America's college campuses, who marched, rioted and occupied buildings in protest. There was open resistance to the military draft, and some youths fled to Canada to avoid military service. The cost of the war, about $25 billion in '67 alone, was kicking up inflation to a level then considered alarming—4% to 6% a year.

Facing challenges within his own party, especially from presidential candidate Senator Eugene McCarthy, Johnson decided in '68 not to run for reelection. He began to limit the scope of the war and called for negotiations with communist North Vietnam.

Protest at home

But the war raged on, and violence in America escalated, too. The spring and summer of '68 were darkened by the assassinations of civil rights leader Martin Luther King Jr. and Robert F. Kennedy, who was John Kennedy's brother, a senator from New York, and a candidate for the Democratic nomination for president. Outside the Democratic convention in Chicago that summer, local police beat anti-Vietnam protesters. In the fall, a sharply divided Democratic Party, under nominee Vice-President Hubert H. Humphrey, narrowly lost the White House to former Vice-President Richard M. Nixon, who said that he had a secret plan for ending U.S. involvement in the war.

Nixon entered office in the last year of a wild decade, seeming to offer solutions to the lawlessness, unwinnable war, social turmoil and rising inflation that troubled many Americans. But he made no major reversals of Johnson's programs, either in Vietnam or domestic affairs. Like Johnson, he pressed for a negotiated settlement in Vietnam while continuing to support the anti-communist

U.S. OFFERS PANAMA NEW CANAL TREATY.	OMNIBUS CIVIL RIGHTS BILL PASSES. GULF OF TONKIN RESOLUTION PASSES.	U.S. BEGINS BOMBING NORTH VIETNAM.	JOHNSON SENDS TROOPS TO DOMINICAN REPUBLIC. WATTS RIOTS IN LOS ANGELES.	CULTURAL REVOLUTION BEGINS IN CHINA. "GREAT SOCIETY" PROGRAMS VOTED.	MEDICARE BEGINS.	NATIONAL ORGANIZATION FOR WOMEN FORMS.
1964		**1965**			**1966**	

South militarily. But opposition to the war mounted with the abolition of draft deferments for postgraduate students. Like undergraduate deferments, they had insulated America's more-fortunate families from military service and the tragedy of losing their sons in an unpopular war. The war in Southeast Asia, unlike World War II and Korea, was fought disproportionately by America's poor.

Nixon, an ideological moderate with a strong pragmatic streak, tried to calm the anxieties of rapid social change by slowing the growth of federal welfare programs and court-ordered school desegregation. And he sought to reorient the federal judiciary toward the political center by appointing conservatives to the Supreme Court and lower federal courts. He vowed to fight rising inflation, too, but there were few tools available to him in an economy running flat out with strong consumer spending, massive government spending on warfare and social welfare, and—as a result—rising federal budget deficits. Even as war raged in Southeast Asia, Nixon in '69 entered into discussions with the Soviet Union on reducing the two nations' arsenals of long-range nuclear weapons.

Amid the explosive social change, American businesses and their employees generally enjoyed good times. The economy expanded continuously from 1961 through 1969, pushed by consumer demand, military spending and social welfare program. Productivity rose strongly, and so did inflation-adjusted worker pay. Unemployment was low, and the poverty rate fell. The U.S. stock market surged to new heights. Energy was abundant and cheap. Suburban growth pressed outward from every big city. America's high-tech innovations—semiconductors, photocopiers, pharmaceuticals, mainframe computers and jet aircraft—flooded the world and maintained American dominance of world exports, largely unchallenged since the U.S. emerged uniquely unscathed from the devastation of World War II.

The U.S. launched the first satellites capable of relaying telephone and television signals around the world, which would later lead to the transmission of TV news images as events were taking place.

Economic troubles ahead

But there were ominous clouds on the economic horizon by the end of the '60s: mounting budget deficits, with small surpluses in only 1960 and 1969 (the last balanced budgets Washington would achieve for decades to come); rising inflation; military overcommitment; soaring costs for social welfare programs, soon to be considered entitlements of citizenship; a growing dependence on oil imports from the politically volatile Middle East; slowing productivity growth, due to high inflation, underinvestment in capital goods, growing government regulation, and a surge of inexperienced baby-boom youths into the workplace.

By the end of the '60s America was also beginning to feel the pinch of competition in international trade. After 20 years of rebuilding their industrial bases, with extensive American financial and technological aid, Japan, Germany and other manufacturing nations were now tough competitors. Imports were rising strongly, as Americans—especially young adults—developed a taste for smaller, fuel-efficient imported cars and inexpensive consumer electronics. And the "green revolution" of agricultural science, spread by the U.S. across the globe, was turning former importers of American food into self-sufficient nations—and sometimes new competitors of the U.S. in food exporting.

As the tumultuous '60s came to a close, America was still the world's strongest economy, but the rules of the game were changing. Technology and capital were spreading around the world, raising living standards and improving competitiveness. Other nations—big and small, industrialized and undeveloped—were flexing their muscles and beginning to question whether America had any special claim on wisdom, ingenuity or hard work. A lot of America's own citizens were wondering, too.

ISRAEL WINS
SIX-DAY WAR.

VIETNAM
PEACE
TALKS
OPEN.

AMERICANS LAND
ON MOON.

RACE RIOTS IN
NEWARK AND
DETROIT.

DEMONSTRATIONS
AGAINST VIETNAM
WAR SPREAD.

NIXON ELECTED
PRESIDENT.

NIXON BEGINS
VIETNAM TROOP
WITHDRAWALS.

TET OFFENSIVE
IN VIETNAM.

KING AND
ROBERT
KENNEDY
ASSASSINATED.

1967   FIRST HEART
TRANSPLANT.

1968

1969

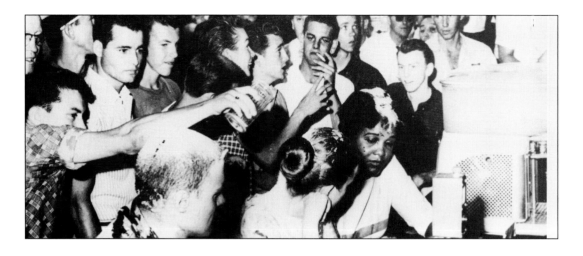

1960

March 12, 1960

Negro demonstrations are going to spread to Northern cities...
in protest on eating places, hotels, soda fountains, jobs and housing.
Confidential reports direct from Negro leaders on plans for extension
have been given to the White House and the Nixon committee, and officials
are "much concerned." A public statement may be forthcoming soon.
"Passive resistance" and "non-violence" are Negro keynotes.
The philosophy and the operating techniques are modeled after Ghandi.
If there's violence (and there may be), "it must start only with whites."

April 2, 1960

Great changes are occurring in the patterns of business.
Some lines are growing fast, some slowly, some are shrinking.
The most spectacular point is the rapid ascent of "services"...
as distinguished from other retailing. Services cover a wide range...
hotels & motels, restaurants, amusements, movies, repairs of all kinds.

April 9, 1960

The thing to watch is the TREND...it is toward liberal-social.
Even though the measures finally enacted this year are not wild & woolly,
they show the leaning...toward popular benefits...more in the future.
What you see in next 3 months is the start in that general direction.
Or, to be more accurate, a re-start, a new start...under the influence
of lessons the New Deal taught...that benefits make millions of votes.
Observe that this trend is in BOTH parties, not limited to one.
It is stronger among Democrats, but even the Republicans have shifted,
from right to middle, or from former middle to a bit left of middle.

April 16, 1960

Blunt truth about Cuba now is that there's no chance of friendship
with Castro regime...no hope of cooperation...just more abuse to come.
Anti-Castro sentiment is rising in Cuba, but it's not centered anywhere
in any one group. Instead, a number of little bands, each ready to jump.
This will make Castro seem a martyr and strengthen him...temporarily.
Our sources within Cuba think a successful revolt will be postponed
for a good many months, perhaps even until next year. Dangerous for us.

Campaigner John Kennedy greets a clergyman. Concerns that Kennedy's Catholic religion would prevent his nomination proved unfounded.

May 14, 1960

Politics, W. Va., Kennedy: The dominant factor, his personality. Demonstrated his pulling power as an attractive individual on the stump. As for church issue, it isn't dead but it's cut down to the normal size. Also...W. Va. shows how wrong a lot of political prognosticators can be.

Looks as if Kennedy is headed goalward, with no one in between. This impression is strengthened by some advance information which we have on forthcoming announcements for Kennedy in Calif., Mich., Ill., and N.J.

June 4, 1960

Politics of the next 10 years will focus sharply on the aged. You see it in the sudden burst of interest in health insurance programs. This is partly for election campaign purposes, but it goes much deeper. It reflects what the politicians know: That with 20 million past age 65, with that many people interested in income, pensions, health insurance, there's sure to be great mass pressure for gov't action for the aged.

June 11, 1960

There's some hope of Castro's overthrow by counter-revolution. The Cuban groups opposed to him are numerous, but they are not united. The Catholic Church is now anti. So are all the liberals...privately... but most of them are afraid to speak out. As for former Batista men, the "white rose" groups in Miami & N.Y...they are tarred, out of favor. Anti-Castro forces are trying to coalesce, but are not doing very well.

So...overthrow is NOT expected within the next 7 or 8 months. And when it comes there will be a new administration in Washington. (Both parties dread a crisis with Cuba during our domestic campaign.)

June 18, 1960

The riots in Japan do not disclose fully the basic trouble. It's NOT just domestic politics and NOT just commie agitation. True, the riots were organized by reds, financed from Russia & China. True, the reds gained face, and we lost face badly in the whole world.

But it goes deeper. It's the horror of war among all Japanese, even among the great majority who are not communists and not socialists. Even many of them dislike the tie-up with the U.S..."a warlike nation." They remember Hiroshima, Nagasaki. They are the only people in the world who have had actual experience at the receiving end of atomic bombs.

This widespread sentiment is bound to weaken the Tokyo gov't, weaken the ties with the U.S., and make our relations less friendly. Kishi's successor will have to bow, and be less subservient to the U.S.

Japan began to compete for the TV market. Here, workers assemble Sony sets.

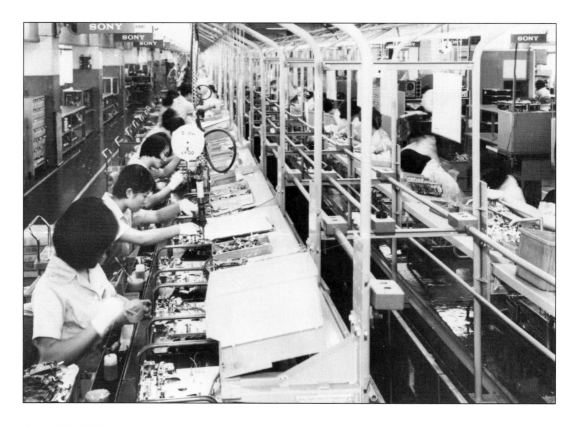

June 18, 1960

    <u>At the root of all the trouble is trade</u>...freer foreign trade...
for it's a MUST with the Japanese. They MUST have outlet for their goods.
It's a matter of national life or death. They fought one war to get it,
and they lost, but the push is still there...toward the ultimate goal.
    <u>They'd like to get rid of the bossing by the U.S. on trade</u>.
They'd like to sell us more...compete in our markets and world markets.
    <u>The Japanese CAN compete</u>, are doing it now, can do it much more.
    <u>They have lower labor costs, can run rings around us on prices</u>,
and are satisfied with narrow profit margins. They imitate, they copy,
and their imitations are now pretty good. As for quality, it was shoddy
before the war, but the Japanese have learned and quality now is good.
    <u>Look at our imports from Japan</u>: Last year, a billion dollars...
up 50% over previous year. And this year, almost certain to be higher.
We take about a third of Japan's exports...the proportion likely to rise.
    <u>Look at what we buy</u>...competitive with our own domestic things.
    Note that each of these items is subject to great expansion:
    <u>Clothing & textiles</u>, men's & women's...wool, cotton and silk.
    <u>Iron & steel products</u>...our steel strike gave them a boost.
    Radio sets. Plywood. Toys. Pottery & chinaware.
    Sewing machines. Nuts, bolts, nails. Carpets. Optical goods.
    Photo apparatus. Sporting goods. Lighters. Costume jewelry.
    Canned fish...tuna, crab, others. Frozen tuna, for our canners.
    Typewriters, adding machines, calculators. Boats. Appliances.
    <u>And now Japanese autos are coming along</u>...medium-small, sturdy.
    <u>We've got to get ready for more competition</u>...it's coming fast.
    And a lot of our American businesses are going to be affected.
    We in the U.S. in the next couple of years must face the facts,
that our export business is not the big dog that it has been for years,
the past 10 or 15 or more years. Now we are up against stiff competition
from Western Europe, even from Japan, discussed earlier in this Letter.
    If we see all this coming, and take steps, we'll avert a crisis.
If we don't, we'll run into trouble...and not quite know what hit us.

July 16, 1960

<u>Kennedy: He lives, works, plays hard</u>. Drives an open car FAST.
A "regular guy." Drinks a little but not much. Wears natty clothes,
changes often to suit the occasion...usually plain styles, not extremes.
A "family man," and his family life is often gay. Plays with his child,
and has another on the way, due to arrive about the time of the elections.
Close to brothers and sisters in all matters, even outside of politics.
The whole Kennedy family would doubtless take part in the Presidency.

September 3, 1960

<u>TV as an influence</u>: Practical politicians in both parties say
that TV will bring out bigger percentage of voters this year than usual.
Early tests are now showing that it even splits families to an extent.
That's why both parties are now paying extra attention to the women vote.
And the TV debates may prove to be THE determiner of final outcome.

October 22, 1960

<u>Kennedy is more "conservative," less "liberal," than he talks</u>.
This is said to allay the extreme fears of a business bust if he wins.
Business climate better under Nixon. More stir & excitement under Kennedy,
and a little more chance of inflation. Business ups & downs under either.
Big bust under neither.

October 29, 1960

<u>Cuba: Invasion by anti-Castro forces from Florida is the bunk</u>.
Ranks are too thin...risks too great...and our gov't would prevent it.

November 5, 1960

<u>Nixon's spurt is probably too late and too little
to overtake Kennedy, who still seems to have lead</u>.

November 26, 1960

<u>"Youth Corps," Kennedy's plan</u>, training young men to go abroad,
isn't merely campaign fluff. It will be pushed in Congress next year.
Idea is to sign up thousands of young men for 3 years, send them abroad
to backward nations as teachers, technicians, farm experts, engineers.

January 7, 1961

<u>Might as well prepare to accept YEARS of bigger gov't spending</u>.
Not just the normal increases that go along with a rising population,
and a branching-out of old ideas...but also because of things added on.
 <u>One reason</u>: <u>The usual social motive</u> of providing more services
for the people, such as health & welfare, social security and the like.
 <u>The other</u>: <u>The notion that "we must spend to grow,"</u> a notion
firmly held by many of Kennedy's key brains. Over the next few months
you will often hear such phrases as "budgeting for full employment,"
"spending to produce surpluses." What all of this will mean is:
 <u>Gov't is to push us into prosperity</u>...spend enough to assure
full employment, full use of capacity. Then we will grow fast enough
to produce the taxes needed. That's the way the theory runs, anyway.
 <u>What effect will this have on business</u>? Stimulating, of course,
at least in early stages. There is a great deal of unused capacity now.
Unemployment is high, and more gov't spending will help prime the pump.
 <u>Tax cuts</u>? Possible, short range, as an anti-recession move,
or to provide more purchasing power, to encourage people to spend more.

Cubans in Miami demonstrate against Castro and the growing Russian presence in Cuba.

February 18, 1961

<u>Castro in Cuba will be overthrown within months</u>. There will be an invasion by revolutionary Cubans, now under training in Guatemala. They have been supplied with good arms and equipment...as guerrillas. The U.S. will not interfere with the movement of the troops by water. The landings will be at a number of strategic points on the coastline. They will be timed to fit local uprisings, to look like an inside coup. The preferred time is late spring, when unemployment will be rising, and unrest among the Cubans at a high...and trust in Castro at a low. Big-scale desertions from Castro forces have already been "arranged." When the signal is given they'll join the revolutionists against Castro. But this won't make the affair bloodless...there will be great slaughter.

March 18, 1961

<u>The big row over gov't aid to schools will be settled this way</u>: <u>Public schools will get federal help</u>...grants to the states and localities for new buildings, but probably not for teachers' pay. <u>Parochial schools will NOT get such aid</u>. They will be kept out of the main bill on the promise of separate legislation for them later.

<u>Tariff: Once the manufacturers yelled loudest for protection</u>. <u>Now labor unions are becoming leaders in protection demands</u>. <u>Against Japanese goods, strikes & boycotts are being planned</u> by clothing workers and electrical workers...some to start on May 1. They'll refuse to work on Japanese materials, may even picket stores. <u>The gov't is very much agitated</u>, lest these few unions gum up diplomatic relations with Japan, and is looking at the antitrust laws to see whether there are ways to proceed against the strikes & boycotts.

<u>Unions will campaign for new import restrictions in a few weeks</u>. Manufacturers may enlist on certain angles. Here are the high points: <u>A double or sliding scale of tariffs</u>. <u>And a bill for relief of workers, firms & areas</u> hurt by imports. Special unemployment pay. Earlier retirement. Retraining for new jobs. Paid transportation to new areas. Business loans for suffering firms. Accelerated amortization to promote a quicker shift to new products. <u>Title of the bill</u>: "Trade Adjustment Act"...(not "tariff").

April 15, 1961

     <u>He's vastly popular</u>. People like him, regard him as President,
accept him as such, don't think of him any more as too young for the job.
     He's spectacular, a good show, looks strong and acts vigorously.
People have the impression that he knows what to do and is doing it.
     He's a leader, and he shows it, and is anything but synthetic.
He dares to go out ahead and advocate new goals which are glamorous.
     <u>Trouble is, he's too far ahead of his followers</u>. They applaud,
and give him lip service, but don't really back him up to the limit.
     <u>This is true of Congress</u>...and many of the Democrats in it.
They cheer him, but aren't rushing to vote with him on what he is after.
     <u>It's true of the masses of voters</u>, too...including Democrats.
Most admire him and his ideas, but many haven't gone to work for him.
     <u>Another way of putting it</u>: <u>He's more attractive than effective</u>.

     <u>Russian man in space</u>: A great deed. But we'll soon have one too.
There's obviously a rocket gap, but we ARE narrowing the gap gradually.
As nearly as we can make out from confusing and highly technical reports,
it will take 2 or 3 years to close the gap...IF we keep on at full steam.

     <u>Cuba</u>: There will be a series of landings within next few weeks.
Rebel forces are not well organized. Hope of success is based on reports
by raiders just back from Cuba. They claim the people will help them.

April 29, 1961

     <u>It's a solemn story</u> that we have to tell you this week...
of war weather blowing up a storm, and plans to meet it.
The facts are old, but the frank facing of them is new.
<u>It stems from Cuba and Laos, but goes far beyond them</u>.
<u>The cold war is being replaced by a series of little hot wars</u>,
or threats of them. We've been losing cold war, reds have been winning,
because of their effective techniques: First, political infiltration.
Then revolts of the peasants and the poor against the ruling regime.
Then communist seizure of power of the new regime, and a police state.
Thus communist rule gets dug in and permanent. All this is being done
by red planning, red directing, red training and undercover support,
but without involving the forces of the communist nations themselves.
     <u>So our gov't is about to turn to the fighting of fire with fire</u>,
adopting many of the red methods. Infiltration of our own, stepped up.
Financing of friendly regimes, and training of their fighting forces.
Guerrilla warfare. Little battles, little wars...hot, no longer cold.

Soviet Cosmonaut Yury Gagarin was
the first man in space.

July 1, 1961

     <u>Berlin of course is grave, but...we think it will NOT bring war</u>.
     This is not in line with many of the signs of impending danger,
but it's based on subsurface information, and reflects the best judgment
of men in high places who dare not say publicly what they say privately.
     The mood of tension is expected to mount for next 3 or 4 months.
We are in for a long period of anxiety, with hot new doses almost weekly.
There's no room for complacency, but there's a need for the long view,
and some sense of direction in current confusion about ultimate outcome.

July 22, 1961

     <u>Our whole military establishment is undergoing an overhaul</u>.
     <u>It started even before Berlin</u>...it started when Laos flared,
when Kennedy saw that we did not have sufficient mobility or strength
in our conventional forces to fight in various corners of the globe.
Also that we were weak on guerrilla tactics, where reds were strong.
     <u>We are going to spend MUCH more on defense</u>...on ground forces.
     <u>Probably 6 to 8 billions more</u> will be poured into the military
in next few years, '62-'64...including some extra money this year.

A German woman at the Berlin Wall.

First Cavalry Division helicopters awaiting shipment to Vietnam.

September 30, 1961

<u>Now South Vietnam is about to explode and overshadow Berlin</u>.
<u>Our military is prepared to commit our men</u> as guerrilla leaders,
even in unit strength, if the reds can not be stopped by native troops.
But we would find it tough going...jungle-mountain-guerrilla fighting.
<u>Decision is up to President Kennedy</u>...in a few weeks from now.
Analysis of his speeches shows that he thinks we MUST hold S. Vietnam.
But the words come easier than the actions. He has hesitated in past,
so there is really no way of foretelling his decision in this case.
<u>We are inclined to think he will say GO</u> on using U.S. troops,
because native troops probably can't hold...and we will have to move in.

November 4, 1961

<u>The main point is that the fright over nuclear war is excessive</u>.
It's proper to have anxiety & deep concern over long-range implications,
but it's wrong to assume that the danger is imminent...or overwhelming.
There's no need for getting neurotic, unbalanced, or hysterical within,
or for letting the nervous imagination run wild by assuming the worst.
<u>The reds can not launch total missile war on the U.S. right now</u>.
They are not equipped to start such a war, despite all their gestures.
They do not have the missiles or the bases for any quick all-out attack.
<u>Furthermore, they know it, and they know what we have</u>. And so...
they won't initiate an attack...and this is more than mere speculation.

December 2, 1961

<u>Now another touchy matter...Negro discrimination in housing</u>...
meaning ALL housing that gets gov't financial assistance in ANY form:
<u>Kennedy is under tremendous pressure to end it by gov't order</u>.
<u>It means "open housing,"</u> giving Negroes the chance to buy homes
or rent in public housing developments anywhere. And it also includes
housing for the elderly, urban renewal projects, housing developments
offering FHA or VA mortgages, or loans made by savings & loan assns.
<u>We do not know WHEN he will sign it, but we feel sure he WILL</u>.
The liberal groups needle him daily, quoting his campaign promises.

An Apollo rocket launch at Cape Canaveral.

January 20, 1962

Space plans...a manned moon shot is still years away...1967. Many more rocket shots and manned orbital flights will be tried first.

Four more communications satellites will be sent up this year to see how well they work and whether they are economically practical. Kennedy will recommend joint ownership of communications satellites... by several electronics firms. He wants to prevent dominance by AT&T. Some in Congress want gov't ownership...and are set for a fight on it.

1962

February 24, 1962

The U.S. is edging nearer to war in Vietnam...slowly, gradually.

This is not generally known or understood by many of our people, partly because our attention has been diverted by troubles elsewhere... partly because the administration does not advertise what is going on.

The situation is very delicate...Americans are in the fighting, which is mainly guerrilla and counter-guerrilla warfare in the jungles. U.S. officers are leading natives, teaching and showing them in action.

We have had casualties, and we will certainly have many more... on the ground, in helicopters and airplanes...flushing out red units.

We are holding down the number of U.S. forces in the operation, so as not to provoke Russia or Red China into a big Korea-type action.

March 17, 1962

Aren't imports hurting American companies and reducing jobs? YES, no doubt of it. But the imports also help many kinds of businesses... Nevertheless, some firms are pinched and others are being BADLY pinched.

Then why cut tariffs even further via Kennedy's trade program? Well, the idea is to cut our tariffs in exchange for tariff reductions in other countries, thereby making it easier to sell our goods abroad. The Kennedy theory is that more jobs will be created by higher exports than will be lost by more imports. Companies and workers that are hurt are asked to settle for promise of gov't aid...on a case-by-case basis.

March 17, 1962

       What's Kennedy going to do about Cuba? NOTHING. He's in a box.
Can't invade because UN and Latin America would scream "imperialism."
Our economic tactics squeeze Castro, but can't finish him. Red nations
give him arms to hold power by force...no matter how bad things get.
No opportunity for anti-Castro Cubans to rise up...he would crush them.
Thus Cuba is a communist armed camp and will remain so indefinitely.

April 14, 1962

       The Kennedy regime thinks it can dictate stability of prices.
Thinks this with even more conviction now that it made steel back down.
       But it can not dictate to the big unions...to AFL-CIO leaders.
It can not make them roll over and play dead or sell them "moderation"
in their negotiations with industry. We have talked with AFL-CIO men
this past week and they are very much stirred up over the steel actions.
Their attitude is even more defiant of Kennedy and his moderation plan.

May 12, 1962

       A sizable tax cut is in the cards next year.
       It's to stimulate business then, to ward off possible recession.
       On individuals, Kennedy will ask a 25% cut across the board.
Top individual rate would come down to 65% from 91%. Bottom rate trimmed
to 15% from 20%, other rates will be cut proportionally.
       Tax on corporations will also be cut, to 45% from 52%.

May 19, 1962

       Medical care for the aged probably will pass. That's our opinion
after canvassing party leaders in Congress. Pressure for it is rising...
sparked by the Kennedy speech, the campaigns by old folks and the unions.

August 25, 1962

       We have reason to think that Russian troops ARE in Cuba...
and we say this despite official line that they are only technicians.
The latest arrival of five ships is part of a continuing red build-up.

Which makes it somewhat unanimous

Castro fears a rebellion and asked for protection from Russia,
troops he could use to cut down his own people, or his own military,
if revolt did come and parts of his armed forces turned against him.

There is growing turmoil in Cuba...people hungry, crops poor,
food scarce, prices rising, black markets, equipment breakdowns.

Revolt against Castro seems far off. The U.S. would be willing
to support a rebellion if it took hold, but chances of it are slim now.
Russian force will prop up the regime, despite the growing opposition.
Fact is, Castro and the Cubans are now Soviet captives.

Now it's official!

December 28, 1962

The whole world is going through rapid change, at times violent.
Here, Europe, even behind the Iron Curtain. New rivalry and competition.
Trade rising. American plants everywhere abroad, foreign companies here.
American business challenged, but it has the stuff to meet the challenge.

Our system has many faults...and awareness of them is acute.
They annoy us like an itch...but the awareness will lead to remedies.

Plenty of problems, perplexities, turmoil, in the years ahead.
Plenty of controversy. Some things will get settled, others will not.

But when the prospects are put together and weighed to get a net,
they point to spectacular progress...and warrant confidence in the future.

January 18, 1963

At least 50 million Americans collect money from federal gov't
in one form or another...both at home and abroad...wages and salaries,
social security, veterans' pensions, retirement, farm subsidies, grants,
unemployment pay, research, consultant work. And the number is growing.

Amount paid them is growing. The demand for new payments is
growing.

Pressure is from two directions: From the top of gov't down,
as politicians invent measures to catch votes. And from the bottom up,
as people want more programs, more benefits that seem to be "for free."
These are cold facts of the situation as to WHY the continuing growth.

1963

March 1, 1963

Space...a glamorous subject...also very practical, businesswise.
The fastest growing industry in the whole economy of the U.S.
Touches nearly every business line in one way or another.
Pours out billions...almost 6 billions this year for space alone,
on top of 9-to-10 billions for military missiles, total near 16 billions.
And still a baby, growing...no telling how big in years to come.

April 5, 1963

Business is in the early stages of another economic revolution.
The cause: Impact of computers and automatic data processing
on business management. Companies find it tough to keep up to date.

It's more than simply running a business, keeping its records,
watching inventories, projecting production and sales data with accuracy.
It goes as far as designing a plant, setting up management systems, etc.

Whole scope of business operations is headed for great change...
not 50 years from now, not even 25 years, but within the next FEW years.

May 10, 1963

Equal pay for women: Congress will vote a compromise version
in a month or so...indirectly this affects nearly all lines. We suggest
you get going now on figuring the cost and any changes in hiring policy.

May 24, 1963

New push to open up jobs to Negroes is starting in Congress...
hearings under way in the House on federal anti-discrimination bill.
Little chance of passing it, but the sponsors hope to make hay.
Jobs as the key to the Negro problem...this is the main theme.
Jobs are first on the list of civil rights that the Negroes are after.
So all sorts of methods to get them will be used from now on,
protest demonstrations, boycotts, court actions, appeals to employers,
behind-the-scenes talks with business groups. Peaceful, not belligerent,
but intended to suggest that hiring Negroes makes economic sense.

June 7, 1963

Here are the plans to use politics: First, Negro registrations.
These are to be pushed in big cities...in the North as well as the South.
Second, to threaten the Democratic party. The reason for this
is that most Negroes did vote Democratic, and did back up Kennedy...
because they took his all-out campaign promises at par. But not now...
now they are talking against him..."He hasn't done nearly enough."

This attitude may be mollified by his new civil rights stand.
Bear in mind that Negroes are not yet turning to the Republican party.
They are merely playing both the parties...and may remain Democratic.
They know that Kennedy knows that he needs Negro votes in the cities
for re-election in '64. This is partly responsible for his new burst
of activity on Negro rights...he was prodded and shocked into action.
From gov't itself, a sudden scramble of activity & propaganda:
The civil rights bill, a sort of scarecrow. Plus "voluntaries"
or appeals to groups to do these things as a substitute for legislation.
Non-violence is Negro watchword, but the unspoken fear is that
hotheads on both sides may get out of hand. Regardless, it seems sure
that this is the greatest internal social revolution since early '30s.

July 26, 1963

Public accommodations proposal: Most businessmen are opposed
as a matter of principle...intrusion on the rights of private property.
But more & more you hear this said: "Maybe better to have federal law
to force everyone to drop the color bars and get it over with fast.
Better than piecemeal, some doing it, others not." This feeling now
is not widespread, but it's gaining support gradually. It could force
some softening of the opposition in Congress to the proposed legislation.

September 6, 1963

        <u>Vietnam</u>: There is little chance of winning a real victory there.
Now it's a question of not losing what we've put into it...losing to Reds.
        <u>One thing is clear: In spite of difficulties, U.S. will stay</u>
in Vietnam, for if we quit or got pushed out, it would reverberate
through all S.E. Asia. Other nations such as Cambodia, Burma, Thailand
would undoubtedly get scared and start buddying up to the Red Chinese,
figuring we were no longer a dependable ally...China taking our place.
        <u>So U.S. will continue to spend half a billion dollars a year</u>
to keep Vietnam from toppling into the hands of the Red Chinese.

September 13, 1963

        <u>The economic repercussions of the report will be tremendous</u>.
Tobacco is an 8-billion-dollar business. Farmers get 1.3 billions a year.
Many regions and local areas depend on tobacco as a major cash crop.
South will be hit the hardest...most growers and manufacturers are there.
Federal-state-local gov'ts get over 3 billions a year from tobacco taxes,
will have a hard time finding substitutes if sales of cigarets shrink.
Insurance companies may even boost life insurance premiums on smokers.
Add vending machines, lighters, fuel, matches and other "dependents."
        <u>The whole tobacco complex is strong, of course, but threatened</u>.

SURGEON GENERAL'S WARNING: Quitting Smoking Now Greatly Reduces Serious Risks to Your Health.

September 20, 1963

        <u>In the North</u>, the situation in many ways is even more explosive.
Black ghettos are bursting...no Negro housing outside these boundaries.
Suburbs and other areas set up tight anti-Negro restrictions, enforced.

October 18, 1963

        <u>Japanese competition on component parts</u> is creating havoc here,
especially in radio and electronics fields. Many firms are complaining,
asking for quotas on Japanese parts. Firm action by the U.S. is unlikely,
since many large U.S. makers of finished goods LIKE the cheaper imports.
        <u>But voluntary limits on imports</u> might be set by Japan itself,
at the urging of our government, IF parts makers here complain enough.

November 23, 1963

        <u>Now a new President</u>: What kind of man? What kind of President?
        <u>He's different, and his administration will be different</u>...
regardless of any public statements about carrying on the same policies.
        <u>He is intensely personal</u>. He works with men more than ideas.
Now he will have to blend them, originate ideas as well as action.
        <u>Considered a "liberal"</u> by Southern standards, but in terms
of national standards he is essentially a middle-of-the-roader.
        <u>Essentially a doer rather than a thinker</u>. He follows through
by insisting on daily reports from his staff on what they have done,
whom they have talked with, what they found out, the outcome of it all.
He keeps a personal tab on what he asks for, and demands hard results.

November 29, 1963

        In the history of these changing times President Kennedy may be
the most quoted leader of the period, the incandescent sparker of ideas,
and President Johnson, the plainer man, the executor of the plan.

Letter to a grandson

W.M. Kiplinger occasionally presented his forecasts in a very direct, real-life prespective. In this letter, he offered a particularly long-range forecast in the form of a letter to his grandson.

December 27, 1963

Dear Grandson:

      I feel an urge to write you this Letter for a couple of reasons. There's affection. Also there's respect for you and your generation.
      Advice will be on the meager side, for advice that's plastered on is no good. You'll have to do your own thinking, steer your own course.
      But you CAN accept information and some forecasting of the future, and this, as an old observer of events, I am prepared to offer you.

      <u>You are likely to live until 2020 or 2030</u>. In your middle years, you will see a new century come, the 21st century, with its new ways.
      <u>Let's try to figure out what's going to happen</u> in your lifetime. Not every little thing, not specifically, but in a general way.

      <u>No world war, no nuclear war</u>, the fear of which has gnawed you. Little wars here & there, a world in turmoil, without much stability.

      <u>More mass attention to the improvement of human beings</u>, PEOPLE.
      This trend is not new, but it will broaden out in your lifetime. Physical health. Mental health. Education in all of its ramifications. Advancement of Negroes. Attacks on causes of poverty, delinquency. Some heart-bleeding, but mainly the practical approach. We can't AFFORD such imperfections in our human system and such waste of major assets.

      <u>Your generation will be more affluent</u> or prosperous, materially, than your predecessors. BUT...you will face many tough new problems. Net, your life will not be an easy one. It will call for all you've got.

      <u>And what kind of American system will you be living under</u>?
      At the base, individual freedom, choice, enterprise, initiative.
      <u>Communism</u>? No, not for us, and there's one practical reason: It has been pretty well demonstrated that planning by millions of minds is better than planning done by few at the top. It's more "efficient," it yields more. That, plus all the spiritual qualities of freedom.

      <u>Our system is evolving to fit the needs, and one trend is this</u>:
      <u>More "partnership" between government and private enterprise</u>. More gov't financing, subsidy, participation, sharing of the big risks. Already we have it, for most leading industries are tied in with gov't. And this has come so gradually that it's hardly recognized as a "system."
      <u>This is a modification of pure private enterprise</u> of the past. But it is OUR system, OUR development, not some doctrinaire "ism."
      <u>Communism will go through a similar modification in reverse</u>. It will adopt many of the tried & tested methods of ours. Already HAS.

      <u>Now let's talk of the prosperity that lies ahead for you & yours</u> from advances in science, technology and better methods of doing things. The changes are so great, so varied, that they are not quite believable.
      <u>So let's sneak up from the rear</u>...for comparison and contrast. Look at what your grandparents have seen come, or become commonplace:

      Automobile. Telephone. Airplane. Electricity in general living. Radio. Television. Indoor bathrooms. Gadgets in the home kitchen... gadgets to do housework. Canned foods. Frozen foods. Suburban living. The typewriter. Roads to everywhere. Automatic thises and thatses.
      Your grandfather worked as a boy in the family carriage plant. Your grandmother worked as a girl for Alexander Graham Bell, inventor of the telephone (which your parents say you use too much these days).

      <u>Your income</u> will be much higher than that of your parents... meaning the average of your generation over the average of the elders.

Your prices will be higher, too, but income will have a margin.
It will rise more than prices...adding to what is called "real income."

And here are some more things that are coming along by the time
you reach middle age...to change your thinking and your living.
New houses, new gadgets in them. Automatics. Push buttons.
Microwave ovens. Plastic plumbing. TV on wall screens. Fuel-cell heat.
Irradiated foods to supplement canned & frozen. New foods from the sea.
Synthetic foods, chemically made, with all needed nutrients & vitamins.
Further spread of cities, shrinking rural areas, cities growing together.
Flight to Europe, 90 minutes. The same across the continent.
Autos, double as many as now. Automated highways, guiding cars.
Lifetime tires. Fuel cells for propulsion. Cars more round than square,
plastic bodies, all air conditioned, glass roofs, glare proof. Luxury.
Fast trains, 200 miles an hour, some riding on a film of air.

Better health in backward countries, so life much longer, so...
populations zooming...so birth controls...and here in the U.S., too.
New wonder drugs & vaccines. Cancer, good chance of licking it.
Maybe even a cure for the common cold.
More automation in factories and offices, replacing hand work
and clerical work. Workweek down to 30 hours. More vacations, holidays,
leisure time, both a boon and a problem. And unemployment troubles too,
smack up to you and your generation...your elders bequeath them to you.
Telephone anyone from anywhere by gadget carried in your pocket.
Global TV...to a billion people...all at once...a mighty tie.
Automated supermarkets...press buttons, pick up groceries outside.
Selling by TV, like catalog ordering now. Credit for nearly everyone.
Space...moon and beyond, yes, but too complicated to go into now.

More emphasis on culture, MUCH more. Music. Art. Theater. Books.
And other "finer things of life." Not just for the few but for the many.
Those are just a very few of the developments in years ahead,
but they do go to show that you are going to have quite a lifetime.

About your education to qualify you to fit into the times ahead:
Key positions will still go to people who are educated BROADLY,
liberally, generally..."balanced" rather than narrow or specific.
This applies to public affairs and private affairs, including business.

Girls, too...everything I've said here applies to your sisters
and your girlfriends, except for somewhat different emphasis and angles.
Women are going into everything, more & more...into the realms
once regarded as men's. More married women take jobs outside the home.
This is a trend...and it will become MORE of a trend from here on out.

One more word...on freedom. We have it, need more of it, but...
it is not license to do whatever we have whim to do at a particular time.
Must be harnessed, disciplined, for good of all, for the total.
To devise the best systems for doing it is the great job for the future.
It means laws, regulations, methods, morals, ways of thinking and acting,
both public and private...and the more important of these two is private.

You wonder whether you are up to it all, whether you are able,
whether you have what it takes, for you know your own inadequacies.
Well, every generation has felt what you feel...the internal doubts...
but every generation when forced to face life has done a fair job of it.

You'll make good, you'll meet your responsibilities.
And you'll leave the world better than you found it.
Congratulations on the opportunities, and good luck.

Affectionately,

Grandfather

January 24, 1964

As for Vietnam, we'll eventually step aside there, after making a big military push to strengthen our hand for negotiations, compromise.
Truth is we can't win...can only fuzz the outcome, to save face. In the end, a coalition regime that may or may not work out commie.

March 13, 1964

Further about inflation: We've been warning you to expect it. At the same time many high officials are saying inflation is unlikely, saying they expect to curb it. Is there a way to explain the conflict?
Well, YES...it's mainly a difference in terms and measurements. The gov't authorities expect a general price rise this year of about 2%, and that much or more next year. But that is not inflation, they say, that's only what you'd expect when business gets going full steam ahead. They insist that runaway inflation is something well in excess of the 2%, and it's this they are talking against, and will take measures to curb.

March 20, 1964

Johnson's anti-poverty program: There's little applause for it in Congress, for much of it has been floating around there for some time. But the "war on poverty" label gives it a new face and political glamour, and legislators running for office this year may find it hard to resist.

Food stamps were part of LBJ's "war on poverty."

May 15, 1964

Note this well: A plan to have the gov't test consumer goods is seriously proposed by the President's Consumer Council. It wants the Bureau of Standards to test the things that people ordinarily buy.

June 5, 1964

Goldwater has the nomination sewed up. Nobody will stop him.
Goldwater will be the first avowedly conservative candidate since Landon in 1936...six election campaigns...almost thirty years.
Attempts will be made to "moderate" him, tone him down a bit so Republican liberals can start cozying up to him for the campaign.
To keep the party together will be a main Republican objective. Won't be entirely successful, but you'll see evidence of it from now on. Republicans will remain in turmoil, both before and after the convention.

Changes in voting patterns are expectable in parts of the South when large numbers of Negroes do begin voting. Probably in some states new faces will appear in Congress...replacing some of the standpatters. And in others, state & city gov'ts will be altered...Negroes elected.

June 19, 1964

On private pension plans, a startling new prospect:
There's a scheme afoot to have gov't regulate them severely, put them under stricter supervision, set up much tougher standards, dictate when vesting must begin, perhaps have them insured by gov't, limit what kinds of securities the pension fund may be invested in.

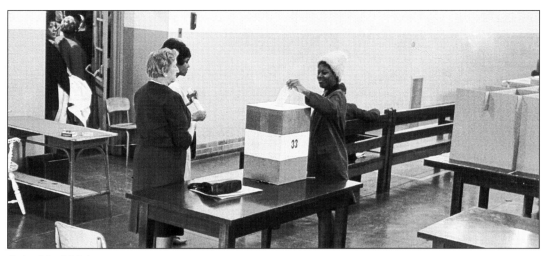

July 10, 1964

    <u>Johnson is sending more troops to Asia</u>...to fight, not "advise."
Many have already been alerted and will be over there in a few weeks.
    <u>By late Aug. the war will be stepped up</u>, more blows at the Reds.
    <u>Raids into North Vietnam</u> will be carried out by U.S. guerrillas
and the S. Vietnamese. Quietly at first, without publicity or fanfare,
but gradually leaking out...and then reluctant official acknowledgment.
    <u>Hope is to push the Reds back</u>, not come out with total victory.
U.S. wants to have a stronger hand to play when the negotiations start
after elections, looking for some way to bring an end to the shooting.
    <u>Johnson is running a risk</u> that war will spread and casualties
will increase. It would make grim reading here in an election period.

August 7, 1964

    <u>The Johnson strategy is to make voters AFRAID of Goldwater</u>...
afraid to switch lest they lose social and economic gains of the past.
    <u>He will use Goldwater's own words</u> on such things as subsidies,
right-to-work, social security, unions under antitrust, many others.
Research men have been digging them out for months, an abundant supply.
    <u>And the charge of "trigger-happy"</u> will get special emphasis.
Was mentioned frequently at the convention...now it's becoming a theme.
Target is the women's vote...most sensitive to any talk of nuclear war.

September 4, 1964

    <u>The Vietnam mess</u> will also go on and on...a long ordeal ahead.
    <u>State Dep't is VERY gloomy</u> about the attempt to establish
a democratic gov't. They know the generals can't win popular support,
but fear the civilians will do worse...making military gains impossible.

November 20, 1964

    <u>The medicare debate may now create a major boom in health plans</u>,
much as passage of social security in the 1930s stimulated pensions.

March 26, 1965

    <u>The space race</u>: We are much closer to Russians than it may seem.
The Reds are spectacular...first space woman, first free-floating man.
We are less dramatic, but our technical excellence is equal to theirs.
    <u>We CAN reach the moon first</u>. While it will require equipment
more complex and sophisticated than either we or the Reds yet have,
we are further along on research and our men are sure we'll make it.

"On ending violence in the streets–
I think I'd cut out that part about
small tactical bombs."

1965

June 11, 1965

<u>Vietnam: Now we're in it up to our necks</u>...our own soldiers,
fighting in the mud against the Vietcong. We're no longer "support"
for the South Vietnam forces, we are running the war and fighting it.
<u>Casualties will mount, the news will be bad</u>...our men dying
in that far-off place, trying to stop a complete Red take-over there.
<u>It's not what Johnson wanted, of course</u>. It's what he hoped
to avoid by the bombings in the north. He gambled that the commies
would fold up under this pressure and finally negotiate a settlement.
He lost the gamble, at least temporarily, and now must take a course
that his critics warned against...putting us in a ground war in Asia.
<u>The odds are strongly against any peace talks...for months</u>.
Instead, the Reds will try to drive us out of Vietnam.
We will have to throw in still more troops to thwart them.
Then later, in the fall, try again to start peace talks.
We have several ugly months ahead of us.

August 20, 1965

<u>The race riots in Los Angeles and elsewhere</u> give new urgency
to the various gov't programs. Overcrowded housing, poverty, illiteracy,
disease...gov't officials here blame these for the uncontrolled violence.
And they fear more outbreaks until steps are taken to eradicate them.
<u>Cost will run into billions</u>, but the new course is already set.

August 27, 1965

<u>A revolutionary policy on agriculture</u> is quietly being developed,
not yet fully formalized but moving definitely in these directions:
<u>Abolish production controls</u>...not suddenly but in a few years,
on some sort of sliding scale. Let anyone raise anything...unrestricted.
<u>Encourage GREATER production</u>...and even put a gov't spur to it.
<u>Gov't itself would buy huge quantities of stuff</u>...commercially,
in the open market. In effect a new type of price support for farmers.
<u>And then pour much of it out as foreign aid</u>, a vast "food bank"
for human relief for millions...and as trading stock for other policies.
<u>This will be a true revolution</u>, a reversal of past three decades.
A veering, then more veering, step by step...a sort of wide U-turn.

September 3, 1965

<u>Amazing...how Congress is voting billions for general "welfare,"</u>
grants & loans to states & localities, insurance and other features.
Amazing, too, that most people are not aware of the rain of "benefits."

September 17, 1965

      <u>Trend to early retirement</u> will be another major cost-raiser.
Retirement age is being lowered to 62 and even 60 in many union plans,
at full pensions...employee's option in some cases, involuntary in others.

      <u>Student unrest on campuses</u> will bring demonstrations this fall,
similar to those at Berkeley. We learn this from school administrators,
who are more concerned than ever before. Also from student conventions.

October 8, 1965

      <u>As for the flow of money from Washington to states and cities</u>,
it's such a big step-up as to make an evolution into almost a revolution.
      <u>Main reason for this is in taxes</u>. The state & local gov'ts rely
heavily on sales & property taxes, which are less flexible than income.
Federal gov't has inside track on income taxes...booming in boom times.
So big & little gov'ts become partners...like a horse & sparrows.
      <u>Is this partnership permanent</u>? We are inclined to say yes.

November 26, 1965

      <u>Credit ratings by computer</u>...a complete profile of each customer
is the prospect within the next two or three years. Local credit bureaus
will feed in data to a local center...from banks, stores, credit card outfits.

December 10, 1965

      <u>Here is some blunt talk about Vietnam</u>: We got it from the men
in gov't who are running the war there, planning and budgeting for it.
      <u>The war is going to get MUCH bigger</u>...approaching Korean war
in both the size and the cost to the U.S. No one in gov't doubts this.
      <u>We now have 200,000 men in Vietnam</u>...air-sea-&-land forces.
      <u>We will build to around 300,000</u> in the next year. Military wants this,
figures it will be necessary, but hasn't yet gotten a go-ahead on it.
      <u>Draft calls</u> will be boosted again, probably next Feb-Mar.
      So you can see the SIZE of the escalation now in the works.

December 31, 1965

As for Mr. Johnson, he faces MUCH tougher going from now on.
He will have to make enemies, which up to now he has avoided.
Business will turn more anti. Many liberals will grow disenchanted.
Unions will fight him on wages. Some Negro leaders will be critical.
The "consensus" he likes to have on public issues will begin to crack.
This may show another side of the President...the testy side
which flares up when he's bucked. He has kept this pretty much hidden
from public view, but he'll find it harder to conceal from now on.

1966

February 11, 1966

The business boom is beginning to hit the wild-blue-yonder stage.
It is confounding even the experts, exceeding their most optimistic hopes.
Prices are rising faster. They've broken out of their "creep,"
and the pace of the rise is expected to accelerate during rest of year.
The cushion of idle capacity is disappearing and new additions
to plant, equipment, manpower resources will not keep up with demand.
Gov't is adding fuel to a hot economy...through military needs
in Vietnam and in still more spending for dozens of welfare programs.

February 25, 1966

The growingest gov't department is HEW. You can see
the reasons for this in all the programs relating to human welfare.
One thing pretty certain: The next 5 to 10 years will bring the
fastest advances in social reform measures in our entire history.
Another certainty: The activities will create a lot of business.
This isn't the main MOTIVE, but it's going to be a major EFFECT.

Read this carefully, if you have youngsters of draft age.
Most of them will probably go...either caught up in the draft
or through voluntary enlistments. That's because we are going to need
far more men in the services to meet our huge commitments in the world.
A tightening of deferments is in the offing.

March 18, 1966

A new outburst of Negro rioting is now feared...and expected...
by men in gov't agencies here who are supposed to know Negro feelings.
Where? Big cities...ANY big city.

Democratic politicians are much worried about Vietnam's effect on the elections next fall. They can sense the voters' dissatisfaction with the Vietnam policies, and they feel it will be taken out on them.

"Remember—return with my shield or on it."

May 20, 1966

An auto safety law will be voted...leaders say it's a "must" to assure consumers that gov't is going to "do something" about autos.

May 27, 1966

There may be ways to shorten the war by escalating it further, by bombing Hanoi, mining Haiphong harbor, blockading N. Vietnam, etc.

But our gov't opposes this as much as it opposes pulling out. The risk is too great...the risk of a major war with no major allies.

That's why it's going to take a long time...years and years. It's also why the spirits will sag and the dissension will increase, why the prospects are unhappy. A drain...in money, materials, men. Sorry to report this, but it's better than false hopes and illusions.

July 29, 1966

The computer will poke its digits into every line and business. Computerized gov't. Computerized teaching. Even computerized medicine. All this is taking hold. After a period of experimenting, it's a fact. Bigger and improved machines are finding new applications every day.

Nationwide computer hook-ups will bring some enormous changes:

Moneyless banking...deposits, charge purchases, payments, all kinds of deals via your account. Less bother, less loss and theft.

Instant credit check-ups, local bureaus tied to national.

Central accounting & inventory systems. The big companies will own computers. But even the smallest will rent time to record stocks, payrolls, profits, taxes...by machine...faster and cheaper.

September 9, 1966

We are going to put tens of thousands more troops in Vietnam within the next year. By summer of 1967, total of nearly 500,000 men.

We are going to spend considerably more to support this force. Early in 1967, Johnson will ask Congress for another 10 to 12 billions beyond what he has now. Hence, he will have to ask still higher taxes.

November 4, 1966

Credit cards issued by banks will be sweeping the country soon. Many of them can be used for cash, shopping, travel and entertainment. Banks are using them as a way to move in on the consumer credit market.

December 9, 1966

Russia is building a widespread defense against our missiles, a complex system to keep our missiles from hitting targets in Russia.

U.S. also has been working on such a system, Nike X, but so far has chosen to develop it further rather than to put it in installations.

1967

January 27, 1967

> On hiring, gov't is going to poke deeper into discrimination.
> Not just against Negroes and women, but older people too.

February 3, 1967

> On pollution of air and water, gov't is starting to get tough...
is asking Congress for a law on air control like the one on water purity.
> Nationwide standards for business AND gov't are the first step.
> These industries especially...utilities, steel, paper, chemicals.
> The cost of cleaner water and air will be borne by business...
the bulk of it. Part of the cost may be offset by the investment credit
that Congress left in the tax laws, applying to anti-pollution devices.
And gov't will pick up part of the bill when the program gets under way,
but this help will be short-lived. Our judgment is that in a year or so
many firms will have to start spending sizable sums on anti-pollution.

May 5, 1967

> U.S. technical lead over Europe is continuing to increase...
especially in lines that rely on computers or very advanced research.
A major reason is all the gov't-paid research, making our bigs bigger.
> And the "brain drain"...flow of trained men to U.S. from Europe
for more pay, better facilities...has the Europeans angry and scared.
> Result: More European firms will have to team with Americans,
cut our companies in on their markets. U.S. firms may get tax breaks
from some nations, too, as a lure to do more of their research there.

July 21, 1967

> Riots. More of them must be expected in the cities from now on
even if the gov't were willing to undertake remedies, which it isn't.
> Business will bear brunt of the cost...not just in the looting
and the destruction, but in being pushed to "make jobs" for youngsters.

July 28, 1967

> A rethinking of priorities...debate will spread in the U.S.
about the wisdom of spending many billions for the safety of Vietnam
while holding in check domestic programs that might aid U.S. cities.
> Will become a hot political issue...growing in intensity.

August 4, 1967

> All this reflects on Johnson and his administration.
Congressmen feel they voted what he wanted, backed him on Vietnam war,
gave him social programs. Yet, the results are stalemate in Vietnam,
riots at home...which isn't what they had in mind as The Great Society.

September 15, 1967

> Keep an eye on the new "ism" now taking hold..."consumerism."
There's mounting interest in "protecting" the public from businessmen,
and it comes not only from gov't but also from scores of private groups.
> Don't shrug this off or dismiss it as just a crackpot scheme.
A recent business survey shows clearly that consumers want more protection
from the gov't, and they do not accept arguments about "free enterprise"
as justification for current practices that are used by many businessmen.
> And it will lead to change...more restrictive laws and rules
that business will have to adjust to. The only question is how well
business can influence the changes...how well it can live with them.

October 13, 1967

The Vietnam war is Johnson's biggest liability. If the fighting is still as bloody there a year hence...if the end still isn't visible, Johnson will be very vulnerable. The Republican candidate needn't claim that he has a "solution" to the war. He need only promise a fresh look at how we can extricate ourselves, since Johnson seems unable to do it.
The voters might then vote for a change...and the hope of peace.

Secretary of State Dean Rusk, LBJ and Defense Secretary Robert McNamara formulated U.S. policy for Vietnam.

October 20, 1967

We are entering a long period of inflation.
In ten years, inflation of nearly 25%, when compounded yearly... up to a quarter of the purchasing power of the dollar blown into smoke.
Why so? Mainly because of gov't policies...big budget deficits, red ink year after year, even in boom times. Also, a general tendency to keep credit as easy as possible and avoid strict tightness of money.

December 8, 1967

Fate of unions is tied to fate of their industries...up or down. Rise of mass production industry brought rise of the big industrial CIO. Now automation and shift to white-collar & services are cutting some down.
Fading are coal, railroads, oil, maritime, many lesser unions. In some cases, it's market shrinkage. In others, it's new machinery... replacing unskilled, even semi-skilled men. Either way, effect is same.
Holding their own or giving ground only slightly are such unions as autos, steel, electrical, construction, metal trades and the truckers.
Rising to prominence are unions keyed to the shifts in industry from blue to white-collar, from production of goods to service lines. Gov't employes, for example, at all levels...due for much more growth.

Union members are changing. They are no longer "working class," now middle-class and affluent...with all the attitudes that accompany it.
Politically, more conservative...most of all on local issues, such as open housing, that rile up the middle-class suburban home owners. This shift to the right is bound to continue...a consequence of changes in economic status, the upgrading of skills and wages across the board.
Means the "labor vote" is no longer automatic Democratic property, even though Meany pledges full support for Johnson. Union men will ignore their leaders and vote own interests...especially at state & local levels.

AFL-CIO President George Meany at a congressional hearing.

December 22, 1967

<u>It will take discipline</u> to cope with the competition of wants.
<u>But the alternative is inflation</u>...of the more rampant kind.
And if we let it happen, we'll kick away our biggest opportunity.
<u>This is the great danger</u> in a future that's basically strong.
To get where we want to go, we will have to appraise the alternatives,
re-examine our scale of values...and set some priorities.

1968

February 23, 1968

<u>Wage-price controls</u>: <u>Businessmen are now becoming suspicious</u>
that the gov't will soon find it necessary to impose wartime controls.
<u>Controls are NOT imminent</u>. None of the preparatory maneuvers
that would have to be put into play are even remotely in the cards now.

March 22, 1968

<u>The dollar is shaky</u> despite the recent efforts to shore it up.
As evidence of just how shaky it is, some businessmen in West Europe
are demanding that the sales contracts they make with American importers
include a clause protecting against dollar devaluation. "Incredible."

April 5, 1968

<u>Martin Luther King</u>: The tragedy is that a voice for moderation
may not soon be heard again...or if it is heard, may not now be heeded.
King was the leader of the older generation...the non-violent.
<u>Now the new generation of militant Negro leaders</u> is taking over.
They are restless, belligerent, aggressive. They were pressing him hard
before his death, and slowly undermining his influence with his people.
Suddenly they have emerged as THE force...with his restraints thrown off.

Martin Luther King Jr. (with aides Jesse Jackson and Ralph Abernathy) in Memphis shortly before he was assassinated.

June 21, 1968

<u>Peace talks are vital to Humphrey</u> this fall for the elections,
to divert the voters' attention away from the war as much as possible.
<u>He is in a bad jam on the war</u>...needs to get himself untangled
from Johnson's policies, if he can, by claiming he stood against them.
<u>The Republicans are growing "sure" they will win</u> the elections
with either Nixon or Rockefeller. Rockefeller aides think he would win
in a breeze and concede that Nixon could win too, by a smaller margin.

July 12, 1968

<u>Medical costs are leapfrogging</u> at a pace considered "alarming"
or "scandalous" by many. In 5 years, they have zoomed 30%, about double
the rise in the over-all cost of living. Question: Can they be slowed?
<u>The gov't is moving in</u>, figures it must if it is to prevent
the cost of medicare and other health programs from getting out of hand.
<u>Drug prices are a target</u>...heavy pressure on makers to cut them.
<u>Also doctors' fees</u>, although here the pressures are more subtle.
<u>Hospital charges</u>...gov't is prodding for better administration.
<u>Will all these steps slow the rise in costs?</u> <u>Not any time soon</u>.

July 19, 1968

<u>Sideburns, beards, mustaches</u>...they used to be for youngsters,
the college set. Now they are spreading into the business world of men.
Fancy hair styles are one reason haircut prices are going up so rapidly,
now over $2 in many cities. The men want razor cuts, hair tinting.
Progressive barbers aren't "barbers" any more...they are hair stylists.

Czech crisis: Will the U.S. get involved? No...we think not.
But Russia is in a very tight spot and seems to be determined
to prevent the Czechs from holding free elections early in September.

August 16, 1968

New small U.S. cars, a bit bigger than VW and with more power,
will start being made next year. Priced tentatively at around $2000.
First, Ford, probably next midyear. Then GM. Rambler later, perhaps.
Why? Imports...the flood of small foreign cars being sold here.
Nearly a million this year, and a market that keeps growing steadily.
The U.S. auto makers want a piece of it. The competition is pinching.

August 30, 1968

As of now, the Democrats are underdogs on winning in November.
Part of their trouble reflects the internal dissent on the Vietnam war
and part stems from Johnson policies at home. His Great Society plans,
once a source of pride, are not so popular now. The public is souring
on some of them despite the many merits that Humphrey can see in them.
Factional bickering among the Democrats is at its highest pitch in years.
The toughest issue Humphrey must face is NOT the war, but crime.
It's what Nixon calls "law and order," meaning thefts, lootings,
civil disobedience, rebellion against authority...breakdown of society.
The Democrats tend to use this term sparingly, for the militant Negroes
regard it as racist, anti-Negro, a slur on their efforts to get justice.
But the masses of voters understand the term to mean an end to violence,
without the subtle shadings ascribed to it by either Humphrey or Nixon.
People are fed up with disorder. Both candidates know this...
Nixon will hammer it constantly while Humphrey pleads for "justice."
On balance, there now seems to be a conservative tide running,
favorable to Nixon. But public sentiment tends to shift back and forth
with day-to-day events. It will be especially volatile this year.

November 8, 1968

<u>As President, he will be middle-road</u>...much as Eisenhower was, but likely to lean more "progressive" rather than "conservative." <u>He believes in "realistic" programs</u> that can be accomplished. <u>He may disappoint many of his supporters</u> who are conservatives and see him as one of their kind. He won't go as far right as they want. Doesn't believe, for example, that deficit spending is necessarily bad.

1969

January 10, 1969

<u>Vietnam</u>: People who are expecting Nixon to settle the war soon are headed for a disappointment. Probably this includes many millions who voted for him last November because they thought he could end it, or at least bring fresh thinking to it that would speed a settlement. <u>The truth is, Nixon has NO new plan for ending the war</u>. <u>He will stick pretty closely to the current Johnson strategy</u>. <u>Simply stated, the strategy is this</u>: Continue to put pressure on the Communists in Vietnam, where we are steadily tightening the vise. And hope that in due time this will force them to make terms in Paris.

January 24, 1969

<u>Then when peace comes, a "dividend" from a cut in war spending</u>. <u>Just how big it will be</u> depends on a lot of horseback guesses. Johnson's Cabinet Com. estimated that it might run <u>22 billions</u> by 1972, but this was the MAXIMUM dividend and was based on optimistic assumptions about the end of the war in Vietnam and the pace of the demobilization. <u>One thing is sure: It won't be big enough to satisfy the claims</u> that are already being staked out by the various special interest groups. Here are a few price tags: The military wants <u>6 billions</u> more each year for new weapons, planes, ships, etc. Another <u>6 billions</u> will be needed to bring up to authorized levels present programs for education, health, crime curbs, housing, anti-pollution. More social security, <u>4 billions</u>. On top of these, proposals for new and enlarged gov't programs to cost conservatively <u>40 billions</u> a year. The "negative income tax," championed by some, might run from <u>15 to 20 billions</u>. A volunteer army, to replace the draft, could add <u>5 billions</u> or more to the present cost. Revenue sharing with states, another <u>5 billions</u> if it is to help much.

May 2, 1969

<u>A broad industrial safety bill</u> covering all industries and lines will also be recommended, despite the opposition of many business groups. And the odds favor passage...late this session or early next year.

May 9, 1969

<u>Reproduction of messages, facsimiles</u>...a rapidly growing service. About a half-dozen firms are in it now...competing with Western Union. They transmit texts, drawings, photos, etc., over existing phone lines. Gov't is watching, in the public interest, and is getting a bit concerned about the rates. So it has plans to step in soon and regulate them.

<u>On welfare reform, there's a struggle within the administration</u>. <u>Conservatives vs. liberals</u> (or moderates). Conservatives want an overhaul of the present welfare & relief programs. But the liberals want to go whole hog and scrap most of the present way of paying relief. Instead, substitute a program that approaches a negative income tax. <u>Cost...nearly 3 billions MORE than now</u>. But chances in Congress aren't too good...probably scoffed at initially. Perhaps better in '70.

Astronaut Buzz Aldrin on the moon. Next step in space exploration would be development of space shuttle.

July 25, 1969

    On welfare, an entirely new approach will be proposed by Nixon.
    A minimum income for the poor, about $1500 for a family of four,
paid for by federal gov't...the cornerstone. To encourage job-seeking,
gov't would scale payments down very gradually as family earns income.
Would increase total welfare cost by 60%...from 5 billions to 8 billions.
    Plus incentives to work via job training and extended child care.
Aim is to expand the labor force, thus stimulate total economic growth.
Also eventually to reduce size of welfare rolls...and the cost to gov't.

August 1, 1969

    Radio-TV ads for cigarets WILL be stopped...that's now certain.
When? Probably about a year hence, the time suggested by the tobacco men.
It will mean a loss of income to broadcasters, but not as bad as claimed,
for the big networks see the end coming and are hustling up new accounts.
    Temporary dip in cigaret sales is expected...and then a rebound.
Other countries have banned such ads, but cigaret sales kept on climbing.

    Re-usable rockets probably will be developed...a space shuttle,
taking men up to a space platform, changing crews, coming home to land.
    Fewer tracking devices...reducing manpower and costly gadgets.
    Further miniaturization of many components, cutting down weight.
    Better fuels, more life from same size & weight of propellants.
These will take years, but they are now the goal...as the moon once was.

December 12, 1969

    Nixon's plans to curb inflation are suddenly in grave danger.
    Now another kicker to inflation: Excessive wage increases.
    Administration has OK'd 10% a year, not in any official way,
but that's how the unions will interpret the recent rail settlement.
    Productivity will go up 3% at the most...output per man-hour.
No matter how you figure it, unit labor costs will continue to climb.
    So prices will keep on rising...forced up by the higher costs.
    Nixon opposes controls, guidelines, jawbone, credit rationing...
any direct action on inflation. But he may change his mind...by spring.

1970s

The economic and political hegemony that the U.S. enjoyed for a quarter-century after World War II waned rapidly in the 1970s. The U.S. was still the world's most powerful nation, economically if not militarily, and U.S. living standards continued to advance. But the once-overwhelming margin of U.S. superiority over other major nations narrowed, in trade, technology and living standards.

American corporations, long the world leader in overseas production, accelerated their search for lower-cost manufacturing centers in foreign lands, to maintain competitiveness in a tightly knit world economy. Foreign corporations based in Asia and Europe, looking for new sales in the world's most affluent and open consumer market, sent vast volumes of products to the U.S.—cars, consumer electronics, clothing and much more. U.S. exports surged, but imports grew more. When the price of imported foreign oil went up more than tenfold during the decade, the U.S. saw its traditional trade surplus melt into a persistent deficit.

U.S. productivity—the value of output per hour worked—continued to rise in the '70s, but at a slower rate than during the '50s and '60s. Productivity gains were depressed by sagging capital investment and by a surge of new, less-experienced workers into the labor force: young adults of the baby boom, older women seeking work outside the home to boost their families' earnings, and a growing wave of immigrants from Latin America and Asia. Labor was plentiful and productivity growth was weak, so real wage gains (adjusted for a high level of inflation) grew more slowly than in the two decades after World War II.

American self-doubts

More than anything else, America's image of itself took a beating in the '70s. Over the course of ten years, America was humiliated by the forced resignation of a president (the first in U.S. history),

			NIXON FREEZES WAGES AND PRICES.	KISSINGER TRAVELS SECRETLY TO CHINA.	CONGRESS VOTES TO END SEX DISCRIMINATION.
FIRST EARTH DAY OBSERVED.	NATIONAL GUARDSMEN FIRE ON STUDENTS AT KENT STATE.	U.S. BOMBS LAOS.			NIXON GOES TO CHINA.
			18-YEAR-OLDS GET THE VOTE.		
1970	U.S. FORCES ENTER CAMBODIA.	**1971**			**1972**

withdrawal from South Vietnam and its subsequent fall to communism, two Arab oil embargoes, Soviet aggressiveness, and the long captivity of American hostages in Iran.

After nearly a decade of growth in the '60s, the U.S. economy of the '70s took a roller-coaster ride of alternating growth and recession, punctuated by bouts of inflation higher than at any time since the late '40s. Stock prices languished for most of the decade. The recession of '73-75, aggravated by the first Arab oil price hike, was the worst economic downturn since 1937.

The federal government continued an unbroken record of spending more money than taxpayers provided each year, in good times and bad. Richard Nixon, long considered a conservative, showed himself to be as much a proponent of an activist federal government as his Democratic predecessors. Federal regulations increased strongly in the '70s. In 1971, with inflation running at a then-shocking rate of nearly 4%, Nixon imposed the first peacetime wage and price controls in U.S. history, and they remained in place into 1974. His administration also saw the creation of the Environmental Protection Agency and the Occupational Safety and Health Administration. In an attempt to break with previous administrations, Nixon introduced the sharing of federal revenues with state governments, and he tried unsuccessfully to replace social welfare programs with a support system that would encourage a work ethic.

In world affairs, Nixon stepped up efforts to reach an agreement with the Soviet Union on reducing nuclear armaments. Given his reputation for ardent anti-communism, the world was startled in 1972 by Nixon's making diplomatic overtures to, and later visiting, Communist China, which the U.S. had not formally recognized since the regime came to power in 1949. In Southeast Asia, Nixon pursued a long, slow policy—not fast enough for opponents of the war—of turning the war over to the South Vietnamese allies, who eventually lost to the communist Viet Cong and North Vietnamese in 1975.

Nixon's Watergate

Nixon's poor choice of political aides, his penchant for secrecy and his us-against-them stance toward political adversaries led to a shockingly rapid downfall for so durable a figure in American political history. Nixon's vice-president, Spiro Agnew, resigned amid charges of political corruption. Nixon allowed, indeed encouraged, unscrupulous White House aides to undermine the 1972 Democratic campaign with a variety of illegal activities, including surveillance and burglary of the Democrats' headquarters at the Watergate office building in Washington. Firm evidence of White House involvement in the burglary was revealed by *The Washington Post* well before the '72 election, but Nixon was reelected anyway. Over the next year and a half congressional investigations showed the scope of Nixon's involvement in the crimes and subsequent coverup. He resigned in 1974 rather than risk certain impeachment.

Energy shocks

The public unfolding of the sordid Watergate scandal depressed an American spirit already bruised by the economic woes of high inflation, recession and energy shortages. In 1973 America's longtime support for Israel in its strife with Arab neighbors caused oil-producing nations in the Middle East to sharply curtail petroleum sales to the U.S. and jack up the price. Overnight, the price of oil soared throughout the world, shortages developed and motorists began lining up at gas stations.

Although the crisis eventually eased, oil prices didn't return to pre-embargo levels, and energy conservation gradually became a serious pursuit of American consumers and businesses. Homeowners turned down their thermostats and beefed up the insulation in their homes, and some

	LAST U.S. COMBAT TROOPS LEAVE VIETNAM.			VIETNAM PEACE PACT SIGNED.	
NORTH VIETNAM LAUNCHES MASSIVE ATTACKS AGAINST SOUTH.		NIXON REELECTED.	SUPREME COURT LEGALIZES ABORTION.		ARABS PROCLAIM OIL EMBARGO.
	SEEDS OF WATERGATE: BREAK-IN AT DEMOCRATIC HEADQUARTERS.		**1973**	DRAFT ENDS.	

installed wood stoves to replace or supplement oil-burning furnaces. Big, gas-guzzling American cars couldn't be given away, as sales soared for small, fuel-efficient cars—mostly imported from Japan. Congress eventually removed longtime federal price controls on energy to stimulate domestic energy production and reduce reliance on imports, but foreign oil remained the mainstay of the U.S. energy supply.

Gerald Ford, a veteran House leader before he became vice-president, succeeded Nixon, pardoned his former boss, and provided two and a half years of honest, capable governance. The economy emerged from severe recession and began growing again, while inflation moderated after the shock of the oil embargo. But the inflation psychology remained, and with it the "indexing" of the U.S. economy. Regardless of productivity gains or the earnings of their employers, workers expected raises—COLAs, or "cost of living adjustments"—at least as big as the rate of inflation and ideally more. Real (after-inflation) corporate profits—and the capacity of business to invest in capital goods—suffered from high inflation, and this was reflected in sluggish stock prices through most of the decade.

Amazing inventions

Technological innovation didn't take a vacation in the '70s, however. Word processors with video display screens—essentially single-function computers—began to revolutionize the American office. Cable television, once a service just for rural areas with bad TV reception, emerged to challenge broadcast TV with an unprecedented choice of programming. Laboratory breakthroughs in genetic engineering began to raise the prospect of new, environmentally safe products for agriculture, waste treatment and human health. Banks started experimenting with electronic banking, using robotic tellers and telephone transactions. And from Japan came a flood of new consumer electronic products, such as videotape players, laser discs and video games, most of which used technologies that had been developed in the U.S. but overlooked by American firms as marketable products.

While federal regulation increased in such areas as the environment, worker health and product safety, the first tentative steps were taken toward deregulation of major markets for transportation, energy, and other goods and services. It began under President Ford and accelerated under the next two presidents.

Government regulation of prices—whether airfares, trucking fees, gasoline, natural gas or interest rates on savings accounts and mortgages—became obsolete in an era of high inflation. With market prices soaring on virtually everything, it was folly to try to control prices on selected goods and services without causing severe shortages in those categories, whether gasoline or mortgage funds. The high-inflation '70s saw the birth of new financial instruments—such as money-market mutual funds and adjustable-rate mortgages—that let both lenders and borrowers roll with the punches of changing interest rates.

The tumultuous world economy of the '70s brought unprecedented instability in currency exchange, as gold was abandoned as an anchor of currency values. The U. S. let the price of gold float freely and allowed private citizens to own gold as an investment. By the end of the decade, the dollar was plunging, inflation exceeded 13%, and the world market price of gold was over $500 an ounce, headed toward a peak of $875 in January 1980.

Carter's woes

In the election of 1976, many voters held against Ford that he had pardoned Nixon. That pardon, plus the continuing fragility of the economy, gave victory to Jimmy Carter, a former Georgia governor, peanut farmer and submarine captain who pledged to restore the lost luster of America's greatness and renew Americans' faith in an effective and forceful government. But that vision was not to be.

1974	1975	1976	1977
U.S. ECONOMY IN RECESSION.	SAIGON FALLS, LAST AMERICANS ESCAPE.	SPAIN'S FRANCO DIES.	CARTER PARDONS VIETNAM DRAFT EVADERS.
EX-NIXON AIDES GUILTY IN WATERGATE.		CHINESE LEADERS MAO AND CHOU DIE.	
NIXON RESIGNS; FORD TAKES OVER.		U.S. SPACECRAFT LANDS ON MARS.	
HOUSE COMMITTEE RECOMMENDS NIXON IMPEACHMENT.		CARTER ELECTED PRESIDENT.	
FORD PARDONS NIXON.			

A fiscal conservative who wanted to trim government spending, an outsider new to the ways of Washington, a cerebral analyst without a love for the give-and-take of politics, Carter had trouble getting his programs through a free-spending Congress controlled by his own party. Another OPEC oil price hike in 1979 put Americans into long waiting lines at filling stations and sent inflation through the roof. Historically high nominal interest rates, coupled with rapidly rising home prices, priced millions of young Americans out of homeownership. State and local government payrolls were growing more rapidly than Washington's, boosted by high inflation, recession relief and relentless expansion of social services. Soon taxpayers were in open revolt against their state and local taxes, flirting with a variety of caps and ceilings to limit taxes.

In foreign affairs, Carter managed to bring together two seemingly implacable foes—Egypt and Israel—in an historic peace treaty that affirmed the right of Israel to exist, but in the process he further alienated many of Israel's other Muslim neighbors. After some tentative steps toward detente in the early '70s, the Soviet Union poured money into military might and went on the offensive in several regions, financing communist insurgencies in the Middle East, Africa and Latin America, often through the troops of its proxy satellite, Cuba. Smarting from the painful and failed involvement in Southeast Asia, the American people were in no mood to counter the Soviet military buildup. U.S. defense spending declined sharply after Vietnam, along with the national will to use American force for foreign-policy objectives.

Trouble abroad

The last year of the troubled decade was one of the toughest for America. In 1979, sensing that the U.S. and its allies would do little to block it, the Soviet Union invaded Afghanistan to prop up its puppet government there. President Carter responded by banning the sale of American wheat to Russia, which made U.S. farmers furious, and by canceling American participation in the summer Olympic games to be held in Moscow the following year.

Meanwhile, in the Persian Gulf, instability was aggravated by the vast oil riches from the high world price of petroleum. Gulf leaders, flush with oil wealth, poured money into the modernizing of their own nations and investments all over the world, including lavish homes and office buildings in the U.S. Their enormous deposits in money-center banks in New York and London were recycled as bank loans to developing nations, especially in Latin America. (The most excessive and imprudent of these loans would haunt the world economy in the decade to follow.) In their home societies, the rapid westernization of traditional Arab societies—with expanding women's rights, freedom of worship and western customs—led to a political and religious backlash by fundamentalist Muslim elements in Iran, Saudi Arabia, Egypt and elsewhere.

The year 1979 would be the time of reckoning. The most pro-western ruler, the Shah of Iran, was overthrown by followers of the Ayatollah Khomeini, and soon after, an unprotected American embassy was captured and its staff taken hostage by radical Muslims.

DEPARTMENT OF ENERGY CREATED.

SENATE VOTES TO RELINQUISH PANAMA CANAL.

1978

ISRAEL, EGYPT REACH CAMP DAVID ACCORDS.

SUPREME COURT REJECTS QUOTAS IN HIRING.

GOVERNMENT BAILS OUT CHRYSLER.

NUCLEAR ACCIDENT AT THREE MILE ISLAND.

1979

AMERICANS TAKEN HOSTAGE IN TEHERAN.

OPEC RAISES OIL PRICES; LONG GAS LINES RESULT.

SANDINISTAS TAKE POWER IN NICARAGUA.

INFLATION HITS 13.3% RATE.

SOVIETS INVADE AFGHANISTAN.

1970

January 16, 1970

<u>Much interest in price-wage controls</u>...many merchants for them as the only way to stop the inflation spiral. And a hint of criticism directed toward Nixon for refusing even to consider broad gov't controls.

March 6, 1970

<u>The aim is to standardize pensions</u>...write precise regulations and minimum standards that every pension plan will be required to meet. That's what many in Congress want and what the Treasury also is backing. The only real opposition comes from business. The unions are divided.
<u>Such things as vesting rights</u> must be improved, proponents say.
<u>Portability</u> needs to be established...to protect job-changers.
<u>And funding</u> must be made safer...where the money comes from.
<u>The pension issue has been boiling for years</u>...under Kennedy and then under Johnson. Now it is coming to a real test under Nixon. This time it looks as though something will be done...a bill passed.

<u>Don't underestimate the power of conservationists</u> in Congress.
<u>They won a stunning victory recently</u>...easily beating a plan to boost timber cutting on gov't land that would normally have passed.
<u>Means trouble for "pork barrel" projects</u> in coming months... dams, reclamation projects, anything that might threaten wild rivers, wetlands, timber lands, seashores, etc. Conservatives are potent. They will pressure Congress into voting more funds to fight pollution, protect farmers, create parklands...reflecting the new public attitude.

March 13, 1970

<u>Japan as a trading nation exasperates most other countries</u>. Outsells them. Outgrows them...10% or more a year. Booming business in its home markets. And booming in the field of international trade.
<u>It is very stingy with its own money</u>. Restrictions on imports. Limits on what tourists can spend overseas. Skimpy on all foreign aid.
<u>Now...pressure on Japan to ease curbs on U.S. goods</u>. It may.
<u>Also much pressure on Japan to revalue the yen</u>, raise its value. But Japan won't do it this year...might hurt Expo '70 tourist business.

March 20, 1970

<u>Look out for the militant women</u>...take their campaign seriously, the "women's liberation" movement for equality in all phases of society. Oh...some crackpotism involved, yes. But an undertone of real meaning.
<u>For employers in particular</u>, a warning in the feminine militancy. Equal employment rights are guaranteed by law...and are beginning to hit the pay-off stage via court rulings that award back pay for inequities. Thing to note is that women are getting aggressive about their rights.

April 17, 1970

<u>Segregation-by-law is on the way out</u>...in the Southern schools and elsewhere...wherever local ordinances or practices are responsible. Justice expects this type of segregation to be nearly ended by Sept.
<u>But the fireworks will continue</u>. For example, about questions such as: Should courts find ALL segregation illegal, however it arose? Gov't says no...argues that Negro neighborhoods are just a fact of life. Civil rights groups disagree...claim local gov't is ultimately at fault, must be forced to take positive renewal and rezoning steps to integrate.

A student anguishes over another student who was killed by National Guard fire at Kent State University during protest against U.S. bombing of Cambodia.

May 8, 1970

<u>The President's credibility is now being openly questioned</u>... by much of the press, by the Democrats, and even by a few Republicans.

<u>On Cambodia</u>, of course...his justification for going in there so soon after he assured the country that peace was at last visible. The switch was too abrupt for Washington to absorb without a reaction.

<u>Even Republicans were thunderstruck</u>, which is significant since most of them have supported Nixon's handling of the Vietnam war.

<u>Politically, this is very serious</u>. And no one knows it better than the President. He saw the credibility of Lyndon Johnson collapse over this war...a collapse so total that Johnson quit the White House.

May 22, 1970

<u>In Indochina</u>, this much is now becoming clear:

<u>The Reds are no closer to negotiating</u> with U.S. on S. Vietnam.

<u>Quite the contrary</u>...they see the U.S. convulsed, angry, divided over both Cambodia and Vietnam. They hear Nixon promising to pull out more & more U.S. troops. No reason to negotiate. They will just wait.

June 5, 1970

<u>Note that demands are growing for some sort of wage-price curbs</u>. Businessmen, union officials, congressmen, even Nixon's official family.

<u>Businessmen want wage guidelines</u>...for example, a ceiling of 6%. They admit this is still inflationary since productivity is not rising. But they say it's at least a comedown from 8%-to-10%...now prevalent.

<u>Unions insist that a FREEZE be applied to prices...and profits</u>.

<u>We think Nixon will move toward controls</u>. Pressures are rising.

<u>Probably not a freeze</u>, for that would catch too many companies and too many unions that haven't "kept up," bringing a flood of appeals.

<u>Not mandatory controls</u>...at least not now, before elections. So...a breathing space for a while. We shall continue to reassess.

July 10, 1970

Turn to soaring imports. A new controversy is about to break,
and it will eventually push the gov't into imposing stiffer barriers.
More U.S. firms are moving abroad to produce the cheap imports.
American capital & know-how are being used to make goods abroad
for sale in our markets, sometimes prices below production costs here.
Smalls say it's "ruinous"...only the bigs can invest overseas.
Now, they claim, they must compete not only with the normal imports
produced by foreign companies but also stuff that is "American-made."
Labor is up in arms about "exporting jobs"...that is how unions
see it. Long run, they maintain that it will mean less total employment
in the U.S. Also, a threat to "decent" wages and working conditions.
What's more, many gov't officials like the trend. Encourage it.
For one thing, they say imports help in the battle against inflation,
since people can buy them for less. For another, they see it as a way
to bolster the economies and standards of living in other countries.
But the gov't is in for hot criticism...for pushing expansion
of foreign investments too long. Especially in underdeveloped nations,
where labor is cheapest. "It may help them, but it is hurting us."
This is sure: More protection against imports IS forthcoming.
Note that protectionists are more vocal and have more political clout
than the free traders. Bit by bit, not fast, new controls and quotas.
And more restraints on foreign investment...maybe even these.

July 31, 1970

The mail service is going to be overhauled. It has bogged down,
overcome by soaring volume and a mechanism that simply can't handle it.
The old Post Office is going...the system we've had for years.
A new Postal Service is coming in, with businessmen running it,
and aimed at making radical changes in the whole works, top to bottom.
Mail RATES will be raised, for example...the new postal managers
will order them after weighing the recommendations of a rate Commission.
Congress has NO say...it can't reject and its approval is not needed.
Also, changes in SERVICES are coming over the next year or so,
and from what we hear, some of them are going to be plenty controversial.
Will they improve service? Not immediately. Confusion at first,
then perhaps a more streamlined system. Perhaps. No one really certain.
Long range they may make money...or at least cut down the huge deficit.

August 14, 1970

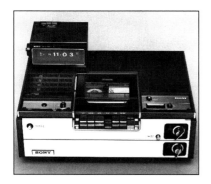

Soon to hit the market...TV tapes...and makers have high hopes.
Will be sold along with a player that is attached to your home TV set.
Thus, "personal" home entertainment, akin to your own stereo or recorder.
Market will be limited at first, for cost will run from $400 to $800.
But if sales increase as planned, prices will be cut to lure more buyers.

August 28, 1970

     <u>Negotiations between the U.S. and Russia on arms</u>...SALT talks...
are making progress, so our diplomats say. A formal treaty or agreement
is probably a year away, but the outline it will take is shaping up now.
     <u>The number of ICBMs</u>...intercontinental ballistic missiles...
will be limited, perhaps to 2000 for each country, land-and-sub based.
     <u>Also, a smaller system of ABMs</u>...the anti-ballistic missile...
only what is needed to protect the capitals...Washington and Moscow.
Could save U.S. up to 30 billions...the added cost for blanket coverage.
     <u>But NO on-site inspection</u>...the Russians will never agree to it.
We can keep track of the number of missiles from the air, but "changes"
to make each more destructive can't be detected. Means that both sides
will go on trying to "improve" their missiles, and costs will stay high.
     <u>A slowing in the arms race</u>, but nothing close to disarmament.

"You see, the more arms we have,
the more we'll be able to *disarm*."

October 30, 1970

     <u>Suppose Japan agrees to voluntary quotas</u> within a few weeks...
would that kill the bill in Congress? Yes, probably would this year.
But textile makers want mandatory quotas, too...don't trust voluntary.
And shoe makers demand help, but know they can't get it by themselves.
So the whole show would just start again next year...where it left off.
     <u>You won't hear the last of this squabble for years to come</u>.

November 20, 1970

     <u>An important change in Red China's attitude</u> toward the U.S.:
     <u>She is acting a bit friendly</u>, more mellow, letting the word drop
among diplomats that a thaw is possible. And we are responding in kind.
     <u>Why? Why the sudden change?</u> <u>Fear</u>, mainly...the fear of Russia
and the long-range fear of Japan, the giants on either side of China.
If the U.S. were a sort of "ally" or friend, neither Russia nor Japan
would be likely to make a rash move against China. Hence, security.
     <u>U.S. will warm up gradually</u>...over the next 5 years.

December 4, 1970

     <u>Let's take a long look at deficits</u>: Starting after World War II
and projecting through 1972, the record will show surpluses for 9 years,
deficits for 17. All the surpluses added together come to 35 billions,
the deficits to 121 billions. This means going into hock by 86 billions.
     <u>And when will it all stop?</u> <u>We don't think it will</u>...short term
or the long range. Doesn't matter about political party, for in the span
of the 26 years the score shows Democrats in the White House 14 years,
Republicans 12 by 1972. There'll be occasional surpluses, but on balance
deficits will overwhelm. This is one reason that we foresee inflation...
nagging, persistent. And why we urge that your plans allow for it.

December 24, 1970

     <u>How pay the cost of zooming demands</u>? By zzzooming the taxes.
     <u>Taxes so high</u> they may soak up gains in income many people get.
All levels of gov't. To pay for expanded services. Medical coverage
for everybody...higher social security payout...control of pollution.
     <u>And who is to pay?</u> As we said, middle-incomers, prime givers.
     <u>How much?</u> By the '80s, enough to make today's taxes look easy.

     <u>Living will become more REGULATED</u>. And industry VERY regulated.
How land is used. How water. How air. Where new building. On and on.
Permits required. New rules, extra paperwork. New era of gov't control.

1971

December 24, 1970

  Standard of living: Perhaps a slowdown in the tremendous rises
of past 20 years. Still, more people will live better than ever before.
  Living will become more cramped, forcing a new trend toward...
  Miniaturization. Almost everything to get smaller. Housing,
smaller units. And more shelf-living...people stacked up in buildings.
Less storage space. Greater use of convenience foods, disposable stuff.
Smaller home furnishings. Most autos will be small, with less power.

February 5, 1971

  There's no issue about what to do in Vietnam. It's to get out.
  Differences arise on how and when, but these are to be expected
considering how unpopular the war is and how fed up with it people are.
  The overwhelming anti-war sentiment and the partisan bickering
do serve as prods to get us out of Indochina as fast as possible.

April 9, 1971

  Bicycles are growing more popular, a proliferation is developing,
for they are being rediscovered by adults...exercise, fun and commuting.
Perhaps crowds of bike-riding businessmen before long, as many big cities
woo them with special trails, parking racks, etc., to cut auto pollution.

April 30, 1971

  Now look at the facts, as pieced together by our intelligence:
  Russia is developing a NEW missile. BIGGER than its biggest now,
the SS-9, which can carry a warhead of 25 megatons...a massive destroyer.
  Have we seen it? No. There hasn't been any showing in public.
In fact, there have been no tests in the Pacific. We can detect these,
put them under surveillance, just as the Russians can monitor our tests.
  But we have seen forty silos from which they would be launched,
much larger "cannons" than are needed to store and fire the SS-9's.

Nixon made tension-easing trips to Communist China and Russia, sharing toasts with Chou En-lai (top left), and Soviet leader Leonid Brezhnev (above).

<u>And that's the only part of the concern</u> over a budding arms race. <u>Russia is also building up ANTI-missile defenses</u> around Moscow. Four sites were completed in 1968, but work was suspended on four others. Now it has been resumed, with evidence that the new sites are designed for ABM's capable of stopping more incoming missiles at longer distances. <u>More missiles for attack, more missiles for defense</u>...net of it. Our view is that U.S. will accelerate its own missile programs. More defense spending, more contracts. And a reordering of priorities as between the military and civilian demands. Ponder the implications.

May 21, 1971

<u>SALT talks, arms limitation</u>: U.S. and Russia will keep talking and keep building missiles...we & they. Any treaty is a long way off.

July 16, 1971

<u>Nixon trip to China</u>: It probably won't hasten an end to the war, it's winding down anyhow. Nor will it bring a burst of trade with China, or affect defense spending here short range. But it does open up doors, it does squeeze Russia, and that may show at the arms limitation talks. Also it helps Nixon...at home and in W. Europe. For him...new status.

August 6, 1971

<u>Wage-price controls</u>: Nixon still is against them...any kind. <u>And so are his principal advisers</u>...in & out of the White House. <u>But we think a control mechanism will be set up</u>, probably in Oct.

August 10, 1971

<u>For inflation, a grim picture</u>. The freeze will put a stop to sharp rises in living costs, but this will probably be only temporary. Gov't is pumping out money, cutting taxes. Fed. Reserve is stimulating via easy money. And when the freeze is lifted, wages will go up faster than productivity, setting in motion the old spiral of wages and prices. The controls to be put into effect after the freeze may narrow the gap but won't close it. Again suggest that you gear plans to more inflation.

August 27, 1971

      Will the official price of gold be raised...above $35 an ounce?
The administration is saying no so often and so loud that many interpret
this as a smokescreen to mask a future increase. That's not the case,
but Nixon may be forced to change. Foreign gov'ts are pressing hard.

October 1, 1971

      The dollar is going to be worth still less abroad. The erosion
has been going on for months via REvaluation of some foreign currencies.
More of these are coming, and the gold price may be raised...DEvaluation.
      So what does all this mean to you, how does it affect planning?
      As a businessman, you are going to have to pay more for imports
from Japan, Canada, Germany, France, Italy, Switzerland, Britain, others.
Also, might pay to scout the big industrial countries as possible markets
for things you make or sell. Our goods will cost foreigners less to buy.

November 12, 1971

      On computers...the latest thing is to hook them up into networks,
use telephone or special lines to link them together around the country.
It's a way of cutting costs...sharing of computers via "teleprocessing."
In its infancy now but likely to blossom fast...into a boom. Still...
      The gov't is worried about possible abuses...within a few years,
when such networks are common. Particularly about two sensitive areas:
      Invasion of individual privacy. Such networks make it easier
to pull together bits of personal information from connected data banks.
      Pirating of business files...data squirreled away electronically.
The experts say that crooks may be able to discover the access codes...
activate computer network, wire-tap data bank, steal business secrets.

November 19, 1971

      A "new" Democratic party seems probable, run by amateurs.
The old guard thrown out, on the sidelines, including the union leaders.
A split party, weakened, unable to focus sharply on the target...Nixon.
      The young liberals and the blacks may take over...the evidence
indicates that they will. Each state delegation has to be balanced...
according to the state's population. By color, nationality, sex, etc.
They may very well exclude hand-picked delegates chosen by the unions,
or by the professional party men...mayors, governors, big contributors.

1972 Democratic Party candidate
George McGovern meets with
influential black supporters, including
Coretta Scott King; Washington, D.C.,
delegate Walter Fauntroy; lawyer
Clifford Alexander; and Gary, Indiana,
mayor Richard Hatcher.

November 26, 1971

    <u>Domestic communication satellites</u>...the future is touted as big. Send TV signals...mail by facsimile transmission...distribute movies... expand computer services...many possibilities. A vast new field opening.

December 23, 1971

    <u>The country is in a transition period</u>, perhaps the greatest ever. A terrible wrenching between the old & new styles of living and working. A great surge of young people, dissatisfied with the time-honored values. A bulge of older people who distrust change or cringe at the speed of it.
    <u>Search for QUALITY</u> will be a chief characteristic of the '70s. Improving products, services, environment, living standards, life style. Making things safer, cleaner, stronger, more reliable, longer lasting. Prettiness, gloss and "looks" to give way to more utilitarian concerns. "Cheapness" that's often associated with mass production is going out.
    <u>It means a wave of new controls on business</u>, demanded by people and imposed by gov'ts at all levels. It's important to anticipate this, allow for it in your affairs...as matters of principle and of profits. Consumer movement will reach a peak in next few years...then quiet down.
    <u>And on pollution</u>...new laws on water, noise, solid waste, etc., tougher regulations on factory air pollution. VERY tough by mid-'70s.
    <u>So, a big up-push on costs</u>...and on consumer prices...and taxes.

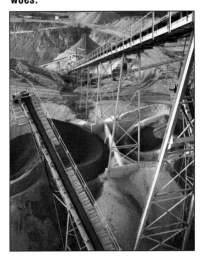

A soft-coal strip mine adds to pollution woes.

December 30, 1971

    <u>Is there any way to reverse the trend toward ever-more inflation</u>?
    <u>Oh yes, but at a price</u>...in jobs, profits, standards of living. Gov't would have to rein in on spending, credit...dampen down business.
    <u>Nobody seems willing not to pay it</u>. Not Nixon, not the Democrats.
    <u>Add it up: Big gov't, big business, big labor</u>...all are marching to the same tune. That doesn't leave much heft for a change in policy. We think the direction for the next 10 years is crystal clear:
    <u>There will be more inflation</u>.

February 25, 1972

    <u>McGovern</u> is also regarded lightly. The pros hate to contemplate the sort of campaign the party would make if McGovern were the nominee. Good-bye to the South. Good-bye to union backing...and union financing. Also, good-bye to many middle-road voters who think he's too left wing.

1972

May 26, 1972

    <u>Now back to the Common Market</u>, for that's the big happening.
    <u>Many changes have already come about</u>. A free flow of trade between the original six...Germany, Italy, France, Belgium, Holland, Luxembourg. A free flow of people...on pleasure or looking for jobs. In the next few years, four more...Britain, Ireland, Denmark, Norway... the same interchange. Plus preferential tariff and trade arrangements with other European countries and the many colonies and commonwealths.
    <u>Just over the horizon</u>: A whole body of Common Market law... American law firms are flocking to Europe. Mergers of very big firms across national borders. Consortiums of banks, other financing groups to aggregate capital. A gradual moving together of the trade unions.
    <u>See the ECONOMIC muscle in all this</u>...not just in Western Europe but throughout the world. New global force for the U.S. to reckon with, at gov't policy levels and in everyday operations of American business.

August 25, 1972

Now about November: Landslide for Nixon? Entirely possible...
even Democrats admit it. Polls so indicate, and Republican politicians
are starting to believe it...which accounts for the jubilation at Miami.
But a scandal might queer it. And the Republicans are very edgy
about charges that some fund-raising activities weren't on the up & up...
and bugging of Democrats' HQ. They hope the smell won't get too strong.

October 27, 1972

Note this about the coal-gas-oil-crisis: It is already here...
and you had better be prepared for it to get worse. Involves the supply
and prices of energy for fuel and electricity in your home and business.
Simple fact is that we are using more fuel than we produce.
Production of energy is limping along, but demand is SOARING...
and will double by 1985 due to growing population and industrialization.
Mostly it boils down to oil, IMPORTED oil...boosting our quotas
for petroleum and liquefied natural gas. That is the stopgap measure
gov't has drifted into due to our lack of any national energy policies.
So temporary help...10 years or so. After that, rely on nuclear power.
Building the Alaskan pipeline will give an important supply lift,
but that is several years down the road. And going to the Middle East...
bargaining there for much of our future needs. That now is a big deal.
So oil diplomacy is on the rise again. Ever since World War II,
oil has played a relatively minor role in intrigues and power struggles
among nations. That's because new finds virtually flooded the world.
Now suddenly EVERYBODY wants oil. Not just U.S...Europe, etc.
We have to bargain with Arab countries for much of our future supply...
therefore oil is again becoming a crucial item in international politics.
Lots of pros & cons about energy crisis...but this seems sure:
Waste of energy is ENORMOUS in this country. All kinds of power
has been "cheap" for so long that it is generally just taken for granted
by the public at large and by industry. Most people will agree on that.
Remedy...general awareness that we are in for serious trouble...
unless the habit of waste is kicked. That time is approaching rapidly.

January 12, 1973

More people between 25 and 34...the nucleus of the work force,
a big increase just over the horizon. The war and postwar baby boom.
These are family-forming people...heavy consumer and major producers.
Hence, a lush market for all sorts of household stuff, food and clothes.
Demand for housing and autos will rise steadily...as families sprout.

1973

Watergate hotel and offices, scene of breakin at National Democratic Party headquarters that ultimately led to the resignation of President Nixon.

January 19, 1973

Watergate scandals: What really happened at Democratic hdqtrs., who was behind the bugging, who ordered it...Senate is planning a probe. Trial here won't turn up anything new...most defendants pleaded guilty.

January 26, 1973

Now luxury imports have Detroit nervous. The demand for these is on the upswing...may cut into the sales of U.S. high-priced cars.

February 2, 1973

The Japanese...the hottest money-makers in the business world.
They can mean big profits to you or can inflict heavy losses, depending on whether you develop some savvy on their fast-moving ways.
They are spreading out in the U.S...not just their products, but also their investments. They now have a hand in scores of lines.
Japanese are good businessmen...no longer riding on cheap labor. Wages there are way up. So, best to face up to their success as a fact of economic life. You may find ways to put their energy to work for you.

March 30, 1973

Men close to Nixon are said to be vulnerable...past & present, including Chapin, Dean, Colson, Magruder. Bright careers may be ended.
Ex-cabinet members...Atty. Gen. Mitchell, Commerce Sec. Stans: Investigators are beginning to link them to the affair in which big sums of unreported Nixon campaign funds were given to men caught burglarizing Democratic headquarters at the Watergate. Both have strong Nixon ties.
Even the FBI is caught up in it...its integrity under question, if not compromised...because White House was given FBI Watergate files.
All this on TV after Easter. A field day for the Democrats... a spectacle. Maybe as gripping as the Army-McCarthy hearings in 1954.

May 25, 1973

Impeach Nixon? Probably not. Democrats see no future in that. They would rather have him here to kick around for the next three years. Besides, the impeachment process would tie up Congress for over a year.
Censure him? Maybe. This is being mentioned as an alternative to formal impeachment...something less time-consuming but still damaging. All depends on whether future evidence ties Nixon closer to the crimes.

June 8, 1973

Autos will get smaller. Plans now on drawing boards in Detroit for models coming in the next few years will show a gradual cut in size. Two principal reasons: People seem to want smaller autos nowadays... and competition from small foreign cars is becoming a tougher problem.

July 6, 1973

Gasoline prices will go up after the freeze. The reason is that the gov't will let the oil companies pass along price increases charged by the Arabs. No way gov't can control what the Arabs dictate. So they will raise the price of crude oil...penny-by-penny, steadily.
Why should the Arabs boost crude oil price? Because they CAN... the demand is heavy, worldwide, and they know how to make a buck.
How long will this go on? Four or five years...maybe longer. Gasoline may go over 50¢ a gallon, despite outcries by motorists.

August 24, 1973

A tough new campaign law is headed through Congress this year.
Stems from Watergate, but it was needed in any event.
Very severe limits on political contributions...and on spending. Gifts by a person to a candidate...$3000 in primary, $3000 in election. That's the limit. And total gifts by one person can not exceed $25,000. Exception: No limit on individual gifts to official PARTY organizations. (This is to prevent rump groups such as Nixon set up.) A formula will say how much the candidates may spend, and this will be enforced strictly.
Enforced by an independent gov't agency...NOT the Justice Dept.

October 12, 1973

On the flow of oil to U.S...it looks strongly as if retaliation will be taken against us for helping Israel, regardless of the outcome. If Israel finally wins, the Arabs will punish us severely. If they win, they may very well cut the supplies for a while as a display of "unity," or to show the world their new strength. Temporary cut, not permanent.
Thus a tightening supply of oil is inevitable...no matter what.

Secretary of State Henry Kissinger
confers with King Faisal of Saudi Arabia.

October 26, 1973

     <u>Impeach Nixon</u>? Still remote, but a growing probability.
House started the preliminary investigation which can lead to that.
Leaders think an impeachment fever may be building up in the country.
     <u>Might he resign</u>? Yes, if the case against him is overpowering,
or he decides the country has turned its back on him, guilty or not.

November 23, 1973

     <u>Detroit must rejigger as fast as possible</u>...bigs to smalls.
Also push economy engines, for that is the next beef people will have.
     <u>Imports are selling like wild</u>. Also the U.S. compacts....Pintos,
Vegas, Mavericks, Novas, Gremlins, etc. And the trades are not too good.
Dealers don't want to get stuck with big cars on their lots. Dead loss.
     <u>Big-car dealers are already singing the blues</u>...can't move stock.
People spurn the heavy, fancy, trim-laden goliaths. Even the well-to-do.

     <u>Recycling is getting a boost</u>...stems from concern over energy.
It's suddenly becoming economical, mainly because of various shortages.
     <u>Old newspapers and boxes</u> are in growing demand by the recyclers.
     <u>Glass, chemicals, woods, metals</u>...business is picking up fast.
     <u>Recovery systems</u> are coming up, too...equipment for recycling.
Many more firms including giants are beginning to market such devices.
But tax incentives for recycling are out, gov't says...not needed now.
     <u>Maybe your firm can profit</u> from recycling. Consult engineers.

December 7, 1973

     <u>In Congress, much talk of WHEN he will resign</u>...not whether.
     <u>The House will begin impeachment proceedings</u> in the new session
that starts in late Jan. Public hearings. Much of the same material
the Senate Watergate committee opened up. Embarrassing, and this time
more difficult for Nixon aides because so much detail is now known...
not many surprises left. Cross-examination to be tougher in the House.
     <u>And remember...now that we have Ford as VP</u>...critics of Nixon
feel a lot freer to go after him than when there was no VP to take over.

1974

"This is where we register for the Postgraduate Economic Course."

February 15, 1974

Business has stopped rising and is now on a sort of plateau... speaking generally, of course. There are ups & downs along the surface, representing lines that are not doing well and others doing very well.

No serious recession is coming. As we said...a high plateau... that's where we think business is going to ride along for a little while. Until sometime in the summer, when most business experts then look for the start of an improvement in things...a slow, gradual upturn again.

March 15, 1974

The Arabs are loaded with dough from the West, will earn more when their oil begins pouring in here again. They want to spend some.

They are looking for investments here, quietly, almost secretly, because they're canny buyers and they know prices of ANYTHING they want would immediately jump up if their interest were known. What they buy: Good real estate. Shares in successful firms, looking to the future, in growth...and in profits (planning for a day when the oil runs dry).

June 7, 1974

Suggest you consider this in the light of inflation:
Saving fuel & electricity now is a hard-boiled business practice. Costs will be rising steadily, and gov't isn't going to do much about it.

June 21, 1974

Oil imports will remain heavy...to provide for an expanding economy over the next decade. There is no other way.

Thus our dependence will go on & on...in the foreseeable future, so talk of becoming totally "independent" fairly soon is just hot air.

July 5, 1974

Inflation will remain high in U.S. But not as high as it is now. It's going to be wrestled down in the next 10 years to a 4% to 6% rate. Not all at once, not next year, not until the late '70s and thereafter.

Remember the U.S. economy is now a part of the WORLD economy. In years past we were somewhat of an island, but now international trade is vital to our fortunes...as it is to Europe's, Japan's and Mideast's. We breathe in & out with them...even though we are still the stronger.

Our exports will increase notably...worldwide...within 10 years.
And our imports. Oil, raw materials, variety of finished goods.
Our money will rise and fall on world markets as conditions vary. There will be "crises" from time to time, but they will be worked out.

July 12, 1974

Now a word on new "floating-rate securities" coming from firms that control banks...bank holding companies. Interest rates on these will fluctuate as the rates on Treasury bills go up & down, except that the floating securities will pay holders more than the Treasury bills.

Are they legal? Yes. Gov't doesn't like them because it fears they will pull money out of savings and loans to grab the higher yields. But it can't do much, can't block them. It has no authority to do so.

August 2, 1974

If Ford has to take over from Nixon, he will have the goodwill of the voters, business managers, union leaders...AND all of Congress. Not unlike sentiment for Eisenhower in 1952-53. That's why Republicans want him to hush now...to keep this goodwill intact. For the country.

Shortly after Nixon's resignation, newly installed President Gerald Ford confers with his appointed Vice-President Nelson Rockefeller in the Oval Office.

August 9, 1974

     <u>President Ford</u>: What does he think? Who will his advisers be? What's he going to do first? Will he continue the Nixon policies? Or does he have a whole set of plans ready? What sort of man is he?

     <u>He is essentially conservative</u>...probably more so than Nixon. But not rigid, not dogmatically right-wing. Flexible when necessary... due to his years in the House as Republican floor leader.

     <u>Example</u>: <u>Ford thinks the gov't should live within its income</u>, except in emergencies...or when economic conditions dictate otherwise.

     <u>Thus not basically different from Nixon</u> in political philosophy.

     <u>But a different kind of man</u>. Friendly, warm, outgoing, genial. In Congress he is very well liked and respected...he's a "decent man."

November 15, 1974

     <u>Now the recession is "official"</u> here in Washington.

     <u>Ford finally agrees that the economy is slowly winding down</u>.

     <u>Will he shift gears and begin fighting the recession?</u> <u>No</u>.

     <u>He intends to sit tight</u>...no basic changes in policies for now. That's the firm impression we get from private talks with his advisers.

     <u>Why?</u> He wants to keep the "game plan" he inherited from Nixon: Let business run flat or even turn down slightly...to cool off prices. Squeeze inflation out of the economy even if it means a mild recession.

     <u>Thus, we think you should expect no substantial help from gov't</u> in the foreseeable future toward getting the economy back on the track.

     <u>Our assessment of the outlook for business is this</u>:

     <u>The slowdown will continue</u> the rest of this year and into next.

     <u>How deep will it go?</u> Not into a depression...nothing that bad. But no blinking the fact that it will squeeze many moderate-size firms.

January 10, 1975

     <u>Look what MAY be happening on wages</u>...no firm trend yet, but:

     <u>Unions seem to be easing up a bit</u>, backing off extreme demands.

     <u>Settlements are lower than expected</u>. Instead of 15% or 20%, they're coming out more in the area of 10% plus escalator for inflation.

Americans evacuating the U.S. embassy in Saigon.

January 24, 1975

    <u>S.E. Asia war</u>: <u>Cambodia is in trouble</u>. Communists closing in, supply lines out. This dry season is critical. May bring Red victory.
    <u>South Vietnam is distressed</u>...running short on military stuff such as ammunition, etc. It wants more from the U.S. to keep fighting, but Congress won't approve. So, in time, probably another Red victory.

February 7, 1975

    <u>Suddenly the Arabs see what is happening here and in Europe</u>.
    <u>There is PLENTY of oil</u>, too much oil...result of the cutbacks. It's becoming a surplus commodity, and the price is now being shaved, here and there on shipments from supposedly united oil-producing nations.

February 14, 1975

    <u>Ford wants to deregulate a number of key industries</u>.
<u>He thinks this would reduce prices</u>.
<u>He has a new standard for measuring ALL gov't rules</u>:
<u>What impact they will have on prices</u>...how they will be helpful in controlling inflation, what good they will do for people, consumers.

April 25, 1975

    <u>On foreign policy</u>, many people now are asking us this question:
<u>Are we headed toward isolationism</u>? That's the general direction, despite official denials...less involvement in affairs of others. Why?
    <u>Mainly because of Vietnam</u>. The war dragged on and most people never saw why we were there. Right or wrong, Americans just grew fed up.
    <u>And because people have lost interest</u> in U.S. worldwide exploits.
    <u>They are weary of "meddling."</u> Past wars and even the "cold war" seem less & less real to voters...not just the young, many oldsters too. The policy looks negative, AGAINST things, mainly Reds, thus uninspiring.

July 3, 1975

    <u>There will be more "two income" families</u>...husband and wife both bringing home the bacon. Thus be able to afford more luxuries... using more of their money for quality things, beyond the necessities.
    <u>Also a greater number of single people</u> in their 20s and 30s... a powerful buying bloc...whether living alone at first or doubling up.
    <u>And older folks will have more money</u> than their ancestors had, hence a fertile field for companies that want to aim for this market.
    <u>All this adds up to great activity</u> and great changes ahead... as people move from the cities. Retailers will use catalog showrooms, warehouse outlets, shop-at-home services, mail-order, telephone sales, even cable TV display and sales...using phones and computers for selling. Emphasis on speed, easier shopping...and higher retail productivity.

July 18, 1975

The Japanese plan a big selling drive in U.S...part of an effort to turn around their recession at home. Heavy promotions and discounts.
Also going to manufacture more here so as to duck transport costs and U.S. duties. Mainly on West Coast now but will be moving inland... the Midwest is next. New plants and joint ventures with U.S. companies.

August 8, 1975

Politics: Reagan will announce for President in a few weeks... and enter several early primaries against Ford. N.H., Fla., plus others where conservative Republicans are strong and he has a good chance to win.
Reagan wants to hold on as leader of conservatives in the party, whether he is the candidate or not. Give the conservatives more voice. That's why he won't team up with Wallace as an independent. Truth is, he hopes to lure Wallace followers into Republican ranks...permanently.

February 27, 1976

The "energy crisis" may SEEM dead & gone, but take another look.
Fact is, prospects are getting worse despite the plentiful stocks and despite the fact that few people can see that the outlook is bleak.
Why? Because our dependence on foreign suppliers is increasing, and that's the REAL problem. Our own production of energy is dropping. But our needs will rise. And that will leave us at the mercy of others, vulnerable to sudden price increases or to any future embargo of oil.

1976

June 18, 1976

Carter: Now that he's pretty much sewed up the nomination...
The smile. It's a genuine basic trait converted to campaigning.
And his ready answers. These tumble from a quick & nimble mind AND meticulous prepping. Cool, calculating, avoids specifics on purpose.
He's highly organized, reflecting his science and Navy training plus business experience...turned his father's place into a money-maker.
Hard-driving and demanding, expects "perfection" from his help.
Understands business. Sees himself more businessman than farmer. Lards his speeches with business jargon..."productivity," "efficiency." He says he will bring business methods to bear on the gov't bureaucracy.
He's familiar with most domestic problems...from the state angle.
But not expert on foreign affairs, which is his weakest point.

June 25, 1976

You might like to know that the world is looking to the U.S.
It is THE place to invest in for future growth and expansion.
Basic reason: U.S. is now a low-cost producer on a broad scale.
Impetus came from the recession. U.S. firms trimmed off waste, reduced work forces, cut costs across the board. In contrast to this, gov'ts in many industrial nations forced employers to maintain employment and pay levels. So foreign industries are still plagued by excess fat. Adding to this misery, wage costs are going up faster than in the U.S.
There are other reasons: The U.S. is seen as politically stable, while other countries have weak gov'ts with a decidedly left-wing bias. U.S. unions are said to be more responsible, in both their bargaining and adherence to contracts. Employes generally have better work habits than in most countries abroad. This may come as a surprise to you in view of absenteeism and idling here. But remember this is in comparison.
The net effect is positive and important. A stimulant both for the total economy and for areas that attract the new investment.

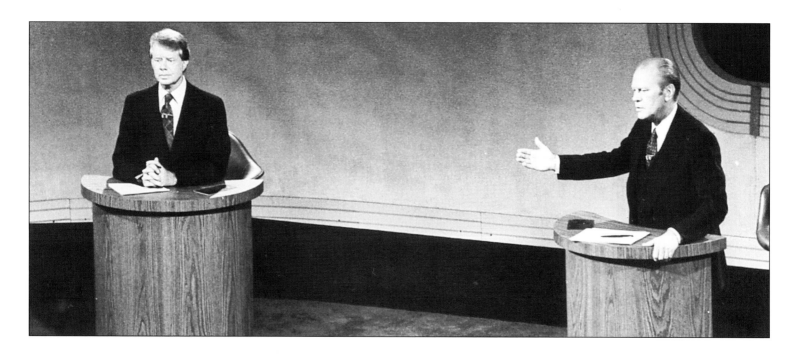

July 30, 1976

> Republican politics: Now almost sure Ford will be nominated...
> on the first ballot. The Reagan gamble this week all but sews it up.
> Reagan has split his followers wide-open, and many will switch to Ford
> to punish Reagan for "betraying" them...a matter of political principle.
> So it will be Ford v. Carter in the fall. Ford the underdog.

August 13, 1976

> Zero-base budgeting: Carter will be making a big pitch for this
> during the campaign, plugging it as a way to get at huge gov't spending.
> Well, the goal is laudable and it fits in with the voter mood.
> But you don't trim budgets by "procedures"...not in Washington.
> It takes political clout to beat back the entrenched interests
> attached to every program. And in this capital, entrenchments are deep.

October 22, 1976

> Question is whether Ford can overtake Carter in the final days.
> Republicans are NOT optimistic about it.
> It's possible, but mood of Republicans is anything but confident.
> The popular vote will be close, electoral vote probably won't be.

November 19, 1976

> Now comes the Republicans' turn to spill blood...their own.
> This always happens when either party loses out in the Presidential race.
> The conservative wing is organizing to take over the machinery.
> Reagan is the lightning rod. His people are doing the spadework,
> and he himself is acting as if he is going to run in 1980...at age 69.
> (We think he will "reconsider" as the date nears, but that's for later.)

February 11, 1977

> Can Carter do anything to moderate inflation this year? No.

1977

May 13, 1977

      <u>The U.S. edge in manufacturing technology</u>: We have enjoyed it
for years in a variety of industries. And it has enabled U.S. producers
to stay in the race for markets with foreign makers despite higher wages.
      <u>The edge is being progressively chipped away</u>...in Germany, Japan,
other industrial nations. Example: Japan is putting equipment on line
to make printed circuits, etc., which will cut assembly time for TV sets
to 1 1/2 hours. Compares with 3 to 5 hours in U.S. This plus lower wages.
      <u>U.S. will become less competitive</u> as our technology lags behind.
In export markets and in meeting import competition in our own market.
Which will bring renewed efforts to provide more protection from imports.

July 29, 1977

      Watch this bill in Congress...it's making headway rapidly:
      <u>MANDATORY retirement before age 70 would be banned</u>...or any age
for federal gov't workers with 15 years' service. For private industry,
however, no company could force employes to retire at 65, as many do now.
An important bill, a "sleeper" in Congress. We will keep you posted.

November 4, 1977

      <u>Look at some of the basic weaknesses that Russia suffers from</u>:
      <u>Farm production is poor</u>. Shortages abound. Productivity is low.
      <u>Skilled labor is scarce</u>. And mismanaged. Most skilled workers
are "European" Russians, not really sold on the advantages of communism.
      <u>Russian technology is lagging</u>, especially on new civilian stuff.
The Red leaders concentrate research & development on military needs.
      <u>One point is clear: Russia can not compete with the West</u>...
not on a sustained basis. The leaders know this and it's VERY worrisome.
Western superiority causes a morbid Soviet fear of dangerous new weapons
being developed as a result of ongoing research in the U.S. and Europe.
      <u>This causes a national inferiority complex</u> that often shows up
in Russian suspicions about the "outside" world, including its allies.
      <u>As a nation, Soviets trust nobody</u>, and waste money & manpower
spying on their own citizens as well as on outsiders...the entire world.
      <u>Nevertheless, the Soviet military machine is good</u>. High grade.
Gets priority on inventors, engineers, skilled workers and raw materials.
Good decision making. Resources are put where they count...big missiles,
"Backfire" bomber, civil and air defense. The Soviet army is enormous.
The navy is being built up and modernized...to match any in the West.
These activities, plus some favorable agreements under SALT agreements,
make the Soviet military a formidable organization. And getting tougher.

A sign of increasing Soviet military might: Soviet Armor in May Day parade in Red Square, Moscow.

November 4, 1977

<u>Might the Reds try to solve their home problems via use of arms</u>?
Keep building up the military machine until it becomes almost invincible?
Then use it to seize some territory that has what the Soviets now lack?
<u>Don't know</u>, of course. Our own officials tend to doubt this.

November 11, 1977

<u>Now consider this</u>...the miraculous gov't inflation machine:
<u>Automatic escalation</u>. By law or by contract, income goes up
for over HALF of all Americans when cost of living rises. One percent
equals 1 billion. Federal & military pensions. Social security checks.
Wage contracts. Food stamps. Some state & local pay. Welfare. Others.
What's wrong with "protecting" all these people against income erosion?
Nothing...except that it all has to be paid for. And you pay for it.

1978

March 17, 1978

<u>Can gov't require you to find & hire minorities</u>? It thinks so,
calls this "affirmative action." Keystone to getting gov't contracts.

April 21, 1978

<u>It's a simple fact</u>: <u>U.S. influence in the world is declining</u>.
We state this bluntly after numerous conversations with business people,
bankers, gov't officials, military strategists...both here and abroad.
<u>Confidence is lagging in our conduct of foreign affairs</u>...badly.
<u>And in the way we handle our domestic problems</u>...a major worry
because of our size. Ripples started here often make tides overseas.

June 9, 1978

<u>How DEregulation may be illusory</u>...more shadow than substance:
<u>Airlines are getting freedom to pick their routes</u>, fly anywhere
they want. Gov't is taking the first big step toward true competition.
<u>But there are constrictions on "freedom"</u> of airlines to choose.
Airports will have to be satisfied on congestion. The environmentalists
will rally against the air and noise pollution. Nothing new in all these,
but it does show that getting out from under the gov't is no easy task.

A Supreme Court ruling on "reverse discrimination" brought on demonstrations like this.

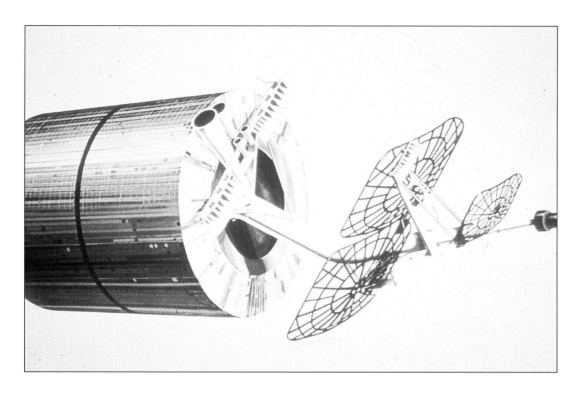

July 7, 1978

New wrinkles in TV, including wider use of pay cables...
special programming on new channels for businessmen, doctors, students.
Computers will be cheaper, smaller, simpler...used EVERYWHERE.
By families, to regulate lights, heating and air conditioning.
To keep records and figure everything from tax returns to homework.
Retailers, bigs and smalls...for checkouts, ordering and billing.
They'll know INSTANTLY what's selling and how much is in the back room.
Electronic mail...using computers, printers at office and home.
Hooking up with other computers via satellites and TV to replay messages.
Electronic banking...special terminals set up in retail stores.
Plastic cards will be used for check guarantees and for instant debits.
And two-way cable channels...allowing you to bank, shop, pay bills by TV.

September 22, 1978

Doing business by computer-satellite hookups is catching on.
Some companies are already setting data from coast to coast by satellite.
This will spread. All sorts of new wrinkles are being developed
for nationwide reservation systems...airlines, motels, automobiles, etc.
Plus financial-data networks, including fast credit-reference checks.
And there is potential for smaller business plugging into these too.

September 29, 1978

Almost everywhere, the theme is anti-spending and anti-taxes.
Both sides playing it to the hilt, even former liberals now in reverse
on both issues...some of them acting as if they invented the new theme.
To old-timers in the parties this causes much behind-the-hand chuckling.

October 6, 1978

New rumors are running wild on wage-price controls...scare talk
that Carter is getting set to spring full-blown controls in a few days.
No...that's bunk. He will stick to "voluntary" measures for now.
So don't worry about any freeze soon. We'll keep watch...and alert you.

The soon-to-be deposed Shah of Iran, Mohammad Reza Pahlavi.

December 1, 1978

      Now look at Russia's plans for the future....the coming decade:
It is trying to get control of areas that have vital resources.
Plus the shipping lanes between them. Using both power AND ideology.
At the same time, trying to buy technology from U.S., Europe and Japan.
      Red targets are already chosen, and they show a clear pattern:
First, the Mideast and Africa. And sometime later...Europe.
It's hoping to get a toehold in Iran as the eventual key to the Mideast.
Controlling the Mideast means controlling Mideastern oil.
Russia will soon have military superiority over the U.S.
Could we catch up again quickly? No...it would take years.
But we can LONG range...toward the end of the next decade.

December 8, 1978

      About foreign investment here...the "buying up" of America,
as some are calling it. Good reason to ask whether effects are healthy.
      Real attractions here are the political stability, huge markets,
good rates of return, certain tax advantages, better labor environment,
and the fact that many U.S. firms are UNDERvalued on the stock market.
      Net...America looks better abroad than it does to many at home.
Maybe distance gives better perspective. Ponder that for a while.

December 15, 1978

      Iran is the gateway to the Persian Gulf. The U.S. and Europe
were counting on the Shah to maintain stability and foil Russia's plans
to edge into the Mideast for a takeover. Now this strategy is melting.
Saudi Arabia, Kuwait and the other Arab moderates are living in fear
as they see how radicals, with Soviet support, can ruin a strong nation.
They also see how hard it is for the U.S...or Europe...to offer help.
      This makes peace between Israel & Egypt paramount...as the start
of a pro-West alliance among the remaining free nations. Against Russia.
Without something of this kind soon, Russia will control all Mideast oil.

Anwar Sadat of Egypt and Menachim Begin of Israel celebrate Camp David accord with President Carter.

December 29, 1978

     Long-term outlook is better...beginning with the early Eighties.
     Productivity gains will start picking up then, rather strongly.
Workers will be more mature, more seasoned...the youngsters of today.
Housewives won't be coming into the work force as heavily as at present.
Fewer teenagers will be starting careers, untrained, untried, unskilled.
     The work force will be between 25 and 55, the best working years.
     These lines will boost productivity dramatically in the Eighties:
Computers. Electronic components. Medical services. Office services.
Synthetic fibers. Chemicals. Drugs. Housing. Air transportation.
     And note that improvement in these will give a lift to others,
which will add up to a rise in TOTAL productivity in years just ahead.

May 11, 1979

     May surprise you to learn that gov't FAVORS a gasoline shortage.
The gov't officials who are in charge of energy are not at all disturbed
about the scarcity, the lines at gas stations or the ever-rising prices.
     Perfectly OK, officials feel, for shortage forces conservation.
Cuts down joyriding, unnecessary driving, the frivolous uses of gasoline.
     If the policy irritates people, too bad. They've been warned,
they aren't heeding the warning...now they can suffer the consequences.

1979

May 18, 1979

     A gasoline rationing plan will be voted by Congress this year,
after the tempers cool off from the recent vote and another try is made.
Most agree that some sort of plan is needed in case of a Mideast cutoff.

     Iran is a big cloud, almost sure to burst. It has NO gov't.
Civil officials ignored as often as not. Religious leaders try to rule
via emotions, but lack real organization. The military is leaderless.
     May be years before anyone can pull it all together again.
     Meanwhile more disruptions in the country's oil production,
putting up-pressure on prices...and a crimp in fuel supplies here.

The Ayatollah Khomeini took power in Teheran in 1979.

June 8, 1979

That's the BASIC reason for Arab oil price increases. Punishment. Other producers...both in and out of OPEC...just ride the rising tide.

It's fury over the peace treaty that's at the bottom of things. The deal between Egypt and Israel. The Arabs are out to make Carter, Sadat and Begin look foolish. And to scuttle the treaty if they can.

What the Arabs want: Force Carter to crack down on the Israelis. Make them stop settling in occupied lands...provide more autonomy there.

Force Sadat to renounce the treaty and return to the Arab camp. (This isn't unthinkable either. We're told Sadat is considering it.)

The price will go up again this month when OPEC producers meet to survey the situation. How much? Not sure. Perhaps as much as 15%.

Then again in December, but recession will put a damper on future boosts. Oil producers are not stupid. Demand is already ebbing.

All of this shows how dependent we are on the whims of others. And the need to work with Europe and Japan on cutting down consumption, softening the price shocks...and somehow finding other energy sources.

June 22, 1979

U.S. position in Central America is sliding...along with Somoza, the Nicaraguan dictator. After his fall, the coming struggle for power will bring in Marxist rulers. Friendly to Castro, who will assist them even though he has played low-key so far. We backed Somoza for years, switched on him too late to avoid the war. So...we end up looking dumb.

Not much the U.S. can now do alone. We have lost the power to sway either side. And any international effort will be cosmetic.

Neighbor nations are shaky too...Salvador, Guatemala, Honduras. With Panama nearby, U.S. business may be affected. And U.S. politics.

June 29, 1979

We're moving toward an "indexed" economy...inflation offsets sought by every group powerful enough to make waves. Example...unions, with their cost-of-living clauses which they strengthen every chance.

Escalator clauses in sales contracts, mortgages, leases, etc. All of which simply means that inflation is being permanently built in.

August 31, 1979

In Afghanistan, there is a revolt against the pro-Soviet gov't. Caught Russia by surprise...the Islamic fervor hadn't been anticipated. As soon as the way is clear, the Russians will try to crush the revolt.

Now another subject...the economic gloom-&-doom peddlers.
Readers often ask whether we agree with them, and if not, why we don't.
No, we do NOT agree. Think they exaggerate...to play on people's fears.
An easy thing to do these days, and profitable. Nothing new in this...
there has been a cult of doomsayers around since World War II was over.
Predicting a crash, depression, ruination. And how to prepare for it.
People who followed them missed out on the greatest growth in history.
There ARE some problems ahead, but they're not insurmountable.
We've looked carefully...with hard-nosed skepticism...at the condition
of U.S. companies, banks, stocks. We find them sound, gaining in vigor.
And bolstered by many built-in stabilizers the system has developed.
No need to panic or turn assets into gold, silver or Swiss francs
or store away guns and food for "survival," to fend off the roving mobs.
That's selling the U.S. short...a bad mistake. The problems are clear.
Business and gov't have noted them. Now they're rolling up their sleeves
and going to work on them, as they've ALWAYS done. Calmly, rationally.
It will take a few years to solve them, but we'll get there.
We've licked far WORSE problems than we are facing today.

September 14, 1979

MOST Democratic officeholders think Carter can not be reelected.
Therefore, they fear that THEY too stand a good chance of being beaten
with Carter at the head of the ticket...bringing out the "anti" voters.

December 28, 1979

Microchips: The leading edge of technology for years to come.
Fantastic reductions in size and cost lead to new applications
in existing products and point to new products. "Computer on a chip,"
tiny circuit board performing functions only big black boxes used to do.
Energy saving...built-in sensors to monitor complex operations
in homes or large buildings...fine-tune energy usage to actual needs.
"Smart phones"...to store often-used numbers, take messages.
Auto carburetion...microprocessors to coordinate fuel mixture,
air intake, spark timing, etc. Far more sensitive dashboard indicators.
Data storage...small units to replace bulky information files
on stuff that needs constant update. Law. Taxes. Medicine. Others.

A bleak symbol of American frustration: Iranians protest outside the locked gate of the overrun U.S. embassy in Tehran.

1980s

The Eighties opened on an American nation that believed itself to be in deep trouble, whipped by double-digit inflation and 20% interest rates, slipping in world trade, bullied by the Soviet Union, humiliated by Muslim fundamentalists.

Ten years later much had changed. U.S. industrial productivity was surging, widening its lead over manufacturing rivals Japan and Germany. Inflation and interest rates had fallen to levels last seen in the early '70s. U.S. exports were booming, the trade deficit declining. American technology was gaining strength, with rising U.S. dominance in microprocessors, telecommunications, software, biotechnology and other fields. There were 18 million more jobs in the U.S. economy than at the start of the decade. Education reform, job retraining and competitiveness were the hot issues of the day.

Most significantly, by 1989 the U.S. was playing midwife to an historic restructuring of the world economic and political order—the most sweeping changes since the end of World War II. The American model of democracy and free markets was being emulated from Europe and Asia to Latin America and Africa. The Soviet empire, America's nemesis for 45 years, was crumbling from its own decay and its inability to compete militarily and economically with the United States. In Communist China, a violent government crackdown in '89 on rapid political and economic liberalization was merely a brief interruption in a halting journey toward freedom.

Although all these remarkable changes occurred between 1980 and 1989, the transformation wasn't a matter of straight-line improvement, and it didn't occur without enormous pain, anxiety and risk-taking along the way. Productivity improvements, mergers and foreign competition led to broad layoffs, first in the manufacturing sector and later in services. While most segments of the work force—especially women, racial minorities and highly educated employees—experienced significant pay gains in the '80s, pay stagnated for workers with inadequate education and training for the skilled jobs of the new economy.

CARTER HALTS GRAIN SALES TO U.S.S.R.

REAGAN ELECTED PRESIDENT.

1980 RESCUE OF TEHERAN HOSTAGES FAILS.

IRAN RELEASES HOSTAGES.

REAGAN WOUNDED BY GUNMAN.

FIRST SPACE SHUTTLE FLIES.

1981

EGYPT'S SADAT ASSASSINATED.

CONGRESS PASSES REAGAN TAX CUTS.

AT&T AGREES TO BREAK UP BELL SYSTEM.

1982 UNEMPLOYMENT EXCEEDS 10%.

America took no vacation from social strife in the '80s. Despite significant advances for racial minorities and enormous growth in the black middle class, race relations grew more tense, with blacks seeking faster gains and many whites resenting a trend toward preferential treatment of minorities in education and the workplace. Citizens divided passionately over whether abortion rights, guaranteed by a '73 Supreme Court ruling, should be maintained or rescinded. Problems of urban poverty—welfare dependency, homelessness, drug addiction, street crime, family violence—seemed to worsen. For homosexual Americans, the satisfaction of winning broader legal and social acceptance was muted by the tragedy of AIDS, an incurable, fatal disease that spread rapidly among gays. AIDS also infected intravenous drug users and, to a lesser extent, heterosexuals.

Technological transformations

Technology was the bright star of the '80s, transforming the way Americans lived and worked. Products engineered by gene manipulation in laboratories were coming to market for uses in human health care, agriculture, environmental protection, veterinary medicine, manufacture of composite materials and innumerable other areas.

Countless new electronic devices went from being expensive novelties to commonplace, affordable tools for personal productivity and entertainment: videocassette recorders; cordless phones in the home, cellular phones in the car, and finally tiny portable phones that fit in the pocket or purse; personal computers, laptops, notebooks and palmtops, ubiquitous in the office, home, schoolroom and wherever business people worked en route; PC software to perform every task from check writing and tax preparation to genealogy and chess; video games in arcades, giving way to super-realistic PC video games that appealed as much to adults as to kids; compact discs, replacing 33-RPM records and chipping away at the convenience of audiocassette tapes; CD-ROM discs that contained entire encyclopedias; interactive computer services that enabled on-line users at home to pay bills, trade stocks, make airline reservations or check the latest weather reports and sports scores. Miniaturization and falling prices were the bywords of the high-tech revolution.

Turmoil in business

The technology revolution of the '80s was accompanied by staggering turmoil in American business. Wealth that equaled the great turn-of-the-century industrial fortunes was created in a few years in software, cable TV, entertainment, retailing, biotech and other new fields. Giant firms that were slow to change, such as IBM, DEC, Sears and General Motors, found themselves playing catch-up with dynamic new competitors like Microsoft, Compaq, Wal-Mart, Home Depot and Honda. Independent banks were gobbled up by fast-expanding regional institutions such as NationsBank and Banc One. Mutual funds surged in popularity, giving small investors the benefits of portfolio management and diversification once available only to the rich.

In the mid '80s, a new breed of financier pioneered a corporate restructuring method called leveraged buyouts, in which companies, often publicly owned, were acquired with borrowed money, trimmed of unprofitable or low-profit divisions and later resold. Many of these turnaround plays turned out well, revitalizing stale firms and increasing value for both stockholders and the broader economy. Others were fiascos in which basically sound corporations were raided, split up and left in a weakened state, with gains only for those who led the takeover. While most takeover financiers used perfectly legal methods, a few, such as Michael Milken and Ivan Boesky, went to jail for violating securities laws forbidding insider trading.

Juxtaposed with the hardship of workers laid off in restructurings, the opulent lifestyle of Wall Street financiers gave the '80s an ill-deserved reputation as the "decade of greed." In fact, charitable giving and volunteerism soared in the '80s. America gave a home to millions of immigrants, including large numbers of political refugees. Small businesses were started in record numbers, creating millions

VOTING RIGHTS ACT RENEWED.

LEGISLATION AVERTS SOCIAL SECURITY BANKRUPTCY.

1983

FIRST WOMAN ASTRONAUT TRAVELS IN SPACE.

U.S. DEPOSES LEFTIST GOVERNMENT IN GRENADA.

SEVERE DROUGHT DEVASTATES AFRICA.

REAGAN VISITS CHINA.

1984

INDIRA GANDHI ASSASSINATED.

of new jobs and modest amounts of wealth for large numbers of Americans, especially new immigrants. While income and wealth distribution did tilt toward the upper brackets, it was due primarily to a strong increase in dual-income households and to rising values for stocks, home equity and pension assets. A much-touted "shrinking middle class" resulted more from upward movement into higher-income brackets than from demotion into lower brackets.

Despite—or possibly because of—cuts in marginal tax rates, total tax revenues grew robustly in the strong economy of the '80s. But federal spending grew even more, especially for entitlements and defense, so big budget deficits were a hot issue in the '80s. Emboldened by the rising value of their assets, especially home equity, many consumers overborrowed and underinvested, and many businesses did the same.

Soaring immigration—legal and illegal—provided U.S. employers with much-needed labor at every level of skill, from physicians and computer programmers to farm workers and cleaning crews. Assimilation problems increased, too, with debates over social-service expenses, bilingual education, English as an official language, and job competition between immigrants and native-born Americans, especially low-income blacks.

Economic recovery

In the first three years of the '80s, the U.S. wrung out many of the excesses of the '70s, going through a recession generally as severe as that of '73-75, and in industry, much worse. The Federal Reserve, under the leadership of Chairman Paul Volcker, tightened the money supply to break the back of high inflation and the high interest rates that accompanied it. American industry slashed employment, embarking on a dramatic modernization that would result, by the late '80s, in the U.S.'s once again being the world's low-cost producer in countless fields. In the fall of 1982, unemployment in the U.S. topped out just under 11%—the highest since 1940's jobless rate of nearly 15%.

Recovery from so deep and long a recession as the '81-82 slump was bound to be strong, and the ensuing expansion was a record-breaker. The U.S. economy expanded steadily for the following eight years, a record of uninterrupted growth exceeded only by the Vietnam-boosted boom from '61-69. And unlike the Sixties boom, this one wasn't accompanied by growing inflationary pressures. Aided by falling world oil and commodity prices, tough international competition and rising productivity and moderate wage increases in the '80s, inflation and interest rates dropped in a jagged but steady line throughout the decade.

Reagan the catalyst

The catalyst, steward and cheerleader for the world's free-market surge in the 1980s was an unlikely figure who was in the right place at the right time with a message that a weary America—and world—was ready for. Ronald Reagan, a former movie actor who had served as governor of California, was long considered too conservative (and too old) to be president. But after the social and economic upheaval of the '60s and '70s, many Americans were ready to try something radically different. Reagan's electoral coalition included large numbers of Democrats who felt disaffected by the increasing domination of the Democratic Party by its left wing. Reagan laid blame for most of America's ills at the door of big government, which, he said, stifled hard work and entrepreneurship with high taxes and overregulation. He called the Soviet Union an "evil empire" whose military superiority over the Western democracies should be opposed by a massive, high-tech arms buildup.

Soon after taking office in 1981, Reagan proposed the largest tax cuts since John Kennedy's proposal 20 years before. Marginal rates were slashed about 25%, with the top rate falling from 70% to 50%. In a sweeping tax reform bill in 1986, marginal rates were cut further, with a new top rate of 33%. But deductions and tax shelters were scaled back, and the longtime tax break for capital gains was eliminated, giving the U.S. one of the world's biggest tax bites on gains from the sale of appreciated assets, such as small businesses, homes, farms and securities.

Reagan also urged large cuts in federal spending on social programs and steep increases in defense spending. The

1985		1986		1987	
GORBACHEV BECOMES SOVIET LEADER.	E.F. HUTTON PLEADS GUILTY TO FRAUD. REAGAN AND GORBACHEV CONFER.	SPACE SHUTTLE CHALLENGER EXPLODES.	U.S. SANCTIONS IMPOSED ON SOUTH AFRICA. ARMS DEAL WITH IRAN DISCLOSED.	REAGAN OFFERS TRILLION-DOLLAR BUDGET.	GORBACHEV LAUNCHES "GLASNOST" AND "PERESTROIKA". DOW JONES CRASHES 508 POINTS. REAGAN AND GORBACHEV AGREE ON MISSILE CUTS.

Democratic Congress, which gladly embraced Reagan's tax cuts and military increases, generally rejected his proposed social-service cuts. While the budget deficit soared through the '80s, the economy grew even more, so the deficit declined as a percentage of gross domestic product from nearly 6% in '83 to half that level by '89.

As the U.S. economy set a world standard for robust job creation between '83 and '90, other nations, especially in Europe, experimented with the American model of tax cuts, privatization of government functions and reduction of trade barriers. Europe took bold steps toward a unified free-trade zone. In China, Communist Party Chairman Deng Xiaoping loosened governmental regimentation and encouraged free-market experiments. When liberalization threatened to spin out of control, with rising inflation, corruption and challenge to the communist leadership, officials responded with force. Student demonstrations in Beijing's Tiananmen Square in '89 were met with a brutal crackdown by the army.

Reagan, believing that the sheer manpower and firepower of the Soviet military couldn't be matched by the U.S., proposed a high-tech antimissile system informally called "star wars." He refused to bargain it away in arms-reduction talks with the Soviets.

In Central America, Reagan authorized an invasion of Grenada to block communist expansion there. He proposed military aid to the "contras," rebels fighting the socialist Sandanista government of Nicaragua, which received military aid from Cuba and the Soviet Union. Aid was also given to the rightist regime in El Salvador fighting its own pro-communist guerrillas. After Congress voted restrictions on U.S. aid to the contras in 1985, the Reagan administration secretly continued that aid under a variety of schemes, including diverting to the contras money from secret arms sales to America's nemesis, Iran, which agreed to release some western hostages. When the Iran-contra affair was exposed in congressional hearings in the summer of '87, White House operative Colonel Oliver North became a villain or hero to millions of Americans, depending on where they stood on Reagan's Latin American program.

By the end of the '80s, governments in Nicaragua and El Salvador were in negotiations with their respective rebel opponents. The Sandinista government was voted out of office by the Nicaraguan people in 1990, and a semblance of order had settled over El Salvador.

Japan becomes powerhouse

Japan, which had spent 30 years investing heavily in dynamic high-tech industries, especially in consumer electronics and automobiles, emerged in the 1980s as a world manufacturing and exporting powerhouse. With high product quality and ease of access to the very rich and open U.S. market, Japan's products gained strong U.S. market share in many consumer sectors, especially when the dollar was strong in the early '80s. But the Japanese economy remained relatively closed to competing products from other nations, so Japan's trade surplus exploded. Japan reinvested its massive trade surplus all over the world, especially in the U.S., where it funded purchases of real estate, whole U.S. corporations, and startups of new manufacturing facilities for cars, office equipment, cameras, tires and other products.

Japanese money was just the most visible component of a surge of foreign investment in the U.S. from many countries, including Great Britain, Canada, Germany and the Netherlands. Heavy foreign investment in the United States, besides being the flip side of the U.S. trade deficit and weakening dollar, was an acknowledgment of the dynamism, high productivity and stability of the U.S. economy. It was a significant contributor to strong job growth in the '80s. Foreign capital also offset the crowding-out effect of high federal budget deficits, which, in the absence of foreign funds, would have sopped up U.S. savings and sent interest rates soaring.

Despite the fact that the U.S. was the world leader in the globalization of business and was still the world's leading owner of overseas assets, surging foreign investment in the U.S. fanned feelings of anxiety in many Americans, leading to a resurgence of protectionist sentiment in trade policy. Foreign investment in the U.S. peaked in the late '80s and then declined, as economies softened in Japan and Europe.

	SOLIDARITY			IRANGATE JURY			BERLIN WALL
WORST	LEGALIZED IN			CONVICTS	S&L		OPENED.
DROUGHT IN	POLAND.	BUSH		NORTH.	BAILOUT		
50 YEARS		SUCCEEDS	EXXON		VOTED.		
HITS FARM		REAGAN.	VALDEZ	SUPREME			U.S. INVADES
AREAS.	NATIONAL		SPILLS OIL	COURT LIMITS		TIANANMEN	PANAMA.
1988	DEBT HITS		IN ALASKA.	ABORTION		SQUARE	
	$2.6		**1989**	RIGHTS.		MASSACRE	
	TRILLION.					IN BEIJING.	

Meanwhile, U.S. exports—aided by a declining dollar, improving product quality and international marketing—grew strongly after '87. The merchandise trade deficit was cut in half over the next four years. The U.S. also became aggressive in the export of services, such as education, financial services, tourism, transportation, and engineering. The U.S. trade surplus in high technology and services was offset, however, by continuing large deficits in petroleum and automobiles.

Nine years of economic growth

The U.S. economy experienced uninterrupted growth for nearly nine years, from the end of the '82 recession until a brief and relatively mild national recession in '90-91. The stock market boomed in the '80s, starting the decade with a Dow Jones industrial average of 875 and finishing at more than triple that level. Along the way, on October 19, 1987, an overpriced Dow tumbled 508 points in one day. But the crash did not cripple either the national economy, which continued growing for three more years, or the stock market, which climbed back to its '87 peak over the following three years.

Growing public concern over rising budget deficits led to the enactment of a spending-control program called Gramm-Rudman, which was often evaded by Congress but at least encouraged more fiscal discipline than Congress would have shown in its absence. Deregulation of markets in trucking, banking, airlines and telecommunications, which began under Gerald Ford and continued under Jimmy Carter, continued to advance under Ronald Reagan.

Problems arose when Congress partially deregulated the banking and savings and loan industry. It gave S&Ls the freedom to lure deposits with high interest rates and invest their deposits in a wider array of assets than just home mortgages. But at the same time Congress insulated depositors from risk—and put the risk on taxpayers—by doubling federal insurance coverage on deposits. Some S&Ls invested their insured deposits in a wild overexpansion of commercial real estate. Many of the real estate projects failed to lease up, causing a wave of foreclosures and thrift institution failures. Depositors were protected, but the U.S. taxpayer was left holding the bag, at a cost of many billions of dollars and an increase in budget deficits well into the '90s.

In the election of 1988, Reagan's vice-president, George Bush, defeated Michael Dukakis, the governor of Massachusetts. Bush pledged to continue the general philosophy of the Reagan administration, but he was not the committed conservative that Reagan was. Bush supported, for example, far-reaching new laws to reduce air pollution and expand the rights of disabled citizens, laws which imposed enormous new costs on American business. In the '88 campaign Bush promised that he wouldn't go along with income-tax increases, but he reversed that promise to win agreement on a deficit-reduction package two years later.

Economic slowdown

The strong boom of the mid '80s was bound to slow down, and in the second half of the decade it did. Auto sales peaked, then declined. Burdened by high consumer debt, many households cut back on retail spending and began paying down debt. Home price cooled off, too, after price runups raced ahead of personal income growth in many hot areas, such as southern California, New England, Washington, D.C., and Atlanta. Construction of new office and retail space collapsed from oversupply. The economy continued to grow through '89 and '90, but rather weakly, and unemployment was rising from a new wave of layoffs at service corporations that were merging, restructuring and generally trimming down to improve productivity and profits. There was little that Washington could do to stimulate growth, because the rising budget deficit tied the hands of Bush and Congress on fiscal stimulus.

Worldwide upheavals

But all the changes going on in the U.S. were nothing compared with much more dramatic changes elsewhere in the world. In South Africa, the first significant steps were taken toward repudiating apartheid and enfranchising the long-oppressed black majority. Mexico was beginning to elect free-market politicians set on privatizing national industries and inviting foreign investment. Palestinians living in occupied territories of Israel began a revolt in '87, and the harsh Israeli crackdown began to elicit world sympathy for the cause of a Palestinian homeland, or at least greater political freedom within Israel. In Asia, newly industrialized nations as large as China and India and as small as Malaysia and Singapore became significant new forces in global manufacturing.

Nowhere was the change so wrenching as in the Soviet empire. Straining under the dead weight of a sick economy, its war in Afghanistan, and trying to match America's growing military spending, the Soviet Union went through a succession of weak leaders as public disgruntlement mounted. In 1987 a new kind of communist leader, Mikhail Gorbachev, embarked on a program of reform he called "perestroika" (restructuring) and "glasnost" (openness). While maintaining the Communist Party's grip on Soviet society, Gorbachev startled the world by freeing dissidents, holding open elections for Communist Party officers and criticizing the harsh rule of his predecessors. In December '87 Gorbachev and Reagan signed a pact to begin the destruction of short- and intermediate-range missiles, and the following spring, Soviet troops began to leave Afghanistan. In the fall of '88, as opposition to the communist regime in Poland grew in strength, Moscow essentially stood by and watched, rather than crushing the revolt as it would have done in earlier years.

Soviet empire disintegrates

The last year of the decade, 1989, turned out to be the tipping point for the tottering Soviet empire. Rejection of communist rule was spreading across the nations of Eastern Europe, captive since the end of World War II. Gorbachev pledged in March that there would be no armed Soviet opposition to the spread of democracy in the region, and the following month saw the beginning of Soviet troop withdrawals from Eastern Europe.

In March Soviet citizens voted in the first free elections in Russian history, electing members of a new Congress. Many Communist Party candidates were defeated, and an emerging figure, Boris Yeltsin, stepped up his criticism of Gorbachev for moving too slowly on democratic and economic reforms. Yeltsin was ousted by the Supreme Soviet but reinstated after popular protests and Gorbachev's intervention on his behalf. Throughout this treacherous period of rapid change, Gorbachev walked a tight rope, balancing between forces seeking accelerated liberalization and opposing factions, especially in the military, calling for a slowdown or reversal of reform.

In September Hungary opened its border with Austria and became the escape route not just for Hungarians but for East Germans as well, and soon the communist premier of Hungary resigned. With the fortified border between East and West Germany now irrelevant, East Germany bowed to mounting public pressure and opened the border in November. The Berlin Wall, erected nearly 30 years before to keep East Germans from fleeing to freedom, was broken apart by jubilant crowds.

Meanwhile, the massive American defense buildup of the '80s was winding down. The U.S. announced sharp cuts in military spending to be enacted over the next several years—reductions in troops in Europe and elsewhere in the world, base closures in the U.S., reduced orders for new armaments, curtailed research on the "star wars" missile defense system. While Americans rejoiced over the prospect of a safer world and politicians began laying claim to the "peace dividend" from reduced spending, others noted that decreased defense spending would be a serious blow to local economies dependent on defense manufacturing and large military base payrolls.

Cold War ends

The rapid crumbling of Soviet communism in the winter of '89 was played out on global television before an incredulous world audience. The Cold War was coming to a close, and the United States had won. For 45 years, with varying degrees of enthusiasm and success, the U.S. and its western allies had militarily contained the expansion of Soviet communism. And with an ideological model more potent than military might, America had demonstrated beyond dispute that democracy and free markets, for all their faults, were the most effective mechanisms for raising standards of living all over the world.

So ended a decade of shocking political and economic change, occurring at a speed that was both exhilarating and troubling. A superpower rivalry that had dominated world affairs for nearly five decades was coming to a close. No one knew whether the result would be a safer world—or a vastly less stable and therefore more dangerous world.

Soviet tanks on the offensive in Afghanistan.

1980

January 4, 1980

<u>The U.S. is reduced to "watching"</u>...monitoring troop movements and HOPING that the Russians will limit their aggression to Afghanistan.
<u>We won't go to WAR over this</u>. Carter ruled out force long ago. He tipped his hand to the Russians...they can now breathe easy on that.
<u>Now the U.S. must try to set up NEW defenses</u> to impede Red plans. Peripheral stuff, since we can't buck the Russians directly without war. Set up bases. Sinai. Kenya. Somalia. Oman. And beef up Diego Garcia.
<u>Send military aid to Pakistan</u> and others who now feel menaced.
<u>Even grope for new relationships in Iran</u> through dissident groups that are starting to see what LOCAL Red organizations may be working for.

January 11, 1980

<u>First, help for the grain farmers</u>, who are hurt by the embargo on sales to Russia. Some arm waving about the cost...several billions. Also sharp questioning of Carter aides on why farmers got hit so hard. There's a suspicion in Congress that using trade as a political club may come back to haunt us at a later date...in competition for sales.

February 8, 1980

<u>This is the start of a long defense buildup</u>...the new budget, and ONLY the start. View it from the perspective of several years ahead.
<u>Little impact on business this year</u>. We're at the talk stage... the early rounds that precede the actual ordering, hiring and production.
<u>This will extend through most of the '80s</u>...a REarmament.
<u>Leading to a boom for the defense industry</u> and its suppliers. Most aerospace companies are bursting at the seams. Soon...even busier.

February 22, 1980

<u>After the release of the hostages in Iran</u>:
<u>A longer range program to bolster Iran</u> will be set in motion. Includes strengthening both its economy and its military capacity. Top officials say it's either this or watch Russia move in by default.

February 29, 1980

<u>What Carter and his aides REALLY want is a mild recession</u>. They're counting on it to solve their problems...wish it would hurry up.

March 14, 1980

     Republican politics: Reagan now seems too far ahead to catch, even if he loses in Illinois. Most of the primaries in the weeks ahead are in states where he is popular and where conservatives are in charge.

     Bush and Anderson are dividing the moderate-liberal Republicans, most of them. The rest, plus conservatives, then swing over to Reagan.

     Ford may be too late to change things. Besides, he'd grab off some moderate-liberal votes...dividing them THREE ways instead of two.

March 21, 1980

     Imports of autos from Japan will NOT be limited by Congress. It wants to put pressure on U.S. auto makers to develop more gas misers, figures protecting them from imports would only undermine this objective. Meanwhile, Japanese are being asked to behave..."restrain" themselves.

April 25, 1980

     New pressure to limit smoking in public is beginning to emerge from a medical report saying smoke can hurt nonsmokers in closed rooms. Gov't buildings, waiting rooms, etc...likely targets for gov't curbs.

May 2, 1980

     The whole Mideast is badly shaken by our botched rescue mission.

     U.S. prestige there is at a new low. Friendly Arab leaders... those basically pro-U.S...are raising questions about just how far to go in continuing their ties to us. They are frightened and disillusioned. Fearful of Russia, but they also fear close attachment to a "weak" ally.

     The hostages in Iran are probably there indefinitely. At least there is little the U.S. can do now to get them out...either by force or by sanctions. The sanctions have the support of our Western allies, but the backing is lukewarm and probably temporary...few months at best.

     U.S. foreign policy is suspect the world over...friends and foes can not fathom it. They find it inconsistent, and very often impetuous. Our friends question whether we are still providing a security umbrella. They HOPE we will embark on a big rearmament...but have their doubts.

May 9, 1980

     Talk of "dumping Carter" is only talk...it hasn't a chance. He has the nomination all but sewed up. But there is little enthusiasm for Carter within the ranks of the party, and that's a serious problem.

     Democratic leaders are worried about Nov., about the prospect that Carter will just turn off SO many voters that Reagan will clean up.

Wreckage of the attempted hostage rescue in Iran.

Line workers installing new fiber-optic cable.

May 23, 1980

"Fiber optics"...glass replacing copper wire. Major innovation in communications, about to take off. Will boost capacity enormously... while reducing cable bulk...and eliminate much reliance on electronics.

May 30, 1980

Texas, California and Florida are the growingest of all states, as the new census figures will show when they come out in a few months. They account for 40% of the total growth in the U.S. since 1970. They're the core of the Sun Belt that stretches across the southern U.S. Think of the political impact...the heft of the South and West. These states now have a majority of the population within them, outstripping the big industrial states of the North for the first time. They will have a majority in Congress in another two years... after the House districts are reapportioned to reflect the new census. They will have the most electoral votes in another four years.

June 13, 1980

Now, take a look further ahead. Through the '80s and '90s. We won't reach energy self-sufficiency, even by the early 2000s. Better crank THAT into your planning, no matter how distasteful it seems.

June 20, 1980

What sort of man is Reagan? What kind of President would he be? These are questions on the minds of many people, including Republicans. They don't feel they know him even though he has been around for years. Is he solidly right wing? No, despite what his opponents say. He's a practical politician. And he was a practical governor of Calif. Is he dumb, as his opponents often claim? No, that's a charge that the liberals make mainly because he used to be a Hollywood actor.

Reagan understands what he's saying. He can stand up and talk in any sort of forum, engage in debate and express himself forcefully. He has a tendency to simplify issues, and this brings him criticism... but it also rouses his audiences and makes them see his point clearly. It's a skillful platform device rather than a reflection of shallowness. He has been consistently underrated in politics. The Democrats made this mistake in California when he first ran. Now doing it again. His views are uncomplicated...few details. Wants sharp tax cuts, really DEEP cuts...for business and individuals. Also wants to cut gov't, reducing its control over personal decisions and over business decisions. Thinks gov't has gotten too big, too complex...needs a thorough pruning. Wants to promote exports, making the U.S. more competitive abroad. Build a stronger defense...giving a green light to new weapons and paying servicemen more money. Will seek to regain U.S. superiority. Is he too old to be President? Many think so. This is a rap that may hurt Reagan in the fall. It's largely unspoken but it's there. He knows it. That's why his choice for VP will be unusually important.

July 11, 1980

For VP, Bush ranks first even though Reagan isn't fond of him, and vice versa. But most delegates think he would be the best choice.

Reagan is not a typical politician. Essentially rather shy... doesn't like to mix socially with other politicians or his own aides. Not much at small talk, seldom makes the rounds in a room to handshake, usually ducks in and out of meetings, doesn't hang around for chitchat.

Lives quietly with his wife...who serves as a sounding board and offers opinions on public policy. She's influential...he listens.
No pretense of intellectualism. Neither is a deep thinker. This is not said critically...it's a fact they don't try to conceal. They fancy themselves "plain people," and this is useful on the stump where Reagan prides himself on "just talking sense" in simple English.

August 8, 1980

Russians are getting the jump on us with new space weapons...
Land-based laser and particle beams to blind U.S. satellites as they fly low over Russia snooping on Soviet military activities.
Next, miniaturized space-based systems which could be used to knock out our satellites and even destroy our nuclear missiles.
Science fiction? No, a real possibility in another 10 years.

November 7, 1980

It's not just an election, it's a turning point...
A veer to the right, nationwide...away from the "new liberalism" that has dominated politics in recent years. It should not be mistaken as a swing to the FAR right, but from the left-center to right-center. This change in thinking among masses of voters didn't happen overnight. There have been signs of it earlier, but the signs were not this clear. And because they were not, they went unheeded...the warnings ignored.

The country now reflects conservative ideals, and this means...
Tax reduction...but more important, tax policies to create jobs via incentives for business to expand and produce more. Old tax notions based on "depression thinking" are obsolete. The voters have shown that.
A gov't that encourages investment...this will get a shove now. Letting people use more of their money to build for their own future.
Wage-price guidelines will be axed. Reagan's inflation strategy will be to squeeze gov't spending and curb growth in the supply of money, prod investment and savings and get rid of impediments to productivity. He will also have to take a hard look at inflationary risk of tax cuts.
Regulatory agencies will get their wings clipped...OSHA, EPA and others. They won't be abolished, but more attention will be given to regulatory COST...dollars & cents...balanced against social benefits. Reagan may call for a moratorium on all nonessential new regulations.
Several Supreme Court vacancies could open up before long... and with a Republican Senate, Reagan's picks should be easily confirmed. He will nominate a woman for the Court...as promised in the campaign.
Defense: A speedup of the Trident sub and MX missile programs. More cruise missiles...land and sea-based. Improving Minuteman missiles. A substantial rebuilding of U.S. defense capabilities in coming years... giving a big lift to aerospace, shipbuilding and other key industries.

Sandra Day O'Connor, first woman named to the Supreme Court.

The B-1 Stealth bomber was touted to be nearly invisible to radar.

Lech Walesa addressing a Solidarity rally in Poland.

November 21, 1980

<u>More strikes in Poland are probable</u>. Economic problems there are going to worsen as winter sets in...and lines for food get longer. Communist officials have had to temporize with the strikers up to now, but their Soviet masters can not tolerate union uprisings indefinitely. They would undermine the system...in Poland and other Red satellites.

<u>A purge may become necessary</u>, getting rid of the union leaders, restoring order before the cancer spreads. A series of "sad accidents," suicides, etc...union shake-ups, leaders replaced by "trustworthy" men.

<u>Or...last resort, Soviet troops</u>. But Russia HOPES to avoid that lest it focus a spotlight on the failure of the Soviet economic system. The gravest situation Russia has faced since WW II.

December 26, 1980

<u>The stock market generally</u> has been in a slump for many years. An extended trough. Prices are up only slightly from the earlier lows. Ten years hence, today's prices will seem like bargains, which they are. So this is a chance for people of moderate means to build a nest egg.

But it requires care...study...advice from competent people.

<u>As for business prospects in the '80s</u>, beyond the current slump: Growth won't be "back to normal" until 1982 or 1983...then picking up.

<u>Investment in new factories and equipment</u> will make bigger gains once the tax incentives are there, encouraging a steadier flow of funds.

<u>Productivity</u> will lag for a while...then pick up more momentum.

<u>Profits</u> also will rise, and more of them will be plowed back into modern machinery, new products, expansion, research...the future.

<u>Inflation</u> will come down gradually as the decade wears on.

<u>Personal income</u>, struggling upward over the years...very slowly. Living standards will improve, but not dramatically until the late '80s.

<u>An important fact about the work force</u>: It will be experienced. More productive. Fewer youngsters and women taking their first jobs.

<u>Now widen the lens and see the changing panorama of the U.S.</u>

The movement of people from the North and East into the South, Southwest and the West, carrying the vigor that comes with migration.

<u>Changing the political face of the nation</u>. Old power centers losing their clout...new developing areas gaining influence steadily.

And a shifting of attitudes...back to more traditional values.
More emphasis on work, output, growth. Less on spreading the wealth.
A major change...noteworthy...a veering away from the previous patterns.
It's the foundation for rejuvenating the whole economy.
The adaptation of the basic American system to a new set of conditions.
Our economy tilting from heavy industry to high technology and services.
New lines being developed, slowly growing more profitable than the old.

January 9, 1981

1981

Television is in for a shake-up in the years just ahead...
some of it already under way...affecting networks, cable TV, public TV.
There will be much less domination by the networks, because...
Viewers will have more to choose from...scads of new stations.
Each area cable-TV system is probably going to offer about 80 channels.
For a small extra fee, viewers will be able to watch first-run movies,
championship boxing, concerts, live theater. Specialized programming:
Business news. Education. Ethnic productions. Hobbies. Music.
And further down the road...direct transmission...satellite to home TV.

February 20, 1981

On foreign affairs, things are starting to look better.
The U.S. and the West are improving their positions gradually.
Not much of this is due to Reagan. It's a slow swing of the pendulum
toward the U.S...instead of away, as has been the case for many years.
The Moslem world is turning toward the West. Key countries...
including Saudi Arabia and Egypt, which both have a stronger Western tilt
than they dare state publicly. And now, Algeria is edging over our way.
This may help Israel feel safer about working out a settlement
with the Palestinians, opening up a chance for calm in the Mideast.

Germany seems headed for strong conservatism...tied to the U.S.
Chancellor Schmidt's party is threatened with a split. If this happens,
the Christian Democrats are a good bet to take over...strongly pro-U.S.,
much more anti-Soviet, anti-communist. More like England...Thatcher.
Even some Latin American gov'ts feel more secure...now bolstered
by the fact that the U.S. won't be pestering them about "human rights."
This will give the radicals in those countries less maneuvering room.

Russia itself has MANY grave problems. Poland. Afghanistan.
China, growing steadily. On top of these...another bad year for crops,
plus the need to try to stay ahead of the U.S. in arms. The Red economy
is being stretched thin by the requirement to balance guns and butter.
At home and in its satellites. And most recently...in Latin America.
This doesn't mean we can relax. The Soviets are past masters
at keeping the world off balance...and provoking troubles for the West.
They still have military superiority over us, which is always dangerous.
But for now at least, their troubles are piling up faster than ours.

"Damned Proletariat"

March 13, 1981

And still ANOTHER type of mortgage is due to be announced soon,
once again to give home buyers a long-term deal without tying the lenders
to a fixed interest rate for the life of a mortgage.
This will help to free up more money for mortgages, by encouraging
lenders who got out of the business to get back in again.

Chairman Paul Volcker of the Federal Reserve held a tight rein.

May 8, 1981

Reagan wants the Fed to be TOUGHER, no matter how high rates go. His advisers say tight money will bring rates down by cooling inflation.

You will probably see some S&Ls go under in the next few months, caught between high rates paid for deposits and low rates on older loans.

Also a lot of mergers...some of them FORCED by the federal gov't.

But deposits in S&Ls are safe...generally insured up to $100,000.

May 29, 1981

Get braced for a disappointment on gov't spending...and red ink.

Spending will be much higher than Reagan or Congress is saying.

Deficits this fiscal year and next will exceed present targets.

This despite painful efforts to bring the budget under control. The most encouraging thing we can tell you is that without these efforts both spending and the resulting deficits would be much worse...hog-wild.

June 26, 1981

This slowdown in inflation is real...and it's lasting.

Look for 9 1/2% this year...compared with 12 1/2 % last year.

Probably around 8% next year, our best early judgment.

August 7, 1981

Will it work...the Reagan program? That's the next question now that he has squeezed nearly everything he wanted out of Congress.

Yes, we think so. Think his tax program will lift the economy out of its stop-&-go rut...into a stronger and more sustained growth. Very little effect THIS year. Too late. Tax consequences too small. But by mid-1982 and beyond, business should be building up momentum.

Air controllers' strike: We don't think Reagan will back down.

This is a crucial test of whether gov't employees have a right to ignore the law and strike. Postal workers and others get the signal, straight from the White House...a hardheaded approach, no pussyfooting.

It may sober other unions too...those that have to negotiate new contracts with industry in months to come. Reagan's tough attitude is likely to stiffen management's backbone before the bargaining begins.

In Central America, Russia is thumbing its nose at Reagan... ignoring his warnings to lay off arms shipments and subversion there.

Going to continue to play tough...whether he likes it or not.

Two Latin dictators confer: Fidel Castro with Daniel Ortega of Nicaragua.

USSR is pouring weaponry into Cuba, at least some of it destined
for redistribution into countries where Castro wants to set up shop.
    And a big arms buildup in Nicaragua...from both USSR and Cuba.
    Nicaragua has a large military force...trained and ready to go.
    Apt to fan out to Guatemala and Honduras...its forces going in
to organize the locals and start a rebellion. And the usual charges
can be expected by interest groups here that those gov'ts are repressive.
    Situation in El Salvador is worsening...gov't is losing troops.
    Even democratic Costa Rica is in danger. Has no army at all...
which was once a plus. Now Nicaraguan leftists move in and out at will.
Threatened strikes could topple the gov't. No military as a buffer.
    Reagan isn't ignoring all this, but he is being very cautious...
not even sure which groups the U.S. should be backing in each country.
Partly because we've let our intelligence system get rusty in that area.

August 28, 1981

    On new weapons for defense, the Reagan program is shaping up.
    There won't be enough money for everything that Reagan promises.
With tax cuts in place, he MUST pull back or face a horrendous deficit.
    Budget outlook is bleak...no black ink by '84 as Reagan promised.
He and Congress ARE getting results in the drive to rein in gov't growth.
Deficits would be even bigger if past trends had been allowed to go on.
It's just that Reagan overpromised...the job is harder than he realized.

November 13, 1981

    Recession: Our judgment is that it will stretch out all winter,
touching bottom toward the end of winter. We think it will be April-May
before there are any clear signs indicating that the recession is over.
The early signs will be weak...growing stronger as we get into summer.
    A broad recovery will become visible by next July or August...
picking up momentum in the fall and running into 1983 at a good clip.
    The market will go up BEFORE business does because these experts
act in anticipation of a business rise. When pressed for a prediction,
they say the market probably will start up smartly in the late spring.
    Now is the time to be thinking of investing, doing the planning
and even some nibbling...while stock prices are at "bargain" levels.

"Oh, those things are the fault of Congress or the past several administrations or something"

1982

March 5, 1982

    There is NOT a depression brewing or a financial crisis ahead.
We say this thoughtfully, after examining the facts, pro & con.
Sure, there's growing speculation about risks of a depression,
a bust much deeper and longer than previous postwar slumps.
Caused by heavy burdens of short-term debt, thin cash cushions,
high interest rates, sputtering growth, defaults, bankruptcies.
Could it happen? A slim chance. Will it happen? We think not.

Our reasons, based on judgments from the best available sources:
The heart of our economy remains sound...steady and resilient.
Strongest anywhere. Tremendous resources and underlying demand.
There are now automatic gov't safeguards against a depression.
The 10% tax cut in July and defense spending will add some lift,
and interest rates will come down a bit more from today's levels.
What's more, if things really appeared to be going kerflooey,
Reagan, Congress and the Federal Reserve would run to the rescue.
Easing credit. Creating jobs. Propping up banks and thrifts.

But there's confidence that the bottom of the recession is close
and that there will be slow improvement in the second half of the year.
Some think recovery will be more sustained because it will be gradual.

PLO Chairman Yassir Arafat, chief spokesman for the Palestinian uprising called the Intifadah.

March 5, 1982

<u>Mideast</u>: <u>Israel</u> is almost being goaded to invade <u>Lebanon</u>... by the PLO, Palestine Liberation Org. Probably will too, when ready, setting off a new Mideast crisis, which may be just what the PLO wants.

March 12, 1982

<u>Another subject</u>, now heating up because of the big deficits: <u>A constitutional amendment to FORCE gov't to balance the budget</u>. The states are pushing hard for a constitutional convention to vote this. Only three more states needed to make Congress act...through a convention or passage of a constitutional amendment for ratification by the states. <u>But any such amendment wouldn't ban red ink under ALL conditions</u>. It's sure to contain loopholes. Still, it would be a permanent restraint on the President and Congress. And that's really the whole point.

<u>Reagan is convinced the Soviets want to control Central America</u>. <u>Nicaragua is the headquarters</u>...and supply depot for uprisings in the neighboring countries, starting with El Salvador and spreading. <u>Our gov't has been asleep on all this</u> and is just waking up. We aren't fully awake yet. There is still considerable resistance here to Reagan's plans for more aid to El Salvador...or further involvement.

May 7, 1982

<u>The FACTS about the future of social security look grim indeed</u>. Without an emergency bailout in Oct., the system will go broke. There's not enough in the retirement fund to cover Oct. checks. <u>But gov't will rescue it</u> by borrowing from other trust funds... Medicare trust fund or perhaps the disability insurance fund. Note that this will happen just a month before the elections. <u>AFTER the elections, maybe some action</u>. Perhaps a lame-duck session will tackle the problem...leaning on the commission's recommendations.

May 14, 1982

<u>Lower inflation is going to keep business on its toes</u>. <u>Stiffer price competition</u>, less distortion of sales & profits. <u>Requiring whole new strategies</u> on inventories, pricing, wages. Prices DOUBLED in the past eight years, inflation averaging close to 9 1/2%. And in three of those years...1974, 1979 and 1980...it ran more than 12%. Now, we're rapidly shifting down...to around 6% or so this year and next. High compared with the '50s or '60s...but it sure beats 12%-13%.

<u>Fact is, inflation has camouflaged mistakes</u> and polished results.
Puffing up sales figures, profits, return on investment, investory value.
<u>It will no longer be hiding sloppy management and top-heavy debt</u>.
<u>Your costs will be much more difficult to pass through</u> in prices.
<u>Variable-rate loans look better</u> for borrowers as inflation cools.
<u>Be cautious about long-term borrowing</u> at current high rates.
<u>Keep in mind that interest rates will ease</u> as inflation slows...
averaging lower in next few years. Important to savers and borrowers.

June 18, 1982

<u>A constitutional amendment for a balanced budget</u> will not pass.
Senate might approve it...needs a two-thirds vote. But the House won't.

August 20, 1982

<u>The sudden eruption of prices Tuesday</u> caught everyone napping.
But before getting too het up about it, see how low prices still are,
even after that spectacular run-up. Dow Jones now, Friday, is...869.
At the end of August 1967, fifteen YEARS ago, it was way up to...900.
<u>Other prices nearly TRIPLED since then</u>...Consumer Price Index.
So if you adjusted Dow Jones to match the prices of 1967, squeezed out
the intervening inflation, it would shrink down to approximately 300.
<u>This suggests that stocks today are a bargain</u>...in true value.
Probably still as low as they will be for the rest of this century.

December 17, 1982

<u>Gov't deregulation of banks & thrifts is moving fast</u>.
<u>This will heat up competition</u>...as it was designed to do...
<u>No rate ceiling on 3 1/2-year CDs now</u>. Moving to 2 1/2 years in April.
1 1/2 years in April 1984...and so on. All such limits will be off by 1986.
<u>We expect even faster deregulation</u>, eliminating all the rules
on interest rates and minimum denominations by 1984 or perhaps sooner.
<u>Clearly there is going to be a scramble for savings dollars</u>.
<u>There's a certain risk in these new accounts</u> for banks & thrifts.
<u>Going to be costly</u>. But competition gives them no alternative...
the race for customers will entail taking chances and trying new things.

<u>The whole shape of the U.S. economy is changing</u>.
<u>Some industries are injured permanently</u>. They will keep going
but on a somewhat smaller scale. Particularly true of heavy industry.
<u>Others will flourish</u>. Service lines. Electronics. Robotics.
High technology. Communications. Science and research. Many more.
<u>New products, new markets, new methods</u> will assume leadership
in coming years...replacing the older markets and older products.
<u>A new generation of industries</u> to add to the total economy.

A day of feverish trading on the New York Stock Exchange.

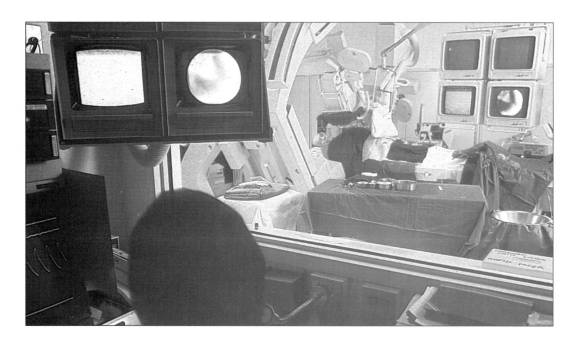

January 7, 1983

The facts about medical expenses and health insurance are grim.
Costs are still SOARING. Hospital room charges up 14% in 1982.
Prescription drugs, rising 12%. Nonprescription drugs and services, 9%.
Physician fees, 8%. Dentists, 6%. Overall medical care gaining 11%.
Compare this with the increase in total Consumer Price Index, of 4 1/2%.
Better look for ways to share these increases with employees.
Have them pick up a bigger part of the premiums, pay higher deductibles,
perhaps switch from basic health-care coverage and major medical benefits
to "comprehensive"...subject to deductibles from the first dollar owed.
And reduce medical bills via second opinions regarding surgery,
advance testing before hospitalization, outpatient clinics and home care.
As for the govt's role...it will be minor.
Congress may vote a limit on Medicare and Medicaid payments...
a schedule of fixed fees for various kinds of hospital care and services.
And perhaps a hike in Medicare deductibles...which is politically risky.
But this could backfire...doctors, hospitals and others reacting
in self-defense by boosting their fees for non-Medicare-Medicaid cases.
Fearing this, some insurers want a gov't cap on ALL medical charges...
but we doubt Reagan would go for that. So rate it as fairly unlikely.
Cost of health coverage for older employees will also be rising.
Congress voted to make private plans primary insurers for those 65 to 70.

January 14, 1983

Three things are required to get deficits back under control:
Slow the expansion of "entitlement programs"...limit how much
gov't will pay in social security benefits, veterans' benefits, etc.
These are a huge part of the budget but mostly off-limits up to now.
Reduce the defense buildup...and obviously this will be done,
well beyond the cuts that have been announced by Reagan and Weinberger.
Increase taxes. This will be done too. We aren't yet sure
which taxes will be raised. Lots of schemes are under consideration.

February 25, 1983

The crack in oil prices...what it will mean in coming months:
The price will stabilize at about $25 per barrel...by June.
Gasoline will ease further...around 90¢ leaded, 95¢ unleaded.

March 25, 1983

Genetic engineering has a big future in farming. Gene-splicing may yet produce super strains of livestock and feed grains. Examples:

Speeding up growth...without dangerous chemicals. Efficient, faster maturing of animals and plants, hence lower production costs.

Controlling many diseases that now hamper crops and animals. Perhaps develop disease-immune strains of cattle, swine and plants.

Could mean vast gains in crop yields as more plants are developed that can pluck nitrogen from the air...sharply reducing fertilizer costs.

April 8, 1983

Foreigners are taking aim at specific industries in the U.S.: Electronics and semiconductors. Business machines. Telecommunications. Textiles and apparel. Shipbuilding. Aircraft and aerospace production. Steel & aluminum. Autos. Petrochemicals. And the list goes on & on.

Goal is to elbow us out of our present markets, here & abroad.

May 13, 1983

Campaign issue to watch: "Industrial policy." Only a slogan in search of a program, but it will be hot stuff in the coming elections. Democrats are touting a mixture of gov't protection for basic industry, gov't incentives for expansion, gov't curbs on dismantling of factories, gov't working with labor and industry on where the economy should go.

Emphasis strongly on gov't: Opposite of Reagan's philosophy... free markets, less gov't interference...thus offering a clear-cut choice. How much ice it cuts with the voters will depend on the economy in 1984.

Communist meddling in the Caribbean is moving into a new phase. a series of small steps by Cuba and Russia to expand their foothold. Grenada has fallen. Nicaragua too. El Salvador is the current target. Then there will be others. Honduras. Guatemala. Costa Rica. Panama.

A systematic takeover, carefully planned over a period of years.

May 20, 1983

Interstate mobile phone conversations will become commonplace via cellular radio...a new network of transmitting and receiving "cells." They will automatically switch calls to unused frequencies as you drive.

Democratic candidates for 1984:
Geraldine Ferraro and Walter Mondale.
VP-candidate Ferraro was the first
woman to be nominated for national
office by a major party.

May 20, 1983

>   Next, word pagers that fit in the pocket. They display messages
> in words, not just numbers. On the market soon, an advance on "beepers."
>
>   Politically, women are THE emerging power bloc...a potent force.
> Women make up more than half of the voting public...52.8%, to be precise.
> And from 1978 on they have tended to vote differently from male voters.
>   Women officeholders will dramatically increase. Some experts
> see women filling 40% of the seats in Congress by the end of the century.
> They'll also make more inroads in state legislatures. A natural result
> of the numbers of young women flocking into law schools in recent years.
>   Women clearly have clout...and are beginning to make it felt.

November 18, 1983

>   Democrats are pretty well resigned to Mondale, he's so far ahead.
> There's not much enthusiasm about him...he's seen as a faithful workhorse
> and a "traditional" Humphrey-style Democrat. He has a big jump on Glenn,
> who is stepping up his attack on Mondale but not yet making much headway.

December 30, 1983

>   Competition with Russia will continue in the years ahead, but...
>   An arms agreement will probably be reached sometime in the '80s.
>   And Russia has an economic mess that it must straighten out soon.
> We think that it will gradually move toward a hybrid marketing system...
> away from central planning, recognizing the present system is a flop.

1984

January 6, 1984

>   1984: Much was written the past few weeks about George Orwell
> and the totalitarian Big Brother gov't that he envisioned for this year.
> And in many parts of the world, his satire turned out to be a grim fact.
> But in the U.S. the trend has reversed...toward relaxing gov't direction
> and to MORE competition rather than less. Muffling the role of gov't.
>   There are even cracks developing within the Soviet satellites.
> And Latin American military dictatorships are gradually yielding control
> to civilian gov'ts. There's more individualism, private participation.
>   1900 to 2000 has been called the "American Century." Perhaps.
> It seems likely, however, that the principles that made our nation great
> will take root and flourish in many more places during the NEXT century.

Deregulation spawned numerous small airlines but ultimately led to fewer, bigger ones.

February 17, 1984

<u>Here's the outlook for nuclear power</u> for the next 15-20 years:
<u>Doldrums after about 20 plants now being built are completed</u>.
About half of those currently under way will just have to be abandoned.
No new starts before cheaper, standardized designs appear in late '90s.
Until then, electrical power demand won't support any big new projects.

February 24, 1984

<u>Shakeout in the airline industry has a way to go</u> before it ends.
<u>Some regional lines will be pushed to the wall</u> in a year or two,
will be battered by fierce competition for some of the popular routes.
And several of the newly formed small lines will have to fold completely.
As for the big national lines, only a handful will remain into the '90s.

April 27, 1984

<u>Turn now to the new Soviet leaders</u>: What kind of men are they?
<u>Chernenko is 72 and merely a caretaker</u>, not truly the big boss.
He has the titles but nothing close to the power of Brezhnev or Andropov.
Shares authority with a collective leadership as the old guard hangs on.
<u>Gorbachev is heir apparent</u>...at 53, youngest among the top brass.
<u>Russians will avoid clashes with the U.S.</u> during this transition,
while home affairs are unsettled. Besides, they respect Reagan's muscle.

June 1, 1984

<u>Most banks are well in the black</u>...although profits are smaller.
<u>Picture is more somber for savings & loans</u>...cause for concern.
<u>Many S&L's haven't recovered from the 1980-81 interest surge</u>...
so are facing this new rise in a weakened position, already losing money.
Still carrying too many long-term fixed-rate mortgages at low interest...
while having to attract new funds by offering depositors HIGH interest.
<u>The FSLIC fund that protects S&L deposits</u> may take a battering.
But there are a number of emergency measures available to the gov't...
IF a transfusion of money should become necessary to cover depositors.

June 22, 1984

On weapons in space, the Russians are attempting a squeeze play.
They have tested an anti-satellite weapon and know that it will work.
So now they want to ban such testing...stop our tests in their tracks.
Soviet goal is permanent space war superiority...nothing less.
They know the U.S. system, when completed, will be better than theirs.
But if we can't test ours, we won't be able to rely on its protection.
Reagan won't go along. He'll stand firm on moves to catch up.

July 27, 1984

As to taxes, Mondale is right on one score and wrong on another.
He's right...taxes WILL be raised next year whoever is President.
But wrong on Reagan's "secret plan" for a hike. There is none.
A tax hike would be Reagan's last resort...accepted reluctantly
only after it becomes clear that a combination of deeper spending cuts
and continued economic growth alone can't slash deficits to safe levels.

August 24, 1984

A few observations about the Republicans...after Dallas:
They're united, but only behind Reagan. There isn't much unity
behind many of the other Republican candidates running for lesser jobs.
In fact, there's a good deal of intraparty bickering and backbiting.
Looking BEYOND this election, Republicans to watch are these:
Bush, of course...the front-runner for the nomination in 1988,
the "man to beat" in the primaries. He will have quite a head start.

August 31, 1984

In Europe, talks between East and West Germany are significant,
perhaps the most significant development since the partition was set up.
Nothing much will happen short range, but the two nations are anxious
to establish something akin to friendship, and this is the beginning.
Other Soviet satellite nations are restive too...Czechoslovakia,
Romania, and Poland again. Romania wants no Soviet nuclear weapons.
The Czechs want more trade with the West. And Poland tugs at its chains,
straining to get free. All seem to perceive current Soviet weaknesses...
another sick leader, economic stagnation (leading to smaller subsidies).
It's a chance to get additional independence...but not REAL independence.
Anything approaching freedom, any little step, is well worth the effort.

Contra forces in Nicaragua depended on American help.

March 8, 1985

    <u>Nicaragua</u>: the Contras are NOT going to be left high and dry. Assuming Congress cuts off funding, other countries will pick up the tab for a modest flow of arms...enough to keep the heat on the Sandinistas.

March 15, 1985

    <u>Resentment against Japan is building up fast here</u>.
    <u>Congress is getting very impatient</u> with all the foot-dragging on opening up markets to more U.S. products and giving us a fair shake.
    <u>Work on retaliatory measures will start soon</u> if the barriers against U.S. telecommunications equipment are not lowered inside Japan.
    <u>Reagan will be pushed</u> to take bolder action than he prefers.

    <u>What got us into this</u>? <u>No single thing</u>. Dollar, of course... higher it goes, the wider the trade gap. But there are other causes: We've overpriced ourselves...our jobs & skills. For what we produce, we are overpaid. People abroad can do the job as well...and cheaper. So more companies are moving overseas to take advantage of lower costs. Or buying from Japan, Taiwan, Korea, Hong Kong, Singapore, So. America.

    <u>Pepping up Russia's weary economy will be his immediate goal</u>. Under Gorbachev, Soviets will start out on a road toward freer markets, and no one knows where it will end. Much opposition from old-line Reds, but Gorbachev knows SOMETHING must be done to exploit resources better.

April 19, 1985

    <u>Boomy sales of compact discs and players</u>, thanks to lower prices. Players are selling for $300-$400...compared with $1000 a year or so ago. Discs, originally $20-$25, are now about $12. They'll get even cheaper.

    <u>Gorbachev wants to finish off Afghanistan</u>...end the war there, calm things down, consolidate the Soviet gains and institute some order.
    <u>He will ease off in Central America awhile</u>...to placate the U.S.
    <u>Also hang back in the Mideast</u>...waiting for new opportunities.
    <u>On arms control</u>, he can't lose the propaganda war. His offer to stop deploying SS-20 missiles in Europe if we stop deploying missiles obscures the fact that he has all the SS-20s he needs already in place. So he will repeat the offer...and even propose it as a PERMANENT thing.

September 6, 1985

Don't kid yourself about gov't DEregulation...
New regulations continue to gush out...300 proposals a month.
A torrent of controls, some of which are bound to affect your business.
True, regulators are more cautious...for word has filtered down
that they'd better not go overboard, that Reagan favors less regulation.
Still...natural tendency of bureaucrats is to spin MORE rules.

September 20, 1985

Reagan's "star wars": Keep in mind that we're playing catch-up.
For years, Russia spent more on missile defense than on missile offense.
Now it leads us in both areas. So why should it care about star wars?
Because it wants to keep its lead. Figures that Reagan's plan will work,
especially with U.S. superiority in use of sensors and data processing.
That's why Reagan is so UNwilling to simply deal it away.

October 4, 1985

A word of caution on tax reform:
Good chance that it will be turned into a tax INCREASE next year,
changing spots before your eyes...and hoodwinking some of its supporters.
That will be clear this winter after Reagan proposes deeper budget cuts.
Congress won't have the guts to trim huge "entitlement" spending.
So higher taxes will be the "solution"...with Reagan going along
once it's obvious that future deficits would otherwise zoom out of sight.

October 11, 1985

Gorbachev BADLY needs an arms slowdown...and he needs it soon.
He's under growing pressure at home to revamp the entire Soviet economy.
That means billions of rubles for new industrial technology & equipment.
It also means cuts in defense spending to pay for such a massive effort.
Reagan knows this...and he'll use it to negotiate with Gorbachev.

November 15, 1985

Watch for a surge of Japanese real estate investment in the U.S.
It's another potential source of friction with American business people,
infuriates the locals who are wheeling & dealing for the same properties.
Close to 5 billions' worth next year...TRIPLE the total for 1985.
Mostly choice downtown office buildings and suburban shopping centers.
By the way, forget about Japan's promise to open up to U.S. goods.
Tokyo isn't serious...figures Reagan will veto protectionist legislation.
So it's back to business as usual...stonewalling U.S. products & services.
Meanwhile, 30 large Japanese companies have built plants here.

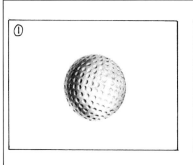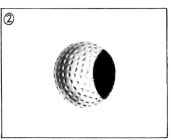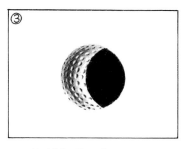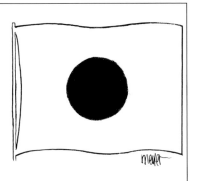

Watching the eclipse at Pebble Beach

January 31, 1986

Space shuttle disaster...what effect on the program? Some delay, but it's unlikely that a complete redesign of the shuttle will be needed. Past flights would have revealed any big flaws. Also, its, vital to SDI, Reagan's Strategic Defense Initiative. Thus, through unmanned satellites and a slightly stepped-up launch plan once the shuttles are flying again, it's a good bet that the program will be back on schedule by early 1987.

April 25, 1986

Interest rates have more room to fall over the next few years. They are still fairly high in "real" terms by past standards. But long run, they'll slip further. Lenders are still hedging more than needed against the mild inflation we expect in the years ahead.

June 6, 1986

The business upturn is nowhere near over, though anxieties abound as it ages...now 3 1/2 years old. Expansions don't die just from old age. This one will soon become a bit friskier, getting stronger, not weaker... with a good chance of going on another year or two, possibly even longer. Not roaring ahead...moderate growth, which is a big reason it will last.

November 28, 1986

Hispanic population of the U.S. will SURGE in the next 20 years, from 18 million now to 23 million in 1996 and 30 million in early 2000s. Accounting for about one quarter of our entire growth during that period.
Sharp rise in births because of a fairly young Latin population.
And a steady flow of immigrants from Mexico and Central America.
A huge increase in older people of Hispanic origin...65 and up... QUADRUPLING in 30 years. Further strain on social security and Medicare.

Iran: It's the acid test for Reagan's leadership and resiliency. Some degree of permanent damage is certain...he will never FULLY recover. However, it's not the unraveling of a Presidency...not another Watergate. There will be other events, new foreign crises that will overshadow it, but the scandal will linger on & on...politicians will make sure of that.

Lt. Colonel Oliver North was a principal Irangate figure inside the White House.

December 19, 1986

Uproar over insider trading will have at least on result...
Congress will boost Securities & Exchange Comm. budget sharply. Maybe 25%-30% more, to copy with the recent explosion of stock trading. Trading up 700% in past decade...four times as many brokers and salesmen. International markets make the SEC job tougher too...it's easier to shift shady deals to overseas exchanges where stiffer U.S. rules don't apply.
Means SEC will have more manpower to discourage funny business. Now actually has FEWER staffers than in 1975 to copy with more problems.
And more fallout from the Boesky affair will be coming soon... probably early next year. High-visibility moves, to scare off repeaters.
All & all, a better situation for investors in the months ahead.

1987

March 13, 1987

<u>Is it time to bail out of the stock market</u>? <u>Well, we think not</u>.
<u>There's room to go higher</u>...plenty of life left in the market.
You've heard many of the reasons: Expected higher corporate earnings,
fruits of past belt-tightening. Money pouring in from foreign investors,
to whom U.S. stocks STILL look cheap. Lack of attractive alternatives...
low inflation & interest rates crimp activity in bonds, real estate, etc.
<u>Stay cool when "corrections" hit</u>...they're inevitable, of course.
But when they come along, don't be spooked. If you panic and sell low,
say the Wall Streeters, you'll just give up future winnings to the pros.

June 5, 1987

<u>AIDS spending is zooming</u>...for research, education, and the like.
Congress has put up $450 million this year, will up that by $75 million.
Next year, $1 BILLION...plus $2 billion in Medicare and Medicaid costs.

June 19, 1987

<u>No effective AIDS vaccine in sight</u>...may take 10 years or longer
because of problems with new strains. But there will be drug approval
to prolong the life of AIDS patients...probably in the next year or so.

July 10, 1987

<u>Take some stock profits</u>. Market's long surge is easing off,
so look over your portfolio and take some gains from the past few years.
Don't just cut & run...think about selectively limiting your stock risks.

October 16, 1987

<u>Stock market</u>: <u>Is it signaling a crisis in our economy</u>?
<u>No, not a crisis</u>...and not doom or a collapse or depression.
<u>But the economy does have real problems</u>...faces serious risks.
The market isn't seeing hobgoblins, although it is exaggerating dangers
of rising interest rates, inflation, excessive debt, trade, the dollar.
<u>Business will slow in '88</u>, but no sign of recession.

October 23, 1987

As you adjust your plans, stay calm, clearheaded, avoid extremes,
both the unwarranted pessimism, the gloominess of the past week,
and the attitude that everything's hunky-dory, business-as-usual.
<u>We'll probably squeak by without a recession</u> in the next year.

<u>It isn't just an aberration</u>, a freak caused by "program trading."
<u>The crash is a symptom of deeper troubles</u>, including heavy debts.
Something like a heart attack...a warning of severe problems,
which causes injury on its own...it CAN'T just be shrugged off.
<u>As for the stock market itself</u>, speculators have been scared,
the high rollers. They'll be forced to sit on the sidelines for a while.
For long-term investors, those who own shares in good companies,
best bet is to ride it out. If it made sense to buy stock originally,
there's probably good reason to hang on to it now. Long-term prospects
are tied to the economy itself. On that basis...no reason for panic.
<u>This is not 1929</u>, despite the scare stories now going around.
<u>Net</u>: We've had a jolt to the economy...<u>but not a knockout punch</u>.

**Soviet President Mikhail Gorbachev
and President Ronald Reagan signing
a missile-reduction pact in Washington.**

December 11, 1987

The new missile reduction pact: Senate review starts next month.
Why is the treaty important? It provides a political breather,
a break in the long, tension-filled and controversial buildup in arms.
And it opens the way for further cuts in nuclear and conventional forces.
So the MOOD it sets may be more significant than what it actually does.
On balance, a deal too good to turn down. We got all we wanted
and gave up far less than the Soviets. The Senate will see it that way.

December 18, 1987

Foreign goods seem to be flooding the stores more than ever.
Makes you wonder if the trade deficit is EVER going to shrink.
But trade fundamentals are improving, a turnaround is in sight.
Exports will be a major factor in whittling down the deficit.
They've risen about 20% so far this year and will do even better in '88.
As for the dollar, we think it's headed even lower, short term...
yen vs. dollar sliding another 5% to 7%. Same story for the German mark.

December 23, 1987

This Letter is all about the outlook for the next 3 to 5 years,
the changes ahead for key industries and for the overall economy.
There will STILL be recessions, at least one before 1993.
Overall growth in the economy will probably be fairly slow...
around 2% a year. That compares with average postwar growth of about 3%.
The sluggishness is part of the cure for trade deficits and foreign debt.
We'll be forced to curb consumption in order to export more, import less.
And we'll pay for failing to save and invest enough in long-term growth.
Expect faster gains from 1995 to 2000 for business as a whole.
By then, trade accounts and finances will probably be in better balance.
We'll restore our credit and reap the benefits of advancing technology.

We think that productivity will be one of the bright spots.
Output of products and services per hour of work will climb 1 1/2% a year,
better than average gains of less than 1% during the past decade or so.
Especially strong in manufacturing industries, topping 3% a year.
Weaker, inefficient companies have already been forced out of business...
survival of fittest. Those that are left are streamlining, diversifying,
closing obsolete plants and investing in new machinery and processes.

December 23, 1987

<u>Interest rates will average 1% to 2% lower</u> over the long haul.
Reasons...moderate inflation, steadier dollar and ample credit available.
<u>Inflation...4 1/2% per year</u>, about the same as we've had this year.
<u>Foreign trade, improving</u>. MUCH lower deficits by the early '90s.
<u>Net...changing markets, new methods, adding to total business</u>,
but they'll also knock out some old markets, old methods, old products.
Thus repercussions, shiftings, ups & downs...lots of new growing pains.

<u>In health care, cost containment will dominate</u>. More controls
over doctors and hospitals as the gov't and private insurers tighten up.
Patients will pay a larger share...and second opinions will be required.

<u>U.S. will import more oil</u>, about 50% of demand within five years,
up from 40% now. That will give foreign producers more leeway on pricing
and increase chances for tighter supplies and costlier oil by mid '90s.
<u>More consolidation in the airline industry</u>...eight major carriers
with 95% of the market. A single airline will dominate each hub airport.

<u>High-definition TV will be a 1990s sensation</u>...sharper pictures,
better technology. Sets with 50-inch screens, more lines, more detail.
<u>A battle royal among TV manufacturers</u> in Japan, Europe and U.S.
for the stakes are huge...BILLIONS of dollars in profits for the winners.
<u>U.S. will set the pace in telecommunications</u>...supercomputers,
artificial intelligence and fiber optics...integrating new technology
into coherent packages. Bell operating firms will have shackles lifted.
<u>Remarkable progress on small computers</u> during the next few years.
<u>"Notebook" types will appear in the early '90s</u>...under 3 pounds,
book-sized...with capabilities that equal those of the existing desktops.
<u>Laptop computers for less than $700</u> will be commonplace by 1990,
capable of handling work that currently requires use of a $3000 desktop.
<u>Biotechnology, super genetics, will be one of the hot industries</u>
in the next five years...transferring the characteristics of one species
to another species. There'll be gene-splicing of plants in laboratories
to develop crops that don't need much water, or to fight disease & bugs.

<u>Summing up, most companies and most industries are running leaner</u>
than they were when the '80s began. They've cut payrolls and other costs
and taken steps to encourage innovation, to sharpen quality and service,
to be more flexible, faster on their feet...in order to compete better.
This is going on in thousands of firms. Quite promising for the future.
<u>There's still plenty of spark and ingenuity in American business</u>.

**An Israeli soldier confronts a
Palestinian protester in the Occupied
Zone.**

February 19, 1988

<u>U.S. and world opinion will eventually influence the Israelis</u>. By making themselves victims, the Palestinians have now gained sympathy, even in Israel. Leverage...to force Israel to adopt softer policies. And long term, bring a form of Palestinian self-rule to occupied areas.

March 11, 1988

<u>Who will face Bush in Nov</u>.? <u>Probably Dukakis</u>. He has the money and organization...others don't. But he doesn't have it in the bag yet.
<u>Who'll have the edge in Nov</u>.? <u>Bush</u>, assuming the economy is OK.

April 1, 1988

<u>Problems of S&Ls and banks are serious and getting worse</u>... <u>much worse than regulators and insurers are now letting on</u>. <u>Federally insured deposits are absolutely safe</u> up to $100,000... and in practice, most accounts above that legal limit also will be safe.
<u>Eventually, Congress will step in</u>...money for deposit insurance plus regulatory changes to help bolster the banking and thrift systems.
<u>And taxpayers will get stuck</u> with at least part of the bailout. Fixing all the problems of the S&Ls could easily run $40 to $50 billion. Last year's rescue won't be enough...FSLIC will be back for more in '89.

April 22, 1988

<u>Auto industry is in for some big changes</u> in the next 3-4 years... a basic shift in the way Detroit makes cars, and the cars that it makes.
<u>Fewer models</u> will be sold, scrapping cars that are getting stale.
<u>More plant closings and automation</u> to replace assembly workers.
<u>Another round of retooling, redesign</u> for quality and efficiency.

<u>U.S. manufacturers will begin to take market share from imports</u>. Prices of foreign cars have been rising rapidly due to the lower dollar compared to currencies in Japan and Europe. The import flood is slowing, even though domestic automakers have also been increasing their prices.
<u>More "foreign" cars will be produced here</u>...Japanese especially. With currency changes, it'll be cheaper to make cars here than in Japan.
<u>And Japan will focus more on exporting luxury cars</u>. New models at $25,000-$40,000 to compete with European and top-of-line U.S. cars.
<u>The Big Three will have to cut fat</u>...consolidating product lines and paring excess capacity while sharpening their assembly operations.
<u>GM will be wrenched the most</u>, shutting more of its older plants and spending billions to make surviving production lines more efficient.

![1988]

Posing in a tank didn't help Mass. Governor Michael Dukakis in the 1988 presidential election.

George Bush campaigning in American-flag factory.

June 3, 1988

<u>A lot of hoopla about doing more business with the Russians</u>... energy and agricultural deals, joint ventures, licensing agreements, etc.

<u>But China is a much better bet</u> for U.S. exporters and investors. Chinese are traders, entrepreneurial by culture...willing to take risks. They're miles ahead of the Soviets in understanding how markets operate. Our trade with China is already TEN times greater than trade with Russia and will keep growing faster. Probably up another 25% or so this year.

<u>Note the economic changes going on there</u> within the past year... decontrol, encouraging for-profit ventures, expanding trade of all types. They're even bringing back old-line managers from the pre-communist days.

<u>If you want to see "economic reform,"</u> look at China, not Russia.

August 5, 1988

<u>How important are the polls at this stage</u> of the campaign?

<u>They can't be shrugged off</u>...Bush is clearly deep in the hole.

<u>But don't rely on current polls to pick the eventual winner</u>. They don't predict...they're simply snapshots of a race at a given time.

<u>Bush will probably cut the Dukakis lead in half by Labor Day</u>... down to 7%-8% or less. He'll stress peace, prosperity and experience, hammering away on specific issues to draw a contrast with the Democrats.

<u>His aim is to close the gap by Oct. 1</u>, then gradually pull ahead.

September 9, 1988

<u>Note the strange goings-on in Poland</u>...communist regime bending to pressure from Solidarity, agreeing to negotiate with the banned union.

<u>A significant development</u>, and a bitter pill for the communists.

<u>Strains in Poland may lead to deeper cracks in the Soviet bloc</u>. There are other basket cases, failed regimes, throughout Eastern Europe. They're watching Poland closely AND the lack of firm action from Moscow.

November 11, 1988

<u>Deficits will cast shadows on EVERYTHING</u>, forcing Bush to squeeze on defense, agriculture and health and limit new spending in other areas. Piling up deficits while business is expanding limits options in a slump.

<u>He'll stand firm against tax hikes, at least for a year or so</u>... banking on spending cuts and higher revenues from a fast-growing economy.

<u>Capital gains tax won't be reduced</u>, despite hopes raised by Bush.

<u>Despite their farm system, the Democrats can't win the big game</u>, because their message and nat'l candidates are out of step with voters. At the nat'l level, they're an awkward collection of diverse interests that have been dominated in recent elections by more-liberal elements.

<u>Moderates and conservatives are shunted aside</u> to favor activists.

Lithuanians rallying for independence.

Finger-pointing has already started...pinning blame on liberals
and their agenda for pulling the party down..."same as '72, '80 and '84."
An effort will be made to turn the party rightward...toward Robb, Nunn,
Gore and Bradley. And away from the likes of Dukakis, Jackson and Cuomo.

December 30, 1988

If you look carefully, the next decade is already taking shape...
the underlying trends in population, in schools, jobs, living standards,
life-styles and other things. That's what this Letter is all about.

The biggest change will be "globalization" of the marketplace.
Competing on the basis of quality...selling world-class products.
Also efficiency, attention to detail and service...all at a fair price.
A premium on innovation, flexible production, beating others to market.
And structural changes...international trading blocs.
Free trade where both sides gain, like the U.S.-Canada agreement,
which will help make North America more competitive with the Japanese.
Also economic integration of Europe in '92...favoring low-cost producers
by getting rid of regulations that impede flow of goods across borders.
Japan will negotiate free-trade deals with other Asian nations.
And perhaps with the U.S. We'll build ties all over the Pacific.
By 1995, our trade with the Pacific Rim will be TWICE that with Europe.
The Far East will produce more Taiwans and Koreas in the '90s.
And that part of the world will be our largest new source of immigrants.

Even more than now, we'll be a melting pot, a nation of nations.
Immigration...legal & illegal...accounting for HALF our population growth
during the '90s. Calif. will eventually have a majority of minorities.
By early 2000s, there will be as many Hispanics as blacks in U.S.
We already have the seventh-largest Hispanic population in the world...
surpassed only by Brazil, Mexico, Spain, Argentina, Colombia and Peru.
All this will affect the foods we eat, clothes we wear, schools,
the workplace, our sports & entertainment preferences. Also politics...
more attuned to needs of the new immigrant population, the new voters.

Expect solid but not spectacular growth in the decade ahead...
not as much boom & bust or wild swings in inflation and interest rates
as we've had in the past 10 years. It will be steadier and healthier.
We're in better shape to compete than we were entering the '80s.
Oil shocks, 12%-13% inflation in '79-80 and two recessions FORCED actions
to cut waste and run more efficiently. And labor has changed its tune...
it's now willing to work with companies on saving jobs, keeping markets.
Managers will concentrate more on LONG-term results...realizing
they can't compete in world markets by going for just short-term profits.
This will show up in research, capital spending and investment in people.

Baby-boomers will be in their peak earning and spending years...
people now 24 to 42 years old. Buying houses, furnishings, raising kids
and sending them through school, all of which will help spur the economy.

Faster productivity gains ahead in manufacturing and services.
This will help offset MUCH slower growth in the labor force.
Fewer young folks...ages 17 through 22...looking for first jobs.
The "birth dearth" generation...those born in the '70s and early '80s.
More women, immigrants and minorities as a share of work force.
Retirees will help fill the gap...second and even third careers.

Summing up: People benefiting from individual freedoms, choices,
enterprise and initiative...still open to ideas and their profitable use.
The new constantly replacing the old in technology, services, products.

January 6, 1989

Preventing a recession will be Bush's No. 1 domestic priority. An economic downturn in the next year or two would be riskier than usual because of heavy corporate debt, shaky S&Ls, jittery financial markets. Budget deficits would soar, making it hard for Bush to get anything done.

February 24, 1989

Why is Nicaragua's Ortega so friendly? It's largely for show... he's offering talks with the U.S., early elections and political freedom in hopes of finally killing off all support for the 12,000 contra rebels. How will Bush respond? He'll demand more than words...some signs Ortega is serious. Meanwhile, Bush will ask for nonmilitary contra aid. The rebels must remain a viable force to maintain the pressure on Ortega.

March 3, 1989

There's growing alarm over the economic outlook for this year... people worried about inflation ahead and increasing threats of recession. Not surprising. Rising interest rates, signs of price escalation and tight plant capacity have folks talking about an end to the expansion. Crucial point is that business will be sluggish, recession or not.

May 19, 1989

Our own gov't isn't sure what Russia is up to or how to react... things are changing so fast there. For years, Russia has been the focus of our defense strategy and foreign policy...affecting everything else. Now comes Gorbachev with his reforms and his smiles and smooth talk. It's a major turning point for the Soviets and for communism... his admission that the system is a flop and his commitment to change. Soviet republics won't be allowed to break loose from Moscow... Lithuania, Latvia, Estonia or others. The Kremlin will coax, bargain and wheedle to put down independence movements without the use of force. If that doesn't work, tanks & troops will be sent in to douse uprisings. No dramatic jump in trade, because Russia lacks the hard currency that's needed to buy much more than what it's already getting from us. And it doesn't have much to offer, stuff we can't easily buy elsewhere.

Soviet leader Gorbachev, Czech party chief Gustav Husak (center) and Raisa Gorbachev in a crowd in Prague.

June 2, 1989

A turn toward free-market economies, away from state-controlled. You can see the first signs of it in eastern Europe, Russia and China.
Democracy and capitalism are on the upswing all over the world, which will open new opportunities for U.S. firms...and new competition.

The U.S. will continue to be the dominant nation in world trade, still the biggest exporter, importer and investor in overseas plants.
Growth in U.S. exports will exceed that of imports in the '90s due to better trade access, quality improvement and smarter marketing.
Trade deficit will shrink and then disappear by the late '90s.
Toughest trade challenge: European economic integration in '92. Lower trade barriers within Europe but plenty of barriers to outsiders. So U.S. firms will scramble to get inside before the gates swing shut.
Trade with Canada, Mexico and China will SOAR during the '90s.
Don't expect much from Russia...still an economic basket case with a lot of bureaucratic drag and very little entrepreneurial spirit.

U.S. economy will grow 3% a year on average in the next ten years. That's normal growth and allows for a couple of recessions along the way. Business will do better in the last half of the '90s than the first half.
Taxes will rise...excise taxes and more trimming of deductions.

We'll retain industrial leadership in most of the major fields, helped by our huge market and fresh focus on innovation and competition.
But trail Japan in some lines, such as consumer electronics.
The Japanese will still be our key competitor in global markets.
However, growth there will taper off as pay pressures build up and more personal income goes for consumer goods...including imports.

Our technology race with Japan will get even tighter in the '90s.
Neck-&-neck competition in some technologies...fiber optics, superconductivity, composite materials, telecommunications, for example.
The U.S. leading in these...supercomputers and microprocessors, software, bioengineering, aerospace, medical technology, food technology.
Japan in these...factory automation and robotics, semiconductors, ceramics, high-definition TV as well as other consumer electronics.
The U.S. will be faster on its feet in moving R&D to market... translating technology into products. Companies will work more closely with universities and gov't...and with each other in joint manufacturing.

Shaping up our schools will be our toughest task in the '90s.
Expect a longer school day and year, more choice among schools, higher teacher pay, testing of teachers, more focus on math & sciences, computers in class. Business will get heavily involved because it MUST. And companies will RE-educate workers who didn't learn in the classroom.

June 9, 1989

Notice that Bush is softening his pledge against tax increases... laying the groundwork to go along with them as part of a budget package.

As for China, the regime will keep using force to restore order. But the people have now tasted freedom and won't settle for the old ways. It's just a matter of time until there's new, more legitimate leadership.
U.S. relations with China will be buffeted but remain intact. Policymakers figure it's up to the U.S. and West to stay the course... encourage China's continuing emergence despite this blow to democracy.
The U.S. will NOT back away and risk deeper, continuing chaos.

**Protesting Chinese youths fill
Tiananmen Square in Beijing.**

August 25, 1989

      During your lifetime, you'll probably see only one or two events
that truly change the course of history...something on the scale of WW II.
      <u>One of these turning points is now under way in eastern Europe</u>...
communist gov'ts crumbling in the face of economic and political chaos.
East bloc nations renouncing communism and trying to cross the threshold
from totalitarianism to democracy...out from under the heel of Russia.
      <u>It marks a breakup of the postwar order in the communist world</u>.

      <u>Gorbachev will allow more leeway</u> for privatizing, running things.
But he won't let the Baltic republics secede, become independent again.
      <u>He'll try to walk a thin line</u> between the rising expectations
throughout the Soviet bloc and growing resentment from party hard-liners.
His hands-off policy in East Europe will improve relations with the West,
thus allowing him more time and money to deal with his own ragtag economy.
      As the seeds now being sown take root, he will be in better shape
to make similar reforms. Until then, he's in danger of being tossed out.
The Soviets aren't known for letting their satellites break out of orbit.
      <u>The risk to Gorbachev is less than 50/50 but can't be ruled out</u>.

      <u>It's the most promising development in years</u> for U.S. and Europe.
But still frustrations ahead, plus the risk that Gorbachev won't survive,
that Soviet diehards will throw a monkey wrench into his reform plans.
      <u>Economic and political changes will relieve pressures on the U.S</u>.
      <u>Making it easier to reduce our troops and arms</u> in western Europe.
      <u>Allowing more breathing room on the budget</u> and domestic programs.

September 22, 1989

      <u>Labor costs in manufacturing are under control</u>...modest pay
hikes, productivity up 3% a year, unit labor costs up only 1%.
      <u>Not so in service industries</u>...retailing, banking and others
that are hounded by rapidly rising labor costs and lagging productivity.
      <u>They're in for belt-tightening and restructuring</u> in the '90s.

October 13, 1989

House prices will rise more slowly than they have in the '80s. There already are signs of a slowdown in the hottest real estate markets as everyone takes a deep breath after years of double-digit price jumps.

There'll be actual declines in some places where current values are not sustainable...markets that simply jumped too far and too fast. Boston, for example. And areas around Los Angeles and San Francisco.

Turning to upheaval in E. Europe...striking changes in Hungary. Noncommunists will win parliamentary control early next year. Democratic changes in Hungary will have great impact elsewhere. In Poland, Hungary's example will accelerate the pace of reforms, putting Polish communists under increasing pressure to simply step aside. Czechoslovakia will begin to crack out of its repressive shell as forces for change gather momentum in neighboring Poland and Hungary. And East Germany...even the Soviets encourage some loosening up. It's clear that the western democracies have won the "cold war" as East bloc nations renounce communism and turn toward market economies. But no one really knows what will follow...or the effects on us.

October 20, 1989

Closer ties between Bonn and East Berlin are likely to develop fairly soon, but molded by U.S.-Soviet and overall East-West agreements. Trade will expand rapidly. East German trade with West Germany, already large, will burgeon...as will West German trade with East Europe. U.S. and Russia will pull some troops out of the Germanys by '92 as a result of the current negotiations on reducing conventional forces. German reunification won't happen soon, despite much speculation in light of East Germany's political upheaval and hunger for freedom.

November 10, 1989

Look at the upheaval in Germany and E. Europe and what's ahead: Will Moscow let it go on? Yes, as long as Gorbachev is in charge and encouraging change, the 400,000 troops in E. Germany won't intervene. The big threat now is that something will happen to Gorbachev... that someone will take a potshot at him or the military will turn on him. A dangerous time as hard-liners see their control slipping away.

Dismantling the Berlin Wall, chunk by chunk.

November 10,1989

There is no turning back the clock...no matter how it plays out. Expectations have been raised throughout the Soviet Union and E. Europe. New freedoms and market-oriented economies about to take root in places that have been under the thumb of hard-line communists for DECADES.

What impact on W. Germany? Short term, disruptions and turmoil. Incredible strains on housing and jobs, social programs and living costs.
What about reunification? It'll begin with economic integration in the next year...joint ventures, massive financial aid from W. Germany.
Then a confederation by the end of the '90s or soon thereafter.

What will the U.S. do to help the new noncommunist systems?
Not much in the way of gov't aid...loan guarantees, grants, food and other giveaways. But Congress will vote more money than Bush seeks.

November 24, 1989

Those defense spending cuts will affect a LOT more than defense. They will have an impact on your taxes, budget deficits, interest rates and investments...the whole economy...over the next four or five years.
Military retrenchment will hurt individual firms and communities, those that depend on Pentagon aerospace, electronics and shipbuilding. Plus local businesses near military bases. Realtors, car dealers, etc.
A unique opportunity to lower our country's defense burden through leaner, more-mobile forces and fewer high-cost weapons systems.
Expect a shakeout of defense companies in the next few years... consolidations, mergers, takeovers and buyouts as spending is cut back. Many defense contractors won't survive, at least in their present form.

December 8, 1989

If you can't quite believe what's going on in eastern Europe...
Wait until you see what's ahead...changes coming faster & faster and in unexpected ways. What has happened so far is merely the prologue to a FAR different world from what we have known for the past 40 years.
What's motivating Gorbachev anyhow, WHY is he shaking things up?
Survival of the Soviet system is at stake, his communist gov't. Gorbachev is firmly committed to Marxism but realizes it must be altered because Russia is falling far behind the other industrialized nations... a military giant and economic midget. He's trying to guide his country into a world of finance, computers, trade and economic competition.

Will he succeed? He already has in some important respects by opening up the system, snubbing the bureaucracy, creating incentives, encouraging people to work and take risks in order to improve themselves.
Even if he's sacked, there'll be no turning back to the old ways, putting the genie back in the bottle. That's the measure of his success.
Will "new-style" communist reformers be acceptable in E. Europe?
No, people are fed up with years of high-handed Soviet lackeys and their sorry results. The new elected gov'ts will be NONcommunist.

Will the winding down of the cold war yield a "peace dividend"?
Yes, though savings from lower defense spending will come slowly, starting in the next few years. Most will go toward nondefense programs, such as roads and bridges, child care, education and the war on drugs. The rest will reduce budget deficits and the size of future tax hikes.
Take note, too, that the cold war has ALREADY paid a dividend... keeping Europe at peace for over 40 years, thanks to the U.S. and NATO.

Will there be a jump in our trade with Russia and E. Europe?
Yes, but from very low levels. Perhaps a doubling or tripling
by the mid-'90s...but small potatoes in terms of our total global trade
or the business that we now do with Canada, Mexico, Japan and others.
East bloc nations lack hard currency for buying much from us.

In time, communist reformers will take over in China, as in USSR.
Meanwhile, China still welcomes investment from U.S. and others,
especially projects that promote new technology or help increase exports.

December 29, 1989

Computers...smaller, faster, more powerful and probably cheaper.
A new generation of microprocessors will make today's mainframes obsolete.
In fact, desktop models will run twice as fast as the current mainframes.
Supercomputers will do in seconds what it now takes hours to accomplish.
Phones will go wherever you go...lightweight, pocket-size units.
And be used for more than talk. They'll help direct appliances,
security systems and other features in the "smart houses" of the future.
No quick payoff on superconductivity ahead...the long-sought key
to sending power without resistance, limitless and less-expensive energy.
Large-scale use of high-temperature superconductors is 10-20 years away.
Same for nuclear fusion. Even with breakthroughs in the '90s,
it will take YEARS of development until commercial projects can be built.

Normal retirement age will probably be phased upward...toward 70.
Pension plans will be rejiggered to discourage people from quitting early.
Here's why: People will be staying well longer...living longer.
There will be concern over social security's ability to meet obligations
after baby boomers retire. And older people will be needed by employers.

More women, minorities and immigrants in the work force.
Means a lot of adjustments ahead for employers. For example,
many will have to teach English to Hispanic, Asian and other immigrants.
And as more companies rely on well-educated and skilled women employees,
they will look for ways to meet the special needs of working mothers.
Result will be more-flexible hours, various types of help on child care
and perhaps job sharing and arrangements for some work to be done at home.
Training programs will be stepped up...teaching essential skills
such as math or communications to those who don't bring them to the job.

Stock market will do well...the Dow Jones reaching 6000 by 2000,
average annual return (price appreciation plus dividends), about 10%.

1990s

The decade of the '90s burst on an American nation that was simultaneously hopeful and anxious. The national economy had been growing steadily for eight years, but growth had slowed under the weight of high debt, rising taxes and a slump in the economies of America's major trading partners, especially Canada, Japan and Europe. Foreign investment in the U.S., a powerful stimulant to growth, was declining from its late-'80s peak.

At the same time, America was hopeful that the spread of democracy and free markets around the globe would bring a new era of peace, prosperity and improved market access for U.S. goods. West and East Germany were racing toward unification, the Eastern European nations were asserting their independence from the Soviet Union, and reforms were accelerating in Moscow.

War in the Middle East

Just eight months into the new decade, the world was shocked by a dangerous development in the volatile, oil-rich Middle East. On August 2, 1990, Iraq invaded and immediately conquered the small neighboring nation of Kuwait, following months of tense arguing over the world price of oil, production targets and disputed ownership of a rich oil field on the border of the two nations. The Iraqi dictator, Saddam Hussein, stated his intention to annex Kuwait, claiming that historically, it was part of Iraq.

The western world reacted with understandable horror, both at Iraq's aggression against a sovereign nation and at the threat to the world's oil supply—not just Kuwaiti production but also that of Saudi Arabia. President Bush acted quickly to condemn Iraq, demand its withdrawal from Kuwait and urge a United Nations trade embargo. The U.N. imposed such an embargo August 6, hoping it would be sufficient to persuade Saddam Hussein to pull back.

When Bush became convinced that Kuwait could not be freed without force and that Saudi Arabia might be Saddam's next target, he put in motion "Operation Desert Shield," a massive movement of U.S. troops to Saudi Arabia. He lined up a narrow majority of the U.S. Senate to authorize the use of American force in the Gulf, and at the end of November

	BALTIC REPUBLICS DECLARE INDEPENDENCE FROM SOVIET UNION.	BUSH SIGNS DEFICIT-REDUCTION TAX HIKE.		YUGOSLAVIA BREAKS UP, CIVIL WAR BREAKS OUT.	SOVIETS, U.S. SIGN ARMS-REDUCTION TREATY.
DOW JONES HITS 3000.			KUWAIT LIBERATED, IRAQ DEFEATED.		
1990	IRAQ INVADES KUWAIT, U.S. SENDS TROOPS.	NEW CLEAN AIR ACT PASSES.	**1991**	YELTSIN ELECTED PRESIDENT OF RUSSIAN REPUBLIC.	NORTH'S IRANGATE CONVICTIONS REVERSED, OTHER CHARGES DROPPED.

the United Nations set a deadline of January 15, 1991, for Iraq's withdrawal from Kuwait.

As in every war the U.S. has fought, opinion in the U.S. was sharply divided. While a large majority supported Bush's aggressive stance, a minority of the public, including many Democratic senators, believed the cause of freeing non-democratic Kuwait and protecting the world's oil supply was not worth the likely cost in American lives and money. As the January 15 deadline approached, frantic diplomatic initiatives around the world sought a peaceful resolution of the crisis.

Hi-tech attacks

The deadline came and went with no indication that Saddam would give in to world pressure. The following day the U.S. unleashed a massive, high-technology air attack on Iraq. Computer-guided cruise missiles targeted military sites throughout the nation and around the capital of Baghdad, but they occasionally hit civilian neighborhoods too. On January 18 Iraq retaliated by firing Soviet-made Scud missiles at cities in Israel and targets in Saudia Arabia. Four days later, Iraq began waging an environmental assault on the air and water of the Persian Gulf region, by setting fire to Kuwaiti oil wells and refineries and allowing crude oil to flow into the Gulf.

In the face of continued defiance by Saddam, the U.S. set a new deadline for an Iraqi withdrawal from Kuwait. When it was spurned, U.N. ground troops under American command moved from Saudi Arabia into Kuwait and Iraq, liberating Kuwait within four days and pushing Iraqi troops toward Baghdad. On February 28 Saddam announced a cease-fire and said Iraq would comply with U.N. directives.

The aftermath of the Gulf War was ugly. The waters and skies of the region continued to be fouled by oil leaks and fires burning out of control for weeks. Hoping for American military help in their fight against Saddam, Shiite dissidents in the south of Iraq and Kurds in the north pressed their rebellion against Iraqi forces. But Bush and Congress chose to limit the conflict to the stated objective of freeing Kuwait, and Saddam's forces soon crushed the internal resistance.

Only when the televised horror of Kurds starving in the mountains of Iraq galvanized public pressure did American forces intervene with air power and humanitarian relief to create a kind of Kurdish protectorate in northern Iraq.

The Gulf War gave the world its first glimmer of how treacherous the post-Cold War "new world order" might be. Despite the unprecedented cooperation of the U.S. and Soviet Union to calm the conflict, with broad support from the whole world community of nations, a tense regional dispute had flared into open warfare. While the superpowers were reaching agreement on the reduction of their nuclear arsenals, smaller nations, including Saddam's Iraq, had been secretly developing nuclear capabilities of their own. And ethnic and nationalist aspirations that had long been held in check by Soviet military might, especially in Eastern Europe, were beginning to be asserted in military conflict, as in the former Yugoslav republics of Croatia and Bosnia-Herzegovina.

Turmoil in the Soviet Union

Meanwhile, the transformation of the Soviet empire was racing forward. In February 1990, Soviet President Mikhail Gorbachev ended the Communist Party's monopoly and allowed opposition parties. Armed clashes were beginning to erupt among rival ethnic groups in Asian republics of the Soviet Union, and in March the Baltic republics of Lithuania, Estonia and Latvia declared their independence from Moscow. Gorbachev faced the toughest test of his career. In May he rejected the Baltic declarations and sent Soviet tanks and troops to shut down the rebellious Latvian parliament and quell unrest in the Asian republics. He denounced calls for the independence of the Soviet republics, and he appointed more hard-liners to his cabinet.

In late '90 and early '91, Gorbachev tried to use foreign summits, arms and aid agreements, and cooperation with the western allies on the Gulf War to bolster his authority in the Soviet Union. But opposition was growing on all sides, from those who feared his reestablishment of a dictatorship and those who found him too soft on the reformers. In March '91 a referendum on national unity showed growing

BUSH SIGNS EXPANDED ANTI-JOB-BIAS BILL.	WESTERN LEADERS AGREE ON FINANCIAL AID TO RUSSIA.	CLINTON WINS WITH 43% OF VOTE.	U.S. SENDS TROOPS TO ESTABLISH ORDER, DELIVER AID IN SOMALIA.	JANET RENO BECOMES FIRST WOMAN ATTORNEY GENERAL.	CONGRESS PASSES DEFICIT-REDUCTION BILL.
SOVIET UNION OFFICIALLY DISSOLVED.	**1992**	POLICE CLEARED IN RODNEY KING BEATING CASE, L.A. ERUPTS.	**1993**	FLOODS DEVASTATE MIDWEST.	

separatist tendencies, and six republics boycotted the vote. In June Boris Yeltsin was elected president of the Russian republic, and the following month hard-liners in Gorbachev's cabinet agitated for temporary powers to deal with the worsening economic crisis. Even as Gorbachev's position weakened, he basked in the international spotlight, with the signing of an historic arms-reduction treaty with President Bush in July '91.

A coup fails

The following month, the hard-liners moved against Gorbachev in an attempted coup, putting him under house arrest in the Crimea and announcing that they were in charge. But it was a short-lived turning back of the clock. Foreign governments condemned the coup, but more significantly, the people of Russia took to the streets in protest and faced down a reluctant Red Army. Yeltsin took control of the volatile situation and engineered the reinstatement of Gorbachev, who returned to Moscow and arrested the conspirators.

The failed coup hastened the demise of the Communist Party and the breakup of the Soviet Union in the fall of '91. Yeltsin, the rising star and Gorbachev's rival, announced that the Russian republic now owned all Soviet and Communist Party property in the republic. Gorbachev, trying to keep his grip on the Soviet Union, resigned from the Communist Party and recognized the independence of the Baltic republics. But the union was crumbling. In December '91, Yeltsin and the leaders of the other remaining 11 republics proclaimed the dissolution of the Soviet Union and the establishment of a loose Commonwealth of Independent States, and Gorbachev resigned. In the year that followed, Yeltsin, as president of the largest republic, became the de facto head of the old empire, announcing troop withdrawals from the Baltics, negotiating further arms reductions with the U.S. and picking up the pace of economic restructuring in Russia.

After 75 years of imposing political tyranny, inept economic management and military aggression on a large part of the globe, the Soviet communist empire was dead. Indeed, communism itself was discredited worldwide as a political system. It survived intact only in North Korea and Cuba. In the largest communist nation, China, communism was rapidly being transformed amid growing personal freedom and surging capitalism.

But in the former Soviet Union, the hard part was just beginning—the challenge of building, almost from scratch, democratic institutions and an economic framework for free-market growth. Everyone knew it wouldn't be easy, but the short-run dislocations—soaring inflation, lack of hard currency, joblessness, corruption and crime, capital flight to foreign nations—were even worse than expected. While savoring the new freedom, the people grew very impatient with the halting progress of Yeltsin's reforms and the pain of transition.

U.S. economy slows

Back in the United States, the Gulf War had a negative effect on an already slowing economy. The problem wasn't the cost to America of the war itself, which was eventually covered largely by contributions from its allies, especially the Arab nations. The problem was the war's short-run impact on American consumers, who were already in a debt-reduction mode. It removed hundreds of thousands of American military personnel—consumers all—from their home areas and sent them to Saudi Arabia. Their families at home in the U.S., concerned about the fate of their loved ones, cut back on their spending, and retail sales, auto sales and home sales plummeted around U.S. military bases. As war tensions grew through the fall and winter of '90, millions of Americans were glued to their TVs, and traffic at shopping malls fell off sharply.

The war was the last straw for the record-breaking economic expansion of the '80s, which had been slowly running out of steam for a couple of years. National economic activity contracted that fall and continued to contract through the spring of '91. American unemployment rose to near 7.5%, still much lower than in the last recession in '82 but higher than the U.S. had seen in the 10 years since. With Japan and much of Europe also in recession, economic Cassandras heralded the arrival of a deep worldwide slump they said would last through most of the '90s. Some portrayed the U.S. slump as penitence for overspending and underinvesting in the '80s, and many Americans seemed to take delight in the financial collapse of dozens of high-flying real estate developers and corporate financiers. The more thoughtful pessimists feared for America's continued economic success in cutthroat competition among newly productive, low-wage industrial nations in both the West and the Third World.

Drastic downsizing

But by the middle of '91, the U.S. economy had begun to grow again, although the growth was weak. Sluggishness was aggravated by a slowdown in Europe, where Germany was having trouble digesting unification, and in Japan, where the burst bubble of the '80s boom had brought falling stock and real estate prices, recession and unprecedented layoffs. Some economists predicted a "double dip" recession for the U.S. in '92, with an interval of anemic growth followed by another contraction. It did not happen, but consumer anxiety was heightened by almost weekly announcements of layoffs at giant U.S. companies going through drastic downsizing and restructurings, reducing the ranks of middle management and selling or closing whole divisions. Lots of jobs—good jobs at good pay—were being created in fast-growing new businesses, especially in high-tech fields, but many of the laid-off workers, whether managers or factory workers, were not trained to fill the new jobs. Consumer spending was depressed not just by the impaired income of households with laid-off workers but also by the insecurity of gainfully employed workers who feared that they might be next.

It was becoming clear that the U.S. economy was not going through just another phase of the business cycle. It was in the middle of—indeed, leading—a worldwide revolution in productivity and market access. Many of the laid-off workers would not be rehired when business picked up, as usually happened after a recession. Many corporations would not go back to business as usual even when their profits improved.

Reductions in defense spending

Superimposed on this global restructuring was a transition from a Cold War economy with high military spending to a peacetime economy—a transition in many ways as profound as that after World War II, and in many ways trickier. The Pentagon was reducing forces and canceling orders for equipment. Defense contractors from New England to southern California were laying off engineers and production workers and exploring ways to convert their capabilities to civilian products. And unlike the conversion after World War II, there was no pent-up consumer demand that would pick up the slack as military spending declined.

The national recession of '90-91 was shorter and milder than most, but there were pockets of severe distress by region and sector, even as other areas were booming. California experienced the worst downturn since the Depression. Layoffs in aerospace and defense aggravated a slide in home prices that followed a decade of double-digit increases. For the first time in decades, more people were leaving California than were coming in from other states. The opportunities were better in high-growth western states like Utah, Texas, Arizona, Idaho and Nevada, where lower taxes and business operating costs were bringing a boom in small-business growth.

The east and west coasts, which led the mid '80s boom, were now lagging behind the industrial and agricultural heartland of America, where manufacturing and export sales were now strong. Among the weaker metro economies of the early '90s were Los Angeles, New York, Washington and Boston. Interestingly, these are also America's major media centers, and press coverage of the national economy in the first three years of the '90s often reflected not only the weakness of those local economies, but also a severe slump in newspaper and magazine publishing, broadcasting and advertising.

President Bush was slow to acknowledge the recession and sometimes awkward in showing compassion for its victims, many of whom were white-collar workers who usually voted Republican. In the afterglow of the Gulf War, Bush had very high approval ratings, but these began to slip as economic sluggishness dragged into '92. Bush had a plan for fighting recession, and the plan was to do nothing but let the recovery proceed at a natural pace. He believed this was preferable to boosting inflation and an already soaring budget deficit by enacting stimulative public works and relief programs.

Clinton & Perot vs. Bush

It is always difficult to sell a laissez-faire program when times are tough, but it's especially hard in an election year, and especially challenging for a President who lacks verbal flair. In early '92 Bush found himself attacked from all sides and proved inarticulate in his own defense. In the Republican Party, former political adviser, speechwriter and columnist Pat Buchanan attacked from the right, challenging Bush in GOP primaries and claiming that the president had abandoned the principles of Reaganism. In the spring, billionaire businessman Ross Perot entered the fray as an independent populist. He attacked Bush and the Democratic Congress for letting the budget deficit swell out of control, and he called for tough, protectionist measures against foreign competition.

Many of the potentially strongest Democratic candidates—including New York Governor Mario Cuomo and Senators Sam Nunn, Bill Bradley and Jay Rockefeller—decided to sit out the '92 race, perhaps believing that George Bush would be easily reelected. The declared candidates bloodied each other throughout the Democratic primaries, until the young, moderate governor of Arkansas, Bill Clinton, beat back all comers. But he, too, was badly wounded in the primaries by evidence of marital infidelity, avoidance of military service during the Vietnam War and other questions of personal integrity. From polls before the Democratic convention, it looked as if Clinton would finish a distant third to Bush or Perot in the November election.

Things can swing quickly in election years, of course, and '92 was full of surprises. Perot faded from a high of 45% preference in the polls as his program and catchy slogans came under closer scrutiny, and he lost a lot of support by canceling and then reinstating his campaign. Clinton came out of the Democratic convention with a head of steam and a new centrist message that set himself apart from the liberal Democratic candidates who had failed to win the White House in 12 years.

Bush never quite got his act together, failing to persuasively rebut his opponents' questionable arguments that the U.S. was in terrible economic shape. When Perot stated that "America isn't making anything anymore," Bush couldn't find a clear way of showing that manufacturing was booming in America, even if the mix of manufactures was constantly changing in a high-tech economy. When Clinton stated that U.S. wages were only "13th in the world," Bush had trouble explaining that, adjusted for purchasing power, U.S. wages were still at or near the top. Clinton promised a tax cut for the middle class and higher taxes on the rich. Bush, smarting from the memory of his broken promise on "no new taxes," promised a tax cut for everyone. The economy continued to grow through '92, but not strongly enough to make people feel much better, and it wasn't enough to save the incumbent Bush. Clinton won with a scant 43% of the vote to Bush's 37% and Perot's 19%—the highest independent tally since Teddy Roosevelt's losing effort in 1912.

Promises kept and broken

In the postelection euphoria, Clinton acted as if his slender plurality were a mandate for fundamental change in America. And he also seemed to forget that many of his supporters were attracted to the middle-of-the-road views he expressed as a "New Democrat." Clinton's wife and most influential adviser, Hillary Rodham Clinton, set out to create an ambitious new health care plan for America, aimed at universal coverage with cost containment built in. Many of the components of the plan aroused concerns about cost and loss of choice in medical care, and release of it was delayed.

Fulfilling a promise to homosexual activists, Clinton proposed that gays be allowed to serve openly in the armed forces, but his proposal ran into a buzz saw of opposition in the military and on Capitol Hill before a compromise was reached.

In his first few months in office, Clinton also backed away from several significant campaign promises. After promising that he would cut the annual budget deficit in half in four years, he now declared that wouldn't be possible. After promising a tax cut for the middle class, he now said that wouldn't be possible either, and instead he proposed raising taxes on everyone except the working poor.

Staffing of the new government proceeded more slowly than usual, and several of Clinton's early nominees for key posts had to be withdrawn when questions arose about their ethics or philosophies. Meanwhile, key elements of Clinton's deficit-reduction plan—especially a broad tax on the consumption of energy throughout the economy—had to be scrapped to win approval from a Congress controlled by the President's own party. In the end a compromise plan raised gasoline taxes, the percentage of social security benefits taxed, and income taxes on wealthy households and businesses, while mildly slowing the growth of federal spending.

In the foreign realm, Clinton grappled with the issue of whether the U.S. should intervene in the war in the former Yugoslavia, at first seeming to favor intervention and then backing off when public opinion cooled to the idea. He continued Bush's policy in Somalia, where U.S. troops participated in an effort to end famine and bloodshed in a chaotic nation without civil government. He supported a North American Free Trade Agreement with Canada and Mexico, even while urging tough "managed trade" agreements with Japan. After learning that Iraq had planned to assassinate George Bush during the former president's visit to Kuwait in early '93, Clinton authorized a punitive missile attack on the Iraqi intelligence in Baghdad.

Clinton refocuses

Public opinion is fickle, and Clinton's high approval ratings of the postinaugural period began to tumble during a rocky period of rookie bungling and policy flip-flops in the spring of '93. Approval of his performance soon sank to even less than the 43% who voted for him as president. But Clinton had a long record of learning from his mistakes, and by mid '93 he refocused his administration, trying to avoid the distraction of too many initiatives and emphasizing such key policies as opening trade access for U.S. firms, boosting U.S. technology and keeping deficit reduction on track. He also remembered that he was elected as a Democrat of a moderate stripe. So he began to move cautiously back to the center, even at the risk of alienating supporters on the left wing of his party, including the black civil rights establishment, trade unions, feminists and gay-rights advocates. It would be three long years until the election of '96, plenty of time for Clinton to get his act together and plenty of time for improving economic conditions to give him a boost.

By the middle of '93, things were trending up for the U.S. In a worldwide economic slump, the U.S. had the strongest large economy. It had been growing continuously, albeit weakly, for more than two years. Unemployment had dropped below 7%, and job growth was adding between one and two million new jobs to the economy. Consumers and businesses had worked down debt and were resuming normal spending patterns, with capital investment especially strong.

The federal budget deficit was poised for a modest decline, although the hard task of reducing entitlement spending was being conveniently sidestepped by Clinton and Congress. Auto sales were enjoying their best year since the mid 80s, and the Big Three American automakers were gaining market share over foreign competitors. Benefiting from the lowest interest rates in 20 years, home resales and new construction had rebounded nicely. Dynamic U.S. firms such as Intel, Motorola and Hewlett-Packard were running circles around their world competitors in the introduction of leading-edge microprocessors, laser printers and other devices. The U.S. had strong trade surpluses in high technology and services, and U.S. exports were growing despite continued softness in the economies of our major trading partners. There was a new recognition throughout America that the nation's future required better public education and job training, and steps were finally being taken to improve schools and apprenticeship programs.

Throughout the world, the new magic word was *openness*—the opening of economies to the freer movement of products, capital, labor, ideas. In all the world, only one nation knew the rules of this new game. Only one nation knew that openness is both a blessing and a curse, giving consumers a high standard of living but also subjecting producers to a constant barrage of world competition. This one nation, the United States, was well positioned to continue its role of world leadership in the last decade of the 20th century.

**Gorbachev confronts Russian citizens
in the streets of Moscow.**

1990

January 5, 1990

There's growing concern about Gorbachev's precarious position
among top-level gov't people, more than they dare talk about publicly.
He's popular abroad but shaky at home and has two Achilles' heels...
a deteriorating economic situation and explosive separatist movements.
Soviet military chiefs are his main threat...starting to growl
about dissent in the Baltics, lack of "discipline" around the country.
They're leaning on Gorbachev to crack down, to establish limits.

February 23, 1990

Just back from a quick trip to Russia...Moscow and Leningrad...
a country setting out on a long irreversible course away from the past
and toward some semblance of democracy and privatization of industry.
Many ordinary working people are AFRAID of change, uncomfortable
with the uncertainties it will bring...competition, layoffs, price hikes.
So reforms will be hotly debated and resisted by the rank & file,
giving bureaucrats an excuse to dig in their heels, slow down perestroika
or foul it up. They blame current shortages on Gorbachev's fancy ideas.

East Germany...already looking to Bonn for direction and money.
West Germany will bankroll unification with hard cash, speeding it along.
(Other East European nations fear that will mean fewer marks for THEM.)

March 9, 1990

We recently visited Japan to size up changes and opportunities
for U.S. businesses wanting to sell there. Talked with many people...
American and Japanese business leaders, trade specialists and others.
We noted an important shift in attitude among the people there.
A feeling that Japan should open its markets for its OWN good...
not just to satisfy us. A sense that it will probably strengthen Japan.
Japanese consumers are still pinched...especially younger adults.
Their standard of living ranks no higher than fourth in world, if that.
After years of sacrifice, Japanese want to ENJOY their hard-earned wealth.
Young Japanese are starting to act differently from their parents.
More individualist, less committed to a group. More international-minded.
They're impatient with promotion by seniority...want merit pay, mobility.

May 4, 1990

U.S. will face stiffer economic competition for years to come...
just when our political ideas are winning and the arms race is slowing.
Can we hold our own? Sharpen our competitive edge? Open a lead?
Yes, if we fix some fundamental problems, but it won't be easy.
Weak saving and investment...now our worst competitive handicap.
As a nation, we save too little of our income, so we can't invest enough.
We often shortchange R&D, automation, employee education and training.
A subtle tilt from consumption to investment may be under way.

May 11, 1990

Why is Bush relenting on taxes, his party's best political issue?
He sees stormy weather ahead, direct links between big deficits,
inflation, interest rates, recession...problems that may hurt him in '92.
Deficits threaten to spin out of control due to the S&L bailout,
rising interest rates and lagging tax revenues that reflect weak profits.

July 20, 1990

Castro's dictatorship will keep fraying around the edges.
Cuba's living standard is declining at an accelerating rate.
And other Latin American countries are turning their backs on Castro.
Soviet support of Cuba will drop fast...has already leveled off.
Gorbachev has his OWN thorny problems...won't keep paying for Castro's.
Odds are good that change in Cuba will be violent, when it comes.

August 10, 1990

This Mideast showdown may be the last straw for the economy...
the business expansion that we've had for almost eight years.
We were teetering on the edge of recession anyhow.
Iraq pushes us OVER the edge to a drop in gross nat'l product.
A short, fairly shallow recession running into early next year.
That's probably the best we can hope for. It's by no means certain.
Costlier oil reduces buying power...working through the economy
much like an added tax. There is no quick cure for a consumer slump.

September 14, 1990

Bush is not out to pick a fight with Iraq...wants to avoid one
if possible. But if the embargo doesn't work, he WILL use force.
So during the next several months, he will tighten the noose,
increasing pressure on Saddam to knuckle under without a fight.
Then, if there's still no headway, look for a military strike.
That's our own judgment after private talks with top officials.

**Iraqi leader Saddam Hussein rallies
his troops.**

Mexican President Carlos Salinas de Gortari meets with Bush.

September 21, 1990

Figure on a U.S.-Mexico free-trade deal within five years...
a counterforce to economic unity in Europe and Far East trading blocs.
Both gov'ts are firmly behind it...negotiations will start in the spring.
But unions in U.S. will raise a fuss...fearing a loss of jobs to Mexico.
Same for a number of industries in both nations...prefer the status quo.
Eventually, a North American free-trade zone will be set up.
A freer flow of goods and services between Canada, Mexico and the U.S.

September 28, 1990

Figure on Germany and Japan pumping less money into the U.S.
W. Germany will spend more on E. Germany due to unification...
well over $500 billion merely to modernize its rickety old factories.
Plus even more to jump-start the economy and build roads and bridges.
Adding up to the biggest leveraged buyout in the history of the world.
This will divert much of the money Germany WOULD have invested here.
And Japan is having problems at home. A sagging stock market.
High interest rates. Unprofitable lending. And its own money squeeze.

A grim Russian winter will complicate Gorbachev's problems.
Gorbachev will be squeezed even more by angry political forces,
ranging from fiery populist Yeltsin to growing calls for "law & order."

October 12, 1990

Watch for a move to limit congressional terms, similar to efforts
in several states to cap the number of terms state legislators can serve.
The threat of such action is ANOTHER sign voters are fed up with Congress.
May not get far, but it will give the politicians a scare.

November 23, 1990

Commercial real estate will continue to decline...VERY overbuilt
in most metro areas, with office vacancies averaging 20% and on the rise.
Real estate is cyclical. So housing markets WILL bottom out
once consumers pay down their debts and feel better about the economy.
Commercial glut will last longer, easing only after business recovers.
Meanwhile, there are excellent opportunities for savvy buyers.
And a need for patience and realism on the part of sellers.

Don't expect any major effort by Bush to fight recession...
no new public works, tax cuts or other standard moves to prime the pump.
It's doubtful such measures would do a whole lot to help the economy.
And the new budget law severely crimps legislation that costs more money.

A breakup of the Soviet Union by mid-'90s can't be ruled out...
a split into independent states. But it wouldn't come without a fight.
Gorbachev will go along with more autonomy in the Baltics and elsewhere,
realizing that outright independence for one will open the gate for all.
Officials in our gov't are speculating on possible successors
to Gorbachev. Economic and social conditions are chaotic in the USSR...
political and military order is breaking down. The people are fed up.
Boris Yeltsin, head of the Russian republic, is considered the best bet
but regarded as a loose cannon by those who've had dealings with him.
They think that he would soon be replaced by a sterner leader.

Russians demonstrating in support of Boris Yeltsin.

Nov. 30, 1990

<u>The recession will probably stretch well into next year</u>...
but spotty from company to company, industry to industry, area to area.
<u>Recovery will be as gradual as the decline</u>. No burst of strength
next year. But there will be a lift from lower interest rates, exports
(helped by low dollar) and a retail pickup as consumers gain confidence
from reduced debts and probable easing of the standoff in the Mideast.

December 21, 1990

<u>Business will be on much firmer ground a year from now</u>,
after all the shakeouts and restructuring under way in most industries.
<u>Followed by a long stretch of slow growth</u> through the early '90s.
<u>Then accelerating by mid-decade</u>, business showing fresh bounce...
boosted by exports and the world's biggest and most competitive market.
<u>The next five years will be a time of flux</u>...here and overseas.
A different world...economic competition replacing military competition.
There will be ups and downs as U.S. businesses adjust to global markets.
<u>But in five years, we'll be stronger, leaner, more productive</u>...
well positioned for solid growth through the rest of the '90s and beyond.

<u>Living standards will inch up</u> during the next several years...
still comfortably ahead of Canada, Germany and Japan in purchasing power.
<u>Increases in savings and investment</u> will put us on a growth track
for the final years of the century...a head start going into the 2000s.
<u>U.S. automakers will flex their muscles</u>...gaining market share
on imports and Japanese transplants as quality rises faster than prices.
<u>We'll stay in the catbird seat in international agriculture</u>...
advantages in production, processing & distribution will keep us on top.
But if GATT talks aren't revived, our farm exports will grow more slowly.

<u>Expect an overhaul of schools</u> after years of talk and planning.
Principals, teachers and parents will get more say-so on what's taught.
More work on basics, better training for teachers, longer school years.
<u>And gradual improvement in test scores</u>...expanded preschool
and programs targeting "at risk" children will begin paying dividends.
<u>U.S. students will narrow the gap</u> in test-score comparisons
with math/science pupils in Japan and Europe but won't catch up soon.
<u>School choice will be common</u>...district boundaries breaking down.
<u>Computers and interactive videos</u> will be used in most classrooms.
First graders will be required to learn at least some computer basics.
<u>By '96, there will be nat'l standards for teacher certification</u>
and licensing...probably tougher than any of those the states now have.
Examining knowledge of subject matter as well as basic classroom skills.
<u>Involvement of business in schools will no longer be a novelty</u>.
Providing curriculum guidance, guest lecturers and management expertise.
And more apprenticeship programs to ease students into the world of work.

<u>The end of the cold war won't necessarily mean a safer world</u>...
as we've seen in recent months with our commitment in the Middle East.
<u>The Iraq crisis will set the tone</u> for the rest of the '90s...
whether the new int'l order will be able to control upstart dictators.
<u>The USSR will be a far different place</u> five years from now.
Gorbachev won't last that long...he'll be the scapegoat for growing ills.
The Russian republic will probably emerge as the major power center.
Other republics may break off as autonomous nations by the mid-'90s.

<u>Regional blocs will control world trade in the '90s</u>...Europe,
Far East, North America. Growth will be strongest within these blocs.
For example, double-digit growth in our trade with Canada and Mexico...
less growth in our trade with Europe, which will be more protectionist.

1991

January 4, 1991

<u>A North American Common Market will be set up</u> in 2 to 3 years, one of the most significant developments of the decade for U.S. business. Expanding the free-trade pact between U.S. and Canada to take in Mexico.
<u>One huge market of 360 million people</u> buying, selling, investing. It will more than match Europe '92, the integration of European markets, which is seen by some as a threat to U.S. economic power and leadership.

January 11, 1991

<u>Mideast</u>: One way or the other, the long ordeal will soon end. Unless Saddam seeks martyrdom, he'll budge at the last moment. If not, the U.S.-led coalition will strike, and fairly fast.

Not much thought or planning yet on what comes AFTER the crisis. How to repair the strains all over the Mideast and here at home. What to do about the menace of Iraq's army and nuclear potential. How to make sure the sparks that remain don't cause new troubles. We won't be able to walk away with an attitude of "that's that."

January 18, 1991

<u>About the war again</u>: It will continue to weigh on all minds. <u>Impressive as an example of coordination among many nations</u>... cutting across traditional geographic, cultural and religious lines. <u>But leaving many of the old problems</u>...even aggravating a few: Palestinian refugees. Arab-Israeli hostilities. Fundamentalist rage. Income extremes among haves & have-nots. And territorial disputes. <u>Before long, Palestinian homeland will move to center stage</u>. The White House will support initiatives and an international meeting. This will strain relations with Israel but may lead to a breakthrough. Even at low points, U.S. ties to Israel will be close and comprehensive. One thing's sure, the Mideast will top U.S. priorities for YEARS.

March 1, 1991

<u>The U.S. emerges as the ONLY true superpower</u> among world leaders. A superpower nation must have 1) military might, 2) economic strength and 3) a political & social system that other peoples wish to emulate. USSR has the first factor, Japan and Germany the second, U.S. all three.

On the eve of Desert Storm, President Bush confers with (from left) General Colin Powell, chairman of the Joint Chiefs; White House Chief of Staff John Sununu; Defense Secretary Richard Cheney; Vice-President Dan Quayle; Secretary of State James Baker and National Security Advisor Brent Scowcroft.

Is Saddam finished? Yes. He's a liability to Iraq's recovery. If Saddam stayed in power, United Nations sanctions would stay in place. Iraq wouldn't be able to sell its oil to help pay for its reconstruction, and few, if any, countries would lift a finger to help Iraq rebuild.

What about political effects of the war? A huge boost for Bush, but he's at the peak of his popularity now. He will face tough sledding when he returns to domestic problems...economy, banks and S&Ls and drugs. Thus, while he's a strong favorite for reelection, he's not a sure bet.
Democrats want to shift to domestic issues as soon as possible... deposit insurance, job discrimination, etc...worried about their OWN jobs.

May 17, 1991

Democratic politics: Party pros figure an outsider would do best against Bush in '92. Someone not in the Wash. mob...to run AGAINST Wash. A number of them think Gov. Bill Clinton of Ark. would fill the bill... mainstream Democrat, five-term governor, 44 years old and Yale law grad. Good record on education, economic development and support for military. No foreign policy record. (Some Democrats WISH they didn't have one.)
Democrats are pessimistic about '92. Republicans are cocky... ignoring the fact that many elections are lost through overconfidence.

June 14, 1991

Turning to Russia...elections, political and economic changes:
Look for a shift in the White House attitude toward Yeltsin. He's now seen as the catalyst for a market economy and democratic change in the Soviet Union. The White House underestimated Yeltsin in the past.
He's now the favorite to beat Gorbachev in next year's elections.

How far will Russia go in moving away from old-style Marxism?
It'll change more in the next year than at any time since 1917. Moving rapidly toward a democratic constitution, nationwide elections and a market economy...even letting the Baltic states go their own ways. No matter who's in charge...Gorbachev or Yeltsin...there's agreement to privatize much of the economy, loosen up. The course is being set.

August 16, 1991

<u>America's meager savings rate</u>...where is it headed in the '90s?
<u>By mid-decade, savings will be much higher</u> in all categories.
The reasons are many, and some of the trends are already under way.
<u>As a nation, we won't assume foreign capital will bail us out</u>
with huge, '80s-level equity investments in new plants and real estate.
The U.S. will STILL be a highly attractive market for world investors,
but so will an increasing number of other nations, due to freer markets.
<u>We'll have to meet more of our own capital needs</u>, and we will.

August 23, 1991

<u>Keep in mind, the failed coup doesn't SOLVE Soviet problems</u>...
merely clears the air, giving leaders a better chance to find solutions.
<u>For the Soviet people, the road ahead will remain painfully grim</u>.
Making the transition after nearly 75 years of communism will be painful.
There are no quick cures for rickety old plants or thickheaded managers.
<u>Now Gorbachev HAS to deliver</u>...turn the Soviet economy around,
move faster toward democracy and self-rule for the republics.
<u>If things keep sliding, he'll be pushed out again</u>...by voters.
<u>Much of the pressure will come from Yeltsin</u> and his followers.
<u>What about the communist party?</u> It's already a dying influence
within the system after opposing political, economic and social changes.
The party is considered a dinosaur, responsible for ills of the country.

**Changing leadership in Russia:
Gorbachev with his successor, Yeltsin.**

October 11, 1991

<u>Fragments of the old Soviet Union will gradually come together</u>
in new shapes...federation, alliance or broad partnership of some kind.
<u>Cooperation is essential</u>. Most republics can't hack it alone.
They must develop resources, establish a new economy, arrange security.
<u>Republic of Russia will dominate</u>, as in the days of the czars.
Twice the area of the U.S., it has 150 million people, vast resources
and controls most of the Soviet nuclear arms and conventional forces.

<u>Running against Congress will be big stuff</u> in the coming year.
Bush will, of course. So will challengers to entrenched incumbents.
And even incumbents...pushing reforms so that they can pose as outsiders.
<u>Congress will be hammered as selfish, arrogant and privileged</u>...
living high on the hog at taxpayer expense. Exempting itself from laws
it imposes on others...including affirmative action, other civil rights.
Approving more & more perks for its members while also raising their pay
to $125,100. Annual pensions for 30-year members will approach $100,000.
And they will be indexed to inflation...probably unlike your own pension.

November 8, 1991

<u>Back to the economy...politics</u>. <u>Bush got a scare this week</u>.
Defeat of incumbents around the country...Republicans and Democrats.
<u>The Gulf War and the defeat of communism won't save his skin</u>
if people are still worried about their jobs and how to make ends meet.
<u>Pocketbook issues usually decide elections</u>...how people feel
about their own financial well-being, whether they're getting ahead.
Rightly or wrongly, the President gets the credit or catches the blame.

"Excuse me...I'm here to report a little collateral damage"

December 13, 1991

European unity summit: There's a lot at stake for U.S. business.
Fact is, Europe is out to rival the U.S. and Japan commercially
and politically, writing a new set of rules to favor its own businesses,
often at the expense of American firms that don't have a foothold there.
By the end of this decade, a common currency and a central bank.
Perhaps undermining the standing of the dollar in international finance.
A European federation will probably be set up in the early 2000s.
A federation with common judicial, immigration and defense policies...
each member country retaining its borders, its language and sovereignty.

December 20, 1991

VP Quayle won't be dumped from the Republican ticket next year.
In fact, dropping him would do more harm than good to Bush's campaign...
would look like he's panicking. Quayle is popular with conservatives,
does all right on the job and is the party's hardest-working fund-raiser.
The President's real problem is the economy...not his VP.

January 3, 1992

Now comes the acid test for Russia...free of the communist yoke
and moving toward private markets, a democratic gov't and a better life.
The commonwealth probably won't last long, at least as is.
Its authority is vague...no legislature, few responsibilities, no money.
It will eventually crumble or evolve into a Moscow-dominated coalition.
How about Yeltsin, Russia's first democratically elected leader?
If his reforms work, he will be a hero, overshadowing Gorbachev.
He's taking a tremendous risk...turning cold turkey to a market system.
Freeing prices. Raising pay. Cutting gov't spending. Adding taxes.
All intended to reduce runaway deficits and help strengthen the ruble.
If they DON'T work, he'll get the heave-ho, perhaps by year end.
Russians will swallow his bitter medicine for a while if they see results
and feel better...an acceptable price for moving to a free-market system.

The middle-aging of America...a phenomenon in the next 20 years
that will affect business, living patterns, retirement, social security.
By 2010, 80 million people born from '46 to '64...the largest generation
in American history...will have reached middle age and begun to retire.
Many repercussions, no matter where you live or what you do for a living.

1992

Democratic hopefuls at their first TV debate: Left to right, Kerrey, Clinton, Tsongas, Harkin, Brown and Wilder.

January 3, 1992

Clinton is the early front-runner for the Democratic nomination
now that Cuomo is out of the picture. But front-runners often stumble.
Harkin should win Iowa caucuses...his home state. Clinton must do well
in the New Hampshire primary to maintain momentum over Harkin and Kerrey.
Tsongas, Brown and Wilder aren't hacking it. They'll soon be also-rans.

Many readers wonder whether the U.S. will prosper in the '90s.
Odds are that it will. People tend to emphasize our problems
and shortcomings, downplaying the underlying strengths of this country.
Fact is, many of our problems are being corrected, albeit slowly.
Corporate and consumer debt are being whittled down...but not gov't debt.
A new urgency to improve our schools. Drug & alcohol abuse, declining.
Productivity, increasing smartly in manufacturing...but not in services.
Tough challenges still ahead: Taming excessive gov't spending.
Boosting an anemic savings rate. Beefing up investment in capital goods.
Absorbing new waves of immigrants. And helping people out of poverty.

Industrial restructuring isn't finished...not in computers,
steel, autos or other lines. Means much turmoil, but higher profits too.
Same thing is happening now in services, where productivity gains
have lagged manufacturing. Retail, banking, health care and other lines
stand to benefit from more automation and less administrative overhead.

Recent world events will strengthen the U.S. in global markets.
Other nations will become more open to products from our plants
and farms and to our services. Already the No. 1 exporter in the world,
the U.S. will do even better as other countries compete by fairer rules.
America's openness often seems to be a curse, our own businesses
and workers facing a daily barrage of foreign competition from all sides.
It's actually a blessing, as other nations are now discovering.
Openness makes us a magnet for world capital, talent and goods.
Teamed with America's world-leading productivity and scientific research,
the result is abundant and reasonably priced food, housing, other goods.

January 17, 1992

Electric cars will grab up to 15% of the market in 20 years...
more if the driving range expands to 300 miles or so before recharging.
Stringent clean air requirements in Calif. will spur sales of electrics.
   And alternative fuels will make inroads as fleet owners switch
to natural gas, propane, methanol, ethanol and others in next few years.
Federal and state rules will require a lot of converting starting in '95.
   A train that travels on air will be ready for trial runs by 2000.
The gov't will spend over $700 million on high-speed magnetic levitation,
the route still to be decided. Defense companies are eyeing the project.

January 24, 1992

   If things don't turn around soon, Bush may get licked in Nov.
He will need more than just a few upward wiggles in gov't statistics.
Ordinary voters will have to feel better about their own well-being.
Rightly or wrongly, Presidents get the credit or blame for the economy.

   Pessimism over the economy is deeper than justified by the facts.
   White-collar workers have been hit hard...managers, engineers,
bankers, real estate agents, gov't workers, sales people and journalists.
They do a lot of talking and are more visible than blue-collar workers.
When they're out of work or their incomes slip, EVERYONE hears about it.
   And the East Coast and southern Calif. are the weakest areas...
big media centers trumpeting gloom. They also account for a large share
of the electoral votes needed to win next Nov...more bad news for Bush.

   Odds are that the economy will brighten in time to save him...
housing, retailing and business spending improving enough to be noticed.
   Many current business changes will make the economy healthier
in the long haul...cost cutting, downsizing, automating, restructuring.
Bush's problem is that short term, they mean disruption and unemployment.
   Democrats have a fighting chance this year...a FIGHTING chance.
But their nominee will probably be an underdog to the sitting President.
Besides, even state party leaders are only lukewarm on Clinton, Kerrey
and the rest...figure it may take more than the economy to put them over.

Displaced workers, homeless families
underscored the issue that ultimately
decided the 1992 election: the
domestic economy.

Federal Reserve Chairman Alan
Greenspan defended his policies
before congressional committees.

January 24, 1992

The twin deficits...budget and trade...long a source of concern
to politicians, economists and recently to business people and consumers.
They're now headed in opposite directions, and people ask why,
wonder what's going on and about the effects on business and investment.
Trade deficit has been heading down since peaking at $150 billion
in '87. It slid to $65 billion in '91, the lowest level in eight years.

But the budget deficit is rising sharply, despite ballyhooed cuts
in the agreement Bush made with Congress. Pushed up by a pokey economy,
which reduces tax revenues, and spending for deposit insurance, Medicare.
This is bad news. Huge deficits retard growth in the economy
and living standards. Gov't borrowing drains money that could be spent
for productive investment...essential for growth and future prosperity.
On the brighter side, '92 will be high tide for gov't red ink...
a shortfall near $350 billion, up 30% from the previous high last year.
Gradual ebbing will begin next year. Recovery will boost revenue.
Defense cuts will start to take hold. Deposit insurance funds will shift
from spending to net income for gov't as assets of failed banks and S&Ls
are sold off. Also helping will be mild inflation and low interest rates.
With luck, deficit may dip to $200 billion by '95, still too high
at more than 2% of gross domestic product, a serious drag on the economy.
A trend in the right direction, however, over the next few years.
IF major changes in taxes and spending patterns get the budget on track,
there's a fairly good chance for continuing progress in the late '90s.

A word on the massive reshaping of U.S. military now under way.
Amounts to a reappraisal of future military needs, not JUST cuts
in budget. Congress, think tanks and others will debate the fine points
in '92...setting the stage for putting major changes in place next year.
Expect defense spending to be down a third by '95, which will mean
cutting back on the B-2, fighters, attack subs and other advanced systems.
But U.S. military will still pack a mighty wallop if called upon.
Better prepared to meet threats of today's world despite big cuts.
It will be molded to respond very quickly and efficiently to terrorism,
regional conflicts and nuclear proliferation. Also very important...
defense policy will help maintain U.S. industrial & technological prowess.
It will add up to a better return on the taxpayer's dollar.

February 7, 1992

"Buy American" mood will have a temporary impact on business.
Most noticeable in the Midwest, but rippling out to both coasts too.
Should help sales of Big Three cars...a boost for GM, Ford, Chrysler.
    But anti-foreign feelings will subside as U.S. economy recovers.
    Eventually, buyers' old habits will return. Gov't budget cuts
will make procurement chiefs pick low bidders regardless of who they are.
Most consumers will still shop for the best product at the best price.
And it's getting more difficult to distinguish imports from domestics.
Which is the American car...a Honda from Ohio or a Ford built in Mexico?

March 6, 1992

    Good chance that half the oil we use this year will be imported.
    That would be a first...exceeding '77, when imports reached 46%,
and last year, when we brought in 46% of what we used. Weak oil prices
are keeping exploration and drilling activity at low levels in the U.S.
As the economy improves, increased demand for oil will be met by imports.

March 13, 1992

    The real election surprise may come in the congressional races.
    Over 100 House seats will change hands because of redistricting,
retirements and outrage over check kiting and other high-handed practices.
It'll be the biggest shift since '48, but Democrats will still run things.
    Many senior members will quit for ANOTHER reason...last chance
to pocket cash from their campaign funds. That will be banned after '92.

    Bush still rates the edge in Nov., assuming a stronger economy
and that he does better in convincing voters that he is up to the job.
    But he's far from a shoo-in. The slump hit millions of families
and parts of the country with big electoral counts...Calif., Ill., Mich.,
Fla., N.Y., N.J. and Mass. A lot of voters are worse off than in '88.
    Clinton stacks up as a formidable opponent...middle-of-the-road,
popular governor with big network of party loyalists around the country.
A co-founder and chairman of the centrist Democratic Leadership Council.
    Democratic officeholders, however, have doubts, fear more stories
about his personal life will pop up AFTER he captures the nomination...
that Republicans probably have a few tucked away in their back pockets.
They're afraid that Clinton will hurt other Democrats down the ballot.

March 27, 1992

Don't fall for the talk that exports are about to take a dive because of weaknesses in the Canadian, European and Japanese economies.
Exports to Latin America will jump 20% this year. Capital goods and other products bound for Mexico, Colombia, Venezuela, Peru, Brazil, Argentina, Chile and elsewhere...taking up the slack from other places.
And big sales to Pacific Rim...Malaysia, Singapore, Hong Kong, Thailand, South Korea and Taiwan. They buy more as their incomes rise.
Both manufactured and service exports will increase this year... aerospace, computers, chemicals, paper, machinery, lumber and aluminum. Also movies, TV shows, videos and recordings, engineering and legal work.

April 3, 1992

Ross Perot may be the wild card in how the election turns out. There's growing support in nearly all states to put him on the ballot. And he can spend as much as he wants if he doesn't accept matching funds.
Perot could tip the balance in Texas and Calif. and other states where he has a large following...taking just enough votes away from Bush. Usually, independents hurt incumbents more than they do other candidates.
In '68, George Wallace attracted close to 14% of the total vote. In '80, John Anderson took nearly 7%. Perot might be able to top them.
Not enough to win, but enough to give the White House fits.

April 10, 1992

Independent presidential candidate Ross Perot rattled cages in both political parties.

Doubts about social security are common among young workers.
Many figure they would do better investing the money themselves.
They're probably right...those who have discipline and know-how.
And that they will get a smaller return than present retirees.
That's true...gov't keeps taking a bigger bite out of their pay.

Others figure that the money just won't be there when needed, that the system is just a big Ponzi scheme on the verge of coming apart. And that in years ahead there'll be too many retirees, too few workers.
That's NOT true. Social security system is no great bargain, especially compared with what earlier retirees paid in and then received. But it is solvent...the gov't will not renege on the fund's obligations.
It will remain solvent for decades...about 45 years by estimates of fund trustees. Estimates are sound...based on reasonable assumptions about wage trends, inflation, births, life expectancy and immigration. Retirees will get back what they contribute within about 10 years...tops.

April 17, 1992

Overhaul of welfare programs will spread from state to state... driven by rising caseloads and budget problems and spurred along by Bush.
Important to business, which pays a lot of taxes for welfare and stands to benefit from new job training and schooling requirements.
Some plans will be blocked by the courts after they're in place, but the mood in the states is to take a leap of faith, TRY something new.

Big league baseball will adopt revenue sharing in next few years, giving small-market teams...Pittsburgh, Milwaukee, Minn., Seattle, etc... a cut of local TV money from New York, Chicago, LA and other big markets. National TV money is already split evenly among the major league clubs.

Political gridlock over the deficit won't be broken this year...
candidates don't have the guts to offer tough remedies before an election.
    The solutions ARE known. Either get a grip on gov't spending,
including popular "entitlement" programs, such as Medicaid and Medicare.
Or raise taxes on high incomes, gasoline, oil imports, alcohol, tobacco.
Or, most likely, some combination of spending cuts and tax increases.
    Fact is, those who understand the problem aren't THAT far apart.
In private talks, leaders in both parties agree there is a budget crisis
and that interest on the debt alone will be a heavy drag for many years.
    They agree that entitlements have to be curbed, like it or not.
    That defense must be cut further...deeper than Bush would like.
    And that taxes will go up no matter what anyone promises now.
Otherwise, no curbing the debt, which is already approaching $4 TRILLION.

May 1, 1992

    Gov. Clinton's strategy for gaining momentum is quite simple...
keep harping on changes needed to get the economy on track and make jobs.
And keep nailing Bush for runaway deficits and lack of ideas, leadership.
Aim is to put the Republicans on the defensive, replying to HIS charges.
    Even with the economy picking up, he'll stick with this strategy,
figuring that unemployment will remain high through the fall campaign.
And he'll talk a lot about the course of the economy over the long haul,
the growing debt..."what that means for your children and grandchildren."

May 15, 1992

    Perot's balloon will lose altitude...his 35% in the polls.
He's giving Bush and Clinton fits. They don't know what to make of him.
    He'll face tougher going once he announces his candidacy in June.
No matter what side he takes on touchy issues, he'll step on some toes.
    Many of his backers really don't know him or what he stands for.
For now, Perot is the perfect candidate...he's all things to all people.

    Economic slowdown in Japan has raised interest rates there.
    Japanese firms will lose an important edge over competitors...
the lower cost of capital they've enjoyed throughout the 1970s and '80s.
Easier money helped Japanese companies grow rapidly and expand exports.
Also kept the yen undervalued...helping Japan build a big trade surplus.
    It's a new ball game for Japan. Its companies will be squeezed.
Big Japanese manufacturers will no longer be so dominant in world trade.

Japanese traders at the Tokyo exchange.

Growing ethnic diversity personified on the M.I.T. campus.

May 29, 1992

> The term "minorities" soon won't mean much in many communities.
> It's ALREADY obsolete in California. No racial/ethnic majority
> in LA, San Francisco, San Jose, Oakland, Stockton and many other cities.
> We're now more mosaic than melting pot...a racial & ethnic quilt
> of whites, blacks, Hispanics and hundreds of nationalities and subgroups.
> Asian-Americans are increasing 24 times as fast as non-Hispanic whites.
> Hispanics 12 times as fast. Indians six times. And blacks three times.
> A mosaic varying city to city...Hmongs in St. Paul and Missoula.
> Cambodians in Atlanta and Providence. And Salvadorans in Arlington, Va.
> All told, 20 million foreign-born people in the U.S...8% of the total.
> Immigrants will keep pouring in...close to a million a year.
>
> Big impact on schools...teaching kids who lack basic English.
> More than 100 languages are spoken in New Jersey and California schools.
> Over half of California school kids belong to one minority or another.
> In another seven or eight years, that share probably will approach 65%.
> And business...growing markets for filling needs of immigrants.
> A Los Angeles company enjoys boomy sales of cosmetics to Japanese women.
> Others carve out profitable niches in foods, banking and communications.

June 12, 1992

> No big surge in hiring. Many companies had to let people go...
> don't want to go through THAT again. Hiring is much easier than firing.
> Besides, there has been a major shakeout and restructuring of industries.
> Employers have slimmed down, automated. They won't need as many people.
> Two million new jobs this year, mostly at small or midsize firms.
> That's barely half as many as in the year following the last recession
> and just about offsets the number of jobs lost in the past 15 months.
> Companies won't add high-pay, low-skill jobs as they did before.
> They can't while competing in worldwide markets with cheap foreign labor.
> That's bad news for young high school graduates with no special skills...
> won't be able to land $15-an-hour jobs at auto-assembly plants anymore.
> But strong demand for these specialists in the years ahead:
> Skilled machinists. People who know plumbing, heating, air-conditioning.
> Biochemists. Doctors & nurses. Therapists. Radiologists. Paralegals.
> Accountants. Information-management specialists. And systems analysts.
> Environmental engineers. Math & science teachers. People who can SELL.

More talk of a value-added tax to whittle away at the deficit
and compete better with foreign firms that get tax rebates on exports.
It would be applied to goods and services at each stage of distribution
from producer to consumer. A 5% VAT would raise roughly $160 billion.
Strictly in the talking stage...no action in the next few years.
But there's a good chance that some type of VAT will pass in the '90s.

June 26, 1992

Democratic convention only two weeks off, and leaders are worried
about Gov. Clinton's slow start, money problems and third place in polls.
Clinton will get a boost from the convention...he needs it badly.
Doing better lately, but still must climb a mountain of voter distrust.

July 2, 1992

Eastern Europe on the road to free markets...encouraging signs
are popping up: Nearly half of Poland's jobs are now in private sector.
In Hungary, about one-fourth. The switch to capitalism will take longer
than many experts thought, but trends still point in the right direction.
In Russia, it's another story...30-40 years for free enterprise
to fully take over. Many state-owned operations will NEVER be converted
into private firms, but pieces of them will be spun off successfully.

No turnaround in sight for organized labor...in a long slide.
Union membership is now just 16% of the work force, down from 35%
in the '50s. The old-line manufacturing unions have suffered the most...
jobs have disappeared in the face of technology and foreign competition.
Shift to gov't, clerical and professional workers will continue
as unions push organizing campaigns in growing sectors of the job market.
They will appeal to women and younger workers by promising to bargain
for benefits such as child care, flextime and better health insurance.

July 10, 1992

Clinton will climb in the polls in the next couple of weeks.
It's a good bet Clinton will soon take a clear lead over Bush and Perot.

Candidates Clinton and Gore out for a morning jog.

**Indonesian workers assembling
Japanese trucks in a Jakarta factory.**

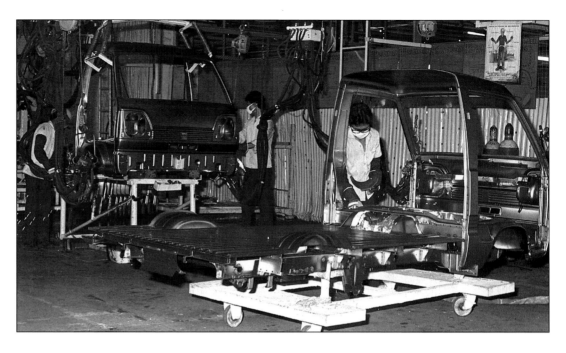

August 7, 1992

<u>Historic transformation is taking place in the world economy</u>...
far-reaching productivity revolution with many facets, including these:
<u>Lessening of gov't economic control</u>...the collapse of communism,
grudging progress against protectionism. Pragmatism replacing ideology.
<u>The spread of technology and production</u> to once-backward nations.
<u>Downsizing by giant corporations</u> in all countries, not just U.S.,
to meet the competition of lower-cost, nimble, innovative small firms.
<u>Soaring world trade</u> despite the seductive song of protectionism.

<u>Ability of governments to steer their economies is declining</u>,
due to the fluid, rapid movement of capital and goods around the world.
In the U.S., the deficit-strapped gov't can't afford to prime the pump.
<u>Reasserting gov't control sounds tempting</u> to workers being hurt
by competition. Perot and some Democrats have pitched a popular theme...
that gov't aid and protection for certain industries will boost the U.S.
<u>But it probably wouldn't work</u>. Gov't intervention in business
usually fails, doesn't help our industries keep pace with competitors.

<u>In the short run, these changes will create massive problems</u>...
falling defense spending, layoffs, brutal competition, capital shortages.
<u>But in the end, stronger economies</u> for the well-prepared nations
with educated and skilled work forces and pro-growth business climates.

August 14, 1992

<u>The westward movement of Americans may be ending</u> after 200 years.
People are still flocking into western states from Asia and Latin America
but not from other states. Net internal migration to the West declined
throughout the 1980s. Nevada was the main exception to this trend.

August 28, 1992

<u>Back to economic ups & downs</u>...the effect on moods and attitudes.
In the '80s, some economic wise men felt the economy had so much momentum
that it could absorb downslides in individual industries, one at a time,
without going into a recession. That was strictly bunk, and we said so.
Now gloom & doomers are out in force, talking of "depression,"
high unemployment for many years, a decline of American competitiveness.
They're as wrong as the wise men of the '80s...and do even more damage.

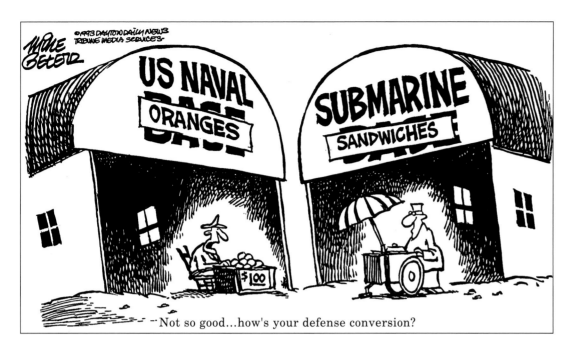

© 1993 DAYTON DAILY NEWS
TRIBUNE MEDIA SERVICES

US NAVAL ORANGES

SUBMARINE SANDWICHES

$1.00

-- "Not so good...how's your defense conversion?"

September 11, 1992

Jolts from defense cuts will go on for another five or six years.
Sharp reductions in weapon systems, fighter planes, ships and submarines.
Base closings all around the country and cutbacks in military personnel.
A big factor in economic woes, both in this country and overseas.
It won't kill the recovery, but it's a definite drag on growth.
Think of it as a post-war transition at the end of the Cold War.

Military spending now accounts for about 5% of our total economy.
It will drop to 3 1/2% or less by '97, the lowest in about 50 years.
Net: Defense cuts will slow economic growth in the short term
due to downsizing & restructuring...impact varying by industry and area.
But over the long haul...the next decade or so...cuts will save money,
make deficit control more possible and result in more private spending.

September 18, 1992

Business won't turn around in time to help Bush.
Statistically, the recovery got under way in the spring of '91.
Economists can see it, but no one else can. Voters read about layoffs
at big companies and figure the economy is headed in the wrong direction.
They're used to recovery starting off with a bang, not with a whimper.

Yeltsin's "shock therapy" isn't working. His efforts fall flat
due to lack of an adequate banking system, credit, solid managers, etc.
Capital is fleeing at an astonishing pace, $6 billion this year.
And with everything in disarray, western investment is slow to show up.
So Yeltsin will buy time by blaming others, dumping some senior aides
and consolidating his power by replacing acting Prime Minister Gaidar.
Support will grow for a firmer hand at the top but not a return
to the old-style communist regime. Even conservatives don't want THAT.

October 2, 1992

Microwave clothes dryers will be on the market by the late '90s.
They will do the job a lot faster, with less wear and tear on garments
and 20% less energy. (Save even more if you put popcorn in the pockets.)

Moscow retail outlet: plenty of nothing.

October 2, 1992

Politicians will handle the deficit like a live hand grenade.
They all remember defeated candidates who wanted to cap social security,
slash subsidies or increase taxes to get a grip on the mounting deficit.
Any serious deficit-reduction solution will hurt SOMEONE...
retirees, high-income homeowners, farmers, physicians, gov't pensioners,
veterans or others. They all have one thing in common...they're voters.
That's why Bush and Clinton will dance around specific proposals.

October 30, 1992

Bush is rallying just about everywhere, gaining a lot of ground.
But probably not enough to catch Clinton. A close popular vote,
but Clinton has more big electoral states sewed up, Calif., Ill. and N.Y.
What effect will the election have on the economy next year?
Very little. It will keep inching upward no matter who wins.
Business scraped bottom in April '91 and has been recovering since then.

November 6, 1992

President-elect Clinton:
He's "middle"...middle class in origin, in outlook and policies.
Pragmatic. Not liberal or conservative in the usual sense of those words.
Clinton tries to steer a wide path down the center, where most voters are.
His natural inclination is to compromise, to avoid confrontation.
Or drop an issue entirely if it draws too much heat from interest groups.
A hard worker, Clinton will get personally involved in lobbying lawmakers
for his proposals...starting soon in meetings with congressional leaders.

Gov't policy will be tilted toward the high-tech industries...
more federal research and development aimed at bioengineering, robotics,
telecommunications, medical services & equipment and factory automation.
Continuity will be stressed in foreign and military affairs...
no sharp swerves away from the policies carried out by Reagan and Bush.
Continued efforts to help Yeltsin and dismantle Russia's nuclear arms
and to advance talks between Israel, Arab countries and Palestinians.
Count on a more aggressive trade policy under the new President.
Clinton will be more willing to pull the trigger if foreigners cheat...
using retaliatory measures when they discriminate against U.S. exports.

Clinton will send a health-care plan to Congress in early '93.
Proposals to expand employer-paid health insurance, control drug prices
and increase regulation of insurance companies and health-care providers.
But major changes will take several years to get through Congress
and be put into effect. There are sharp differences between lawmakers,
employers, doctors, hospitals and insurers about what ought to be done.

Many bills WILL pass, bills that fell short in the last Congress:
Unpaid leave for family emergency. Bush vetoed. Clinton won't.
Ban on hiring replacements for striking workers. No. 1 priority
of the unions the past few years. Now looks like a sure bet for passage.
A crime bill, including gun control. Nearly made it this year.
Easier voter registration...while renewing a driver's license
or getting gov't aid. Bush felt it attracted too many Democratic voters.

December 4, 1992

The productivity of U.S. business is soaring.
Layoffs, mergers and downsizing are key factors, making companies
lean and mean. They plan to stay that way as the economy strengthens...
automating and making better use of current employees instead of hiring.
Strong foreign competition is another big incentive to keep running lean.
That's good news for investors. It will fatten the bottom line.
But bad news for the jobless because fewer new jobs will open up.

Long-term continuation of this trend would be a big plus for all.
It would lead to a DOUBLING of living standards in the next 25-30 years,
creating demand for more products and services...and more employment.
And high productivity means firms can pay more without raising prices.
But gains probably won't continue at such a high level for long.
It's partly a cyclical phenomenon...a spurt in productivity that's common
early in a recovery when orders outpace hirings. Gradually slowing down.
However, there's a good chance gains will stay above levels of the '80s
because service industries, 75% of all workers, are much more efficient.

Note these population trends important for business planning:
U.S. will add 25 million people in the '90s. Means that by 2000
we'll have 275 million people. During the '80s, 22 million were added
because of heavy immigration and "natural increase"...births over deaths.
Sharpest growth will be among Hispanics each year after '95.
By early in the 2000s, there'll be more Hispanics than blacks in the U.S.
A huge increase in Asians too...growing faster than whites after 2002.
Immigrants will continue to pour in. A steady flow of illegals
and many legals admitted to reunite families or as political refugees.

A big jump in 5 to 13-year-olds...increasing four times as fast
as during the '80s. Many of them immigrants or children of immigrants.
That will increase the demand for language specialists in grade schools.
And more 14 to 17-year-olds, following a drop during the '80s.
Means more people entering the labor force starting around 2000,
after further declines in 18-21-year-olds during the next several years.
By 2010, the entry-level group will hit a record high, 18 million people.
The elderly population will grow more slowly from now until 2010.
Then it will start shooting up as the oldest baby boomers reach age 65.

Typical scene in Mogadishu, Somalia: starving children.

December 4, 1992

   Haiti: Neither Bush nor Clinton will open the door to refugees.
They will lean on the generals who run Haiti to improve conditions there
or face possible intervention. All Haitian refugees will be interviewed.
Some who can prove they've been politically persecuted will be admitted.
But most will be classified as economically motivated and sent home.
   Somalia: Amounts to a LONG-term commitment by the U.S. and UN.
Achieving order, establishing legitimate rulers and a functioning society
will take a lot of time and money. U.S. pays for 25% of the UN's budget
and 30% of its peacekeeping. Clinton will get more money from Congress
to finance assistance for Somalia, Bosnia and other down-&-out places.

December 11, 1992

   Probably a slowing in the longtime trend toward early retirement.
   Here's why: Longer life spans. Questions about future benefits,
including company-paid health coverage for retirees. Low interest rates,
which mean puny payoffs from CDs and other forms of savings/investments.
And more people balking at buyout offers because of the poor job market.
   Ten years ago, 72% of men ages 55 to 64 were in the work force.
That's down to 67% now but probably won't go much lower during the '90s.

December 23, 1992

   Is the U.S. "not making anything anymore," as Ross Perot says?
   No. Not only are American-made goods growing in value, but...
   Manufacturing is holding its own as a share of our economy,
about 20%, similar to 1960 and '75. The MIX of products keeps changing,
with declining production in some manufactures, like shoes and clothing,
and rocketing growth in things that didn't even exist 10 years ago...
new drugs, advanced microprocessors, MRI scanners, laptop computers, etc.
   Some people confuse employment with output in a given sector.
Sure, manufacturing jobs are a falling share of the U.S. labor force,
just as farmers dwindled from 8% of the 1960 labor force to about 3% now.
But as with agricultural production, industrial OUTPUT continues to rise.
That's productivity...more value from fewer workers with better tools.
   Now it's the service sector's turn to boost productivity.
In '70s and '80s we added more service firms and jobs than sustainable.
Now, shakeouts in banking, airlines, retailing and other service lines.
   Trimming will keep jobless rate higher than normal in expansion.

Affordability of housing suffered in the '70s and early '80s,
when home prices and rents outpaced income in many parts of the country.
Getting better now...overbuilding has softened housing prices,
and lower mortgage rates are helping many more young people buy homes.
The percent of homeownership has fallen a few points from 66% in '80.
Probably has bottomed and will rise to its former peak in a few years.

American health continues to improve in most categories.
Life expectancy increases, but not at the rate of past decades,
when new antibiotics brought many infectious diseases under control.
Infant mortality has dropped 50% since '70 and continues to fall,
although the U.S. rate is still slightly above other industrial nations.

December 30, 1992

There will be plenty of energy available the next 10-20 years,
but the mix will be different, and prices will be a bit higher.
Oil will still be the main source of energy throughout the '90s.
Geothermal, solar, natural gas, propane, methanol and ethanol will gain,
but we're set up to use petroleum for everything from heating buildings
to fueling cars & planes and as a feedstock for chemicals & plastics.
People feel comfortable with it...they're not so sure about alternatives.
We'll import more oil and oil products, raising our vulnerability
to supply disruptions and price hikes from Mideast and other suppliers.

Clinton-Gore will promote natural gas as a way to cut pollution
and oil imports. It will be the "politically correct" fuel of the '90s.
Energy conservation will also be pushed by Clinton and Gore...
carrying out requirements of recently passed energy and clean air laws.
More emphasis on renewable energy sources in coming years.
And no big expansion of nuclear power until well into the 2000s.
The combination of alternative fuels and conservation lessens the need.
U.S. will export more coal, offsetting loss of domestic markets.
Europeans and Asians will buy from us...we have better and cheaper coal.
Electric vehicles will make inroads in the next five years...
new clean air laws in Calif. and other states will help increase sales.
Big buyers will include gov't, utility firms and other commercial fleets.
Families won't buy them until costs come down and batteries last longer.

December 30, 1992

New U.S.-Russia deal on reducing nuclear arms will help Clinton.
He'll begin his administration with a major agreement already in the bag.
It'll be up to him to carry out Start II. That won't be easy...
missiles loaded with nukes are also in Ukraine, Kazakhstan and Belarus.
And leaders in those countries want more say about arms on their soil.
Top-notch intelligence will be required to keep track of Russia,
Yeltsin and his opponents. Following Reagan's rule: Trust...but verify.
Note that the treaty does NOT require destruction of warheads
on missiles or nuclear materials inside them. Preventing their transfer
to Iran, Iraq and other Third World countries is a job left unfinished.

Watch Clinton shift the emphasis to LONG-term deficit reduction,
bringing it down gradually over many years, through the end of the '90s.
He'll soft-pedal short-term actions for trimming the deficit.
And he'll cast a wider tax net than outlined in his campaign...
going beyond the well-to-do and foreign-owned companies in this country.
Clinton is already considering the pros and cons of higher energy taxes,
reducing the amount companies can deduct for employee health insurance
and taxing employer-provided health benefits above a certain level.

1993

January 8, 1993

Clinton will backpedal on a number of his campaign promises.
A tax cut for the middle class will be downplayed by Clinton.
He promised it in the campaign, but the economy is recovering without it,
and the deficit is worsening. Very few in Congress think it's needed.
More tax hikes than cuts. Clinton is looking under every rock.
Only a small dose of stimulus will be offered, not the bold plan
that was talked up in the campaign...roads, sewers, fiber-optic networks.

Congress will approve more research on "smart" highways and cars.
Speedier weighing systems for trucks...checking them on the move.
Only trucks found to be overloaded or oversized will have to pull over.
Collision warning systems to guide you through fog and signal
if a car is in your blind spot. (Could drive you nuts in heavy traffic.)
Cruise control that brakes automatically if a slow car is ahead.
Computerized road signs to minimize variations in vehicle speeds
and direct drivers to alternative routes BEFORE they're stuck in traffic.
And on-board computers for directions and road conditions ahead.

Big changes in the works for television and telephone technology.
Some in the next few years. Others not until early in the new century:
    High-definition TV by '95 or '96...sharper pictures, better sound
on $5000 big-screen sets. U.S. companies have a jump in HDTV technology.
    Interactive TV by the mid-'90s. By using your remote control,
you'll be able to answer questions on TV, order tickets and take classes.
    Cable TV with up to 500 channels by '95. 50 games every Saturday
plus 100 movies. But you'll pay $3 to $5 each and a $20-$50 monthly fee.
    Direct-broadcast satellites by the end of '94...18-inch dishes
that will cost $700 and a monthly fee. Mostly for folks in rural areas.
The smaller dishes will cut into the market for larger and costlier ones.

    Fiber optics will revolutionize telecommunications by 2010...
phone and cable companies spending billions to install cables of glass
that can carry much more information than present phone and TV systems.
Also multimedia networking...interaction of TV, phones, computers, faxes.
    Phones will handle more tasks...mobile phones linked to pagers,
faxes and computers. By '95, small portable phones will be available
for $100 or less plus 15¢ to 20¢ per minute for those making local calls.
Before then, Federal Communications Comm. will approve extra frequencies.
    "Personal digital assistants" this year...combination of phone,
fax and electronic notepad. Selling for $2000...strictly for big shots.

February 12, 1993

    Big shifts in the population mix will affect your business...
probably even changing the makeup of your own customers and employees.
    There will be fewer young families, more people 45 and older,
more minorities...a third of our population by 2010, up from 25% now.
    First of all, don't assume that everyone will ACT their age...
they won't. Bottlers worried that baby boomers would switch to coffee
as they grew older. But they stuck to soft drinks...sales are booming.
Now bottlers are playing up fruit content, lack of artificial coloring
and other traits that appeal to health and environment-minded boomers.
    The 55 & over crowd will keep buying sports cars and Walkmans.
They'll give up on fitness clubs but will use exercise machines at home.

February 12, 1993

        <u>Home and family will take on more importance</u> in the years ahead.
Many more people in the prime family-raising and grandparenting years...
increasing demand for home entertainment gear, furnishings, casual dining
and conveniences that free up TIME for family, friends and goofing off.
For example, dry cleaners and auto mechanics who'll pick up and deliver.
        <u>People will spend less time browsing the malls</u>...want efficiency,
convenience, in & out fast. Exception...those in teens and early 20s.

        <u>Women already outnumber men in college graduating classes</u>...
more & more will move to top ranks of business, education and politics.
        <u>Women will continue to marry later and have their babies later</u>.
In 1960, over 60% of women ages 20-24 were married...half were mothers.
Today, fewer than 40% are married, and only a fifth of them are mothers.
Births will decline now to 2000...fewer women of prime childbearing age.

        <u>Politics will be driven by these changes</u> in our population mix.
Population and political representation will keep shifting to the West
and South. Today's hot issues...child care, family leave, health care...
will give way to pension rights, social security and immigration control.
Sometime in the early 2000s, will probably elect a minority President.

March 12, 1993

        <u>Clinton's plan to boost technology and open foreign markets</u>...
        <u>It will be a two-pronged approach</u> to make aerospace, electronics,
automotive and other industries stronger and more globally competitive.
        <u>More money for gov't labs and to form gov't-industry partnerships</u>
to speed technology transfer. Congress will honor President's request.
        <u>Plus a tougher stand with trading partners</u>. Telling the Japanese
and others the U.S. will vigorously prosecute trade cases against them
if they don't drop their barriers to exports of U.S. goods and services.
        Outcome will be crucial to thousands of companies and investors.

March 19, 1993

        <u>French abortion pill will be approved</u> for marketing in the U.S.
within a few years. Clinton is leaning on FDA to make it available.
The Reagan and Bush administrations did their best to keep the pill out.

March 26, 1993

  <u>Ross Perot</u>. <u>What's he up to?</u> Clinton and Congress want to know.
They see him as a force to be reckoned with in the '94 and '96 elections.
  <u>He'll keep harping on the deficit</u>...attracting media attention
and new members for his political organization, United We Stand America.
If the deficit gradually comes down, Perot will take much of the credit.
If it increases, he'll be in position to make hay on voter frustration.
  <u>Perot wants to be President</u>, take another shot as an independent.
He won't try for the Republican nomination...that would be too confining.

April 2, 1993

  <u>Gays in the military</u>: The Pentagon must draft a plan by July 15
for carrying out Clinton's directive. He won't back off his commitment
but is willing to compromise on the timing and ways of implementing it.
  <u>Congress will have the final say</u>. Most members will support
an end to asking recruits about their sexual orientation, nothing more.
There's no support for changing the laws that specifically ban sodomy.
  Any eventual compromise will be based on standards of conduct.

April 9, 1993

  <u>Brace yourself for a regulatory blitz in the next year or so</u>...
the gov't nosing deeper into your business, adding rules and paperwork.
  <u>We're now at a crossroads regarding govt's role in the economy</u>.
Not a radical or wrenching change, but a subtle drifting toward control.
Buzzwords are "managed competition," "managed trade," "global budgets."
  <u>Adds up to more gov't direction</u>, more setting of priorities.
It's Clinton's idea of activist gov't rather than market orientation...
let the gov't decide which industries OUGHT to be encouraged to expand
and allow some collaboration among companies in a handful of industries.
A similar approach on taxes...hit some industries while favoring others.

  <u>On federal debt</u>: <u>More than $3 TRILLION is owed to the public</u>...
that's the amount we're in the hole. Compares with $700 billion in 1980.
  <u>It'll be at least $4 trillion by '97</u>, the end of Clinton's term.
  <u>The main culprit is automatic spending</u> for Medicare and Medicaid.
Unchecked, those programs will swamp the cuts now being made in defense.
Clinton and Congress must control gov't health costs and other programs
or else debt will spin out of control. Even if his health plan is OK'd,
costs will keep rising awhile...no real impact on debt until about 2000.

April 30, 1993

<u>Allow for tax increases in your planning</u> for the next few years.
<u>Congress will approve a tax bill before it adjourns</u> this fall.
<u>Much tougher on business than Clinton proposed</u> a few months ago.
<u>Some sort of energy tax will pass</u>, but not a straight Btu levy
as outlined by Clinton. Exceptions are already in the works for coal,
home heating oil, barges, int'l airlines, ethanol/methanol, other uses.
Farmers want out. And other industries are waiting in line, hat in hand.
<u>Compromise may be a sharper gasoline tax hike</u> and milder Btu tax.

<u>Higher taxes on upper-incomers are SURE</u>, top marginal rate rising
to 36% from 31% for marrieds with taxable incomes of more than $140,000
or singles over $115,000. And a 39.6% bracket on incomes above $250,000.
<u>Business deductions for meals will be cut</u> from the current 80%.
<u>Deductions for club dues will be ended</u>...country clubs, others.
<u>And moving expenses</u>...cost of buying & selling a house, meals.
<u>No scrapping of lobbying deductions</u>. Clinton wants to end them,
but he'll hit some snags in Congress. Trade groups are strongly opposed.
They would have to figure the percentage of dues that goes for lobbying,
then tell each of their members the amount that could NOT be deducted.

<u>Forget about line-item veto</u>. Senate won't go along with a plan
to strengthen Clinton's hand in cutting individual spending projects.

<u>States will move faster than the federal gov't on health care</u>.
Employers are pressuring legislatures to help control insurance costs.
And the states are getting eaten alive by runaway expenses for Medicaid.
<u>Clinton wants states to experiment</u> in controlling health costs.
The President thinks that creative state programs should serve as models
for federal health reform...may even grant them waivers from his own plan
if they provide coverage for everyone and actually get a grip on costs.
<u>States are delighted to oblige</u>...get credit from their voters
plus a possible exemption from federal rules that will be coming along.
Besides, states know it will be YEARS before nat'l reforms take effect.

<u>New VCRs that will tape programs by subject</u> or favorite star...
"Chicago Cubs" or "Robert Redford"...will be in stores in a year or two.
Cable networks will code each program by category, title, stars, etc...
information carried on part of the signal, similar to closed captioning.
<u>Coming later</u>...automatic parental lockout of R-rated movies.

<u>Bosnia</u>: Pressure is forcing the President to do SOMETHING...
probably combine limited air strikes with an arming of Bosnian Muslims.
<u>Clinton won't send ground forces</u> to fight the Serbian militia.
However, U.S. troops will be part of an eventual UN peacekeeping force,
working with other countries to carry out a cease-fire and partitioning.

<u>Note sweeping changes just ahead in Asia and the Pacific Rim</u>...
China, Taiwan, S. Korea, Singapore, Malaysia, Thailand, Indonesia, India.
<u>For perspective</u>: HALF of the people in the world live in Asia...
close to 3 billion. It already accounts for roughly 40% of world trade.
By 2000, Pacific trade will be twice as big as trade across the Atlantic.
Billions are being spent on new plants, warehouses, railways and ports.

<u>China will be the biggest growth story</u>, surpassing even Japan.
Tremendous investments are going on in the southern Chinese provinces...
factories & equipment for making textiles, apparel, footwear, machinery
and parts, consumer electronics, tools and even lawn & garden goods.
This industrialization will gradually spread to other parts of China.

Relief supplies for Bosnian refugees.

Chinese are eager to deal...putting entire towns on the block. Everything you need to get started...factory, equipment, raw materials.

There's a new generation of entrepreneurs there...younger people who ignore Marxist ways and are willing and able to work with foreigners.

China/Hong Kong marriage in '97 will get off to a rocky start... Hong Kong entrepreneurs fighting interference and China seeking control. But Hong Kong will emerge as the money center of a more prosperous China.

May 7, 1993

Health care has gone from an apple-pie issue to a can of worms, with the earthiest question being how to pay for it all. Clinton's delay in releasing his plan shows what a spot he's in. Middle-class Americans with health insurance think that covering the uninsured is a noble idea. Clinton hopes they'll still feel that way after they're handed the bill.

Nothing will pass this year. Just too much for Congress to chew.

A limited measure is likely next year. Insurance-buying co-ops to help small firms get better prices. A ban on refusing to cover people because of ill health. Simpler claims and billing...all using one form.

Not enough bipartisan support for more-ambitious steps, including price controls, quick universal coverage. GOP senators will block those.

'94 congressional campaign could be a referendum on health care. Clinton will call for the election of more Democrats to finish the job.

No statehood for Wash., D.C., despite Clinton's campaign pledge and an all-out push by Jesse Jackson, Sens. Kennedy and Simon and others. GOP is strongly against idea...doesn't want two more Democratic senators, another Democratic House member and governor. Some Democrats in Congress oppose statehood...they hold D.C.'s purse strings and want to keep them.

Defense manpower will shrink by about 25% through '97, with cuts of about 560,000 active-duty, 260,000 reserves, 270,000 civilian workers.

Emphasis will be placed on military readiness at lower levels... a smaller force that can fight is better than a large one that is hollow.

Regional disputes pose the greatest threat. As bad as Bosnia is, a blowup in Kosovo or Macedonia would be worse. There's plenty of worry over events in Russia...no return to Cold War days but rife with turmoil. Iran is a growing problem...backing terrorism and menacing its neighbors.

Driven from their homes by Bosnian Muslim forces, thousands of Croats sought refuge in the south.

May 21, 1993

<u>Now watch Clinton use trade policy to push his economic goals</u>...
attempting to create more jobs in this country by twisting arms overseas.
<u>Expect a hardball approach</u> toward the Japanese and Europeans.
Demands for reciprocity, market access and an end to dumping practices.
<u>Managed trade will be pursued</u> for key industries...electronics,
autos, personal computers and others. Clinton will seek market shares
in Japan and elsewhere...quantitative goals to be measured regularly.
The Japanese don't like Clinton's idea but will give in to some degree.
If not, they'll face more restrictions in the U.S., their key customer.

<u>Put defense cutbacks in perspective</u>: Spending now, $300 billion.
Spending in '98, $230 billion...smallest share of our economy since '40.
A loss of a million defense jobs, but that's less than 1% of total jobs.
<u>An uneven impact area to area</u>. Hitting some especially hard...
Conn., S.C., Texas, N.M., Calif., Wash., Alaska, Hawaii and Wash., D.C.
<u>$20 billion will be available to help communities</u> make adjustment
to nondefense work...for retraining and the like. And more may be voted.

May 28, 1993

<u>Bosnia</u>: Clinton threatens with more gusto than he can deliver,
more bark than bite. Americans aren't clamoring to get involved there.
That's why there will be no unilateral action ordered by the White House
or proposal to join Europeans in going to war against Serb aggression.

<u>Don't read TOO much into the presidential approval ratings</u>...
they jump around a lot. Only 50% approved of Bush when he took office.
His approval soared to 85% after the Gulf War and fell to 35% last Oct.
<u>Such ratings reflect the headlines</u>...tax hikes, gays in military,
dickering over health care, White House travel office, the $200 haircut.
They're snapshots, not forecasts of future attitudes or election results.
<u>A brighter economy will help Clinton recover</u> from his bad start.
As conditions improve further, people will feel better about their jobs
and their financial well-being. He'll end up getting much of the credit.

<u>And the Senate will OK a tax & spending bill</u> that he'll trumpet as a major achievement, even though his proposed Btu tax will be gutted. Voters will forget the details as long as the economy is healthy in '96.

<u>Clinton has a pattern of bouncing back from political setbacks</u>, including the Gennifer Flowers episode and other problems in early '92. He will try to get his presidency back to the themes of his campaign... concentrating on the economy and jobs from a middle-class perspective.

<u>Democrats in Congress will eye him like hawks</u> or maybe vultures. The President has plenty of time to recover from his stumbling start. But THEY don't...all House seats are up next year. And 34 Senate seats. If a year from now Clinton isn't viewed as a strong consistent leader, high in approval, members will go their own way to save their own skins.

June 4, 1993

<u>Too much negative talk about jobs</u>. The market has NOT dried up.

<u>About 1.7 million more people are now employed than a year ago</u>... not just low-skill and low-pay jobs but managerial and professional work.

<u>And employment will increase another 2 million in the year ahead</u>. That compares with an average 1.8 million jobs per year during the '80s. Average for the '90s so far...284,000, dragged down by big losses in '91.

<u>Good job growth in many states</u>: Nevada. Utah. Montana. Idaho. Colorado. Arizona. Texas. N.D. S.D. Minnesota. Wisconsin. Kansas. N.C. S.C. Georgia. Mississippi. Arkansas. Alabama. Delaware. N.H.

<u>Small business will do most of the hiring</u>, as it normally does. Overall, it's a gradually improving situation despite gloom & doom talk.

June 11, 1993

<u>Clinton's troubles aren't just growing pains</u> of a new President. The flip-floppery, botched appointments, one bungled mess after another.

<u>They're self-inflicted wounds</u>...an eagerness to please everyone and inclination to cave in easily, to cut & run as soon as he's pressed.

<u>But don't write him off yet</u>...his ability to bounce back.

<u>He's scrambling for the middle of the road</u> to regain lost ground even though that's sure to cost him support among liberals in his party. The President realizes that he lurched too far from the political center.

<u>Other things being equal, his fortunes depend on the economy</u>. If it keeps inching ahead, as we expect, he'll be in better shape too. Besides, there is a herd instinct in the media. Within a few months, the papers and TV will discover "the new Clinton"...the comeback kid.

Picture Credits

*Where more than one picture appears on a page
credit is listed from top to bottom, left to right.*

Dust jacket/slipcase: Steve Gottlieb/FPG.

1920s

2-3: AP/Wide World Photos. **2:** Brown Brothers; Boston Public Library; National Air and Space Museum, Smithsonian Institution Photo #89-20586; Hoover Presidential Library; Library of Congress. **3:** Photography Collection, Harry Ransom Humanities Research Center, University of Texas at Austin; Culver Pictures. **8:** Photography Collection, Harry Ransom Humanities Research Center, University of Texas at Austin. **9:** Culver Pictures. **10:** Library of Congress. **11:** National Air and Space Museum, Smithsonian Institution Photo #A-44561; Photo #A-44773-F. **12:** Library of Congress. **13:** Brown Brothers. **14:** Library of Congress. **15:** National Air and Space Museum, Smithsonian Institution Photo #87-8992. **16:** Henry Ford Museum and Greenfield Village. **17:** The B.F. Goodrich, Co. **18:** Hoover Presidential Library. **19:** Boston Public Library.

1930s

20-21: Library of Congress. **20:** *The Detroit News*; Hoerchst Celanese Corp. of Somerville; Library of Congress; Franklin D. Roosevelt Library; Library of Congress. **21:** AP/Wide World Photos; Smithsonian Institution Photo #63531; Library of Congress. **26:** Library of Congress. **27:** National Archives. **28:** *The Detroit News*; Franklin D. Roosevelt Library. **29:** Library of Congress. **30:** AP/Wide World Photos. **31, 32:** Library of Congress. **33:** Archives of Labor and Urban Affairs, Wayne State University. **34:** The Bettmann Archive. **35:** Franklin D. Roosevelt Library, *Sioux City Journal*; Library of Congress. **36:** Library of Congress; Brown Brothers. **37, 38:** Library of Congress. **39:** Library of Congress; Franklin D. Roosevelt Library; Fitzpatrick in the *St. Louis Post-Dispatch*. **40:** Hoechst Celanese Corp. of

Somerville. **41:** Library of Congress; Hugh Hutton. **42:** Brown Brothers; Library of Congress. **43:** United Steelworkers of America; Franklin D. Roosevelt Library © 1937, *The Washington Post*. **44:** Smithsonian Institution Photo #63531. **45:** National Air and Space Museum, Smithsonian Institution Photo #81-12157; AP/Wide World Photos. **46:** Library of Congress. **47:** Culver Pictures; Library of Congress. **48:** National Archives. **49:** Library of Congress. **50:** Stock Montage. **51:** Smithsonian Institution Photo #59708-C. **52, 53, 54:** Library of Congress. **55:** Smithsonian Institution Photo #63536; Library of Congress.

1940s

56-57: National Archives. **56:** Library of Congress; Library of Congress; Library of Congress; Franklin D. Roosevelt Library; Library of Congress. **57:** Library of Congress; National Archives; National Archives. **62:** Culver Pictures; Library of Congress. **63:** The Bettmann Archive. **64:** Library of Congress. **65:** Culver Pictures; The Bettmann Archive. **66:** Library of Congress. **67:** AP/Wide World Photos. **68:** National Archives; Library of Congress. **69, 70, 71:** Library of Congress. **72:** AP/Wide World Photos; Library of Congress. **73:** Franklin D. Roosevelt Library. **74:** National Archives. **75:** AP/Wide World Photos. **76:** Library of Congress; National Archives. **77:** Library of Congress. **78:** National Archives. **79:** National Air and Space Museum, Smithsonian Institution Photo #89-1176; Library of Congress. **80:** Library of Congress. **81:** National Archives. **82:** Library of Congress. **83:** National Archives; Library of Congress; Raytheon Company. **84:** Library of Congress. **85:** The Embassy of Israel. **86:** Library of Congress; Walter Sanders, *Life Magazine* © Time Warner Inc. **87:** The Bettmann Archive; Library of Congress. **88:** New China Pictures, Magnum. **89:** Library of Congress.

1950s

90-91: National Archives. **90:** National Archives; Library of Congress; National Archives; National Archives; National Archives. **91:** The Bettmann Archive; Library of Congress; AP/Wide World Photos. **96:** Library of Congress. **97:** National Archives. **98:** National Archives; Library of Congress. **99:** Richard Nixon Library. **100, 101:** National Archives. **102:** Library of Congress. **103:** National Archives; From *Herblock's Here and Now* (Simon and Schuster, 1955). **104:** AP/Wide World Photos; Library of Congress. **105:** National Library of Medicine; H. Armstrong Roberts. **106:** NYT Pictures. **107:** AP/Wide World Photos. **108, 109:** National Archives. **110:** Smithsonian Institution Photo #61483-F. **111:** U.S. Council for Energy Awareness. **112:** Library of Congress. **113:** National Archives; The Bettmann Archive. **114:** Library of Congress; National Archives. **115:** Library of Congress. **116:** Library of Congress; The Bettmann Archive. **117:** Library of Congress; British Airways. **118, 119:** National Archives. **120:** Library of Congress. **121:** Cadillac Corp. **122:** National Archives. **123:** AP/Wide World Photos; John F. Kennedy Library. **124:** AP/Wide World Photos; National Archives. **125:** Library of Congress; National Office Machine Dealers Association.

1960s

126-127: Flip Schulke/Black Star. **126:** Magnum/Library of Congress; NASA; National Archives; Lyndon Baines Johnson Library; Library of Congress; Nixon Presidential Materials Staff/National Archives. **127:** National Archives; Paul Conklin/*Time Magazine*. **132:** AP/Wide World Photos. **133:** Library of Congress. **134:** The Bettmann Archive. **135:** National Archives; David Battle/Peace Corps. **136:** National Archives. **137:** TASS/Sovfoto;

Index

Page numbers in italics refer to photographs. Photographs of persons mentioned in text on the same page are not indexed separately.